ARCHITECTURES OF SCIENCE

Berlin Universities and Their Development in Urban Space

Edited by Arne Schirrmacher and Maren Wienigk

In cooperation with Gabriele Metzler (concept) and Konrad Angermüller (design) with further contributions by Nils Exner and Sascha Morawe

jovis

CONTENT

FOREWORD

This book examines architectures of science in an urban setting. The origins and development of these architectures are traced over the course of centuries for the city of Berlin, and in this manner the emergence of a topography of the sciences is sketched, one in which the universities represent nodal points. The interactions between science, architecture, and the city are at the center of our interest. To this end, from the great abundance of science buildings in Berlin, we have chosen to focus our attention on those ensembles of university buildings and affiliated institutions which on the one hand exemplify the establishing, interconnectedness, and also conflicts inherent in the simultaneous growth of the sciences and the city or which on the other hand have provided especially important impulses for the development of science.

With a primary focus on ensembles instead of single architectural works, the present guide foregoes highly detailed building descriptions, opting instead to direct interest to questions regarding the function and representativity of buildings, as well as concerning interrelations or synergies found within the context of associated urban planning efforts. While the greatest amount of space is devoted to the development of scientific sites in the various districts of the city, accompanying essays exploring overarching themes open up and deepen further perspectives of Berlin's science architecture.

A selection of multifarious images expands upon the text and serves as a counterpoint. Frequently though, these images have a weight of their own, that is to say, they can be viewed, but also "read" in diverse ways. As such, they occasionally supplant texts about a building's architecture, use, or city planning considerations. In addition, the guide features info boxes and indices as a service to the reader by providing quick overviews, while also offering further points of entry into the chapters and essays. For instance, the journal-like index of architects invites readers to spend time browsing its entries, while simultaneously cataloging the science buildings treated in this volume and providing some additional information about exemplary cases of non-realized buildings to boot. Finally, a bibliography facilitates the initiation of further-reaching independent research.

If this multi-dimensional structure motivates readers to familiarize themselves with a part of Berlin's science landscape in various ways or perhaps even calls them outside to see its subjects up close in the real world, and if this results in the perception of the still new or previously unknown when it comes to science locations in Berlin, that would be entirely in keeping with the spirit intended by the editors and authors.

The present publication is part of the more extensive Science in the City project, which was initiated in the context of the European Cultural Heritage Year 2018. An exhibition, *Architectures of Science: The Universities of Berlin from a European Perspective*, has already been curated and shown at the three larger Berlin universities involved in this project, and an open lecture series was also organized, entitled "Building for Science", which took place during the summer semester 2019 at the Technical University's Institute of Architecture and brought architects of current science buildings into dialogue with representatives of historical and social-science disciplines. In addition, in the run-up to the overall venture, project and research seminars conducted in parallel at the HU and TU incorporated this topic into the university curriculum and involved students in its exploration.

This project was conceived, submitted and realized by Gabriele Metzler, to whom we are extremely grateful, above all for the wonderful project team that she assembled. Not only did she conceive this publication together with us, see it through with good advice and hands-on assistance, and carry it forward with just the right stimulus and important suggestions she also composed central chapters and sections and edited the text of many others.

Special thanks for financial backing goes to the Department of Historical Preservation and World Cultural Heritage of the German Federal Government Commission for Culture and Media, namely Romy Ruhnke, who has given sterling support to the project throughout the process, to the Berlin Senate Administration for Culture and Europe, as well as to Humboldt-Universität zu Berlin and Lotto Stiftung Berlin.

This publication would not have been possible without Konrad Angermüller, whose graphic design makes up a substantial part of the book (as was previously the case for the exhibition). He has seen the book project through from the very beginning and advised us wisely and with great good sense in order to realize a form that supports the content to the utmost extent. If we have attained our shared goal of creating a book as beautiful as it is useful, with which one can get to know Berlin, one equally suited to being read at home or serving as a reliable guide when out and about in the science city of Berlin, and last but not least, a book that sits comfortably in one's hand, then all credit is due to Konrad Angermüller.
Our special thanks go to Nina Kremer for administrative support and two students of history, Nils Exner and Sascha Morawe, who made significant contributions as authors and have supported the entire research effort from the beginning. Big thanks are also due to Paul Morawski, whose thorough proofreading of the texts provided the necessary formal consistency, the right finishing touch and valuable suggestions as well as to Leon Blohm for final research.
For their review of individual chapters and valuable commentary, we would like to offer special thanks to Martina Schilling, Hans-Dieter Nägelke, Dieter Hoffmann, and Ralf Streckwall.
For their thoughtful and intensive support in research related to images, as well as their particularly generous co-operation, we would like to thank the Architectural Museum and the university archive of the Technical University of Berlin, the university archive of Freie Universität Berlin and the Stadtmuseum Berlin Foundation. Big thanks are also due to the archive and the custody of Humboldt-Universität zu Berlin, Berlinische Galerie, the Architecture Archives of the Academy of Arts, the Berlin State Archive, and the Berlin Monument Authority.
Special thanks goes to Norah C. Allen, Heidi Börner, Ludger Derenthal, Kerstin Diether, Verena Feltes, Matthias Hahn, Anne Herdin, Gregor Hitzfeld, Klaus Janetzki, Tanja Morgenstern, Aleksandra Pawliczek, Frank Schütz, Irina Schwab, Anna Seidel, Andreas Teltow, Kathleen Waak, Bernd Wannenmacher, Robert Wein, Susanne Uebele and Claudia Zachariae.

In addition, we would like to thank all photographers for their impressive contemporary photographs, as well as all architectural firms for providing us with illustrations.
This book is being published in both German and English versions. We would like to thank our translators James Campbell and Alexander Zuckrow in particular for their careful rendering into English. Due to technical reasons and in order to limit costs, no translations of labels within illustrations were made. However, the translations of the building and institution names on the maps can be found in the building directory.
Finally, we would like to thank Nina Bergeest of Jovis Verlag for her extremely supportive, dependable and professional support.

The editors

Science Architecture City

9

No other place in Germany is home to more buildings for science than Berlin. The city's three large universities alone and the research facilties affiliated to them – whether for medicine, archaeology, or high tech – have covered the greater metropolitan area with a web of scientific sites: from Adlershof or Buch to Wedding and Zehlendorf. At the same time, there are probably only very few cities in which the awareness of the significant role played by the sciences and their buildings in shaping the urban landscape and development of the city is as low as it is in Berlin. While many other cities that possess a university refer to themselves as "university cities", for instance by stating the label clearly on their town signs, the list of places in Germany that greet their visitors as a "science city" is a short one: only Darmstadt, Fürth, Straubing, and Burghausen have been given this title by their respective state governments. In Ulm, the university district also goes by this name, and Hamburg is planning to transform the district of Bahrenfeld into a science city. The competition of the Stifterverband für die Deutsche Wissenschaft (or "Donors' Association for the Promotion of Humanities and Sciences in Germany") for the distinction as a "City of Science" awarded annually between 2004 and 2013 was also reserved for medium-sized cities from Lübeck to Dresden which showed particular commitment to supporting the expansion of their scientific institutions.

One encounters another use of the term science city wherever large settlements for universities and scientific research institutes themselves take on the size and form of an independent city for science. The new universities established during the expansion of higher education in the 1960s in Constance, Bochum, or Bielefeld did not arise within existing urban structures, but were instead effectively founded as scientific satellite towns outside of historical city centers and residential areas.

Berlin is not a science city in any of these senses. And yet, it is a city of science, one in which universities and research institutes have been profoundly influenced by specific circumstances of the growing metropolis. Indeed, Berlin is a place where city and science are connected with one another in a special way due to their deeply entwined lines of historical development.

What makes Berlin exciting in this regard are particularly the processes of co-creation of science and city whose breakthroughs to modernity did not just coincidentally occur in parallel. Co-creation here always also means: superimposition, repurposing, the reinvention of places and structures. In this way, buildings of the royal stables were transformed into accommodation for the Academy of Sciences and Berlin's first anatomical theater. The "Fireland" of iron foundries and engineering works outside of the city limits in front of the gate Neues Tor became the science and museum mile at Invalidenstrasse.

The royal hippodrome at Tiergarten became the main grounds of the Royal Technical College. Prussia's largest institute building for the natural sciences took over the area of Berlin's inner-city military workshops. Age-old barracks, still in use by the National People's Army in the GDR era, would be transformed into educational science institute buildings for Humboldt-Universität. The list goes on and on.

Against this backdrop, it is all the more astonishing that the city and its inhabitants seem to take precious little notice of these buildings of science – if one excludes a handful of prominent exceptions. Moreover, among the many individuals who are currently studying at or have already graduated from one of Berlin's three large universities, whose combined enrollment totals over 100,000 students today, the majority of them may only be able to consciously recall the small number of science buildings where they themselves were active. In addition, many university sites are well and truly hidden from those who do not study or conduct research within their walls, and are largely cut off from the urban life surrounding them. This applies to Campus Nord of the HU in Mitte for instance, whose entrances are rather hard to find, but the TU grounds are also shielded by wide streets and thus isolated from the non-academic world, while the Rostlaube, Silberlaube, and Holzlaube complexes in the village-like villa district of Dahlem form their own tight-knit little academic town.

It is only in recent years that the universities themselves have made deliberate attempts to open up their buildings to a broader audience by publishing guidebooks. For instance, in this context art historian Martina Schilling has produced an architectural guide for Freie Universität; the Technical University has already been the subject of two extensive descriptions of its buildings (by art scholar Christoph Brachmann and art historian Robert Suckale, as well as by architectural historian Michael Bollé). Aside from texts treating its main building, such a description has been lacking up until now for Humboldt-Universität. And certainly to date hardly any energy has been devoted to surveys venturing beyond the scope of a single institution. Indeed, a systematic attempt has not yet been made to examine and discuss the development of Berlin's universities and the science conducted within them together, and in this manner to trace the emergence of the academic science landscape in Berlin as a whole. For neither did the universities evolve independently of one another, nor do they exist separately of one another today. Students did not start commuting between them just yesterday, as they are able to receive credit for coursework at all of Berlin's universities, and when it comes to tomorrow's challenges the HU, TU, and FU are increasingly finding that there is great strength in collaboration, as for instance in the national Excellence Strategy Competition, in which they participated successfully as a unit in July 2019. The HU and FU have teamed up to train future doctors, and Charité already serves as a bridging institution in this regard. And, at the moment, Charité is embarking on a medical technology collaboration with the TU at the new Seestrasse Campus in Wedding.

Whether motivated by historical interest or in regard to current development potential, the question of how research and teaching institutions have shaped urban space here is just as relevant for Berlin as the question of the different urban functions that evolved to meet the needs of the inhabitants of the respective districts on the one hand and those of researchers and professors on the other. To a great extent, the answers to these questions lie before us in stone, wood, and metal. However, in order to understand them, we must first decode the architectures of science. The volume at hand endeavors to accomplish just that, at least for the city's three large universities, whereby, however, attention is also paid to many associated and co-operating non-university institutions – from Charité and the Kaiser Wilhelm Institute of Chemistry to the University

Sketch from 1836

of the Arts and the State Libraries. True, the scientific landscape of Berlin always was and still is far larger than these institutions. By focusing on the universities, the backbone of this urban scientific landscape, and some of the scientific institutions affiliated to them or in their immediate proximity, we aim to delineate the major lines of this development.

Architectures

It is self-evident that the central connecting link for the development of science in and along with the city are the buildings where the former has been practiced. What is perhaps not so obvious, however, is the role architecture plays here. Of course, a building's exterior often represents its function. Columns, the arrangement of floors, and the preciousness of the materials, as well as the artful design of facades all signal significance. Inscriptions and sculptures, for example of scientists and artists, communicate the mission and aspirations of the institutions housed within such buildings. Aside from that, there are far more fundamental functions of architecture, so that it appears meaningful to speak of architectures in the plural.

One of the tasks of architecture is to create and arrange spaces, to define both the inside and out, and thus create enclosures for specific purposes. A further aspect applies to the production of relationships and connections between rooms and buildings and the definition of their functional interaction. However, architecture also always has the function of including and excluding. For instance when entrances and stairways for rulers or aristocrats and service personnel are separated, when scientists and laborers have different designated points of entry into a research institute, or when, as in the prominent case of Lise Meitner, the accomplished female scientist was obliged to use a rear door to enter the university's Institute of Chemistry in 1907.

Similarly, urban orders of the social realm are also an architecture, to the extent that they manifest themselves in decisions concerning urban development that assign respective individual places to specific demographic groups, trades, state facilities, or institutions of culture and leisure. This spatial allocation has always included the assessment of social, political, or cultural significance. In this way, for instance, Charité was initially established as a plague house and lazaretto for the poor far from the Spree in front of the city's gates, while the Royal Library, together with the Opera House and the Prince Heinrich Palais, at the disposal of the university since 1809, defined the representative cultural forum of the Frederician era in direct proximity to the palace. This architecture of a cultural forum was taken up once again after the division of Berlin with the Philharmonie, State Library, New National Gallery, Gemäldegalerie, and further museums, though without a university.

Architectures of Science

Science is related to all of these architectures, if not perhaps to the same extent in all respects when it comes to the natural sciences and the humanities and social sciences. With the scientific revolution brought about by the experimental natural sciences, the scholar's parlor had become

Schinkel column in the garden of the TU

obsolete, and more and more often special spaces had to be created for laboratories, collections, libraries, and lecture halls for the demonstration of experiments. On top of that came the fact that scientific knowledge was itself increasingly conceived of in the form of architectures: classifications and systems of elements, minerals, living creatures, languages, symbols, or even architectonic artifacts were spatialized. The objects of science were arranged on paper, ordered in card indexes, separated in different display cases, assigned to different laboratories, or, as in the case of the Technical College, exhibited in back gardens, where diverse columns, arcades, and art objects still form a sort of open-air museum of technical artifacts today.

It was precisely through this architectonically characterized processual nature of knowledge that the development of the architecture of university and science buildings became interlinked with the development of science itself – to wit, both as regards the differentiation and specialization of fields of knowledge and in the organization of science into faculties, disciplines, and institutes. This development took the imagined single, shared house of science and made it into an elaborately arranged ensemble of building sections, if not small-scale science cities. Here, we observe the appearance of a form of architectures of science that structures spaces in a comprehensive manner as a system of ordering – including spaces of communication. This also serves the implementation of certain scientific concepts. Thus, architecture becomes a means of both executing science policy and imposing discipline on scientists – according to subjects as well as by behavior and habitus – and those they educate.
Architectonically, the main building of the university at Unter den Linden follows the palace construction model – after all, it was originally built as a palace for the brother of Friedrich II. However, from the perspective of science architecture, it conveys the idea of the unity of the university in keeping with the ideals of Wilhelm von Humboldt and Friedrich Schleiermacher.
This is even more evident for the main building of the Technical College in Charlottenburg, which united all of its subjects (with the exception of chemistry). All of those assembled here to instruct and learn were virtually inoculated with the significance of the technical sciences via architectural means: through the sheer size and materiality of the building, the originally grand ramp, and above all the entranceway through a vestibule into an imposing atrium. The largely egalitarian accommodations and uniform rooms for all disciplines found here demonstrated this unity.

Alexander von Humboldt for his part stands for the concept of using the university building not only for the imparting and discussion of knowledge, but instead also as a place to store the objects of knowledge themselves. So it is that large

Vestibule, TU

portions of the university building at Unter den Linden were occupied by collections and exhibits, which were used as visual aids to facilitate instruction but were also made accessible to interested members of the general public. This was also not realized any differently at the Technical College in Charlottenburg. Architectures and systems of order, such as those we find in university buildings, in science itself, and in urban space as well, were linked to one another by universities in this manner, if not altogether synchronized. Only in Dahlem did the settlement of museums, collections, and archives play out on a separate timeline from that of the establishment of the university, which is of course hardly surprising in light of their history of founding in Kaiserreich and Cold War, respectively.

The architectures of science present in Berlin are neither inevitable nor are they typical. Other types can also be found throughout history: for instance, the collegium or college follows the model of the medieval or early modern university; conversely, the university for the masses set upon an expansive green lawn is typical for the second half of the twentieth century. The latter model breaks completely with established structures in an attempt to arrange and connect all of the sciences within a sort of university machine, the built expression of the quest to reconnect the now differentiated individual sciences. This model too has only been realized to a certain degree in Berlin by Freie Universität, and, what is more, in a manner that almost negates the predominant massive mode of construction.

Between the college as an effectively town-like site for science and the university machine as science city – without really being a city – lie the architectures of Berlin's science. Here, other forms of expression have been found for science. The cultural forum has already been mentioned; in analogue fashion, the Museum Island evolved into a space for archaeology and art history. The quarter, frequently defined by a street, is a further form. It evolved, for instance, along Dorotheenstrasse behind the main building of the university in Mitte, or around the Museum of Natural History on Invalidenstrasse. In the nineteenth century, a small science quarter also existed near Hallesches Tor revolving around an astronomical observatory built by Karl Friedrich Schinkel alongside Lindenstrasse which no longer exists.
For medicine, the case was once again different: Charité and the clinics in Buch surpassed the size of a city quarter and evolved into hospital or even health cities within and beyond the city itself. These are to be differentiated from campus structures – a true campus in the sense of American universities was never realized in Berlin. However, Reuss Garden with the Veterinary Anatomy Theater from 1790, whose grounds became home to the disciplines of veterinary medicine and later the life sciences, forms the site known as Campus Nord right in the heart of Berlin. The former parts of the Royal Hippodrome in Charlottenburg that remained behind the main building of the Technical College also form a small campus-like main grounds that make the technical laboratories accessible. Following World War II, as the "free" Freie Universität was set up to counteract the socialist-occupied

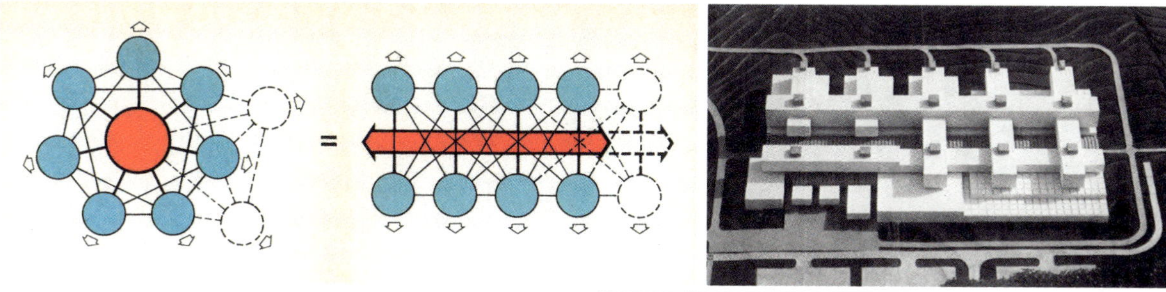

University Bielefeld: system sketch and competition modell, 1969

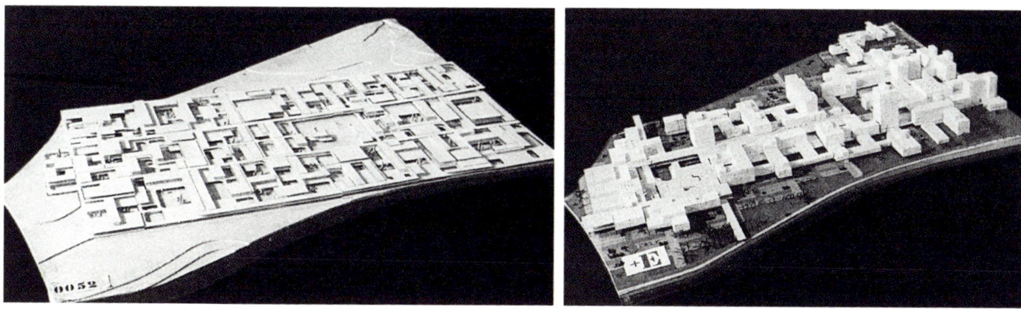

FU Berlin: competiton modells, 1963

University of Berlin, it first took up quarters on the site that the abandoned Kaiser Wilhelm Institute of Biology had used for its test fields. This "south campus" of the FU is the closest thing in Berlin to the widespread American campus model, while the original ideas of Thomas Jefferson are perhaps most likely to be found at Campus Nord in Mitte.

Whether forum, island, quarter, health city, or campus structure – the building ensembles that define the functional units of Berlin's science architecture consist of segmented building structures which in turn delineate spaces for science. In this respect, the fundamental vocabulary of architecture can be applied to its effect on science. The institute building is the most commonly found architectonic form that structures scientific life. Walls separate departments, which are themselves compartmentalized. Struts are usually realized in the form of columns lining the representative rooms for the communication of scientific knowledge. Activities that take place under a common roof are connected and coordinated with one another. However, the director's villa has its own roof, and, as is still the case for Emil Fischer's institute, a little bridge leading first into a private laboratory and then into the rooms of the spacious Institute of Chemistry. The latter is, however, then dissolved in a purely functional manner into a fissured ensemble of rooms, in order to ensure the ventilation and lighting conditions crucial to research and to enable the surveillance of the working processes of innumerable staff members. Indeed, a unique conglomeration of walls, departments, basement rooms for animals, power generators, or refuse can be found in the quarter of the Nobel Prize winners referred to today as the Koch Forum. Four branches of the natural sciences combined their research facilities into one city block, communicating a sense of unity to the outside world through a richly ornamented facade and a small trench running around the whole block. However, on the inside, walls, gardens, ponds for breeding frogs, and ventilation shafts divide private, scientific, student, and public areas from one another. Elaborate procedures

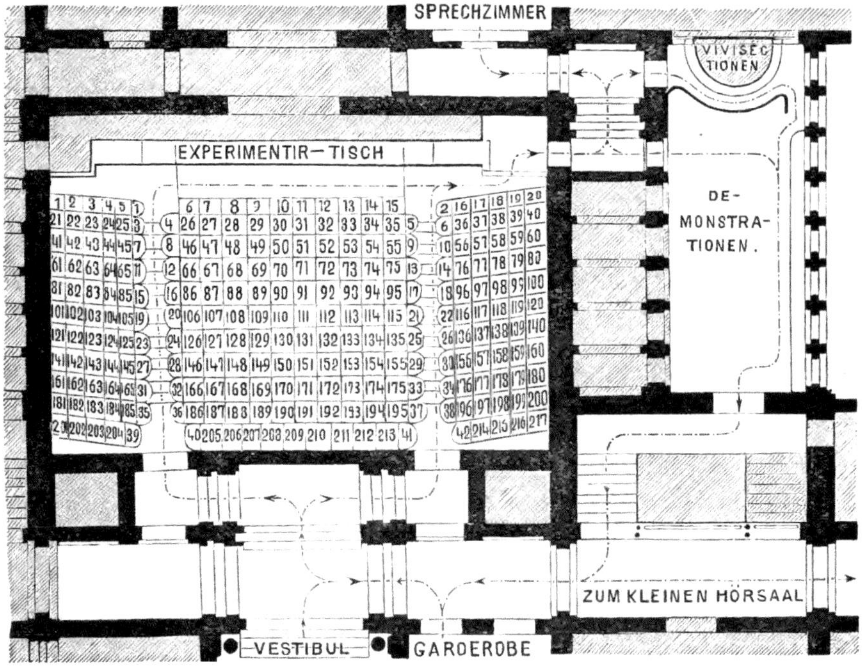

Entrance card to a lecture from Emil du Bois-Reymond, approx. 1880

govern the work of staff members or the flow of students through lecture halls and rooms for the acquisition of practical experience.

Only when one is willing to consider architectures of science in this multiplicity does it become possible to truly understand the origins and present structure of Berlin's science landscape. To that end, however, it is still necessary to take a look at a further dimension: that of city development.

Urban Space and Its Economies

Growth, concentration, and conflicts are key terms in the basic vocabulary used to describe the development of urban space. Areas previously situated just outside the city gates later become part of the Berlin-Mitte district. Such was the case for instance for the so-called Neustadt, or "New City", of Dorotheenstadt with Dorotheenstrasse, Friedrich-Wilhelm-Stadt with Luisenstrasse, or the Oranienburger suburbs too with Invalidenstrasse, all of which became science districts as well. The locations for science spread out along with the city, although their interests frequently conflicted with developments within the city.

The boulevard Unter den Linden offered little in the way of potential expansion for the University of Berlin in Prince Heinrich Palais, and extension to the rear along Dorotheenstrasse was only successful to the degree that properties were available, along with funding for their acquisition and development at more remote locations, though still reachable on foot.

In part, buildings realized for other purposes were acquired little by little and repurposed to fit the university's needs, such as the Chamber of Commerce and a series of commercial buildings. The Academy's astronomical observatory, which the university initially shared and ultimately took over, was, however, already rebuilt on the edge of the city in 1835, on one hand in order to open it up to the general public, and on the other as a reaction to the fact that conditions for making astronomical observations were steadily worsening due to nearby industrial estates. Schinkel's observatory building was itself torn down in 1913

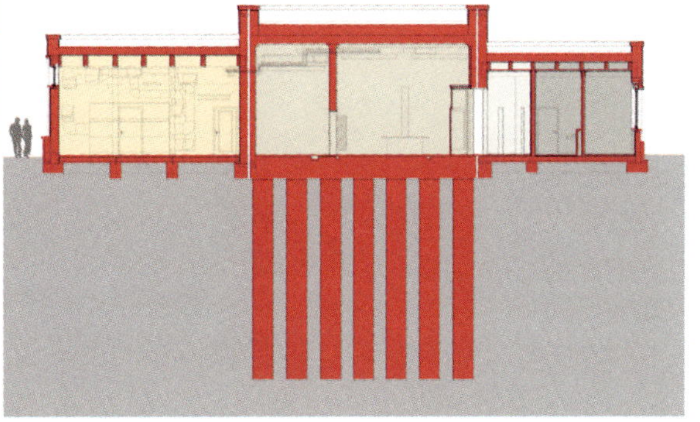

Foundation constructions: Natural Sciences Quarter (→ 47), Electron microscopy building (→ 137)

for similar reasons. The combination of smog and sharply rising land prices compelled and enabled the university to build a new one in Babelsberg, since the sale of the old property was able to cover the cost of a new building outside the city. It is these sorts of interlocking processes of urban and scientific development that lie at the heart of the present work. The development of Berlin's universities will be traced in order to provide a point of access to the architectures of science. This quite obviously includes the transportation infrastructure that made it possible to integrate Charlottenburg or Dahlem into the network of science locations. What is less well known, however, is how substantially these infrastructures, particularly in the areas of transportation and electricity, or the combination of the two, caused continual conflict between the city and science, indeed have done so all the way up to the present day.
Hermann von Helmholtz had to take great care in 1872 to ensure that vibrations caused by carriages, trams, or subways would not disturb his sensitive physical measurements; just like Michael Lehmann, who required freedom from external influences on the north grounds of the TU for his transmission electron microscope, which went into operation in 2011. In both instances, an architecture needed to be found that would keep vibrations, electric currents, and temperature fluctuations at bay in the laboratory, albeit on different levels from a technical point of view. Helmholtz and Lehmann – as well as many other scientists – share the attitude that in spite of all of the inherent difficulties they prefer to conduct their research within the city, in order to nurture equally vital scientific exchange with their colleagues and maintain their involvement in the university.

The last example underscores the fact that the interest in the co-evolution of city and science is by no means merely fixated on history. Today as in the nineteenth century, building for science is a task that must reconcile thoroughly different demands for functionality and representativity while at the same time never losing sight of the urban environment in which architectures of science unfold their long-lasting effect that far exceeds the moment of their emergence. (AS)

MITTE, DOROTHEENSTADT

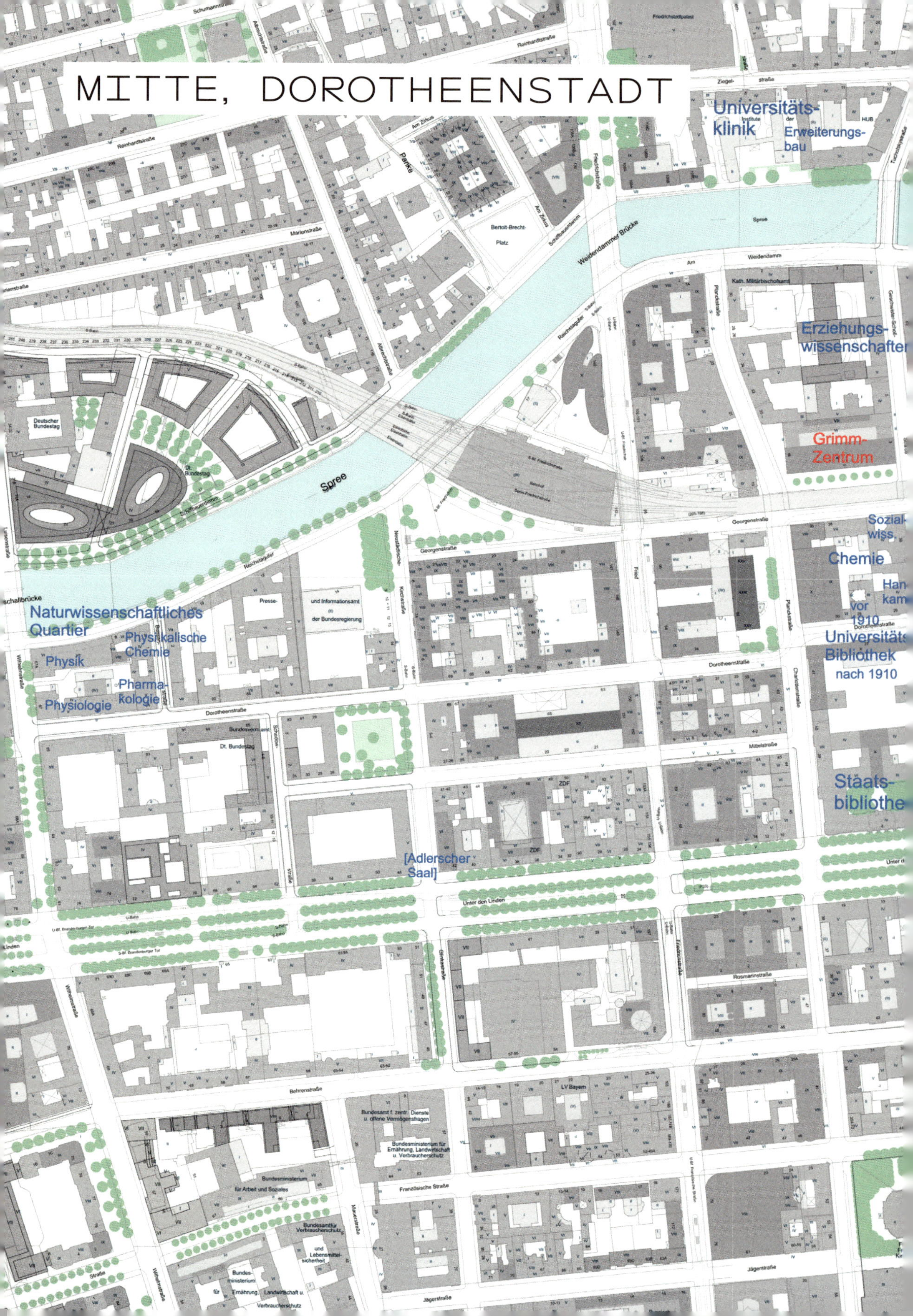

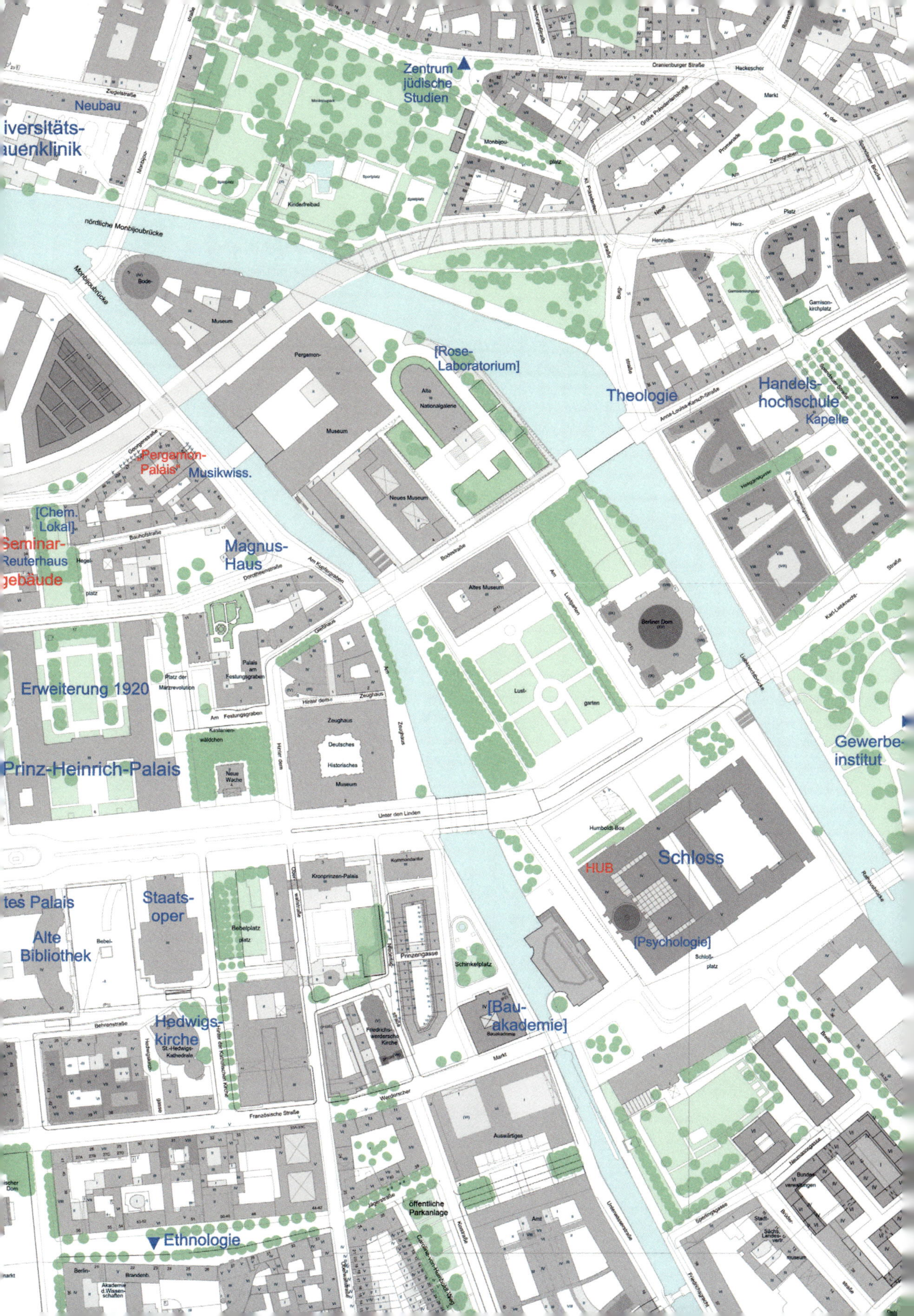

Zentrum jüdische Studien
Neubau
iversitäts-
auenklinik
Oranienburger Straße
Hackescher
Markt
Monbijouplatz
Kinderfreibad
nördliche Monbijoubrücke
Monbijoubrücke
Bode-Museum
Pergamon-Museum
[Rose-Laboratorium]
Alte Nationalgalerie
Neues Museum
Theologie
Handels-
hochschule
Kapelle
Anna-Louisa-Karsch-Straße
„Pergamon-Palais"
Musikwiss.
[Chem. Lokal]
Seminar-
Reuterhaus
gebäude
Magnus-Haus
Bodestraße
Altes Museum
Berliner Dom
Lustgarten
Erweiterung 1920
Palais am Festungsgraben
Zeughaus
Deutsches Historisches Museum
Neue Wache
Prinz-Heinrich-Palais
Gewerbe-
institut
Unter den Linden
Humboldt-Box
HUB
Schloss
[Psychologie]
Schloßplatz
Kronprinzen-Palais
Prinzessinnenpalais
tes Palais
Staats-
oper
Alte
Bibliothek
Bebelplatz
Schinkelplatz
Hedwigs-
kirche
St.-Hedwigs-Kathedrale
Friedrichswerdersche Kirche
[Bau-
akademie]
Behrenstraße
Französische Straße
Auswärtiges Amt
öffentliche Parkanlage
Ethnologie

ORANIENBURGER VORSTADT &

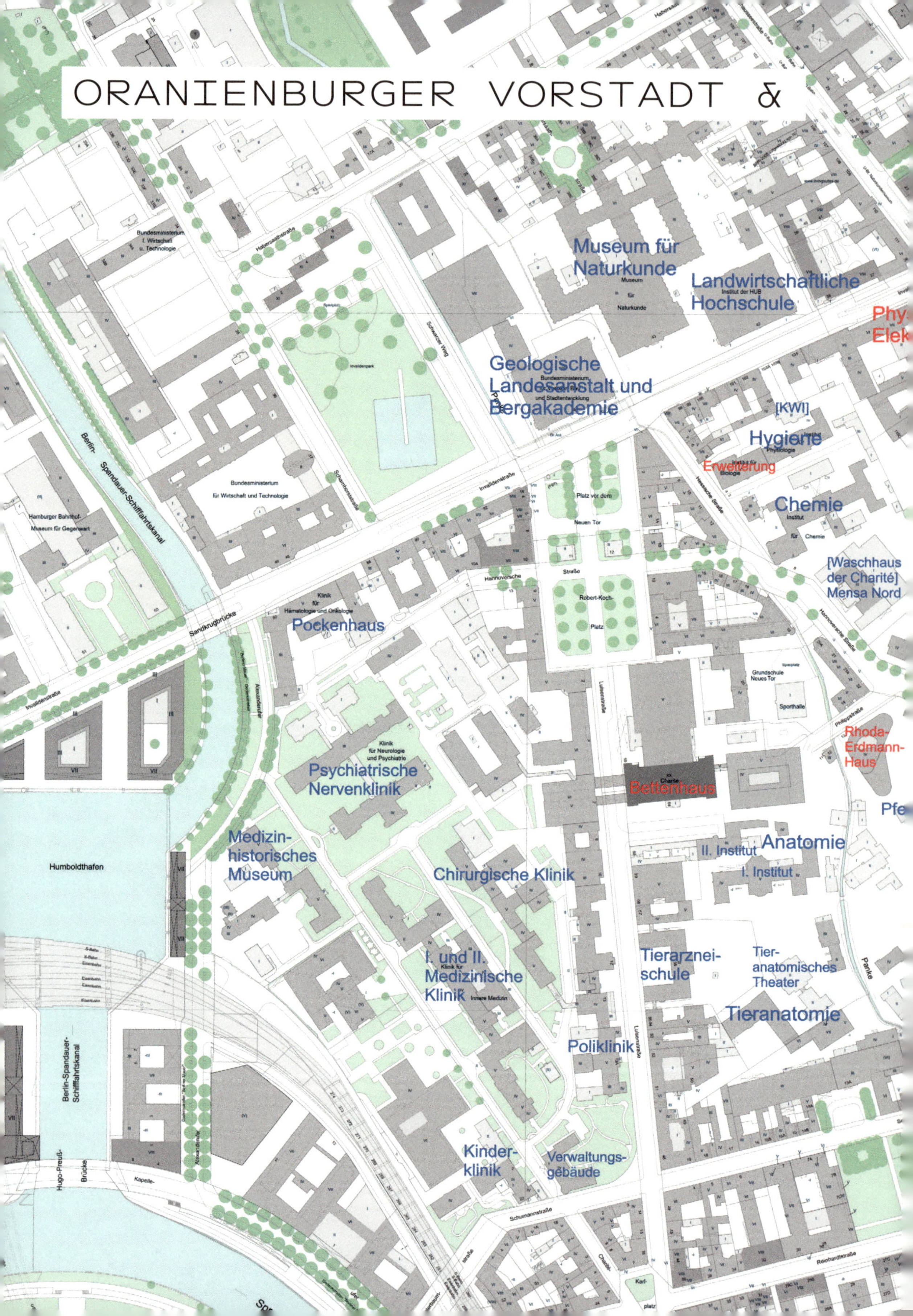

FRIEDRICH-WILHELM-STADT
Sektion Physik
BIMSB
Physikalisches Praktikum
Elektronik-praktikum
Torstraße
Friedrichstraße
Oranienburger Straße
Linienstraße
Johannisstraße
Friedrichstadtpalast
Schule
Hemingway-Oberschule
Sporthalle
Stadtbad Mitte
Golgatha-kirche
Ev. Kirche
Kath. Akademie
Brecht-Weigel-Gedenkst.
Hannoversche Straße
Chausseestraße
Bundesministerium Gesundheit
Bundesmin. f. Bildung u. Forschung
Reinhardtstraße
Ziegelstraße
Institute der HUB

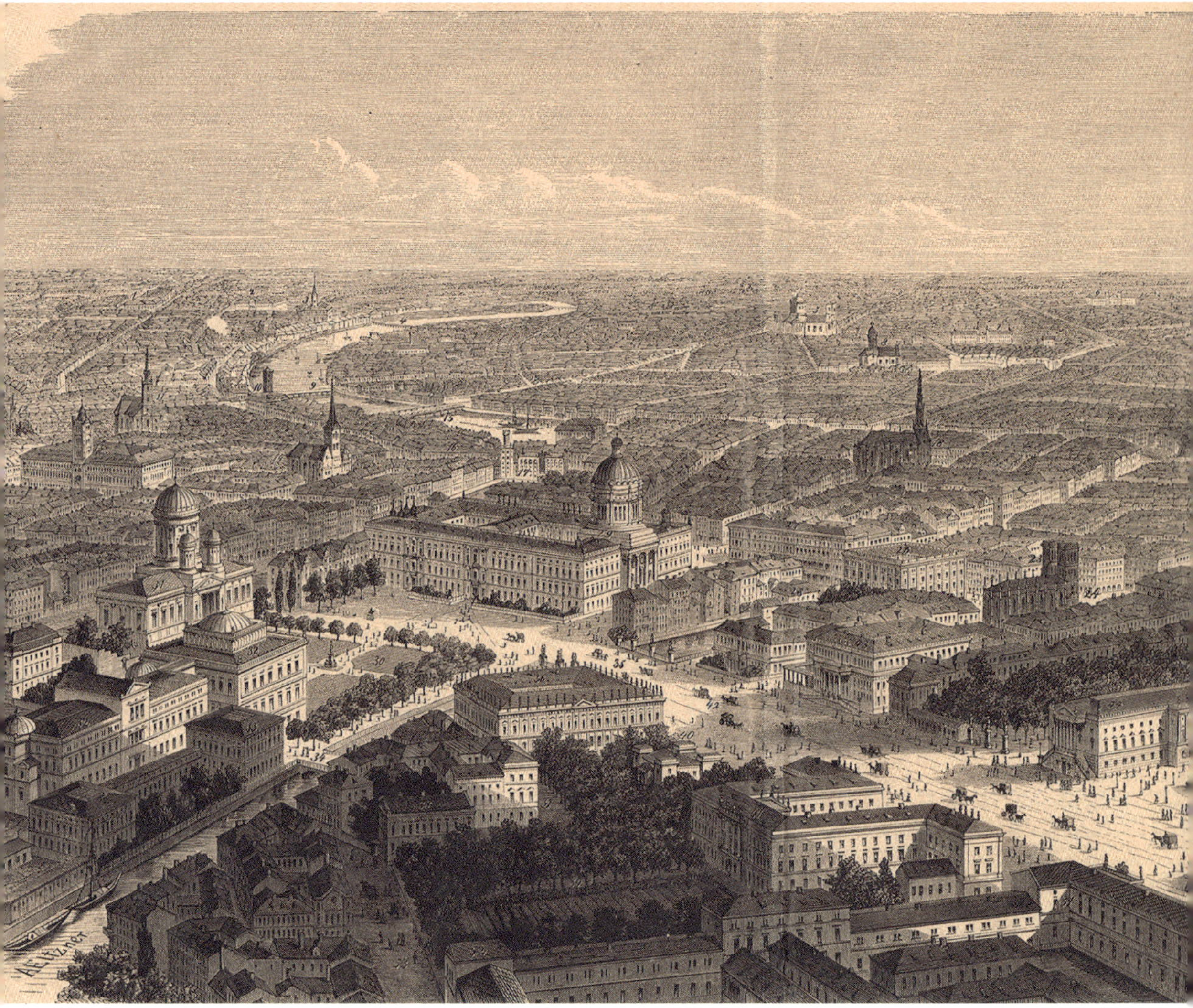

City veduta with city palace (counterclockwise): (old) Berliner Dom, Zeughaus, Neue Wache, Prinz Heinrich Palais, Marstall with Academy (in the foreground), Altes Palais, Königliche Bibliothek, Sankt-Hedwigs-Kirche, Staatsoper, Friedrichwerdersche Kirche, Bauakademie

In Berlin's historic Mitte district, there where on the banks of the Spree alongside Cölln and Alt-Berlin the core of today's metropolis was born in the thirteenth century, one can find the first-ever historical center for science in Berlin. Prince-elector Joachim II's cabinet of curiosities, established in the early sixteenth century and after its destruction in the Thirty Years' War significantly expanded by Prince-elector Friedrich Wilhelm after 1640, formed the nucleus for later scientific collections and thus for research as such. From the beginning

of the eighteenth century, the collections were housed in the palace, which was built out by Andreas Schlüter in the style of the Protestant Baroque, and then ultimately used as a city palace starting in the nineteenth century. Further scientific facilities and teaching institutions were later built in proximity to the palace: the Academy of Sciences (founded in 1700 as the Kurfürstlich-Brandenburgische Societät der Wissenschaften and which took over part of the cabinet), the Bauakademie, established in 1799, as well as the Gewerbeinstitut, founded in 1821.

The development of the Mitte district as a central location for the sciences received a decisive stimulus with the founding of the university in 1809. The educational institution was able to take up residence in the rooms of the late Prince Heinrich's former palace, which, together with the Staatsoper, Sankt-Hedwigs-Kirche, and the Königliche Bibliothek, formed a unique ensemble as the Forum Fridericianum. Teaching started in the Palais in 1810. In the area directly adjacent, buildings for art, as well as for church, monarchical and state representation found a home: from its location next to the Lustgarten, Karl Friedrich Schinkel's classical Altes Museum represented the starting point of the Museumsinsel, today a UNESCO world heritage site with the Alte Nationalgalerie, the Neues Museum, the Bode Museum, and the Pergamon Museum. The Berliner Dom, a replacement structure for one of Schinkel's churches and a Baroque cathedral on the same site, represented the Protestant church in a Roman Renaissance style. With its reconstructed facade and Schlüter courtyard, newly constructed along the lines of the original, the rebuilt city palace is slated to open its doors in 2020. Located a bit further to the west at Unter den Linden, the Staatsbibliothek, built by Ernst von Ihne rounds out this marvelous area. From its origins in Prince Heinrich's palace, the university, and with it the sciences, began its further geographical expansion. New buildings were required, ones specially tailored to the needs of scientific disciplines that were in the process of differentiating themselves and becoming specialized fields of knowledge. They found a home north of the palace on Dorotheenstrasse and Ziegelstrasse. Subsequently, buildings associated with the university would spread out all the way to Invalidenstrasse and the grounds of Charité.

Humboldt-Universität has had a continued role in shaping the urban face of Berlin's central district up to the present day. Its buildings do more than simply meet functional needs – they also possess a representative character. As such, the university stands alongside the ensembles in its immediate vicinity, which were used to stage political power, from the city palace to the armory – today's Deutsches Historisches Museum – all the way to the Neue Wache.

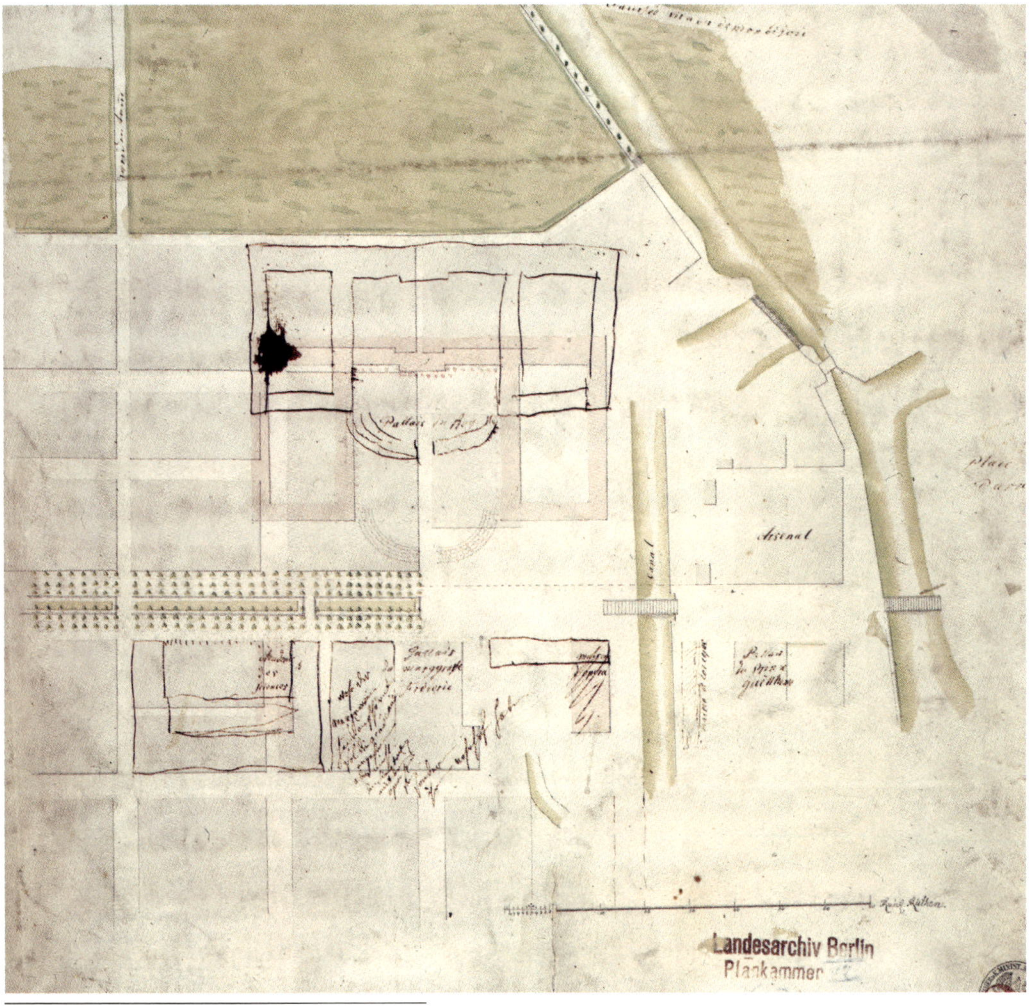

Sketch with entries by Friedrich II, approx. 1740

THE PRINZ HEINRICH PALAIS AT FORUM FRIDERICIANUM

Prinz Heinrich Palais
main building of HU

Unter den Linden 6 | 1748–1753 | Friedrich II (builder), Johann Boumann the Elder (design) | built as a palace for Prince Heinrich | since 1809 main building of the university | 1913–1920 addition of the garden wing, Ludwig Hoffmann | 1943–1944 sustained heavy aerial bombing damage during the war | 1945–1961 rebuilt in two construction phases

The main building of Humboldt-Universität at Unter den Linden, the **Prinz Heinrich Palais**, is today the most renowned building for scholarship in Berlin-Mitte. As a popular photographic motif, foregrounded by one of the two monuments to Wilhelm and Alexander von Humboldt respectively, which stand to either side of the entrance to the front courtyard, it virtually symbolizes the idea of the university. The building's past points to a completely different historical context, as it was originally planned and built around the middle of the eighteenth century for Prince Heinrich, brother of Friedrich II, and thus for a totally different purpose. Alongside a series of other stately buildings in the immediate vicinity, today's main building was part of a representative complex, the Forum Fridericianum, which is located on the left and right hand sides of the boulevard Unter den Linden. Over the course of time, the university has managed to occupy significant portions of this complex, making new use of them for academic purposes.

Since its transfer to the freshly founded university in 1809, the history of the building has been one of refurbishments that have profoundly altered its original substance, of additions, and – after the massive destruction of World War II – of reconstruction. The original structure is only perceptible today in the court of honour, facing Unter den Linden. On the building itself, the facade alone hints at the structure's Frederician past, in particular the eye-catching median risalit with its columns and pilasters spanning two stories, the crisp, unembellished ribbon windows, as well as the Attica sculptures (which are in part copies of the Frederician originals, and were in part transferred there from the Potsdamer Stadtschloss on loan, a source of political friction today).
As soon as the university took up quarters in the palace, extensive renovations were undertaken in the interior. Rooms had to be redesigned for teaching and research activities, or created from scratch. Lecture halls needed to be constructed, space had to be made for the comprehensive collections, but also a number of official residences for professors and university employees had to be created. From this point on, the university would use the majestic ceremonial hall and audience chamber on the first upper floor as an assembly hall. Alexander von Humboldt gave a portion of his Cosmos lectures inside the resulting large auditorium during the winter semester of 1826/1827. The remaining ones were held in the neighboring Singakademie, today's Gorki Theater, managed to draw a sizeable audience from beyond the university as well.
This building gave expression to the idea of the unity of the sciences: here scholars from the humanities and the natural sciences pursued their teaching and research activities in direct proximity to one another; here the collection of paintings and the

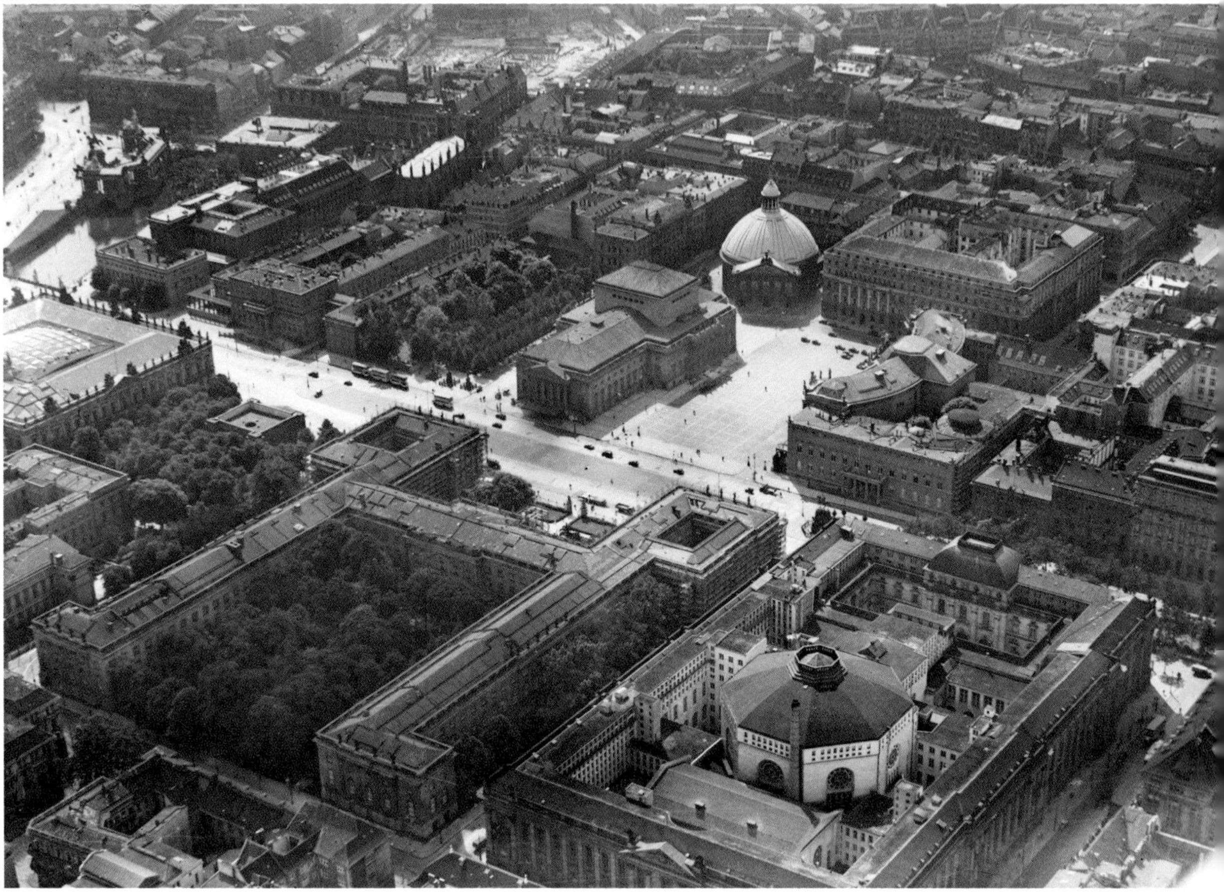

HU, approx. 1934 (above) and 1951

cabinet for physical instruments (from 1844) were both housed; the Anatomical Museum as well as that for mineralogy could both be found here, in addition to further collections. On the ground floor, facing the garden, professor of medicine Christian Wilhelm Hufeland operated a little polyclinic. The growth of the university, the expansion of the collections, which were taking up more and more space, as well as the poor structural condition of the building combined to make refurbishments and a fundamental restoration necessary again between the years of 1836 and 1846. However, these efforts failed to yield a permanent solution to the issue of inadequate space. Shortly thereafter, in 1863, the senate and rector authored a memorandum calling attention to "the university's growing need for the creation of new space and the expansion of existing rooms for teaching activities, collections, and institutes".

As a matter of fact, starting in the 1860s the institutes for the natural sciences did indeed begin to move out, to buildings in the immediately surrounding area built to house them individually (→39, 47). From the 1880s, large portions of the collections followed, with storage relocated to the newly established Museum für Naturkunde on Invalidenstrasse among other places (→79). The guiding notion of the unity of science had run up against its own limits when it came to space. In spite of these undertakings, the main building remained crowded, and barracks erected temporarily on the grounds provided scant relief in this regard. A truly substantial extension would have to wait until 1920, with the completion of construction of the twin garden wings, which give the originally three-winged building its characteristic H shape today. The exterior design of the two wings was realized in such complete harmony with the existing building that the naked eye does not at all register the fact that the extension was carried out more than a century after the university first occupied the space.

Some two decades later, World War II also left its miserable mark on Prinz Heinrich Palais. After aerial bombing in the years 1943 and 1944, the east wing was completely burned out, and all that was left of the central section were its external walls. The west wing had also sustained considerable damage. After carrying out makeshift repairs, the university nonetheless managed to re-open its doors at the early date of January 1946 – now under radically different political circumstances. In 1949, it was rechristened Humboldt-Universität after Wilhelm and Alexander. While for the most part the interior received a fresh design, the restoration of the facade adhered to the original aesthetic. The fact that a new understanding of science had become predominant was most visibly expressed in the building's design in the eleventh Feuerbach thesis from Karl Marx (→259), whose words have been engraved on the red slabs of the main staircase (made of knotted limestone, not marble) in the foyer for all to read since 1953.

The facade was not the only thing restored – the court of honour at Unter den Linden was also reconstructed following war's end. Here the outsized monument to Hermann von Helmholtz dominates until today (1899, Ernst Herter), flanked by monuments to Theodor Mommsen (1909, Adolf Brütt), Max Planck (1948–1949, but not installed in the main courtyard until 2006, Bernhard Heiliger), and Lise Meitner (2014, Anna Franziska Schwarzbach). Helmholtz, Planck, and Mommsen had all in fact conducted

Interior view of the Bauakademie

Bauakademie
general school for construction

Schinkelplatz | 1832–1836 | Karl Friedrich Schinkel | originated from the Berlin Academy of the Arts | 1799 Building Academy | 1801 in the New Mint at Werderscher Markt, 1806 at Zimmerstrasse 25 | 1945 destruction and start of rebuilding efforts, halted however in 1956 | torn down in 1962, to make room for Foreign Ministry of the GDR

Gewerbeinstitut

Klosterstrasse 36 | 1821 | Martin Heinrich Böhme | built as the Royal Technical Institute in Creutz-Haacke Palace, modified by Karl Friedrich Schinkel | 1827 renamed Gewerbeinstitut, then 1866 Gewerbeakademie | 1827–1829 first expansion phase | 1861–1865 second expansion

research and taught in the main building, as many other renowned scientists have done too, in this space originally conceived for royal representation and not for research and education.
Although it wasn't intended for the purpose, as a university building the former palace fit in seamlessly alongside the surrounding ensembles, in which science and research were already very much present. Of the scientific collections that had initially been given special rooms in the royal palace since the start of the eighteenth century, quite a few were passed on to the university. Beyond that, science education was already taking place at this location too. Situated at changing locations not far from the palace and the university, the **Bauakademie,** an academic teaching facility for the "theoretical and practical education of capable surveyors and builders", as the royal order decreed, had already been founded in 1799. In 1836, the Bauakademie found a new home in a building designed by Karl Friedrich Schinkel. Together with Peter Beuth's nearby **Gewerbeinstitut**, founded in 1821, the Bauakademie formed the nucleus of what would later become the Technical College, which would however be established in Charlottenburg.

However, from an architectural perspective the university building was above all directly connected to the ensemble on today's Bebelplatz square, from which it is merely separated by the boulevard Unter den Linden. In reality, Prinz Heinrich Palais was from the start an inherent part of the plans for the representative square created at this location starting in 1740. Friedrich II had intended to erect a magnificent royal residency palace with a large ensemble for the square after his coronation as King of Prussia. Participating actively in the planning, the young king proved to be a builder of both great ambition and creativity. Though the residency palace was never built, as the king ultimately chose to place it in Potsdam, nevertheless an impressive complex, the **Forum Fridericianum**, was built starting in 1740, one which broke consciously with the fundamental rules of Baroque architecture, namely symmetry, axiality, and uniformity. The ensemble, consisting of the Staatsoper, Sankt-Hedwigs-Kirche (which became a Cathedral in 1930), and the Staatsbibliothek, conceived by Friedrich II and Georg Wenzeslaus von Knobelsdorff and framed by Prinz Heinrich Palais, the Old Palace, and the academy building on the opposite side, was driven by an absolutist desire for

Forum Fridericianum
planning: Friedrich II of Prussia, Georg Wenzeslaus von Knobelsdorff

Bebelplatz
originally Opernplatz | 1910–1937 Franz-Josephs-Platz | 1937–1947 Unter den Linden | on May 10, 1933, site of book burning by members of the National-Socialist German Student Association | 1995 ceremonial dedication of the monument in memory of the book burning, Micha Ullman (design)

other Forum buildings
Staatsoper
1741–1743 | first building of the ensemble | modeled after Italian villas in the style of Andrea Palladio

Sankt-Hedwigs-Kirche
1747–1773 | takes up design motifs from the Roman Pantheon

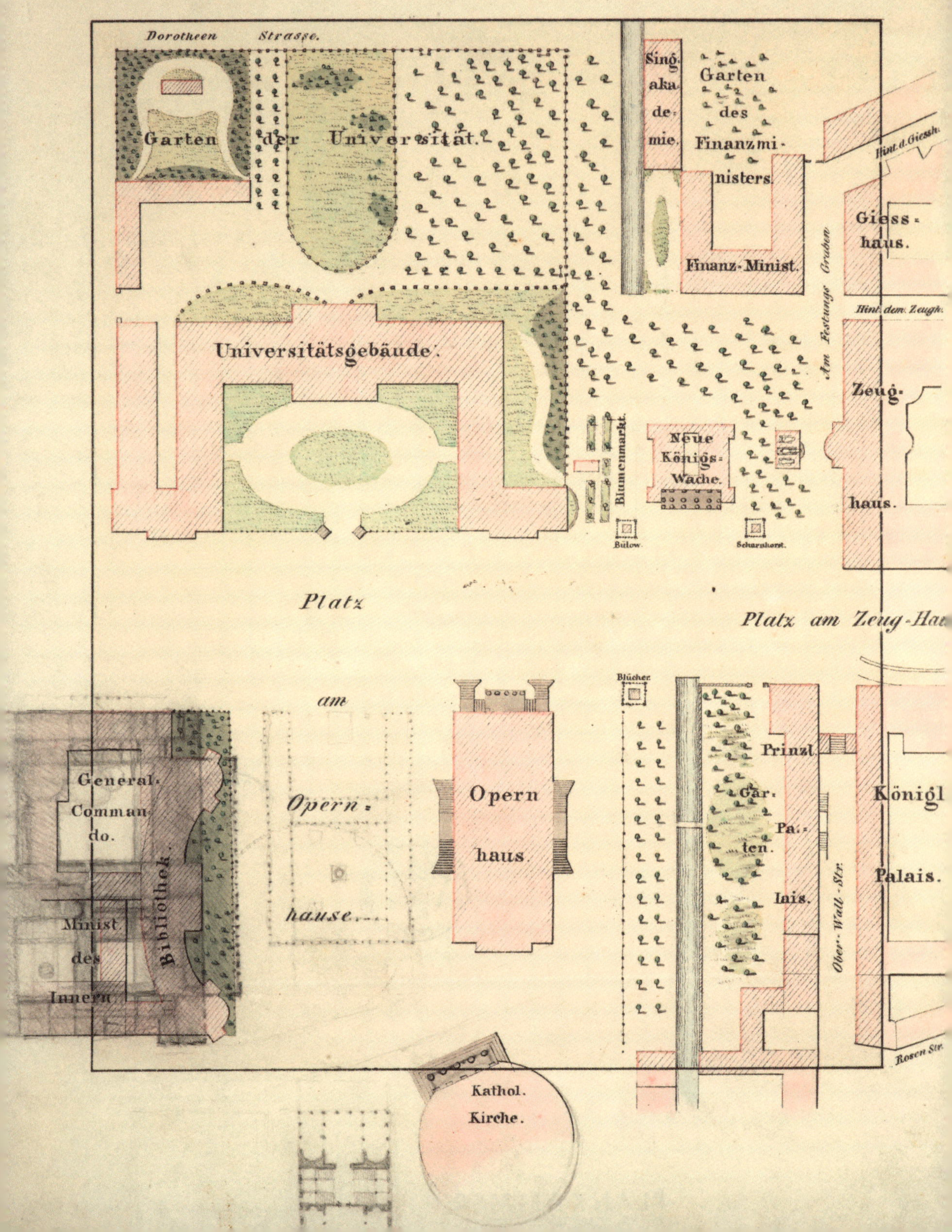

Dorotheen Strasse.
Garten der Universität.
Sing-akademie.
Garten des Finanzministers.
Finanz-Minist.
Hint. d. Giessh.
Giesshaus.
Hint. dem Zeugh.
Am Festungs Graben
Universitätsgebäude.
Blumenmarkt.
Neue Königs-Wache.
Zeughaus.
Bülow.
Scharnhorst.
Platz am Opernhause.
Platz am Zeug-Hau
Blücher
General-Commando.
Bibliothek.
Minist des Innern.
Opernhaus.
Prinzl. Garten.
Palais.
Ober-Wall-Str.
Königl Palais.
Rosen Str.
Kathol. Kirche.

Prinz Heinrich Palais and Alte Bibliothek, at the time of Friedrich Wilhelm III

Auditorium (1922), facade (1967) and new rear building

representation. The complex was meant to equally express both religious liberty and the high value placed on education and culture in Prussia.

The first structure to be built on the square was the Königliches Opernhaus, and just a few years later work commenced on the construction of the catholic Sankt-Hedwigs-Kirche. It was meant to serve as a symbol of reconciliation following the Second Silesian War. Though not completed until nearly three decades after ground had first been broken, the diagonal placement of this building already made a break with the guiding conceptions of Baroque square design. Finally, on the opposite side of the majestic boulevard Unter den Linden, itself incorporated into the design of the square, the Prinz Heinrich Palais, whose facade revisits the design of the opera house, was created between 1748 and 1753.

Alte Bibliothek

Königliche Bibliothek, "commode", Faculty of Law of HU

Bebelplatz 2 | 1775–1780 | Friedrich II (builder), Georg Friedrich Boumann the Younger (construction supervisor), Georg Christian Unger (design, based on well-known etchings by Salomon Kleiner, among others, and models of a proposed design for the St. Michael's Wing of the Vienna Hofburg by Joseph Emmanuel Fischer von Erlach from 1725–1726) | the ground floor was also used as a warehouse by the opera, and as a uniform store by the army | 1910 modification, Georg Thür, Anton Adams, Paul Emmerich | 1963–1969 reconstruction, Werner Kötteritzsch

On Bebelplatz square, the **Alte Bibliothek** today houses Humboldt-Universität's Faculty of Law. At the time of its construction for the Forum Fridericianum, Friedrich II specified that the external design of the building be based upon a proposed design for the St. Michael's Wing at Vienna's Hofburg that was widely disseminated and well known in Europe in the form of etchings and cork models. The fact that the proposed design was able to be realized in Berlin far in advance of the structure in Vienna was for Friedrich II (further) proof of Prussia's superiority over its Habsburg archrivals.

The origins of the Königliche Bibliothek can be traced back to collections from the Churfürstliche Bibliothek, located in the pharmacy wing of the palace, founded in 1661 by Prince-Elector Friedrich Wilhelm and consistently expanded in the years to follow. Practical considerations as well as the intention of setting an example for the promotion of science and education led to the creation of a representative new building in the High Baroque style. Seen from the outside, Georg Christian Unger's design, namely the arrangement of the windows and the rendering of the facade, indicates four stories, though in fact there are only two on the inside. Carl von Gontard was responsible for furnishing the newly established library on the upper floor.

In 1905, a new building became necessary in order to provide adequate storage for the dramatically expanding inventory of books. The library moved into a new building on the opposite side of the street, today's Staatsbibliothek (→198). The Alte Bibliothek, having lost its original function, was converted into a modern lecture hall facility by Georg Thür in 1910, to mark the centennial of the Berliner Universität, and equipped with several large lecture halls. Particularly impressive was the large auditorium, which was graced by a monumental mural: Fichte's Addresses to the German Nation by history painter Arthur Kampf. Having already suffered massive damage during air raids in November 1943, the building was completely consumed by fire in 1945, leaving only the enclosing walls standing.

Reading room in reconstructed Alte Bibliothek with glass painting window

Academy of Sciences and old observatory

As with the main building, the rebuilding work carried out by the university in the 1960s took its cues concerning the reconstruction of the exterior from the aesthetics of the original, while the courtyard side and the interior were redesigned. 1968 saw the addition of the large arched window "Lenin in Germany" by glass artist Frank Glaser, which can also be viewed from the outside, a piece commemorating Lenin's study visit in 1895.

Altes Palais

Faculty of Law of HU

Unter den Linden 9 | 1834–1837 | Prince Wilhelm of Prussia, later Kaiser Wilhelm I (builder), Carl Ferdinand Langhans (design) | used by Wilhelm as a city palace | 1943 heavy destruction by aerial bombing; residential and ceremonial rooms extending to Behrenstrasse completely destroyed by fire | 1960 demolished | 1964 reconstruction, Fritz Meinhardt; towards Behrenstrasse supplemented by pre-fab buildings | 2007 reconstruction of the pergola

Directly adjacent to the Alte Bibliothek, one finds the **Altes Palais**. This classical building by Carl Ferdinand Langhans served Kaiser Wilhelm I, who moved into the premises while still a prince, as a primary office and personal residence until his death in 1888. After 1945, Humboldt-Universität was given possession of the war-ravaged building. The facade and the eye-catching access ramp, above which a jutting balcony floats upon Doric columns, were restored in the 1960s. Today this building is also used by the Faculty of Law.

Directly opposite the Altes Palais, on the other side of the street, the Staatsbibliothek building is merely separated from the main building of the university by the narrow Universitätsstrasse. It is on this spot that one could find the royal stables (modified by Johann Boumann in 1743) from the late seventeenth century on, which were also used jointly by the Academy of Sciences, which maintained an astronomical observatory there. The observatory was shared by the university from its inception, later it was relocated to the edge of the city. There, in the vicinity of Hallesches Tor, Schinkel realized a building in 1835 that would in turn be demolished in 1913 and replaced by a new building in Babelsberg. The discipline of astronomy was the first to flee Mitte, while the other natural sciences initially pursued attempts to become better settled in the immediate vicinity of the main building. (GM)

DOROTHEENSTRASSE

With Prinz Heinrich Palais, the university had gained a prominent location in the city within the Forum Fridericianum, but, alas, Unter den Linden offered very little potential for expansion or cultivating connections with other institutions. Thus, gradually, the university built up a presence in the Dorotheenstadt quarter, where it was able to acquire, among other locations, for its scientific pursuits a series of properties that had formerly been used for military purposes. So it was not the Linden side of the university, but instead the rear side that would progressively open and expand into a tighter-knit academic district, which extended above all along Dorotheenstrasse.

The amount of space available in the main building remained unchanged for over a century after the university took up quarters in the former palace – and was thus unable to satisfy any additional demand. Two generations of scientists had justifiably harbored little hope of ever being granted more extensive or better facilities, or even additional rooms. However, through a clever approach to faculty appointments, the university still managed several times not only to recruit brilliant scientists, but also to incorporate their existing research facilities into the university. With the passage of time, however, few traces of them remain to be seen today.
This applied primarily to the experimental sciences of chemistry, technology, and physics. In 1810, Martin Heinrich Klaproth first incorporated the Academy's laboratory into the university's teaching activities, by holding his experimental lectures there. However, nothing remains of the lab, which was located at Dorotheenstrasse 30. On today's undeveloped Hegelplatz square, in front of the new seminar building at Dorotheenstrasse 24, prior to the founding of the university there already existed the "chemical saloon" of Sigismund Friedrich Hermbstaedt, a residential and laboratory building that the local trade association had financed in 1802. After Hermbstaedt's appointment to faculty in 1811, it was considered the university's "Chemical Institute". The private laboratory of his successor Heinrich Rose, located on the Museumsinsel, has also been lost to history. Today, only the **Magnus-Haus** at the beginning of Dorotheenstrasse – its facade facing the Museumsinsel – is left as an example of how private houses were used for the natural sciences in the first fifty years of the Berliner Universität.

Gustav Magnus, himself a graduate of the Berliner Universität in chemistry, was named professor of technology and physics in 1834. In 1840, he acquired the Baroque palace, which, with its self-assured architecture, held its own as the bourgeois equivalent of the Prinz Heinrich Palais, and equipped it with a laboratory and lecture hall such that not only he but also his students could work there, particularly in the field of experimental physics.

Magnus-Haus

Am Kupfergraben 7 | 1756 | Georg Friedrich Boumann (the Younger), August Naumann | commissioned by Friedrich II for the secret war councilor Johann Friedrich Westphal | inhabited by mathematician Joseph-Louis Lagrange (1766–1787), German philologist Rochus von Liliencron (1908–1911), and director Max Reinhardt (1911–1921), among others | 1934–1945 transferred to the university | from 1952 used by the Physical Society of the GDR | since 1990 headquarters of the (united) German Physical Society

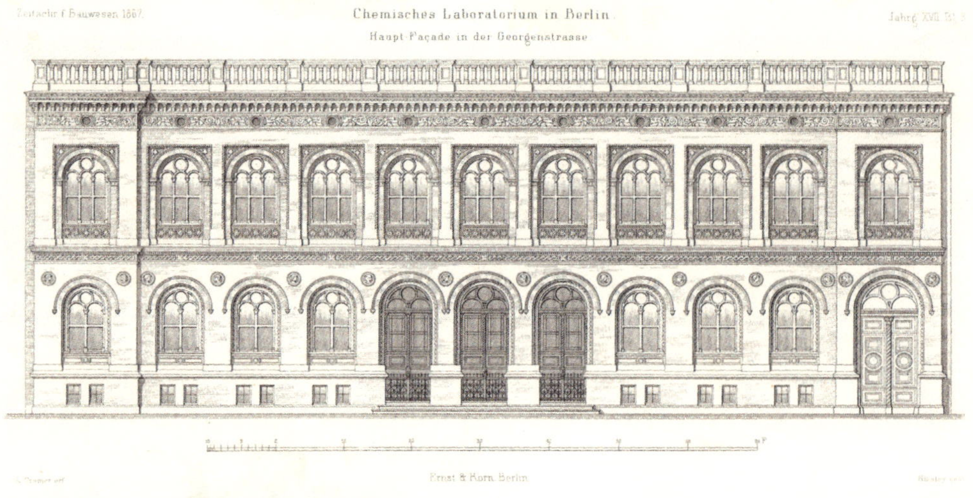
Zeitschr. f. Bauwesen 1867.
Chemisches Laboratorium in Berlin.
Haupt-Façade in der Georgenstrasse
Ernst & Korn Berlin

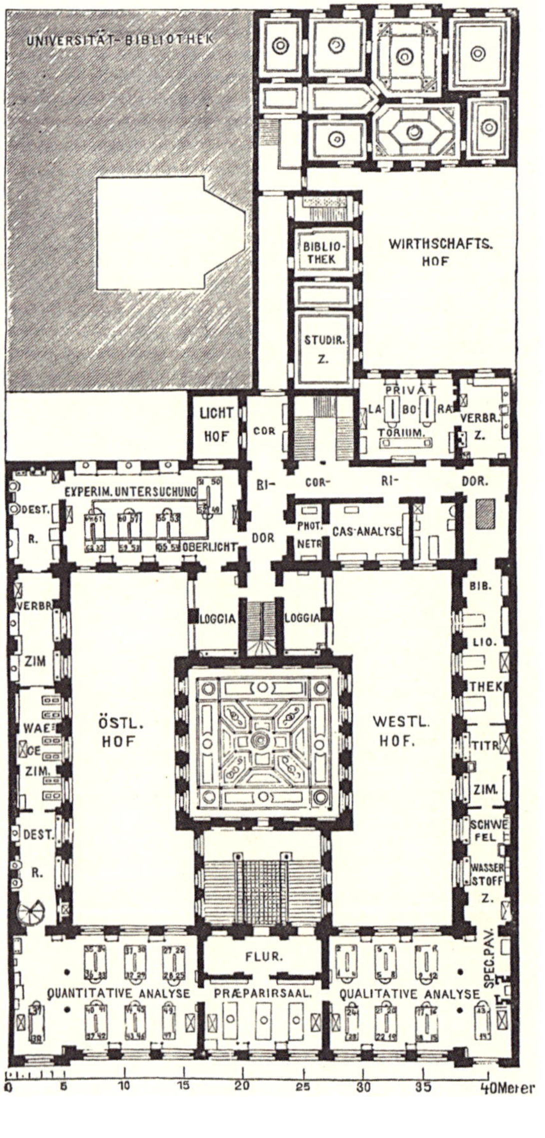
UNIVERSITÄT-BIBLIOTHEK
BIBLIO-THEK
WIRTHSCHAFTS. HOF
STUDIR. Z.
PRIVAT LA-BO-RA-TORIUM.
VERBR. Z.
LICHT HOF
COR
RI- COR- RI- DOR.
EXPERIM. UNTERSUCHUNG
DEST. R.
OBERLICHT
DOR
PHOT. NETR
GAS-ANALYSE
BIB- LIO- THEK
LOGGIA
LOGGIA
VERBR. ZIM
WAE-GE ZIM.
ÖSTL. HOF
WESTL. HOF.
TITR. ZIM.
SCHWEFEL
WASSERSTOFF Z.
DEST. R.
FLUR.
SPEC. PAV.
QUANTITATIVE ANALYSE
PRÆPARIRSAAL.
QUALITATIVE ANALYSE
0 5 10 15 20 25 30 35 40 Meter

This building is also famous as the place where the Berlin Physical Society, later the German Physical Society (DPG), arose from Magnus's physics colloquium of 1845. The DPG is still present here today, using the building for lectures and archival storage, as well as hosting receptions in the garden and its coach shed.

Chemical Laboratory

Georgenstrasse 34–36 | 1865–1867 | Albert Cremer, Karl Zastrau | 1900 repurposing as Institute and Museum of Marine Science

University Library

Dorotheenstrasse 28 | 1871–1874 | Paul Spieker | 1910 within in the Staatsbibliothek complex, first Universitätsstrasse 9 and in 1922 Dorotheenstrasse 27

When the physics laboratory moved into the east wing of the main building in 1870 after Magnus's death, the chemists had already had their own independent premises for three years. With the previous creation of the **Chemical Laboratory** in 1867, the construction of the university's first genuine natural science institute was completed. It was extended in 1874 with the addition of the **University Library**. The front of the structure is still intact. Together, the two buildings formed a rectangle between Dorotheenstrasse 28–30 and Georgenstrasse 34–36, whereby the academy laboratory was incorporated as a residential wing. In the person of August Hofmann, the university was able to hire on a luminary in the world of chemistry from London, who would also have a determining influence on the laboratory architecture. The enormous windows arranged in an arched style, intended for ventilation when the building was used for chemistry, continued to acquit themselves well after 1900, when the ensemble was transformed into the Institute and Museum of Marine Science.

Before a dedicated building could be readied for the university library, the institution's books had to weather an even more eventful journey than that of the laboratory. The Königliche Bibliothek provided too little space, a fact that could not be mitigated by an 1831 cabinet order to create a separate section for the university. The "Adlerscher Saal" at Unter den Linden 76, a building bridging the (Neue) Wilhelmstrasse which was rented eight years later, soon proved too small; the same was the case for the two stories of a residential house at Taubenstrasse 29, near the Gendarmenmarkt, which were occupied after 1854.

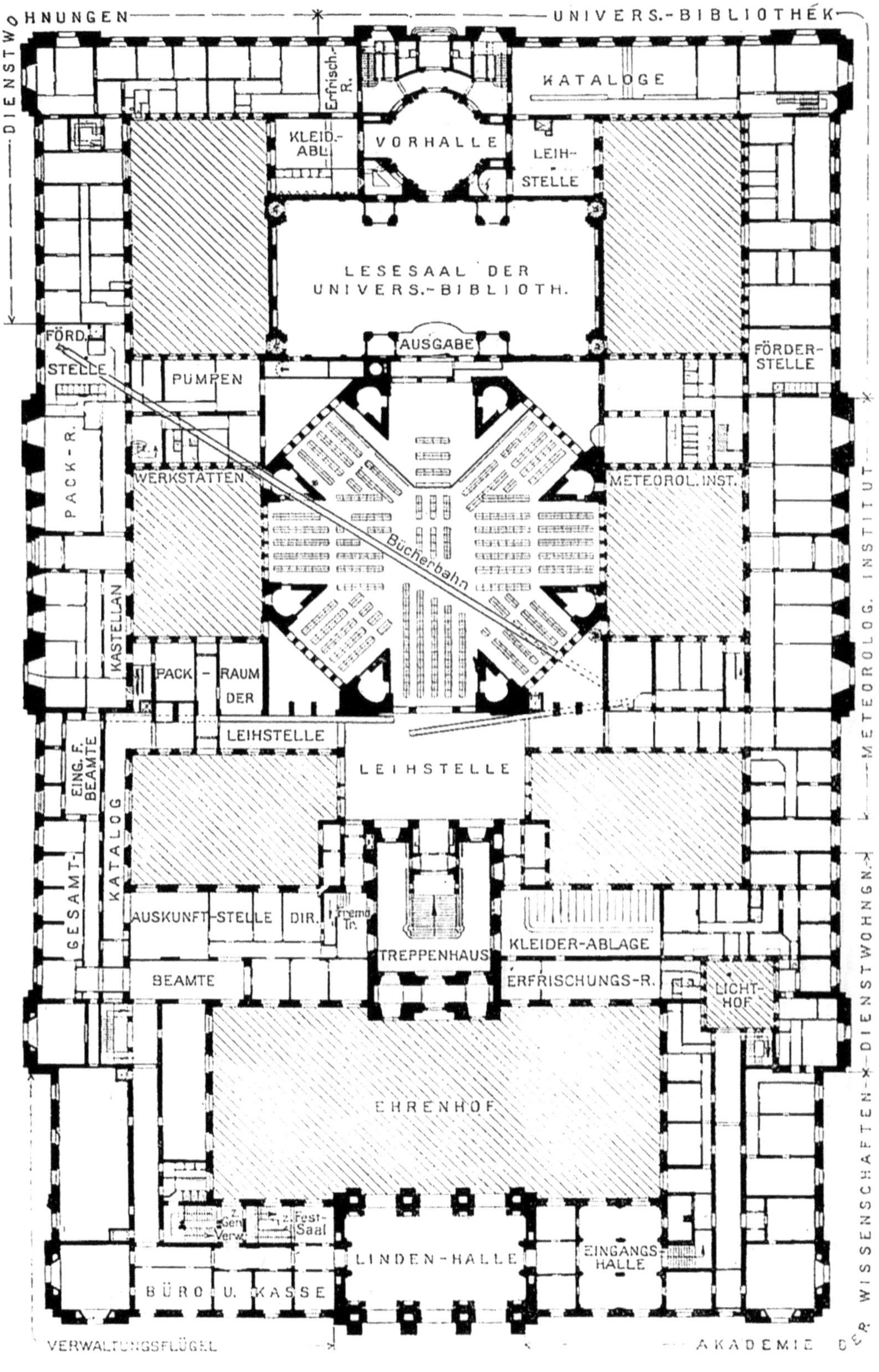
DIENSTWOHNUNGEN
UNIVERS.-BIBLIOTHEK
Erfrisch.-R.
KATALOGE
KLEID.-ABL.
VORHALLE
LEIH-STELLE
LESESAAL DER UNIVERS.-BIBLIOTH.
FÖRD.-STELLE
AUSGABE
FÖRDER-STELLE
PUMPEN
PACK-R.
WERKSTÄTTEN
METEOROL. INST.
Bücherbahn
KASTELLAN
PACK-RAUM DER
LEIHSTELLE
LEIHSTELLE
EING. F. BEAMTE
GESAMT-KATALOG
METEOROLOG. INSTITUT
AUSKUNFT-STELLE
DIR.
TREPPENHAUS
KLEIDER-ABLAGE
BEAMTE
ERFRISCHUNGS-R.
LICHT-HOF
DIENSTWOHNGN.
EHRENHOF
z. Fest-Saal
LINDEN-HALLE
EINGANGS-HALLE
BÜRO U. KASSE
VERWALTUNGSFLÜGEL
AKADEMIE DER WISSENSCHAFTEN

Staatsbibliothek

Unter den Linden 8, Universitätsstrasse 6–8, Dorotheenstrasse 27, Charlottenstrasse 39–41 | 1903–1914 | Ernst von Ihne | building complex with parts for the University Library, the Academy and some insitutes
(→ 198)

Jacob-und-Wilhelm-Grimm-Zentrum

Geschwister-Scholl-Strasse 1/3 | 2005–2010 | Max Dudler
(→ 199)

In the years before World War I, an older ensemble between Unter den Linden and Dorotheenstrasse consisting of the royal stables, the academy, a barracks, and a telegraph station was replaced – originally the observatory and the anatomical theater stood at this location as well. With Ernst von Ihne's **Staatsbibliothek**, erected exactly on this spot, with its boastful neo-Baroque architecture meant to represent Wilhelminism, one is dealing in the interim more with a further ensemble than an individual building. From Unter den Linden one could enter the Königliche Bibliothek – from 1918 known as the Preußische Staatsbibliothek – and the Academy, while from Universitätsstrasse one could access institutes such as that for meteorology, and Dorotheenstrasse provided an entrance to the new university library. Situated right across from the old library, the books only had to cross the street in 1910. After World War II, the war-damaged library had to make do for decades with a temporary solution, until almost exactly one hundred years after the opening of Unter den Linden the **Jacob-und-Wilhelm-Grimm-Zentrum** was inaugurated as the university library of Humboldt-Universität, some one hundred meters to the north, beyond the S-Bahn tracks.

Institutes for Library Science and Social Science

Seminar Building at Hegelplatz

Dorotheenstrasse 24 | 1905–1906 | Georg Thür, Max Guth | auditorium building (Reutersaal still intact) | 1981 and 2006 expansions into seminar building

Chamber of Commerce

Dorotheenstrasse 26 | 1903–1904 | Wilhelm Cremer, Richard Wolffenstein | sculptural work by Ernst Westphal | used by HU since 1946 | 1950 conversion | today the location of the School of Library and Information Science

Institute of Social Science

Universitätsstrasse 3b | 1903–1904 | Otto Richter | facade design with sandstone figures and decorative motifs by Erich Blunck | building initially used exclusively as office space, possibility of functional repurposing already foreseen in planning stages | used by the university since 1936 | 1993 occupied by newly founded Institute of Social Science

Theological Faculty

Burgstrasse 26 | 1910–1911 | Siegfried Weile | built as a commercial building across from the then-location of the Berlin Stock Exchange | used by the university since 1950 | 2001 occupied by the Theological Faculty | 2007 renovation, reconstruction of the historical facades, extended with a new building for the branch library

The area between the Staatsbibliothek and the Grimm-Zentrum, as well as east of Universitätsstrasse and Geschwister-Scholl-Strasse, was "scientified" in different ways. The mighty **Seminar Building at Hegelplatz** from 2006, with the Institutes for German and Nordic Languages and Literature, encompasses the older Reuter-Haus, which was built one hundred years previously as a lecture hall and seminar building. Little has remained visible of the first enlargement at the beginning of the 1980s. Before that, this area was home to a maternity clinic, as well as residential and commercial buildings, which at times also housed seminar libraries.

The building of the former **Chamber of Commerce** belongs to a whole series of houses which were not originally conceived for academia, but which were taken over by the university in the course of its expansion and differentiation. These also include the **Institute of Social Science** and – in a direct extension of Dorotheenstrasse beyond the Museumsinsel – the **Theological Faculty**, which were built in 1904 and 1911 as commercial houses, but have been used by Humboldt-Universität since 1936 and 1950 respectively.

Musicological Seminar

Berlin Palace, 1930

School of Commerce with chapel and Royal Artillery Barracks

School of Commerce

Spandauer Strasse 1 | 1905–1906 | Wilhelm Cremer, Richard Wolffenstein | part of the Faculty of Economics since 1946, in use since 1951

Berlin Palace

since 1443 | Renaissance buildings (especially pharmacy wing) in the 16th and Baroque buildings at the beginning of the 17th century by Schlossbaumeister Andreas Schlüter | numerous alterations and extensions | 1661–1780 Churfürstliche Bibliothek in the pharmacy wing | 1920–1945 Psychological Institute in the southwest wing | 1945 destroyed | 2013–2020 modified rebuilding | from 2020 home of Humboldt Laboratory of the HU

Further repurposed structures

Musicological Seminar
Am Kupfergraben 5 | 1829 three-story residential house | Johann Börner (builder) | war damages | 1972–1982 reconstruction | in possession of the university since 1949 | today the location of the Institute of Musicology

Institute for European Ethnology
Mohrenstrasse 40/41 | 1787 | Carl Gotthard Langhans' "Mohrenkolonnaden" mark former bridge | 1952–1955 restored for the Academy's Institute of Physics after sustaining damage in the war | 1992–1993 conversion for the Institute for Ethnology

Berlin-Brandenburg Center for Jewish Studies
Sophienstrasse 22 | 1899 residential and business park complex | Gebert & Söhne (construction company) | used by HU since 1993 | since 2012 location of the Selma Stern Center for Jewish Studies

"Pergamon Palais"
Am Kupfergraben 4, 4a, Georgenstrasse 46–48 | 2009–2011 | Rüthnick Architekten | office and residential building with institutes in building segment Georgenstrasse 47

Institute of Educational Sciences

Geschwister-Scholl-Strasse 7 | built around 1898–1901 as Royal Artillery Barracks | Josef Wieczorek, Julius Boethke | damaged severely in the war | used in the GDR as Friedrich Engels Barracks

One more block down the street, one finds the former **School of Commerce** from 1906, later also the "Gau Economic Bureau" under the Nazis, in which the Faculty of Economics is housed. Incidentally, this building includes as a lecture hall the Heilig-Geist-Kapelle, constructed in 1300, making it the oldest building used or repurposed by the university.

The **Berlin Palace** too was reused after World War I with the abdication of the emperor, and so the Psychological Institute of the Linden University moved into a wing and experimented there in the stately rooms.

Further repurposed structures can be found within a wider radius of the main building. In recent times too, university institutes have been integrated into residential and commercial buildings; for instance, the Pergamon Palais is home to several institutes for fine art, culture, and media studies.

The **Institute of Educational Sciences** is an example of another repurposing for science: since 1773 the Royal Artillery Barracks had stood on the grounds east of today's Geschwister-Scholl-Strasse. The barracks, renovated in 1900 in the style of the Weser Renaissance, became the Friedrich Engels Barracks in the GDR. Only after German reunification did science finally take up quarters here.

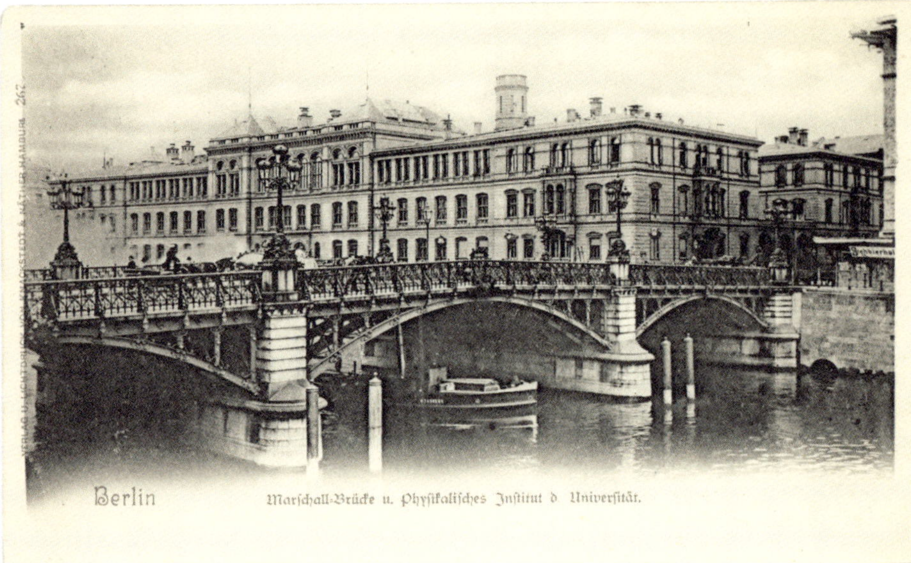
Berlin
Marschall-Brücke u. Physikalisches Institut d. Universität.

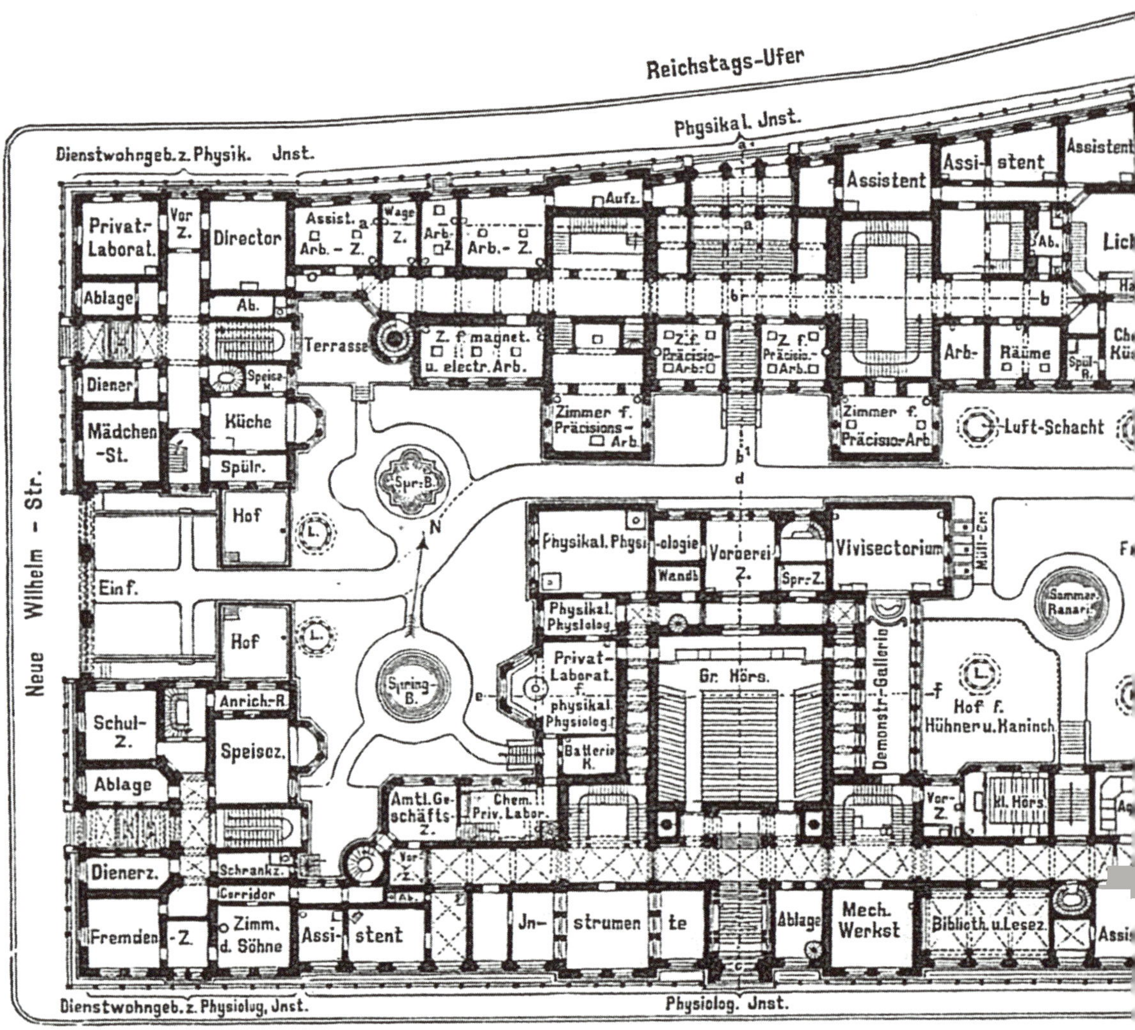
Reichstags-Ufer
Physikal. Jnst.
Dienstwohngeb. z. Physik. Jnst.
Privat-Laborat.
Vor Z.
Director
Assist. Arb.-Z.
Wage Z.
Arb.-Z.
Aufz.
Assistent
Assi- stent
Assistent
Ablage
Ab.
Terrasse
Z. f. magnet. u. electr. Arb.
Z. f. Präcisio-Arb.
Arb- Räume
Spül-R.
Diener
Speise-A.
Mädchen-St.
Küche
Spülr.
Zimmer f. Präcisions-Arb.
Zimmer f. Präcisio-Arb.
Luft-Schacht
Hof
Spr.-B.
N
Physikal. Physi-ologie
Wandb.
Vorbereit. Z.
Spr.-Z.
Vivisectorium
Müll-Gr.
Neue Wilhelm-Str.
Einf.
Physikal. Physiolog.
Sommer-Kanari
Privat-Laborat. f. physikal. Physiolog.
Gr. Hörs.
Demonstr.-Gallerie
Hof f. Hühner u. Kaninch.
Spring-B.
Schul-Z.
Anrich-R.
Speisez.
Batterie K.
Ablage
Amtl. Geschäfts-Z.
Chem. Priv. Labor.
Vor-Z.
Kl. Hörs.
Dienerz.
Schrankz.
Corridor
Fremden-Z.
Zimm. d. Söhne
Assi- stent
Jn- strumen te
Ablage
Mech. Werkst
Biblioth. u. Lesez.
Dienstwohngeb. z. Physiolog. Jnst.
Physiolog. Jnst.

Natural Sciences Quarter
Koch Forum

Institute of Physics
Wilhelmstrasse 67 | 1873–1878 | Paul Spieker | 1945 largely destroyed | 1996–1999 new building for ARD capital studio

Institute of Physiology
Dorotheenstrasse 94 | 1873–1877 | Paul Spieker | 1960–2009 Robert Koch Museum in library section | since 2017 Einstein Center Digital Future in former residential wing

Institute of Physical Chemistry
Second Chemical and Technological Institute
Bunsenstrasse 1 | 1879–1883 | Karl Zastrau

Institute of Pharmacology
Dorotheenstrasse 96 | 1879–1883 | Paul Spieker

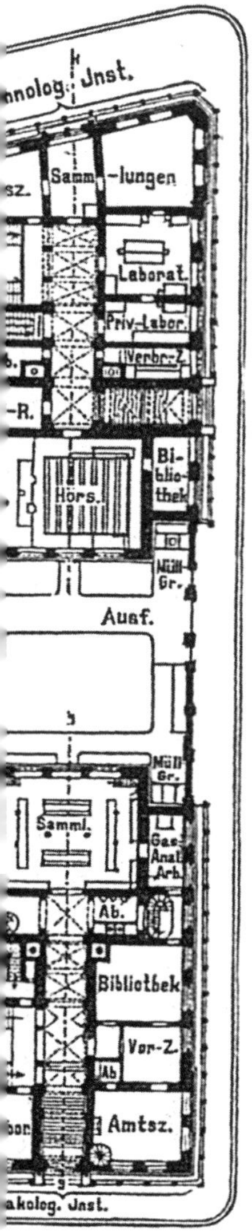

The property formerly occupied by the artillery workshops on the western end of Dorotheenstrasse was already acquired for the experimental natural sciences immediately following 1871. In the **Natural Sciences Quarter**, the Institutes of Physics and Physiology could be established on a grand scale first from 1878 on. With that, promises made to Hermann von Helmholtz upon his appointment, as well as to Emil du Bois Reymond, were fulfilled. Both presided over the furnishing of the laboratories and received directors' residences along Wilhelmstrasse. Soon the building ensemble was expanded with the addition of the Institutes of Physical Chemistry and Pharmacology on Bunsenstrasse.

On the outside, the German Empire's largest and most expensive institute building complex of the time formed a single entity characterized by high-end architectural design, while examination of the interior revealed surprising partitioning and differentiation. Apartments and private laboratories were separated clearly from research and teaching areas of nearly industrial proportions. Distributed throughout the complex, one found gardens, frog ponds, and stalls for animals. Vibration-free pedestals, rooted in special foundations, were intended to make it possible to record precise measurements. The entire building complex was isolated from vibrations emanating from heavy city traffic by a trench running alongside the sidewalk.

Alas, the local S-Bahn train line planned for the same time very nearly nullified all this effort to facilitate the attainment of precise measurements in the new institutes. For not only were the sciences growing in Berlin –

Nernst auditorium at the Institute of Physical Chemistry and Koch auditorium at the Physiological Institute

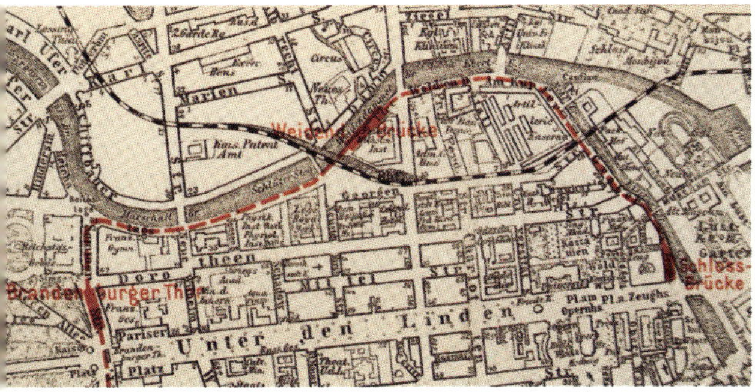

Another proposal for an under pavement railway, Siemens & Halske, 1897

the transportation infrastructure was too, and the plans of the day called for a railway line from Lehrter Bahnhof on the left bank of the Spree that would run directly past the Institute of Physics as a subsurface line. It was only thanks to a vehement petition from Helmholtz and the university senate to the king and cultural ministry that this plan was thwarted in 1872. So it is that even today the S-Bahn still makes a gentle double curve here and first crosses the Spree at Friedrichstrasse station – an inconspicuous reminder of Dorotheenstadt's status in times past as a district for natural science research of the highest order.

In direct proximity to the Reichstag building which was taking shape at the time, the "Reich Chancellor of Physics", as Helmholtz was also called, went about his business, and the most important expert associations for the natural sciences held meetings in the institute libraries. Here, Robert Koch announced the discovery of tuberculosis bacillus in 1882, and Max Planck promulgated his quantum theory in 1900, before Walther Nernst discovered the third law of thermodynamics in 1906, supposedly during a lecture in his lecture hall. The former military property had become a seedbed for Nobel Prize winners.

Today, the former site of the destroyed Institute of Physics is occupied by the capital studio of public broadcaster ARD, while the buildings of the three remaining institutes remain standing, and were in use up until the relocation of the natural sciences to Adlershof was completed in 2003, after which they fell into a deep slumber and stood vacant for years. One section of the complex has awakened again, with the creation of the Einstein Center Digital Future, a co-operative undertaking by Berlin's three big universities. The Berlin University Alliance and the Hertie School of Governance are slated to join it in the very near future. (AS)

UNIVERSITY MEDICINE ON ZIEGELSTRASSE

Reclining hall on the roof of the University Clinic for Gynecology

When the university's Faculty of Medicine was founded in 1810, it was far from the first site for the training of physicians-to-be in Berlin. As early as 1723/1724 there was the Collegium medico-chirurgicum, then the Pépinière starting in 1795, and above all Charité, founded already in 1710, which provided practical training to military doctors in the making, army surgeons, and surgical medics, and cared for a large number of predominantly poor patients. In order to distinguish itself from the practice-oriented training at Charité, the university medicine department wished to prepare subjects for the medical profession scientifically, and it took in the Collegium medico-chirurgicum and the latter's collections to this end. In order to create space, the university built a bridge across the Spree to the north of the main building at Unter den Linden – only in a figurative sense back then, though today the river can indeed be crossed at that particular location: from 1818 on, dedicated buildings for university medical studies were created between the Spree and Oranienburger Strasse on Ziegelstrasse. Admittedly, the university was not entirely able to resist the attraction of the practical potential offered at Charité, and, thus, between 1828 and 1927 the facilities of the Faculty of Medicine were gradually relocated to the Charité hospital grounds.

In the beginning the newly founded university had a hard time providing its Faculty of Medicine with adequate facilities for the education of doctors-to-be. Moves towards locating the university's medical division on the premises of Charité came to naught initially due to objections from the first tenured professors for medicine: they wished to maintain a healthy distance for the time being from the practically oriented training of military doctors conducted there. They were also skeptical whether it was wise to let their students be confronted with the chaotic conditions involved in treating the masses, in this case primarily "impecunious" patients. Thus, improvisation reigned supreme at the outset: the first "clinics", Johann Christian Reil's medical clinic and Carl Ferdinand von Graefe's surgical clinic, initially shared two little rooms in a rented house on Friedrichstrasse. In both establishments, patients were assigned in the closest of quarters to one of twelve beds. These humble beginnings are nevertheless to be considered as the germ cells of the university clinic, since, in addition to the fact that patients were being treated there, students were also being trained. The crowded space was smothering and, on top of everything else, the locals complained constantly about disturbances through foul odors, the pained screams of patients being treated without anesthetic, or the removal of corpses. For a time, the university physicians continued to improvise, occupying further rental properties, until the decision to establish a separate clinic building was finally made.

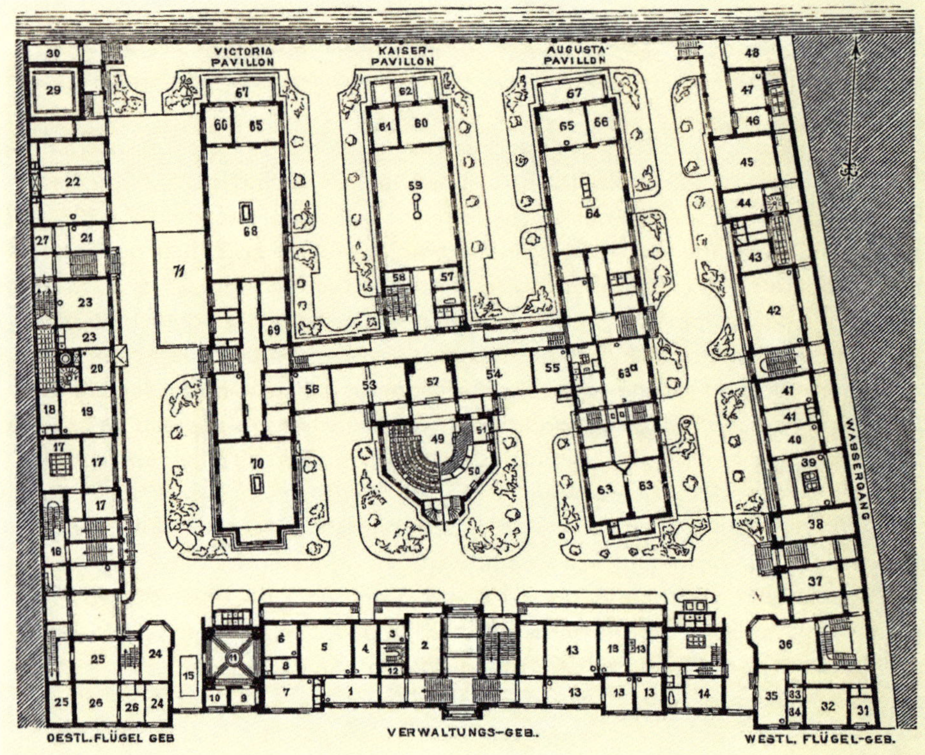

University Clinic, plan and facade, extension building on the left side of the picture

University Clinic

Ziegelstrasse 5–9 | 1818–1819 repurposing of an existing factory building after plans of the doctors Christoph Wilhelm Hufeland and Carl Ferdinand von Graefe | 1878–1883 construction of new building for Surgical Clinic and Eye and Ear Clinic, Martin Gropius, Heino Schmieden | further floor added in the 1920s | conversions in 1951 and 1990 | 2014–2015 conversion to nursery school facility of HU

Annex building

Ziegelstrasse 10–11 | 1893 | 1891–1893 Eduard Haesecke, Friedeberg | administration and technical division of HU

Gynecological Clinic

University Clinic for Gynecology

Ziegelstrasse 14–19, Tucholskystrasse 2, Monbijoustrasse 2 | 1880–1883 | Martin Gropius, Heino Schmieden | 1886 autopsy house added | 1892–1893 addition of a lecture hall | 1927–1933 fundamental redesign and modernization, new construction of Ziegelstrasse wing in the style of the New Objectivity, Heinrich Wolff | 1952–1956 reconstruction | 1982 move into "Bettenhochhaus" of Charité | since 2015 parts of the site are in the process of being converted into rental apartments and office spaces according to plans by David Chipperfield

To gain space for a new **University Clinic**, the university had to take a step across the Spree: within walking distance from the main building, an appropriate location for a dedicated clinic building was found in a former lead acetate and starch factory on Ziegelstrasse. The factory was refurbished for medical purposes and occupied by the medical and surgical clinics in 1818. Alas, soon enough it become clear that – contrary to previous assumptions – large numbers of patients were no disadvantage when it came to the training of future doctors: a mere ten years later, the medical clinic was relocated to the grounds of Charité, as the location turned out to offer better opportunities for co-operation in medical education. Nevertheless, the university held onto the site on Ziegelstrasse. The surgery department in particular was able to make a name for itself at this location. Under the direction of Bernhard von Langenbeck, Berlin developed into Europe's true center for surgery.

The clinical disciplines continued to evolve and become more and more differentiated in the second half of the nineteenth century. These developments left traces on the premises at Charité for all to see, but they also brought significant new impulses to the university site on Ziegelstrasse. Here, in the 1870s, impressive new clinic buildings were erected between the Monbijou and Weidendamm bridges. With the new construction of the clinic a three-winged pavilion complex was created with the Victoria, Augusta, and Kaiser Pavilions, each with its own risalits. Further down towards the Spree, the isolation ward and surgical clinic found new homes in a pavilion group of their own. The primary advantage of the pavilion form lay in the fact that both light and air intake could be regulated flexibly and easily to best meet occupants' individual needs. About ten years later, the **annex building** opened as a polyclinic, which carried on the architectural design.

The new structure built to house the university's **Gynecological Clinic** introduced a powerful new accent to the Ziegelstrasse ensemble. This building followed in the footsteps of the maternity hospital on Oranienburger Strasse which had already been opened in 1816. After an intermezzo in Dorotheenstrasse 5, which also soon proved insufficient to meet the institution's requirements, starting in 1880 the construction of an "obstetrical-gynecological clinic" finally took place at the Ziegelstrasse site. In addition to the two houses in front, the three-winged complex contained three pavilions in the courtyard. Further buildings followed. A dedicated clinic building for "women with refined lifestyles" was created right at the water between 1909 and 1911, based on designs by Georg Thür.

Gynecological Clinic, original facility and annex from the 1920s

Here, female members of the upper classes were hosted in welcoming patient rooms featuring their own south-facing balconies and loggias. Whereas the influence of the Wilhelmine neo-Baroque could still be felt with this structure, a fundamentally new design would take hold in the Gynecological Clinic from 1927: the New Objectivity had arrived. Particularly striking here was the new round building on the corner of Monbijoustrasse, which took up elements from the Bode Museum across the way and interpreted them in a new light. With its white facade, glazed superstructure, and flat roof, the building added a modern accent to this area.
The buildings of the Gynecological Clinic, largely protected by preservation orders, are being converted today within the remit of the "Forum Museumsinsel" project. A hotel complex, as well as rental properties, offices, retail spaces, markets, and restaurants are to be created here – recently, the architect David Chipperfield converted the site into a luxury quarter.

The site of the Gynecological Clinic today

LUISENSTRASSE: FROM PLAGUE HOUSE TO UNIVERSITY CLINIC

As the university's medical division began construction for a dedicated clinic building on Ziegelstrasse in 1818, to the north, within walking distance, there had existed for already some one hundred years a medical facility still familiar today – first as a plague house and then as a center of care for the poorer classes, and finally as a training site for military doctors: Berlin's Charité. Wilhelm von Humboldt wished to keep the academic and rather more theoretical and scientific approach to university medical instruction at a safe distance from Charité's efforts to serve the masses. Alas, the research and teaching opportunities offered by the large number of patients soon led the university to move closer to Charité after all. As early as 1828, a part of the medical clinic was relocated from Ziegelstrasse to Charité. Further clinics would follow. When a comprehensive overhaul of the historical Charité grounds west of Luisenstrasse began in 1897, Charité had already effectively been merged with the university clinics. The resettlement of the surgical clinic in 1927 completed this process. The structural expansion on the Charité site coincided with the transformation of the training facilities for Prussian military doctors into a modern university clinic.

Plague House and first Charité

1709 commissioned by royal decree | 1710 completed | used as a hospital for the poor and not as a plague house | from 1727 used as a public hospital | additions made to plague house | expansion with kitchen building, dining room/church hall, as well as a baking house and brewing house| demolished to make way for construction of Old Charité

Walking around today through the large clinic complex at Charité in the heart of Berlin, one is very unlikely to imagine that this site, at the time of its inception, once lay far beyond the city walls. The **Plague House** built to the northwest of the city in 1710, in which the infected were to be accommodated at a safe remove from urban society, formed the nucleus for the clinics of the present day. Due to the fact, contrary to the fears of the time, that the plague epidemic failed to reach Berlin, though it raged on in East Prussia, the two-story, timber frame structure arranged in a square around an inner courtyard could be used for other purposes. Beggars and vagabonds were brought here for shelter or held and made to spin wool.

In 1726, by cabinet decree, King Friedrich Wilhelm I turned the facility into a "citizens' lazaretto", which he christened **"Charité"** – French for charity or mercy – two weeks after its opening in the beginning of 1727. This was the true birthdate of the hospital that would go on to become the largest university clinic in Europe in the second half of the twentieth century.

Now penniless elderly folk came here as well, the "infirm", as they were referred to. In addition, unwed pregnant women and sick individuals unable to afford a doctor's care were treated here too. Thus, strictly speaking, the very early Charité was three institutions in one: it provided care for the poor, took care of patients, and also contributed to training doctors for the Collegium medico-chirurgicum, founded in 1724, whose members manned the hospital wards in front of the city walls at regular intervals. At first, the emphasis lay on the practical formation of military doctors. The official founding of the Pépinière in 1795, a boarding school for military doctors in the making, would reinforce this orientation once again towards the end of the eighteenth century (this institution was known from 1895 on as the Kaiser Wilhelm Academy for the Education of Military Doctors, and located on Invalidenstrasse from 1910).

Old and New Charité

Following 1727, outbuildings, as well as a residential house for the inspector general, were erected In rapid succession on the grounds of the plague house. An extra floor was added to the building as well: in the new third story, "the infectious" – most of them suffering from venereal diseases – received medical care. For several decades, this ensemble remained intact, although it soon struggled with overcrowding in light of the rapidly growing population of Berlin.

In 1785, construction began on a new wing on the north side of the plague house, followed by another, until finally the old plague house had to be demolished to make way for the central section of the new building. Thus, fifteen years after the first ground was broken for expansion, Charité possessed a new, functional clinic, commonly referred to as **Old Charité**. The late-Baroque three-winged structure now housed an "insane asylum" among other things, in which mentally ill individuals were not merely detained but also received active medical treatment. All in all, the facility boasted some 680 beds, rendering it a large-scale clinic according to the standards of the time. And with that, the former institution for the care of the poor outside the city gates had become a genuine hospital within the city limits.

After the university's founding in 1809, featuring its own Faculty of Medicine from the start, a close collaboration soon developed – against the will of the university founders as it were – between the military and civilian approaches to the training of physicians. In 1828, the medical clinic became the first university facility to be relocated to the grounds of Charité. It was soon joined by a number of new buildings, including **New Charité**, which provided treatment for the "mentally ill", but also housed the clinic for skin and venereal diseases. The **Pox House**, erected in 1836, is today the oldest intact building on the premises of Charité, as both structures, Old and New Charité, had to be torn down to make space for a large-scale visionary and courageous development project at the end of the nineteenth century.

Friedrich Althoff, the hugely influential Prussian science manager, and Georg Diestel, who was charged with the overall planning, shaped this new phase of construction. Between 1897 and 1917, numerous new clinics were created, which Diestel graced with eye-catching structural features drawing on neo-Gothic, Art Nouveau, or neo-Renaissance styles, all while taking great care that the buildings would come together to form a homogeneous architectural ensemble through the uniform use of brick construction. The advent of these new buildings also marked the end for all of the temporary structures, the barracks and tent infirmaries, which had been erected throughout the years. The otorhinolaryngology clinic on Luisenstrasse was the first new clinic to open its doors in 1901.

Where New Charité once stood, the buildings for the **Psychiatric and Neurological Clinic** were created beginning in 1899. Towards the end of the nineteenth century, an entirely insufficient mental health care situation was the rule of the day: the treatment of mentally ill patients

---

Old Charité

1785–1800 | Karl von Gontard, Georg Christian Unger | from 1800 inside the city limits following relocation of the city walls

---

New Charité

1831–1834 | Ludwig Ferdinand Hesse | torn down in 1905

Pox House

Virchowweg 21 | 1836–1837 | probably Ludwig Ferdinand Hesse | 1854–1951 used by the gynecological departments | 1951–2008 Department for Experimental Endocrinology | from 2001 Aschheim Zondek House | today Institute of Neuropathology and Neurosurgery

---

Psychiatric and Neurological Clinic

Charitéplatz 1, Virchowweg 19 | 1899–1905 | Georg Diestel

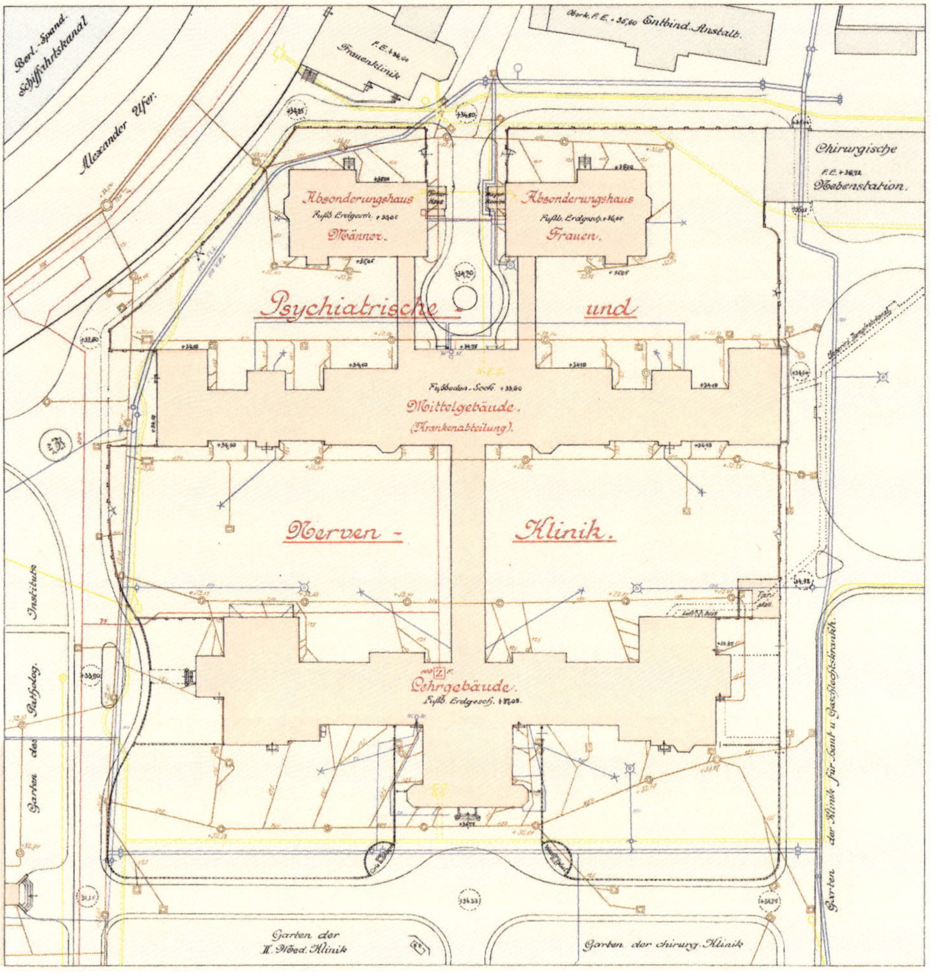
Berl.-Spand. Schiffahrtskanal
Alexander Ufer
Frauenklinik
Entbind. Anstalt
Chirurgische Nebenstation
Absonderungshaus Männer
Absonderungshaus Frauen
Psychiatrische und
Mittelgebäude
(Krankenabteilung)
Nerven - Klinik.
Lehrgebäude
Garten der II. Med. Klinik
Garten der chirurg. Klinik

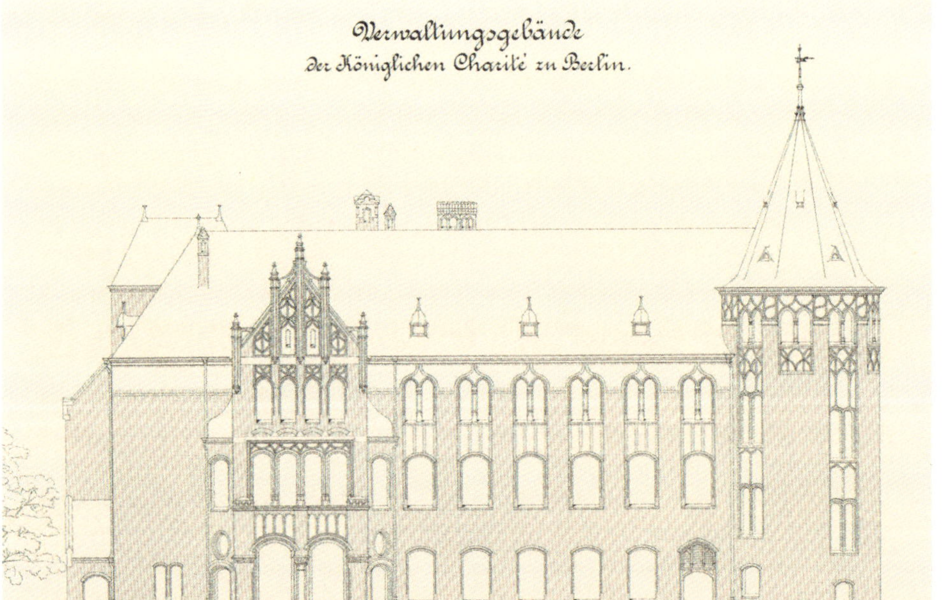
Verwaltungsgebäude
der Königlichen Charité zu Berlin.

was spread across several buildings, and the number of available beds was by far no match for the existing need for medical care. Laboratory facilities were inadequate, and there wasn't even a single lecture hall. For all of these reasons, it was decided that New Charité would be torn down in stages, and in its place a new building would be constructed for the clinic. The new three-building ensemble was connected via covered walkways. A teaching building was created to the south, which, in addition to a lecture hall capable of seating 180 students and work places for research, also housed the polyclinic for neurology, as well as several apartments for doctors and care personnel. The middle building was set aside for the accommodation of "calm mentally ill men [and] women", who also had several leisure rooms at their disposal – including one for billiards and another for music. Finally, a closed psychiatric ward accounted for the northern part of the complex: the "isolation house" for "restless" patients. On the one hand, this spatial approach expressed a certain gradation of degrees of illness and separation of the sexes, while on the other hand the garden complex granted the "calm invalids" markedly more space for exercise than had been the case at Old Charité.

On the Alexanderufer side of the Spree, the former pathological museum (today's **Museum of Medical History**), completed in 1899, was the first building to be erected as part of a new phase of construction, soon to be joined by an Institute of Pathology in 1905. The museum incorporated the extensive pathology collections of Rudolf Virchow and made them accessible for research and teaching purposes, as well as to a wider public up until 1914. Situated on the western edge of the Charité grounds, with its unassuming brick architecture the building differed from the surrounding clinics at most due to its stepped gable – the collection was thus also an inherent part of Charité in a visual sense. The building was destroyed during World War II, along with a large portion of the collections. It would take until 1998 for a museum to reopen here.

Museum of Medical History
formerly Pathological Museum

Charitéplatz 1, Virchowweg 17 | 1896–1899 | Georg Diestel | 1899 opening as Pathological Museum | 1998 re-opening | 2018–2021 renovation, Rustler Schriever Architekten | since mid-1990s the ruin of the Virchow lecture hall (Virchowweg 16) in the Pathological Museum has been used for events

A new **administrative building** at the main entrance to the grounds on their southern side was completed in 1901. The stairwell tower gives this building its distinctive form. Here, initial admission of patients and preliminary examinations took place. In addition, the building was home to the director's office, a library, and a pharmacy, as well as apartments for unmarried assistant doctors and pharmacists.

Administrative building

Charitéplatz 1 | 1898–1901 | Georg Diestel

The building of the **Pediatric Clinic**, located up until then on the ground floor of the northeast wing of Old Charité, which had been designated for demolition, was erected on the opposite side. The new building contained space for infirmaries, a polyclinic, examination and operation rooms, and a clinical lecture hall.

Pediatric Clinic

Charitéplatz 2, Schumannstrasse 22 | 1901–1904 | Georg Diestel

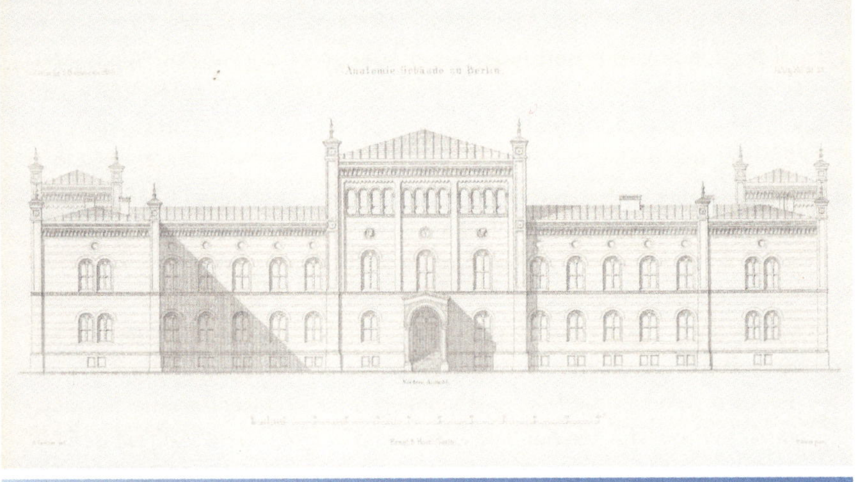

1st Anatomical Institute, redesigned central building

Construction of the new **Surgical Clinic**, previously housed in the summer hospital, a building only used in the warm months, lasted from 1901 to 1904. Now the surgical department had a modern building at its disposal, in which infirmaries were arrayed on both sides of the central section, while the middle part of the building was occupied by a large clinical lecture hall, a spacious operating room, as well as further rooms for microscopic, chemical, and bacteriological research work and tests. Modern surgery, which had received a strong impetus through the introduction and use of anesthesia and x-ray technology, continued its rise here.

In a certain sense, the crowning achievement of this new phase of building was the construction of the **1st and 2nd Medical Clinics** on the terrain of Old Charité. Originally only planned as a single clinic, the high demand for care made it advisable to construct two clinic buildings right next to one another. The facades of the eastern and western segments are designed differently, in order to make the building less monotonous from a visual standpoint. In the arrangement of the clinics, the structure adhered to the template provided by the Surgical Clinic directly opposite, taking up its distribution of the hospital wards in the wings, while the examination and treatment rooms were located in the main section. The medical clinics were pioneering in their generous provision of equipment for laboratory experiments as well as in their integration of laboratories within the wards. The facility was relieved of poly-clinical duties, as a separate **Polyclinic for Internal Medicine** was built at Luisenstrasse between 1913 and 1916.

With the arrival of these new buildings, the clinic district between Alexanderufer, Schumannstrasse, and Luisenstrasse had become a fully differentiated, self-contained clinic complex whose organization reflected the division of labor. East of Luisenstrasse, only the two anatomical institutes were initially connected to the university, from the 1860s and 1890s respectively. The older building for the **1st Anatomical Institute** from 1865 brought a long era of improvised accommodations to a close. In designing this three-winged facility, architect Albert Cremer took his cues from palace typology, while the facing brickwork construction mimicked the form of the surrounding buildings. On the north side, a risalit erected upon a half-octagon also makes it evident from the outside that a large lecture hall lies concealed behind it, one that initially provided room for 260 listeners, before being expanded to seat 460 individuals in 1898. Post-mortem and cold storage rooms lay beneath, supplemented by anatomic dissection halls, built to meet the most modern technical standards of the time.

Surgical Clinic

Charitéplatz 1 | 1901–1904 | Georg Diestel

1st and 2nd Medical Clinics

Charitéplatz 1, Sauerbruchweg 3, Virchowweg 10 | 1910–1914 | Georg Diestel

---

Polyclinic for Internal Medicine

Luisenstrasse 13a | 1914–1917 | Georg Diestel

1st Anatomical Institute

Philippstrasse 12 | 1863–1865 | Albert Cremer | 1887 addition of northeast wing | 1907 further floor added, with the exception of the central section | 1950 middle building plastered

ARCHITEKTUR
DER DDR
9'82
Preis 5,– Mark

Morgue

Hannoversche Strasse 6 | 1884–1886 | 1913 further floor added to side building | police morgue, commissioner's office for corpses, location of forensic medicine department for a long period | used by HU since 2007, initially for housing an excellence cluster, from 2019 for the Institutes of Islamic and Catholic Theology

2nd Anatomical Institute

Philippstrasse 12–13 | 1891–1892 | Paul Boettger, Karl Friedrich Endell

Bettenhaus

high-rise large-scale hospital ward, surgical center

Luisenstrasse 64 | 1977–1982 | Karl-Ernst Swora, Peter Korneli | 2014–2016 total renovation by Ludes Generalplaner; new facade design, SAA Schweger Architekten

The **morgue** was carved out in 1886 and relocated to Hannoversche Strasse. A wing was added to the northeast side of the anatomy building in 1887, containing further dissections rooms; this new space was also able to take in the portion of the zootomic-anatomic collections of the university relevant to human anatomy. Up until that point, these had been kept in the main building at Unter den Linden, and now their contents were split up among several institutes. In the early 1890s, the university's **2nd Anatomical Institute**, a modest utilitarian building for comparative anatomy, was built to the north of the 1st Anatomical Institute.

It was not until the GDR period that the area east of Luisenstrasse regained the attention of clinic planners. The immediate post-war period had been dominated by the need to repair the massive damage to the existing buildings and to get the clinics up and running again at full capacity. The few new builds (notable here are the Tumor Clinic on Invalidenstrasse and the Dermatology Clinic on Luisenstrasse, constructed in the second half of the 1950s) are austere, functional buildings when it comes to their exteriors.

The strongest accent was provided in the end by a building which today, recognizable as it is from a great distance, has become a landmark, Charité's emblematic structural feature: the **Bettenhaus** (literally "house of beds" in German). The Bettenhaus took up operations as the "Surgically-Oriented Center" in 1982. The dimensions of this clinic building were impressive from the beginning, housing two dozen operating rooms and over 1,000 beds on more than twenty floors. Directly adjacent to the high-rise structure was a three-story teaching wing, which was replaced in 2016 with the new construction of a building section for operating rooms and intensive care units. The passage built at the same time as the tower block represented a sizeable rupture in the centuries-old visual axis running along Luisenstrasse to Platz Vor dem Neuen Tor and Invalidenstrasse from the eastern to the western section of the building. Built three stories above the street, it extends right across traffic on Luisenstrasse below, cementing the connection to the functional wing. The basic system and organization of the Bettenhaus, with its two connected purpose-built structures, paid tribute to a new mindset in medicine which represented a shift away from differentiation and specialization towards increased interdisciplinary co-operation. In the wake of various renovation efforts, in particular the new, bright, aluminum-clad facade installed in place of the old, dark pre-fab concrete segments, Charité is also more visually present than ever in the center of Berlin.

CAMPUS NORD

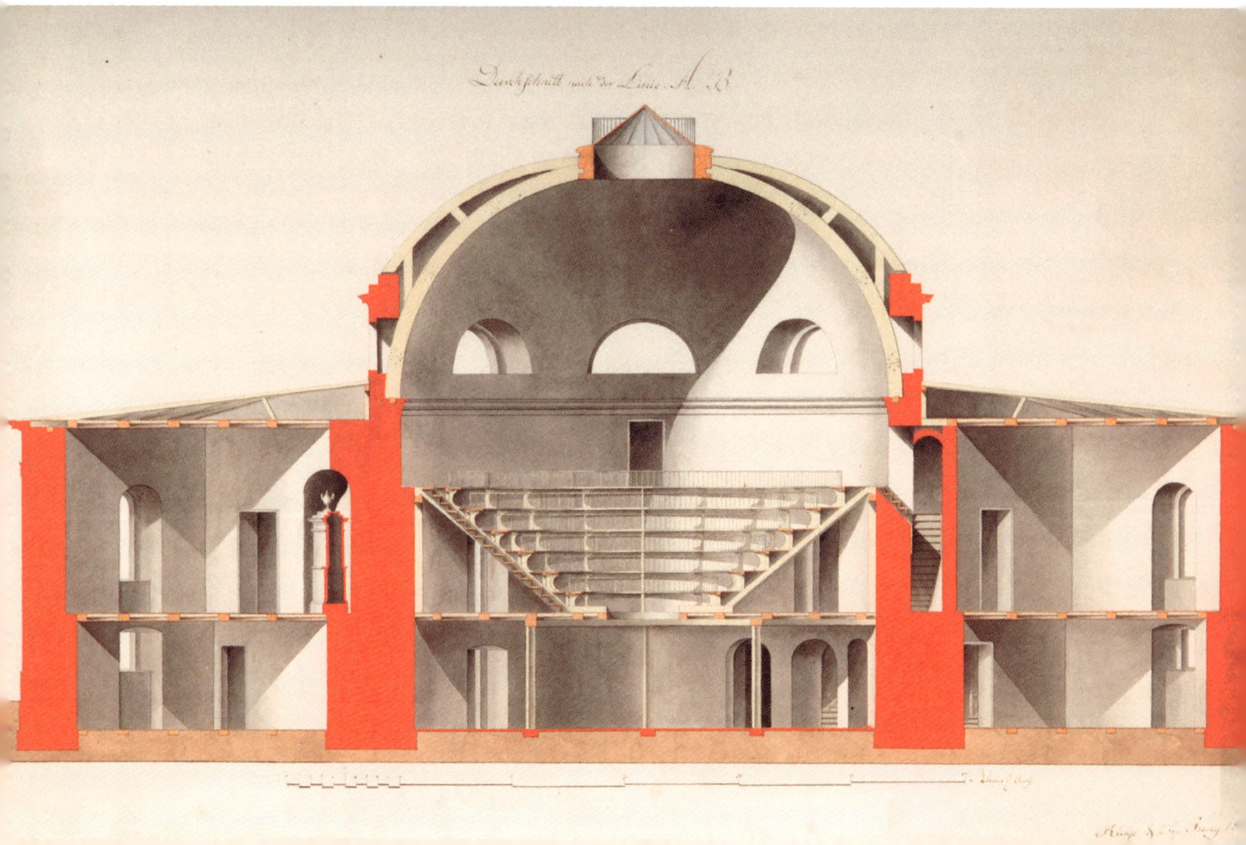

The area referred to today as Campus Nord, situated to the northwest of the university's center at Unter den Linden, is one of the most historically significant and at the same time most dynamic locations for science in Berlin. At first glance, the place does not strike one as such: its origins in a large-scale garden complex from the eighteenth century are still perceptible. Here, in the immediate vicinity of Charité, around the nucleus of the Veterinary School's Anatomical Theater, a unique ensemble of Humboldt-Universität research and teaching buildings has taken shape since 1790.

Tieranatomisches Theater

Philippstrasse 12, building 3 | 1789–1790 | Carl Gotthard Langhans | 1840 library and display collection moved into new main building on Luisenstrasse | 1874 addition (Gerlach-Bau) for autopsies and pathological studies | 1933–1945 extended with addition of a slaughter hall; affiliation with the University of Veterinary Medicine as Faculty of Veterinary Medicine | from 1950 to 1990s section for animal production and veterinary medicine of HU, used for lectures | 2005–2012 renovation by Müller Reimann Architekten | since 2013 used by Hermann von Helmholtz Center for Cultural Techniques of HU as event and exhibition space

Under Friedrich II, the plan had gained support within Prussia to establish a school for veterinary medicine. The rinderpest repeatedly threatened livestock, and the progressive development of the cavalry also made veterinary knowledge a resource of relevance to the military. The plan was ultimately implemented under the king's successor, Friedrich Wilhelm II, who was keen to add his own special touches to the cityscape as well. The first veterinary doctors were systematically sent abroad to be trained. While that was taking place, Prussia's highest-profile architect, Carl Gotthard Langhans, was to oversee planning for the construction of an equally representative and functionally optimized structure.

A location was soon found: the grounds of the Reuss Garden, a Baroque garden complex on the city's northern border, through which the Panke creek flowed. The first distinctive building to be placed there, on the western side of the property, was the **Tieranatomisches Theater**, today the oldest preserved educational building in Berlin science history. Embedded in the existing garden complex, the theater is a striking example of Prussian early Classicism. With this structure, Langhans created a monument to both science and the royal demand for representation. Originally erected on a little knoll, today the building lies somewhat lower than the neighboring structures due to ground subsidence and changes to the terrain. However, this has done little to lessen its effect on the beholder: situated in the middle of Berlin, the Tieranatomisches Theater recalls Renaissance builder Andrea Palladio's Villa Rotonda, an absolutely unmistakable point of reference, in fact. The stucco building erected on a square floor plan is crowned by a cupola, beneath which one finds the building's centerpiece, the round lecture hall. From each seat in rows arranged at a sharp incline towards the back, lecture attendees enjoyed an ideal view of the dissecting table, which was designed to rest upon a hydraulic lift. Thanks to the windows in the tambour, light from the outside could also be used for illumination. The building featured technical advances too, above all in the curved plank roof construction of the dome, which spanned thirteen

HUMBOLDT-UNIVERSITÄT ZU BERLIN

meters. Like the building itself, the motif paintings between the cupola windows highlighted the special significance of veterinary medicine, while the structure offered optimal conditions for training in the field. The lecture hall was surrounded by library and dissection rooms. The other buildings on the premises which Langhans designed for the veterinary school – for instance stables, a large forge building, and apartments – were executed as simple half-timber constructions and are no longer preserved today. Architect Ludwig Ferdinand Hesse played a decisive role in the school's second phase of expansion. The **Equine Clinic** was created to the northeast of the Tieranatomisches Theater according to his plans. More buildings realized in a simple brickwork style followed, housing further stalls, forges, and living quarters and recreation rooms for employees. These efforts were spurred on by the expansion of the veterinary school, which was still able to make do with space for fifty horses in 1790 but had by the 1830s grown to treat several thousand of them, while the number of students was also rising. The focus of veterinary medicine was also changing during this period: instead of concentrating solely on practical training, it was increasingly also concerned with the generation and mediation of scientific knowledge, which in turn necessitated laboratories, dissection rooms, and the like. A new building for a canine clinic also testified to the fact that the era of concentrating on horses was coming to a close.

Equine Clinic

Philippstrasse 13, building 9 | 1836–1838 | Ludwig Ferdinand Hesse | 1874 expansion, Julius Emmerich | 1955 further addition | 2012–2017 conversion and renovation, Bodamer Faber Architekten | since 2017 used by Institute of Biology

Between 1838 and 1840, a main building for the **Tierarzneischule** was constructed for educational and representational purposes. Architectural plans for the building had already existed for quite some time – Karl Friedrich Schinkel had also submitted proposals, which may potentially have been incorporated by his pupil Hesse in the plan drawn up and implemented later. This plan resulted in a three-winged, late classical structure with an axisymmetric layout, whose forecourt opened onto Luisenstrasse. The new addition meant the school now also possessed a thoroughly representative entrance. The visually dominating median risalit was used for teaching purposes, housing two large lecture halls and the library. A hall located on the upper floor was initially used for examinations, and, following an intermezzo as a lecture hall, as an auditorium from 1890 on. The more modest side wings originally contained apartments as well. During the same period, the park was transformed into a landscape garden according to plans by Peter Joseph Lenné.

Tierarzneischule

Luisenstrasse 56, building 1 | 1838–1840 | Ludwig Ferdinand Hesse | significant architectural work of late Classicism | from end of World War II until 1990 used by Soviet military administration and state institutions of the GDR | since 1990 part of HU | today the site of Humboldt Graduate School

The site experienced another surge in development as the university began to locate some of its individual institutes there. The first important facility was the 1st Anatomical Institute, with the 2nd Anatomical Institute following in the beginning of the 1890s. Both belong to Charité today (→ 57).

A fundamental reorganization of the curriculum and research focus in veterinary medicine occurred under Andreas Christian Gerlach, the scientific and

Overview, building age

Lecture hall at the Chemical-Physiological Institute

administrative director of the veterinary school from 1870. He ordered that an addition be built onto the Tieranatomisches Theater, known as the Gerlach-Bau, creating space for the zootomic collections and a further dissection room in the basement. In its external appearance, the building is restrained, its straightforward design blending in with the style of the Tieranatomisches Theater. In 1890, the collection rooms were refashioned into an experimental hall for lectures in chemistry.

Finally, veterinary medicine's reorientation towards the (natural) sciences resulted in a change in status: in 1887 the Tierarzneischule became the University of Veterinary Medicine, which was subsequently granted the right to award doctorates in 1920 and post-doctoral lecture qualifications in 1919, making the institution a full-fledged scientific university. The expansion didn't stop there. Between 1870 and 1918, the faculty grew from five teaching positions to eleven chairs. Veterinary medicine continued to become more professionalized, more highly differentiated, and more specialized. To these ends, additional rooms were necessary, each with its own special requirements for the particular sub-discipline involved. Among other spaces, the **Institute of Veterinary Anatomy** was born in this context on the western edge of the site between 1899 and 1902, after a planning phase driven substantially by anatomist and histologist Reinhold Schmaltz. Here, laboratories, teaching rooms, and collections found a home, especially the specimen collection of animal deformities begun by Ernst Friedrich Gurlt, which was installed on the upper floor. At the same time, the building housed the University of Veterinary Medicine's largest lecture hall of the era, an auditorium with seating for 300 students. The strikingly stepped north gable causes the building to stick out visually from among the surrounding structures. Not only did Otto Poetsch design the Institute of Veterinary Anatomy – he was also the architect for the Institute of Animal Hygiene, which was erected between 1899 and 1900 bordering the Tieranatomisches Theater to the east.

Institute of Veterinary Anatomy

Philippstrasse 12, building 2 | 1899–1902 | Otto Poetsch | today Institute of Biology

The most eye-catching structure of the Wilhelmine era at Campus Nord also marks the conclusion of this expansion period: the **Chemical-Physiological Institute**. Here as well, professors from the university made crucial contributions to the design and planning of the building – namely, physiologist Emil Abderhalden and chemist Georg Schroeter. Abderhalden, who took advantage of contract renewal negotiations with the university to secure approval of more and better equipped facilities, was able to gain forty additional laboratory workplaces. The complex is situated facing the Panke towards the south, where it has an interior courtyard between the two wings, while the north facade faces the main grounds of Campus Nord. Notable for the facade design of this building is the melding of elements drawn from Classicism, Jugendstil, and contemporary modernism. The large lecture hall in the southeast wing is discernible from the outside through a large window arrangement.

Chemical-Physiological Institute

Philippstrasse 13, building 18 | 1909–1914 | Edmund Zastrau | today Institute of Biology, IRI for Life Sciences | 2010 renamed Leonor Michaelis House by resolution of the institutional board of the Institute of Biology (previously Abderhalden House)

Surgical Equine Clinic

Hannoversche Strasse 23 | 1924–1926 | Walter Wolff | today Institute of Sport Sciences

Following World War I, only a single building with noteworthy architecture was added: the **Surgical Equine Clinic** in Hannoversche Strasse, directly adjacent to the Army Veterinary Inspection Office. Walter Wolff, who would shortly thereafter also make a name for himself with an addition to the Gynecological Clinic on Ziegelstrasse (→53), designed a late Expressionist building in which horse stalls, rooms for research and teaching, feed storage, and operating rooms were housed. This multi-functionality is hinted at on the outside by the striking stepped gable, as well as in the idiosyncratic design of the window and door openings in lancet arches on the ground floor.

The University of Veterinary Medicine was integrated into Friedrich Wilhelm University as a joint faculty along with the University of Agriculture in 1934, from whence the Faculty of Veterinary Medicine emerged in 1937. Following grave damage sustained in World War II, a prolonged period of reconstruction began, and the number of new buildings erected during the GDR era proved negligible. In 1992, a merger took place between the veterinary medicine faculties of Freie Universität and Humboldt-Universität, and veterinary medicine was shifted and relocated to Freie Universität in its entirety over the course of the years to come. With that, the most recent development phase of Campus Nord had begun: the buildings were painstakingly renovated and allotted to university institutes for new uses by and large.

Today the campus belongs to the Faculty of Life Sciences of Humboldt-Universität. Among the most notable (re)building efforts are the conversion of the Surgical Equine Clinic for the Institute of Sport Sciences, which has operated a new sports research hall (Building 26) on the campus since 2010, and the transformation of a former horse stall into the ultra-modern research building of the Bernstein Center for Computational Neuroscience (Building 6). Northeast of Philippstrasse, old buildings are also being used for new purposes. For instance, there is today's Mensa Nord cafeteria, located in a former Charité.

Rhoda Erdmann House
"Green Amoeba"

Philippstrasse 13, building 24 | 2013–2016 | Hansjörg Bodamer, Achim Bodamer, Alexander Faber | Institute of Biology

While the remaining university institutes on the grounds are primarily housed in old buildings, a noteworthy new building was inaugurated for the Institute of Biology: the **Rhoda Erdmann House**. Here, working groups for molecular and cellular biology from Humboldt-Universität can pursue research under the most modern conditions. Over fifty laboratories, measurement rooms, as well as twenty refrigerated and incubation rooms are available here. In this striking building, the external design directly mirrors the functions contained within. For this reason, the building is also referred to as the "green amoeba" due to its organic external form. The horizontally segmented banding in shades of green is intended to symbolize the life sciences. The main staircase features an installation of the art work 27° C by sculptor Kathrin Wegemann. Recalling a loose cluster of cells, the piece stretches across three floors, altering its color with changes in temperature. Thus, today's contemporary architecture has also gained a foothold in this predominantly landmarked ensemble at Campus Nord. (GM)

INVALIDENSTRASSE

Borsig's railroad machinery manufacturing company

The tract of land in front of Berlin's New Gate, which opens to the north of the Charité hospital settlement, was known in the mid-nineteenth century by the nickname Fireland. This label was a reference to industrial facilities such as the Royal Prussian Iron Works on Invalidenstrasse or August Borsig's mechanical engineering works on Chausseestrasse, to name only a couple examples from Berlin's industrial nucleus. In addition to these sites, the Lehrter, Hamburger, and Stettiner Bahnhof railway stations, all situated on Invalidenstrasse, demonstrated the growing significance of the Oranienburger suburb. The relocation of heavy industry, which occurred around 1870, freed up space in this urban setting for culture and education as well.

Between 1868 and 1917, a series of museums, colleges, and academies was created, with exhibition halls, laboratories, and lecture hall buildings, as well as new places for university institutes, which turned Invalidenstrasse into an extension of both the educational institutions located in Mitte and the district's museum landscape. Running from west to east, soon the popular-scientific Berliner Urania, the exhibition grounds at Lehrter Bahnhof, the Museum of Transport in Hamburger Bahnhof, the State Geological Museum and the exhibitions of the Mining Academy, the Museum für Naturkunde, and the Agricultural College with its own exhibit, or the Humboldt Gymnasium on the corner of Gartenstrasse, which opened in 1875, were all lined up side by side.

The Museum für Naturkunde became a central attraction for the general public, for instance as its expeditions returned to the museum bearing dinosaur bones, which became the object of a special exhibition that the institution still presents proudly today. From the perspective of the history of science, the museum additionally represents a center for the natural sciences in East Berlin after 1945, as initially the rooms of the architectural ensemble offered alternative accommodation for destroyed inner-city institutes, and then, after 1984, as the capital city of the GDR received a respectable research center with the new construction of the Physics Institute at Invalidenstrasse 110. This facility, however, proved to be short-lived, since following reunification the future for most of the natural sciences indeed seemed to lie increasingly in Adlershof.

State Geological Institution and Mining Academy

Invalidenstrasse 44 | 1875–1878 | August Tiede | already used as temporary exhibition building in 1868 | 1890–1892 extension by Fritz Laske following Tiede's plans | 1913 north building for director's residence and library storage | from 1916 only State Geological Bureau | 1927 Museum of Applied Geology | building reconstructed in simplified version after the war | Ministry of Geology in GDR | today Federal Ministry of Transport and Digital Infrastructure | 1996–1999 expansion building by Max Dudler

The **Mining Academy**, newly founded in 1860, was initially housed in Mitte, in the old stock market building. Joining forces with the **State Geological Institution**, ground was broken for a shared building in 1873, which was then completed in 1878 as the first structure of what would become a three-part ensemble on the property of the Royal Prussian Iron Works. The relationship between the Mining Academy, whose roots stretched back to 1770, and the universities was however a checkered one. The academy was part of the university from 1810 to 1860, only to become independent once again with the construction of the new building – the

Exhibition in the inner courtyard of the Mining Academy

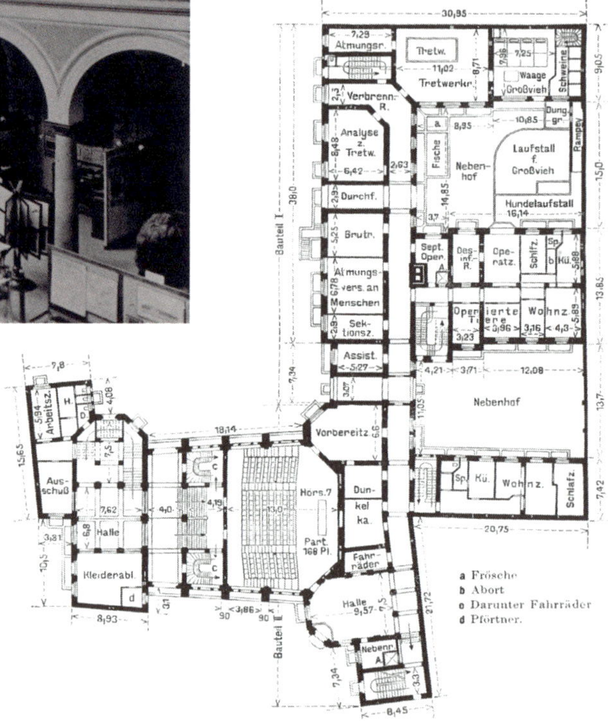

Interior design of the Agricultural College

establishment of the Technical College in Charlottenburg did nothing to change this state of affairs, until the Mining Academy was in fact integrated into the latter in 1916. Architecturally, the building was a precursor to the Technical College on a smaller scale, so to speak: the rooms of the Mining Academy were arranged on the ground floor around a glass-covered courtyard with an ambulatory colonnade, while the state academy, with its offices and geographically ordered exhibition halls, was situated on the upper floor. The collections, which had already been stored in a temporary building on this site since 1868, for the most part had their origins in the Prussian contribution to the 1867 Paris World's Fair which detailed domestic mining activities (→89).

The designation as a building of science was represented outwardly by the use of natural stone of various colors and origins, and the prominent position the academy occupied at Platz Vor dem Neuen Tor allowed its Italianizing architecture featuring round arches to unfold to full effect. Decorative elements wrought in iron and animal sculptures evoked the former presence of metal production here, from which portals and a "Florentine dog" from the old Royal Prussian Iron Works remain preserved today at the eastern entrance.

Agricultural College

Invalidenstrasse 42 | 1876–1880 | August Tiede | 1906–1910 two extensions by Kern, E. Gerhardt | 1983 building for biophysics

The **Agricultural College**, whose construction began a year later, appears from the outside to be an architectural twin of the Mining Academy. On the inside, however, the building is characterized by different materials, such as red granite for the columns, white marble for the stairs, and floors featuring colorful mosaics. Here, the inner courtyard served to present agricultural machines to students and visitors. The museum department also absorbed the collection of the Royal Agricultural Museum, which had been housed at different locations in Mitte since 1868.

As the field of agriculture increasingly required knowledge of chemistry as well, a chemical laboratory, located on the part of the property behind the main building today referred to as the eastern grounds, was annexed with the college from the start. Although the education of farmers was not one of the university's responsibilities, synergies were still meant to be taken advantage of, by having the Institute for Plant Physiology of Friedrich Wilhelm University share its range of instruments on site with the botanical microscopic laboratory of the Agricultural College from the beginning, with the former assuming the expenses for upkeep. Further back on the northeast grounds, institutes for both physics and animal physiology were added in two construction phases, as well as a lecture building with two halls arranged one on top of the other. The physics lecture hall, featuring seating for 354 individuals, was in operation for nearly a century, up to the relocation of the discipline of physics to Adlershof. In 2019, it was meticulously restored and is today once again among the most beautiful auditoriums Humboldt-Universität has to offer.

After World War II, this lecture hall, along with the Institute of Physics of the original Agricultural College, would enable the university's physics department to resume its teaching activities, for the large institute on the Reichstag bank of the Spree had been destroyed. Of the Agricultural College's facilities, only the intermediate wing between

Ensemble of scientific institutions in front of the New Gate

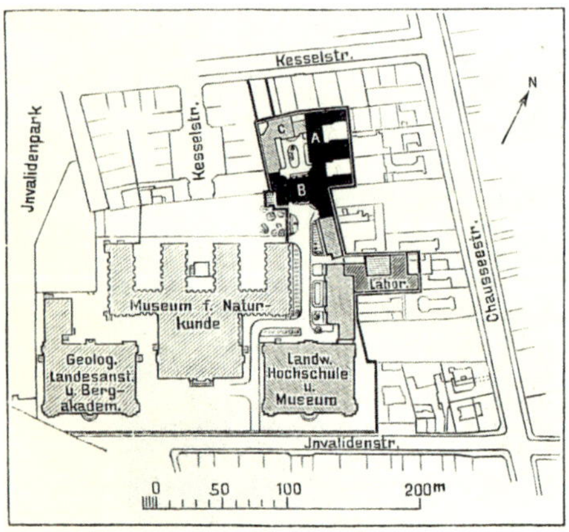

Atrium with whale skeletons, around 1890

the main building and the chemistry laboratory lay in ruins, until a modern functional building for biophysics was created there in 1983.

Museum für Naturkunde

Invalidenstrasse 43 | 1883–1889 | August Tiede | 1914–1917 extension for zoological collection | 1944 destruction of east wing | 2008–2010 reconstruction with warehouse for wet collection, Diener & Diener | since 2009 independent from HU as Leibniz Institute for Evolutionary and Biodiversity Science

Some ten years after the mining and agricultural institutions flanking it on either side, the **Museum für Naturkunde** opened its doors in 1889. The new museum gave both the Zoological Institute and three collections from the main building at Unter den Linden a new home. At the same time, Invalidenstrasse had finally become a university site. The front section of the Museum für Naturkunde fills the space between the two other university buildings to a large extent, though without touching them, and it leaves room for a forecourt, once again a nod to the palace construction model in the context of an ensemble of scientific facilities. The magnificently decorated facade shows relief images of Alexander von Humboldt, zoologist Christian Gottfried Ehrenberg, and crystallographer Christian Samuel Weiss, among others. However, in accordance with the institutional hierarchy in the German Empire, the ensemble had to take its place behind the splendor of the Technical College, which had been completed in the meantime.

Rudolf von Virchow had already called for the establishment of a "national natural-historical museum" in 1875. Although the Museumsinsel would have lent itself well to the purpose, priority was supposed to be given to the development of a new site for the natural sciences and technology on Invalidenstrasse, and thus to a separation of (museum) centers for the humanities and the natural sciences. The Museum für Naturkunde also featured an "atrium for the exhibition of larger objects" – which initially referred more to whale skeletons than those of dinosaurs. Mineralogical, paleontological, and zoological collections were arranged according to the classification systems of the natural sciences around the atrium and in the other four wings of the building.

The museum's architecture and use to this day testify to a controversy in the museum field of the waning nineteenth century. Namely the question of whether scientific collections conceived for university teaching and research purposes could at the same time serve as a public museum, or whether one ought rather to set up separate collections. The latter point of view carried the day, and only the ground floor was made accessible to the general public – the large, representative iron stairwells demonstrate that the initial concept was a different one.

The museum would also become a symbolic place for Germany as a colonial power, as, shortly before World War I, in the wake of an expedition led by the museum, dinosaur bones from German East Africa for instance were brought back to Berlin for exhibition as new "large objects", a total of 225 tons in fact. The museum was expanded substantially to accommodate them while the war was still raging. It wasn't until 1937, however, that the twelve-meter tall brachiosaurus would become the main attraction in the atrium, and take on a new, political dimension – the way it is also a subject of political contention in the contemporary debate regarding colonial plunder. In the divided city after 1945 on the other hand, the Museum für Naturkunde became an

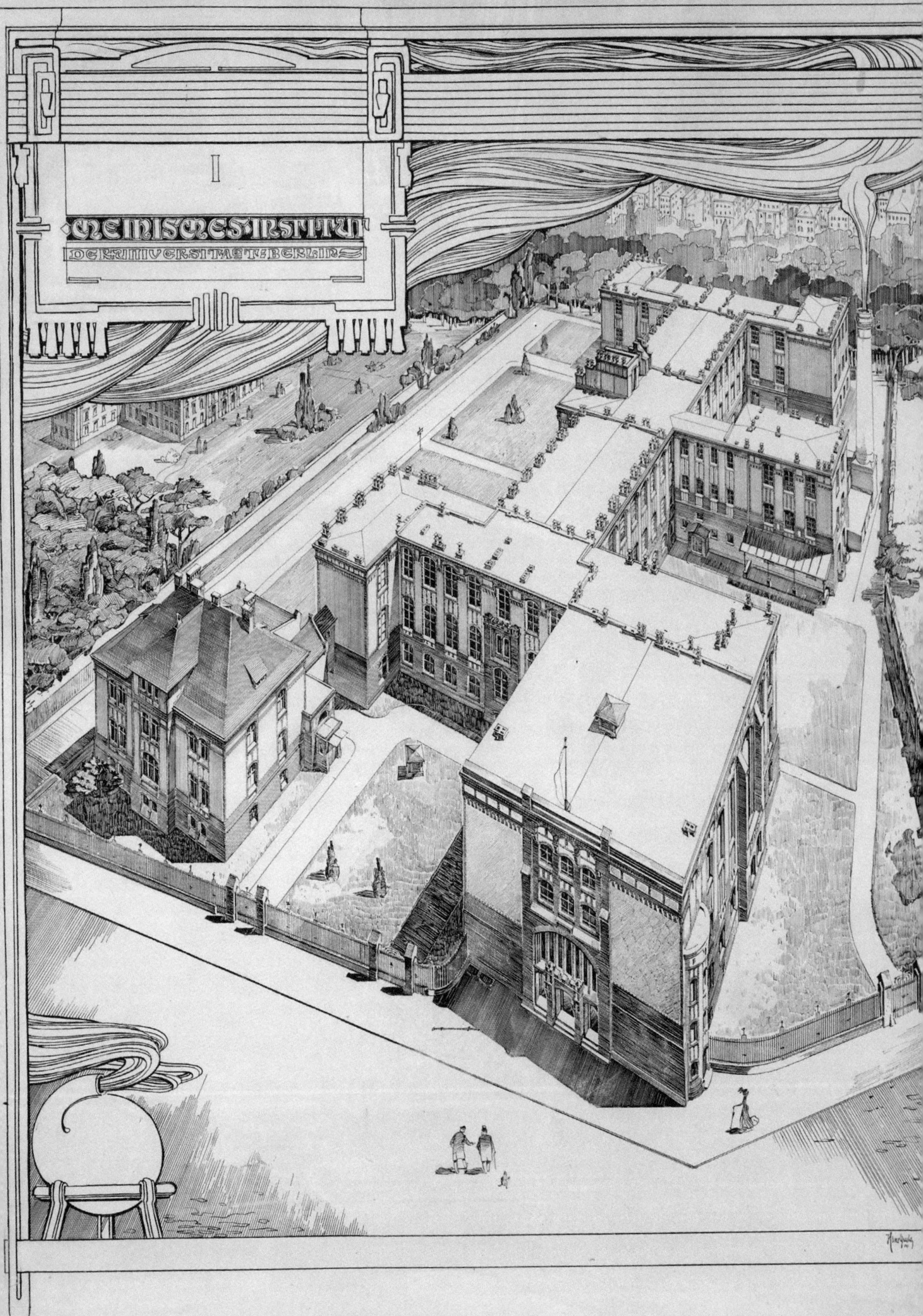
I
CHEMISCHES INSTITUT
DER UNIVERSITAET BERLIN

important cultural figurehead for East Berlin, due also to the fact that the western half of the city lacked a true equivalent. Today, many people feel that Humboldt-Universität's 2009 decision to part ways with the museum was not to its advantage.

The grounds of the former University of Veterinary Medicine, today's Campus Nord, and the ensemble revolving around the Museum für Naturkunde were separated from one another by cemeteries until the turn of the century. Whereas those of the Dorotheenstadt and Friedrichswerder parishes have remained intact, the old Charité cemetery became a building site for scientific institutes. The appointment of Emil Fischer was coupled with the creation of a new **Institute of Chemistry**, which was initially planned for Dahlem. In the end, the Institute of Chemistry was completed in 1900 to the north of the morgue and the Charité washhouse, today's Mensa Nord university cafeteria. Here for the first time architectural aspirations were consistently given a lower priority than the creation of ideal conditions for the achievement of scientific aims, while such artistic ambitions would still play the decisive role in the construction of the Kaiser Wilhelm Institutes shortly thereafter. Fischer himself had insisted on a grouped construction, in which building components with various functions would be arranged next to one another in a row. Towards the street, this is still hidden, however, through the juxtaposition of the lecture hall wing and the director's villa. The jagged arrangement of rooms possessing different functions exclusively served the purpose of both optimizing ventilation and illumination and orchestrating the work of a small army of laboratory technicians in two large halls with adjacent special rooms. The director's private laboratory, however, stood apart, in a wing connected to the residence, while the large lecture hall capable of seating 500 students possessed its own entrance from the street.

Institute of Chemistry
branch library Campus Nord

Hessische Strasse 1–2 | 1899–1900 | Georg Thür, Max Guth | 1946–1984 Institute of Physics in the director's villa

Whereas the Institute of Chemistry chiefly pursued pure research, for instance into the structure of sugars, amino acids, and pharmaceuticals, the **Institute of Hygiene**'s mission was to conduct practical research concerning hygiene and the diseases associated with it. Nevertheless, Robert Koch's appointed successor Max Rubner understood hygiene as a kind of applied physiology, which in turn required description in chemical and physical terms. This is mirrored in the new building for the institute, which had previously been housed in the building of the Gewerbeinstitut on Klosterstrasse in Mitte, after the latter was absorbed by the Technical College.

Accordingly, the new Institute of Hygiene, located just to the north of the Institute of Chemistry, not only closely resembles the latter (aside from its linear disposition) in its architectural sequencing of structural components and yellow brick and light-hued stucco facades, but also in regard to its functional rooms. Chemical and physical laboratories, microscopy halls, as well as rooms for bacteriological work were housed here, and, as in the Institute of Chemistry, separated from the lecture hall. The functional character of the building was emphasized more stringently here, embellished sparsely with only a few, reserved ornamental elements. Rubner moved to the chair for physiology in 1909, which is why the institute

Institute of Hygiene
Institute of Physiology

Hessische Strasse 3–4, Invalidenstrasse 103a | 1903–1905 | Georg Thür, Max Guth | 1913–1916 integration of newly founded Kaiser Wilhelm Institute of Labor Physiology on basement floor | since 1916 in auxiliary building Invalidenstrasse 103a | 1954–1955 extension

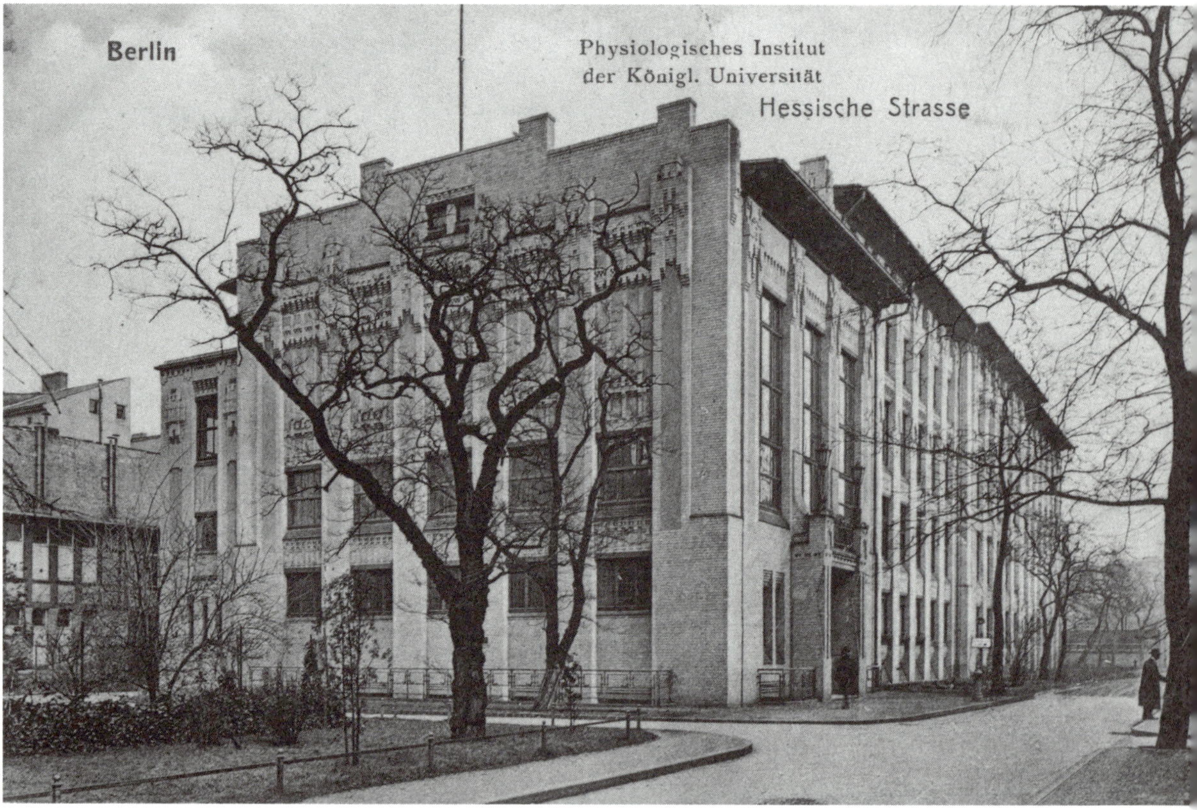

Institute of Hygiene with lecture hall wing and extension

Kurt Berndt Courtyards

was soon considered the Institute of Physiology. In 1913, he allowed the Kaiser Wilhelm Institute of Labor Physiology, which he ran, to move into the basement temporarily, until a new building could be completed next door in 1916, a structure with a view towards the University of Agriculture from its position set back a bit from Invalidenstrasse.

Following World War II, one of the few new builds of the early post-war period was commissioned for medicinal chemist Samuel Rapoport, recruited from the USA, and his Institute of Physiological and Biological Chemistry. To this end, an add-on building was placed in front of the Institute of Hygiene on its lecture hall side, which meant the new addition extended to the edge of Hessische Strasse. This simple, functional stucco structure, adorned exclusively with a thin cornice band above the ground floor, today largely conceals the old institute building.

In the eastern half of Berlin, lack of adequate facilities was one of the primary problems encountered by most university disciplines at war's end, one which they usually attempted to solve through improvisation and co-operation, for instance with the Academy of Sciences. This state of affairs was especially dire for the field of physics. For this reason, in the following passage we will treat this example somewhat more extensively in order to illustrate the situation. This phenomenon certainly extended in similar fashion to the other natural sciences and mathematics, as well as to the humanities.

Even a quarter century after the war had come to an end, Humboldt-Universität was still without a central building for physics. Indeed, the opposite scenario prevailed: the discipline was scattered across the entire city at twelve different locations and frequently housed in repurposed buildings. The 2nd Institute of Physics, for instance, moved into the director's villa at the Institute of Chemistry, where the first research work on solid-state, semiconductor, and nuclear physics would take place after the war. Over a period of three years starting in 1950, first three and then five rooms in the neighboring Institute of Hygiene, sectioned off using makeshift partitions, were added to the facilities at the discipline's disposal. Institutes such as the 3rd Institute of Physics that emerged from the working groups had to make do with the former boiler house of the complex in Hessische Strasse or use more remote sites. A conflict with the prioritized training of doctors, who for their part also complained of lack of space, almost led to the disbanding of working groups from the Institute of Physics, before an **office building and a factory building** with several rear courtyards were finally found in Mitte at the last minute – the working group for solid-state physics was ultimately able to settle here and grow into an independent 4th Institute of Physics. The university was forced to resort to using **further residential buildings** for students' practical training or even for research projects.

Office building and a factory building

Kurt Berndt Courtyards

Neue Schönhauser Strasse 20 | 1911–1912 | Kurt Berndt (for Metropol-Theater AG) | later HU Department of Food Production and Technology | today headquarters of Goethe Institute Berlin

---

Further residential buildings

Practical laboratory for electronics
Reinhardtstrasse 7 | residential building from 1880s | used by HU from 1964

Practical laboratory for advanced physics
Reinhardtstrasse 10 | residential building from 1880s | since 1960 Department of Ultrasound Physics | since 1964 practical laboratory for advanced physics

Department of Physics of HU
Friedrichstrasse 112b | 1894 | Paul Vigdt | used by HU from approx. 1970

Topping-out ceremony of the departmental building for physics and electronics, April 22, 1982

Respected and politically influential scientists such as Robert Rompe were initially able to use former postal facilities in Kleinmachnow, then in Zeuthen, and later a building at Mohrenstrasse 40 in Mitte which had been rebuilt with the Langhans Arcades, or institutes in Berlin-Buch which belonged to the Academy of Sciences, as in the case of Friedrich Möglich. This also led to the establishment of co-operation between university educators and researchers at academy institutes, who frequently had access to better equipment. Many diploma and doctoral students also had to pursue their research at academy institutes, which were often run by professors from the university. Still, the overriding majority of research was conducted in the improvised laboratories of the downtown area.
The construction of the Berlin Wall brought a certain unwanted alleviation of the space problem. Almost overnight, the 2nd Institute of Physics, for example, lost almost its entire management staff, as these individuals resided on Berlin's western side. As a result, the university and the academy institutes had to become even more closely entwined in terms of personnel, which had led by roughly the end of the 1960s to an "integrated history for university and academy" (Dieter Hoffmann). Humboldt-Universität also began to open itself more intensively to technological issues, attempting to develop new technologies to the point of application readiness in the scope of pilot projects. To this end, a number of temporary buildings realized in a light metal construction style were erected in Friedrichsfelde in 1970, with the aim of integrating a "technical center", in particular for the university's optoelectronic specialists.

Plans for a grand solution to unite the physics departments or the natural sciences and technology initiatives as a whole were repeatedly floated. In this regard, the Invalidenpark west of the ensemble around the Museum für Naturkunde was proposed in 1951, a tract of land which had also already been considered as a potential location for the Technical College around 1880, before the latter assumed its familiar form in Charlottenburg far from the downtown university. In the 1960s, Adlershof, the coveted destination not only for physicists, became home to many academy institutes.

Departmental building for physics and electronics

Invalidenstrasse 110 | 1982–1984 | Karl-Ernst Swora, Fritz Kalusche

However, it was the 11th Party Conference of the SED (Socialist Unity Party of Germany) in 1976 that would finally pave the way for a **departmental building for physics and electronics**, a six-story structure diagonally across from the Agricultural College extending 130 meters along Invalidenstrasse and 45 meters along Chausseestrasse. This corresponded roughly to the floor space in the new physics building of Freie Universität and the Technical University in the west, which were built in the previous years (→185, 125). The GDR's capital city university had taken up the challenge. The new building complex, with its x-ray, ion accelerator, and low temperature laboratories, as well as clean rooms and computer terminals, defined the vision of an East Berlin center for the natural sciences, sprawling out on both sides of Invalidenstrasse from the Institutes of Chemistry, Hygiene, and Physiology to the Museum für Naturkunde and the rear lecture hall and research buildings for biology and biophysics.

Chemistry fared somewhat better on the whole. Walter Nernst's institute in Bunsenstrasse had made it through World War II fairly well, while the Chemical Institute in Hessische Strasse had been rendered largely unusable. Research and teaching activities could only be resumed on a small scale in the few still functioning laboratories. It wasn't until reconstruction began in earnest that space became available for inorganic chemistry in particular, while biochemistry was transferred to the medical and agricultural faculties. Portions of the east wing of the Museum für Naturkunde had also been destroyed in the war, and prior to the establishment of the biology department various botanical and zoological institutes were based at a variety of locations, with a more or less coordinated approach, in a similar manner to their counterparts in the field of physics. The loss of the Botanical Museum to the ravages of war and the loss of access to the Botanical Garden, which lay in West Berlin, weighed more heavily. The founding of the Institute for Special Botany in 1960 and the annexation of the Spät'schen Arboretum in the Baumschulenweg district, as a stand-in for the Botanical Garden, were only able to partially compensate for these losses. The architectural ensemble on Invalidenstrasse remained the central location for the natural sciences up until reunification. (AS)

Collections

From the Kunstkammer to the Humboldt Forum

87

It is not only through their buildings that the universities have contributed to research and education in the city: their collections have played a significant role too. One could consider them the main link connecting universities with urban society. Although the collections were mainly used for academic teaching and research, during the nineteenth century most of them were open to interested members of the public. And there were some true treasures to be discovered: to celebrate its founding in 1809, the Universität Unter den Linden was given large parts of the collection that had been in the custody of the Margraves of Brandenburg since the sixteenth century. From the early eighteenth century on, it continued to grow in the *Kunstkammer* (lit. chamber of art) of the nearby palace under the Prussian kings. Gottfried Wilhelm Leibniz had already linked his plan for the establishment of an academy of sciences in Berlin with the Kunstkammer; he wanted the artistic and scientific artifacts there to be brought together and presented as a Theatrum naturae et artis. And although his plan came to nothing, in the early nineteenth century the university was able to benefit from it by establishing itself as a "research museum", as the arts historian Horst Bredekamp described the university. This description might seem somewhat exaggerated given that the main purpose of the university was to produce proficient, academically trained officials, priests and doctors for the Prussian state, though it should not be dismissed out of hand. In fact, ever since the university first opened its doors, the main building on Unter den Linden housed several veritable museums at once: the "Anatomisch-Zootomische Museum", das "Zoologische Museum" and the "Mineralogische Museum". However, these were not static collections; they were continually expanding. It is reported that in the year 1825, the zoological collection in the main building occupied 22 rooms just by itself. Other collections were added, since every faculty purchased its own artifacts to use for educational purposes. For a time, the university took in a large art collection of seventeenth century Italian masters – the Giustiniani collection – which had been stored temporarily (1818–1827) in the Unter den

Linden building after its return from France (where it had been taken during the Napoleonic Wars), before being transferred to the Altes Museum and the Gemäldegalerie. Contrary to the original plans, the university was not granted its own art museum, however even today the HU has custody of a considerable inventory of art works. The ethnological collection in the Kunstkammer was not granted to the university either, and though at some point there had been plans to store its contents in the Königliche Bibliothek (→33), for which Karl Friedrich Schinkel had already planned rooms to house them, they were ultimately transferred to the Neues Museum.

The fact that these two collections were (initially) handed over to the Altes Museum and the Neues Museum indicated the close correlation between the development of the Berliner Universität and the institutions on the Museumsinsel and other museums: firstly, they were linked by the Kunstkammer in the palace, from where artifacts were transferred to the museums and universities; secondly – and more relevant in the current context – in the course of the nineteenth century, the university collections reached the limits of their capacity. This resulted in artifacts being either transferred to museums or forming the inventories of dedicated new museums.

The Museum für Naturkunde is the most prominent example of this. Bredekamp succinctly describes the founding impetus: "In the year 1869, a walrus that was being taken to the taxidermist was found blocking the way to the auditorium [in the university's main building]. This incident led to the decision to found a natural history museum and thus alleviate the overcrowding in the university's main building". Twenty years later the time had arrived, and the natural history artifacts could finally be taken to the new site on Invalidenstrasse (→79). Together with the mineralogical collection, the natural history artifacts were to find their new home in the Naturkundemuseum.

However, this did not mark the end of the era of university collections. On the contrary: in its imposing main building (→97), the Technical College presented impressive plaster and iron casts, and also bronzes from the Bauakademie which were of particular interest to prospective architects. In addition there were mineral samples, a mining exhibit, a construction materials collection and other inventories that have mostly been lost to wartime destruction.

And although the extensive collection of historic building models and plans was also lost during the war, the collection of sketches, designs, photographs and other architectural history media was preserved almost in its entirety. Indeed, after the war it was expanded considerably, and the current inventory of the Architekturmuseum at the Technische Universität comprises around 150,000 digitized architectural history documents that are accessible to the public.

The Friedrich-Wilhelms-Universität also continued to house collections in its main building after the transfer of the zoological collection to the Museum für Naturkunde and the anatomical collection to the Pathologische Museum at the Charité (→61). Even today, the collection of ancient casts is open for public viewing in the Winckelmann-Institut. The special presentation requirements of this collection were given particular consideration during the addition of two garden-facing wings to the main building (→27). The presiding architect Ludwig Hoffmann, who had co-designed the Pergamon Museum, designed suitable museum spaces for the exhibition of the plaster casts in the west wing. However, only traces of these rooms can be found today. After the war, the rooms were at some point used to house the library of the Slavic Institute. In the early part of the twenty-first century, the Winckelmann-Institut was once

Späth-Arboretum, Collection of ancient casts in the Winckelmann-Institut, plaster and iron casts in the TH, agricultural machinery in the Argicultural College

Späth-Arboretum

Späth-Strasse 80/81 | 1874–1879 designed as a landscape garden | Johann Heinrich Gustav Meyer, director of city gardening | part of HU since 1961

HUB der Wissenschaft

"Humboldt-Lab" in the Humboldt Forum | Schlossplatz 1 | replicas of the Old Palace, Andreas Schlüter, new building: Franco Stella, Hilmer Sattler Architekten | opening date: 2020

again able to use these spaces. The plaster cast inventory first had to find its way back to the institute, since part of it was destroyed in the war and other parts were in storage. Three halls have now been restored and are open to the public.

In the nineteenth century it was quite common for higher education institutions to house museum inventories, a tradition exemplified by the Landwirtschaftlichen Hochschule. The design of the new building (→ 77) included plans to house the collection of the Königlichen Landwirtschaftlichen Museum (founded in 1868). Indeed, the large inner courtyard provided the ideal setting for the agricultural machinery and tools brought from the museum. Moreover, there was a steam engine available that allowed the machines to be shown in operation. However, the art historians Katrin and Hans Georg Hiller von Gaertringen see no contradiction in such artifacts being presented in the context of a palace-like building inspired by the Italian Renaissance; on the contrary, they recognize a "Würdeformel" (lit. dignity fomula) in the buildings style which underscored the "rank of an academic institute". This again illustrates clearly that the university collections did not exist solely for research and educational purposes and for the edification of urban audiences, but that they often exerted a significant influence on the architectures of science.

Scientific collections had a direct influence on the urban environment whenever they occupied large spaces. This applies in particular to the Botanischer Garten and to other botanical or agricultural science collections. In Berlin, a royal "show garden" was transformed into a botanical garden which was intended as a Kunstkammer of botanics in which rare, precious or especially useful plants were on display. At first located in Schöneberg, on the site of what is now Kleistpark (where the Botanische Museum was also established), the gardens and museum were relocated to the Dahlem district in the early twentieth century (→ 169). Since 1961, the Humboldt-Universität has also housed the **Späth-Arboretum**, thus compensating for the fact that East Berlin previously had no botanical gardens of its own.

Today the university collections are spread all over the city. Some are to be found in the university institutes, others have been transferred to museums. The guiding idea that these collections should not be solely accessible for research and education purposes, but rather to the broader public in the city, was lost in the course of the twentieth century. This task was delegated to the public museums and other cultural institutions. However, in the twenty-first century there seems to have been a reversal of this trend: the universities and other academic institutions are now rediscovering the value of their own collections. This applies in particular in view of their original function of forming a link between universities and urban society. The Humboldt-Universität has taken the bold step of establishing its own exhibition space in the Humboldt Forum from 2020 onward. In the "**HUB der Wissenschaft**" (the so-called Humboldt-Lab), the university will present parts of its collections – which in this way will return to their place of origin: Berlin Palace. (GM)

CHARLOTTENBURG
Zentrum für Produktionstechnik
Büro-haus
Heinrich-Hertz-Institut
Energie-technik
Technische Akustik
Landwehrkanal
Elektro-technische Institute
Altbau
Neubau
Luft- und Raumfahrt
Elektronen-mikroskop
Villen
Holtz
Stilke
Heizung und Klimatechnik
Mathematik
Pepper-Haus
Architektur
Wasserbau
Technische Chemie
Telefunken-Hochhaus
Otto-Suhr-Allee
Fraunhoferstraße
Marchstraße
Straße des 17. Juni
Bismarckstraße
Ernst-Reuter-Platz
Erweiterungs-bau
Nordflügel
Hauptgebäude
Bergbau und Hüttenwesen
Metallhütten-kunde
Bauingenieuere
[Gewächshaus]
Kirchen-musik
Alte Mineralogie
[Chemie-Ausstellung]
Physikgebäude
Neue Physik
Studentenhaus
Mensa
Hochschule der Künste
Schillerstraße
Schiller-Oberschule
Oberstufenzentrum Körperpflege
Sporthalle
Staatliche Europaschule Berlin
Kindertagesstätte
Friedensburg-Oberschule
Schlüterstraße
Hardenbergstraße
Knesebeckstraße
Goethestraße
Grolmanstraße
Pestalozzistraße

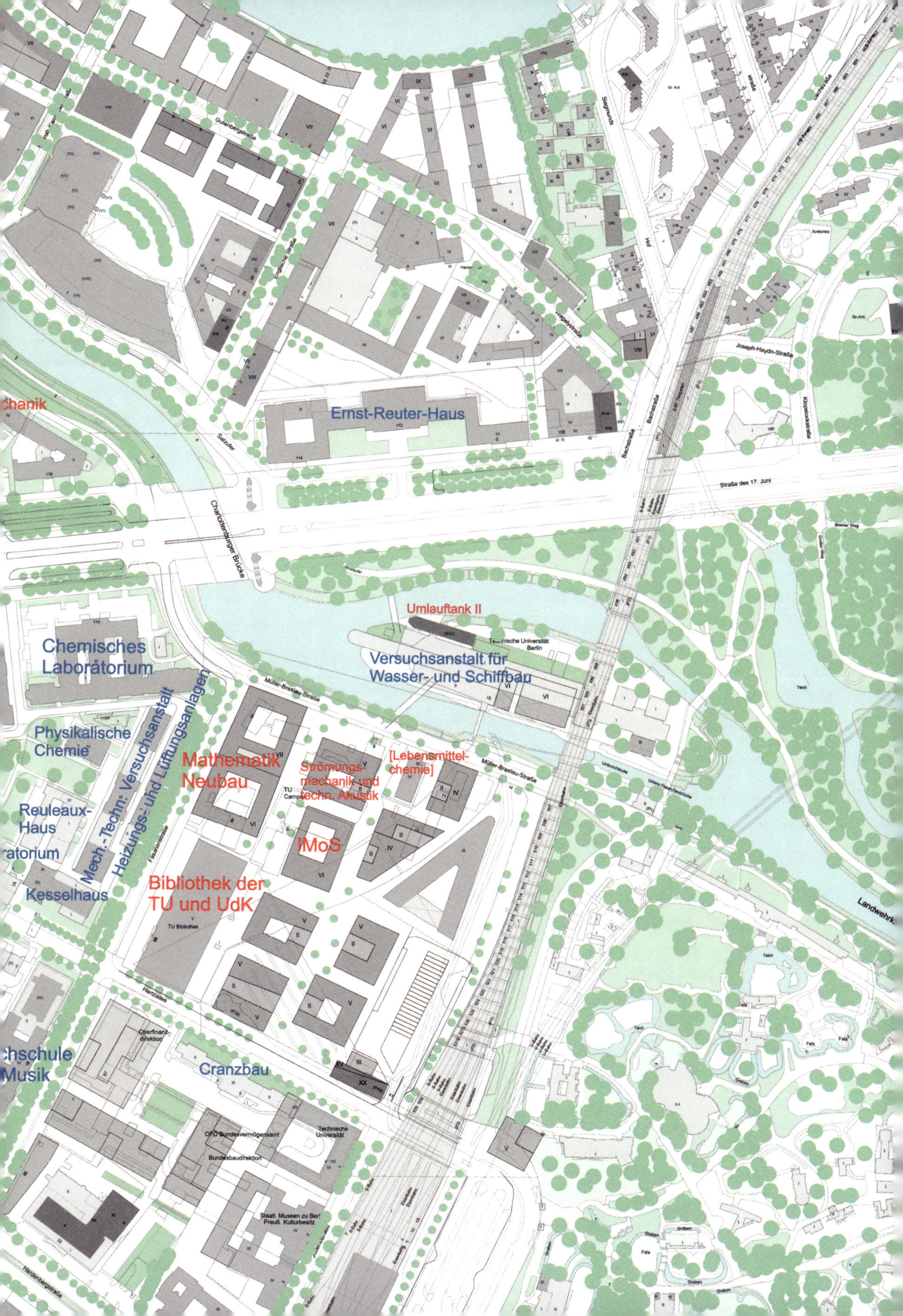

Gutenbergstraße
Englische Straße
Wegelystraße
Siegmunds Hof
Joseph-Haydn-Straße
Klopstockstraße
Bachstraße
chanik
Ernst-Reuter-Haus
Salzufer
Straße des 17. Juni
Charlottenburger Brücke
Umlauftank II
Technische Universität Berlin
Versuchsanstalt für
Wasser- und Schiffbau
Chemisches
Laboratorium
Müller-Breslau-Straße
Physikalische
Chemie
Mathematik
Neubau
Strömungs-
mechanik und
techn. Akustik
[Lebensmittel-
chemie]
Reuleaux-
Haus
ratorium
Mech.-Techn. Versuchsanstalt
Heizungs- und Lüftungsanlagen
IMoS
Bibliothek der
TU und UdK
TU Bibliothek
Kesselhaus
Landwehrk
Hertzallee
Oberfinanz-
direktion
chschule
Musik
Cranzbau
OFD Bundesvermögensamt
Bundesbaudirektion
Technische
Universität
Staatl. Museen zu Berl
Preuß. Kulturbesitz
Hardenbergstraße
Teich
Fels
Graben

CHARLOTTENBURG

By the middle of the eighteenth century, Charlottenburg, with its eponymous palace, had become the seat of royal power. By the nineteenth century, it had developed progressively into a summer retreat for Berliners, some of whom also chose to resettle there permanently. Werner Siemens was among the earlier settlers, moving in 1862 to the "new west", which from 1865 on was connected to the capital via Berliner Strasse and Prussia's first horse-drawn streetcar. In 1882, the Zoological Garden station opened, and the first subway was added in 1902. Between 1875 and 1893, not only did the population quadruple to over 100,000 inhabitants, rendering Charlottenburg itself a metropolis by the standards of the day, but, in addition to a military academy and the Technical College, the Physical-Technical Reich's Institute and a host of industrial enterprises also settled here during this period. Like many other companies, Siemens & Halske did their manufacturing on the Landwehr Canal, while parts of the Schering chemical factory were situated opposite the palace on the banks of the Spree. Training, research, production, and state testing went hand in hand in Charlottenburg, in particular when it came to electrical engineering products and, from 1900, automobiles – first electrically powered ones, and then later those equipped with internal combustion engines. The largest and most visible symbol of Charlottenburg's development into a place for technology was the Technical College with its magnificent main building. Although this institution had always been the Royal Technical College of Berlin (despite widespread use of the appellation TH Charlottenburg), Charlottenburg itself did not become an official part of Berlin until 1920.

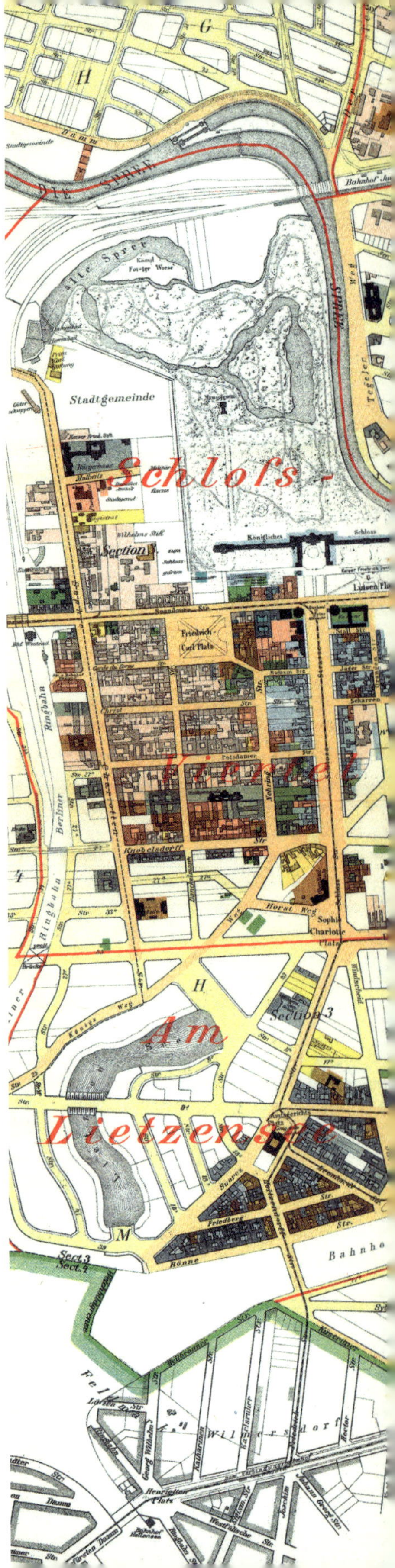

Farbenerklärung.
Bebauung bis zum Jahre
1717
1777
1824
1862
1872
1889
1894
1899
1905
Halb-
Section 2.
Hochschul-
Viertel
Kurfürstendamm
Hippodrom
Berlin
Spree
Lützow
Karl August Platz
Kant
Berliner
Kurfürsten
Wilmersdorf

THE ORIGINAL SITE OF THE ROYAL TECHNICAL COLLEGE OF BERLIN

The technical sciences' desire to catch up with other academic disciplines had finally found architectural expression no later than 1856 in Gottfried Semper's building for the Federal Polytechnic Institute in Zurich. Technical universities in Munich, Karlsruhe, Brunswick, or Stuttgart adapted this construction and earned new cachet for their research efforts everywhere they did so. Unlike Schinkel's Building Academy, which was more along the lines of an architectural sample for his new ideas, with its Prussian simplicity and pragmatic embedding in its surroundings (1836, →29), but also of a completely different quality than Beuth's Institute of Trade, whose most distinctive section was modeled on a factory (1827, →29), the new university architecture in Charlottenburg promised unshackled science and liberal arts. Founded in 1879 from these two earlier institutions, the Royal Technical College of Berlin took up the idea of the unity of the university. The palace building scheme, like that underlying the University of Berlin's Prinz Heinrich Palais, now conveyed this notion of oneness in the technical sciences as well. However, in its unprecedented dimensions, the main building instantly outclassed the university's large institute district for natural sciences on Dorotheenstrasse for example (→47), as well as the ensemble on Invalidenstrasse (→75) – although both had in fact only just recently increased the standing and visibility of science in Berlin in their own right.

Main building of the Technical College

Strasse des 17. Juni 135, previously Berliner Strasse 151 | 1878–1884 | 1876 first plans by Richard Lucae, 1877 revision by Friedrich Hitzig, completion by Julius Raschdorff (atrium in particular)

All this in spite of the fact that the site in Charlottenburg had by no means been firm, and had to be found first. Plans for settling the Technical College on Invalidenstrasse, like the Agricultural College and the Mining Academy, were initially well on their way. Yet the fact that the Technical College received its own swath of land in Charlottenburg instead of merely extending the expanded inner-city university landscape, testifies to the increased significance of technology in the era of high industrialization. And the need for space – for drafting, constructing, experimenting, and testing – exceeded that of the university sciences by quite a lot. The grounds of the hippodrome, which were in royal possession, including a tree nursery (more or less around today's Steinplatz), lent themselves perfectly to this purpose.

The temple of the technical sciences, which the **main building of the Technical College** of Berlin no doubt represented, was in its day the largest non-ecclesiastical building in Prussia. The Technical College surpassed Friedrich Wilhelm University in more than just size, facade ornamentation, and colorfulness (the floors were designed in red, orange, and light-hued sandstone): there were also no comparable counterparts to be found in Berlin for the entranceway, with its vestibule (→14) flanked by exhibition rooms on both sides, or for the atrium overflowing with artworks, or for the grand auditorium either for that matter.

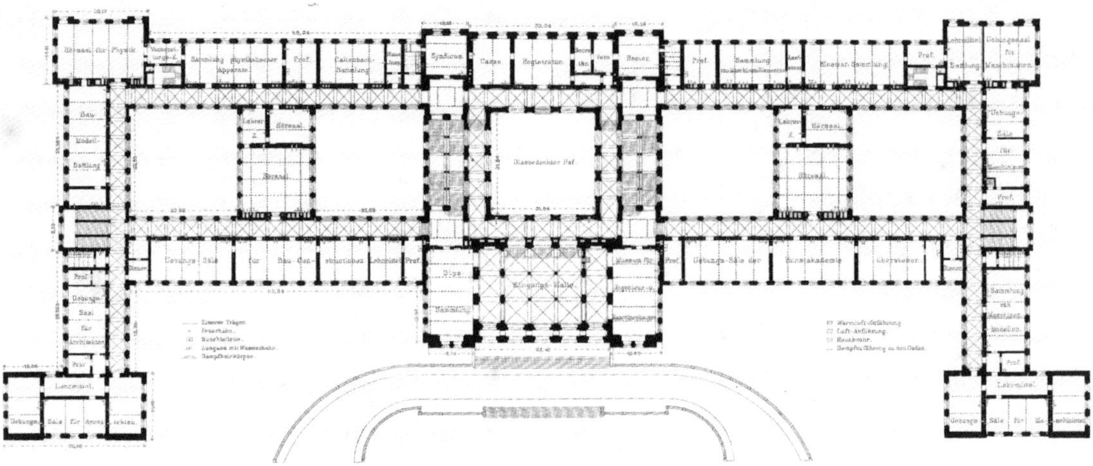

Erdgeschoss.

Walther gez.

Entwurf zu einer polytechnischen Hochschule zu Berlin.

Durchschnitt nach A-B.

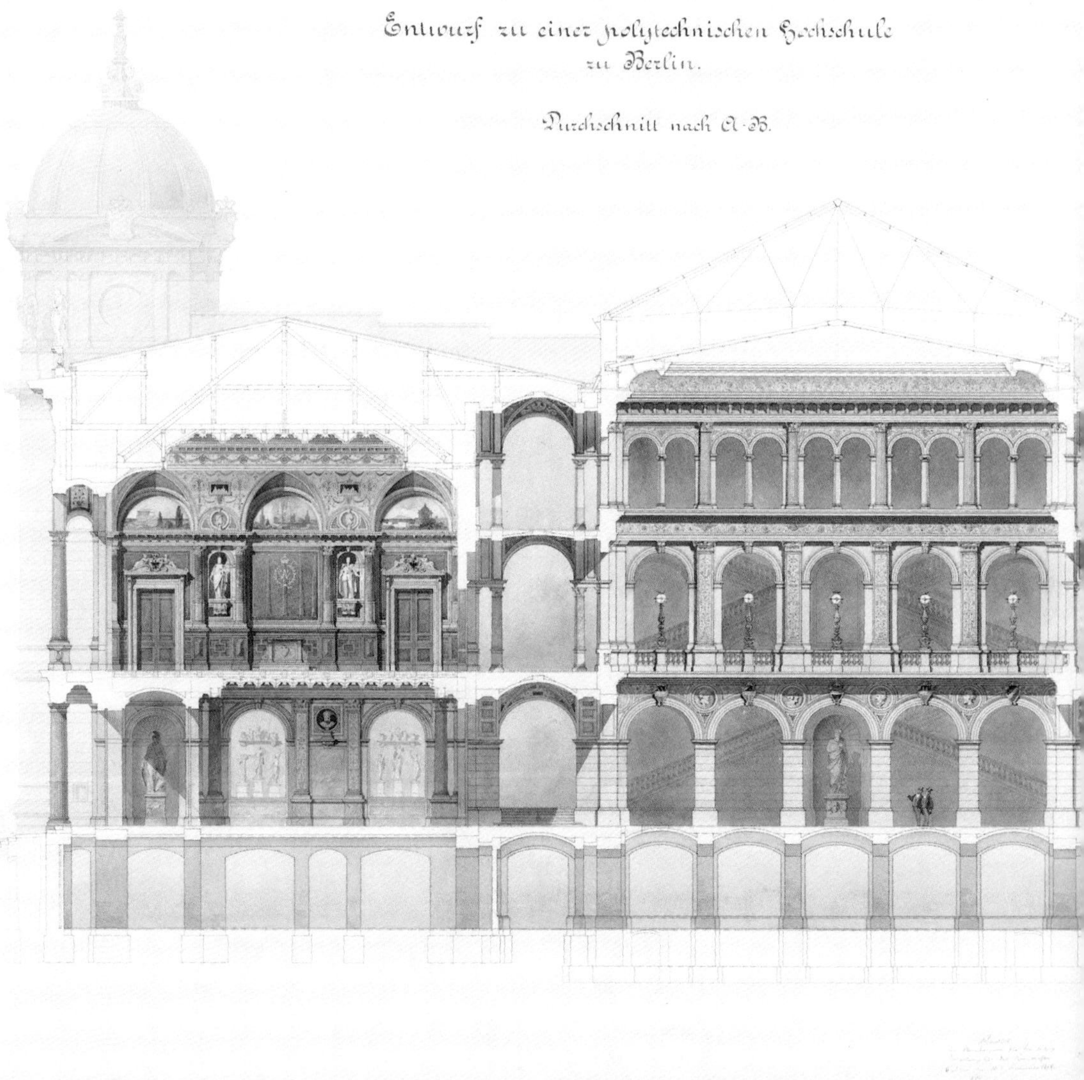

Blatt 13.

North facade, design of the entrance area

Staircase of the Chemical Laboratory

The representation of the claim to validity of the engineers educated here in five faculties for the good of the empire could hardly be clearer. Above the entrance, five individuals sat enthroned: Carl Friedrich Gauss for mathematics and physics, Johann Albert Eytelwein for civil engineering, Karl Friedrich Schinkel for architecture, Ferdinand Redtenbacher for mechanical engineering, and Justus von Liebig for chemistry and metallurgy. To the left and right of the vestibule, the plaster collection, which came from Schinkel's Building Academy, and the Museum for Engineering and Mechanical Constructions, whose roots went back to the Institute of Trade, together represented not only the precursors of the Technical College, but also the adoption of an instructional model based upon sense perception, as also pursued by Friedrich Wilhelm University, with its innumerable collections guided by the ideas of Humboldt and Pestalozzi (→88). In the centrally situated atrium, designed to encourage encounters, as in the cella of an ancient temple one came upon a statue – to be sure, not of a god in this case, but of Friedrich Wilhelm III in the form of an imperator – while murals on the walls featured allegorical depictions of the technical sciences. This clearly demonstrated the institution's aspiration to be a university dedicated to science and the arts, and not merely a school, teaching facility, or technical academy. This aim was ultimately fulfilled in 1899 with the granting of the right to award doctorates. Countless uniformly distributed rooms for research and teaching could be found on four floors along sprawling corridors and encircling four further open atria. In this manner, the unity of the technical sciences was conveyed to every student and lecturer, and the various disciplines were equipped in a fairly balanced fashion, although special attention was paid to subject-specific requirements.

Whether physics, architecture, mechanical engineering, or shipbuilding – all subjects were given equal consideration in the main building. A portion of the rooms was also designated for study collections and public museums, such as the Schinkel Museum or the Callenbach collection, which the well-known Baedeker travel guide recommended to visitors for instance. However, what were admittedly missing for the most part in this temple of the technical sciences were laboratories – and the field of chemistry.

Chemical Laboratory

Strasse des 17. Juni 115 | 1881–1884 | exterior design Friedrich Hitzig, completed by Julius Raschdorff | 1903–1905 new wing added

With proportions and stylistic elements alluding to the Florentine Renaissance and a front facade of light-colored granite, the same architects responsible for the construction of the main building taking place at the same time were able to distinguish the **Chemical Laboratory** from the latter in external appearance, without revealing its purpose-built nature. This is also true for the entrance hall, whose originally elegant double staircase was replaced by a modern solution fashioned from steel. In particular upon further inspection of the inner courtyards with their simple yellow brickwork, the arrangement of the rooms exhibits a purely functional design without embellishment in the interior, while defining the transition from external representation to practical laboratory architecture behind the main building.

Technical College, site plan

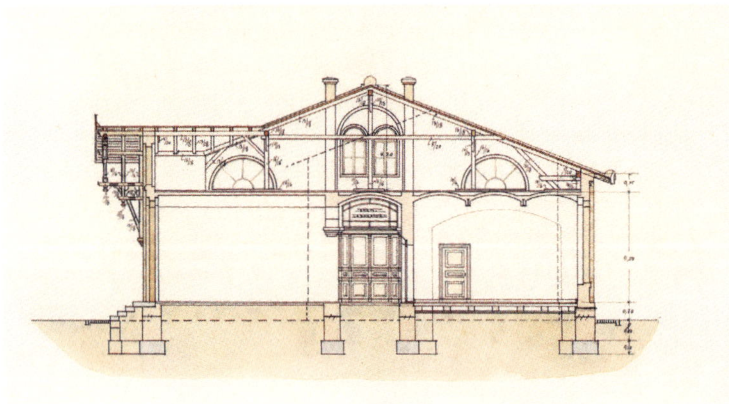

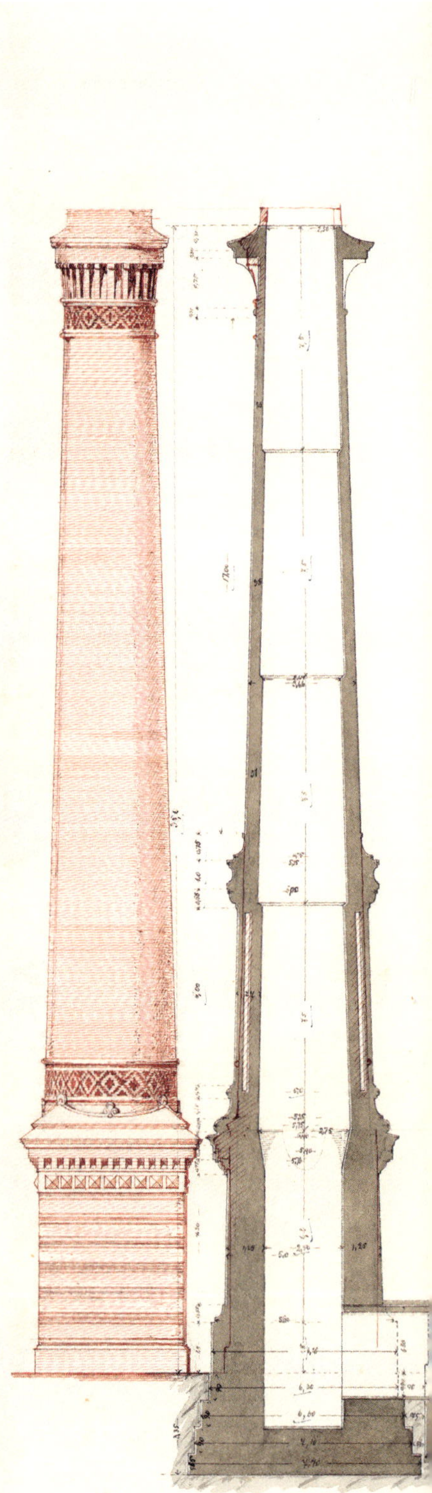

Laboratory for Mechanical Testing and chimney of the boiler and power house

Compared to the Institute of Chemistry in Mitte (→81), the building in Charlottenburg resembles an enlarged version of the former, although it adheres even more closely to the model of a counterpart in Vienna. Having said that, the otherwise typical director's residential wing is missing here, though a private laboratory is still present. The freestanding structure also offers not only more windowed surfaces, and thus better ventilation options, it also enabled Prussia's largest building for chemistry of the day to expand by adding side wings, which is exactly what would take place twenty years later.

First completed at the same time as the chemistry and main buildings in 1884, the Prussian Royal **Laboratory for Mechanical Testing** was a sort of dowry from the Institute of Trade, which was officially incorporated into the Technical College upon completion of the new building. At first, the facility was used to test the strength of paper or iron, for example. Then testing procedures for oils and lubricants were added, to be joined later by building materials, and then, in the emerging automobile age, combustion engines. The exterior design, with yellow bricks broken horizontally by twin stripes of red bricks, would also have a determining influence on the appearance of the laboratory and testing facilities to come. This approach indicated the rooms for experimentation, in which staff were also expected to get their hands dirty from time to time, and divided these rooms from the main building.

The **boiler and power house** covered the main building's heating and energy needs, and those of the other structures as well. Its twin smokestacks are not only the most visible elements of the building, they are also the components that commemorate the original architecture, whereas the current state of the rest of the building is the result of a series of renovations, made necessary by evolving needs. As the demand for heat and power grew, due among other things to the added extension building, and the boiler and power house had to increase its capacity accordingly with the aid of its own conversion projects, ochre-colored bricks were used in 1916, still visible today, instead of yellowish red clinkers, bringing for their part a new architectural form with them in the process. When the university was finally connected to the local district-heating network towards the end of the 1970s, the boiler house was transformed into an institute building.

In the years leading up to the turn of the century, the **Mechanical Laboratory** formed the conclusion of the original ensemble of Berlin's Technical College in several regards at once. From an urban planning perspective, it closed off the campus-like area

Laboratory for Mechanical Testing

different sections of the building house mechanical systems, motor vehicles, mailroom

Fasanenstrasse | 1883–1884 | Julius Raschdorff | 1894–1896 extension to north side, 1904 further floors added | 1906 motor vehicle laboratory added on the southern side | 1928 remodeling of south wing by Otto Weissgerber | 1949 floors added to middle pavilion | 1956 changes made to north wing

Boiler and power house

Institute of Environmental Technology

Fasanenstrasse 1a | 1882 built according to plans by Raschdorff | already planned by Lucae and Hitzig from 1877 | 1903 extension | 1916 remodeling with addition of water tower | around 1930 new south front | 1978–1983 converted into institute by Planungskollektiv 1

Mechanical Laboratory

thermodynamics and cooling engineering

Hertzallee (Kurfürstenallee) | 1894–1895 laboratory for mechanical engineering | 1896–1898 extension | 1956 extension by Emil Josse and Kuertze | 1956 addition on the west side

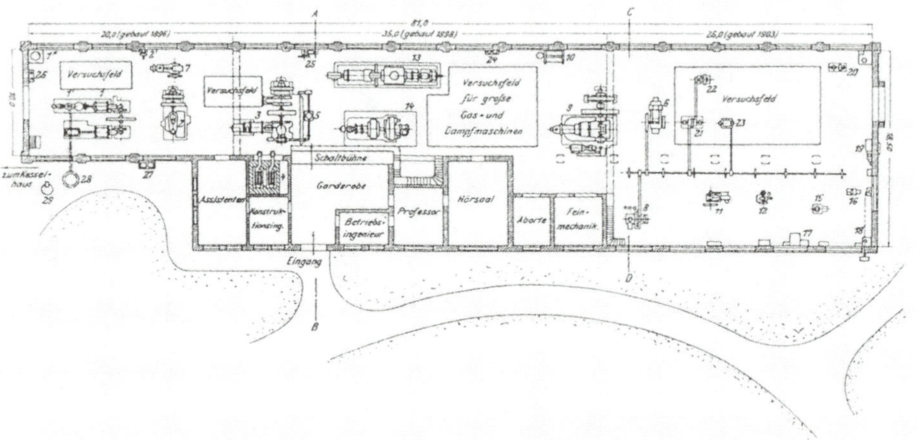

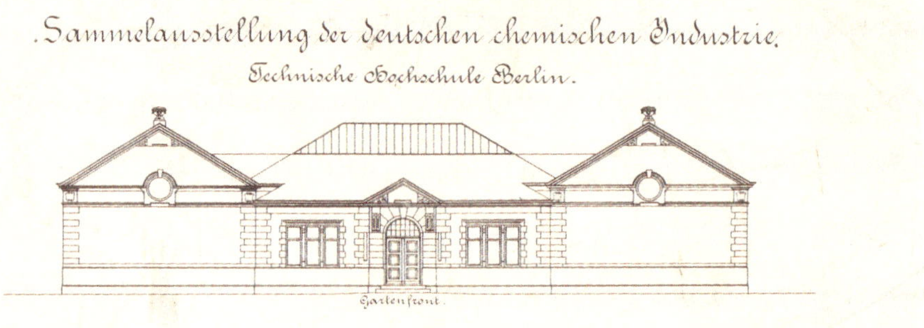

Mechanical Laboratory, Museum of Chemistry, and greenhouse in front of the TU

running along Kurfürstenallee (Hertzallee today), whereby all of the institutes were accessible from the garden side and thus through the main building, and it continued the recurring exterior design in a humble manner with its yellow bricks and red stripes. On the inside, testing areas for steam, gas, and dynamos complemented the furnishings of the university. As an additional special feature, power for electrical illumination was also generated here, making the Technical College a trailblazer in the field of electrification. And, finally, the new laboratory provided the necessary space for the laboratory instruction inherent in an engineering education featuring a heavy emphasis on the practical. This new educational orientation went hand in hand with the appointment of the influential mechanical engineering professor Alois Riedler, who wished to reform engineering education according to the American model and aimed to impart a new self-image to graduates. Of course, it was also Riedler who would, as rector of the Technical College, gain the right to award the Doctor of Engineering title for the Royal Technical College from the emperor.

No longer preserved are two buildings, constructed around the turn of the century, which once closed the last remaining gap between the Mechanical Laboratory and the main building. The greenhouse served to help teach architecture students how to draw ornamentation following the example set by the world of Mediterranean flora, while the building for the collective exhibition of the German chemical industry brought their presentation shown previously at the 1900 Paris World's Fair to Berlin, reflecting the tremendous significance of chemistry for the German Empire. The exhibition, also referred to as the Museum of Chemistry, existed until approximately 1930, and, like the museums in the main building, opened the university up to the general public. In recent times, this former location has been floated in discussions for a new museum pavilion, which is to give tourists and other interested parties an understanding of the collections and research findings of the Technical University.

NEW NEIGHBORS AND EXPANSION AROUND 1900

College of Fine Arts in the middle of the picture, on the right College of Music and Military Academy of Technology

With the settlement of further academies for the fine arts and music, which took up residence south of the original grounds of the Technical College and to the west of the military academy on Fasanenstrasse, the further development of a complex for artistic, technical, and military pursuits became apparent, an expansion which would continue into the 1940s.

College of Fine Arts
Main building of the University of the Arts, Royal Prussian Academy for the Fine Arts

Hardenbergstrasse 33 | 1898–1902 | Heinrich Kayser, Karl von Grossheim | 1936 conversion of antiquity hall into auditorium, ruins in courtyard since destruction in World War II | diverse enlargements during post-war period

College of Music

Fasanenstrasse 1b | 1898–1902 | Heinrich Kayser, Karl von Grossheim | destruction during World War II of two concert halls facing Hardenbergstrasse and Kurfürstenallee respectively (→121)

Institute of Church Music
Royal Prussian Institute of Church Music

Hardenbergstrasse 41 | 1902–1903 | Anton Adams, Paul Mebes

The building for the **College of Fine Arts**, which was founded in 1882 as the Royal Prussian College of Fine Arts, offered an entirely more reserved sight for keen eyes shortly after the turn of the century than the imposing main building of the Technical College. Through its segmentation into components with differing building heights and its three-part neo-Baroque sandstone facade, whose side wings with their stepped structure extending backwards provide better lighting conditions in the rear, the building leaves room at the same time for two pavilions in front, which appear to be separate structures, although they can be accessed from the main section of the building via corridors and bridges. Today, however, only the west pavilion is preserved. In the back, lower studio and drafting rooms encircling a courtyard lay adjacent, thus recalling the structure of the Technical College ensemble that served as a point of departure. The Rauch-Schinkel Museum added on the northwest side in 1916 and 1917 was already forced to clear the way again for a physics building in 1929. This incident succinctly demonstrates the deep connection between the developments of the two institutions, which co-operated with one another on curriculum as well, for instance in the instruction of future architects.

Noise concerns were the reason given for opposition to the idea of placing the academies for the creative arts on Jebenstrasse directly next to the Bahnhof Zoologischer Garten station, evidently referring both to the noise caused by S-Bahn lines and that created by music students. Be that as it may, there was more room on the grounds of the former royal nursery; thus, the construction of the College of Music was realized next to the art academy by the same architects, who merely varied their formal language here. Specifically, the structure featured a palace-like design, with the arrangement of the central building for instruction in a line alongside two flanking concert halls facing Fasanenstrasse, whereby the halls were each given their own entrances, including the large music hall facing Hardenbergstrasse.

Lying some distance from the conservatory, the **Institute of Church Music** on Hardenbergstrasse stands out starkly from

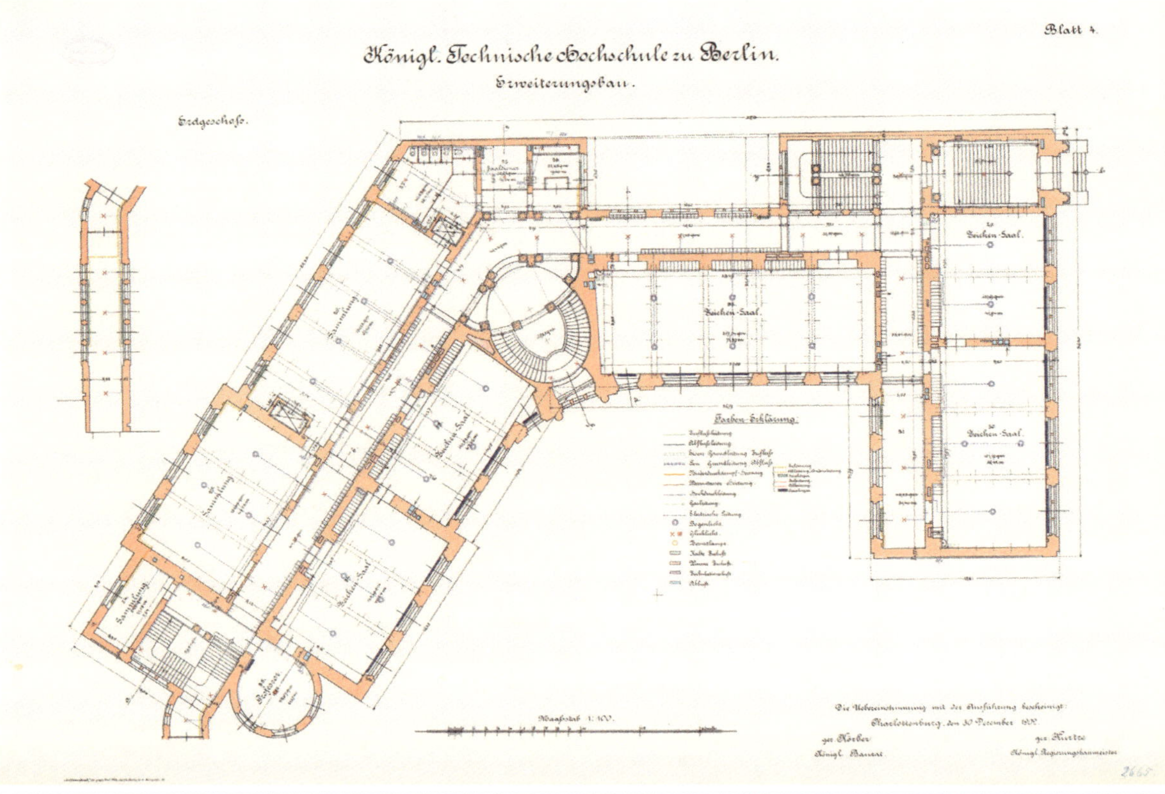

Extension building, floor plan first construction phase, facade along the Hertzallee

the neighboring structures due to its neo-Romanic facade affixed exclusively to the side of the building facing the street. The comparatively smaller sister institute of the music academy, which can also be described as an organ institute, made a churchly impression with its cross vault in the interior. However, how scarcely removed church music was from worldly affairs is evidenced by the institute's efforts to promote "music for the Hitler Youth", which was established as its own subject in 1934.

Extension building

Strasse des 17. Juni 145 | 1899–1902 | Hermann Eggert, Robert Leibnitz (realization) | 1912–1916 extension, Walter Körber | underground: test tunnels from the Institute of Mining and Metallurgy

Inorganic Chemistry Laboratory

old mineralogy building

Hardenbergstrasse 38 | 1912–1914 | J. N. Rackebrandt | 1946–1959 used by mineralogy department, after that as temporary cafeteria, nursery school

Institute of Metallurgy

Hardenbergstrasse, Hertzallee | 1913–1916 | J. N. Rackebrandt | today part of the building of the Institute of Mining and Metallurgy (→121) | 2005 renovation, Kebe + Schoberth architects

At the same time, the Technical College was in the midst of a westerly expansion, rounding out its main and chemistry buildings in a nearly symmetrical manner with the addition of an **extension building**, which was realized in two phases with an approximately ten-year interval in between. Since an elongation of the main building was out of the question, drafting rooms were placed in a building branching off on the street side, while lecture halls and collection rooms were set up towards the rear, with the two wings connected to one another via an unusual, oval-shaped stairwell.

The relocation and integration of the Mining Academy from Invalidenstrasse (→75) made a second building phase necessary, made possible too by the acquisition of the neighboring private property in the interim, so that the Technical College was able to occupy the entire area between what is today Hertzallee and Strasse des 17. Juni. Although the special discipline of mining and metallurgy was able to install a test mine in the extension building for training purposes, there was no room for the required laboratories. The **Inorganic Chemistry Laboratory** was realized as a modest stucco building, the first to conquer the other side of Kurfürstenallee (today Hertzallee) for the Technical College, soon to be followed by the similar-looking building for the **Institute of Metallurgy**, completed during the war years and today only partially preserved. A third building for briquetting from 1916 no longer exists.

LABORATORIES AT THE BEGINNING OF THE TWENTIETH CENTURY

Testing Facility for Shipbuilding and Hydraulic Engineering

sluice island | 1901–1903 | Georg Thür | 1927–1929 extension, Hans-Bernhard Reichow | 1967 conversion and water flow channel, Ludwig Leo | 2014–2017 renovation

The armament of the German fleet at the beginning of the twentieth century also had consequences for science. For instance, the **Testing Facility for Shipbuilding and Hydraulic Engineering**, created in this context, which was situated on the sluice island in the Landwehr Canal and used for the execution of hydrodynamic experiments. Although it wasn't an official part of the Technical College, still it maintained close ties with university instruction, for instance with the shipbuilding department, which was initially located in the main building. The testing facility forms the endpoint of the sluice island with its semi-circular entrance hall wainscoted with brick. At the end of the 1920s, two long towing tanks were added, in which models could be moved in standing water. Following destruction during the war and reconstruction, it was above all the object known as circulating tank II that added a special touch to the cityscape of Charlottenburg. The blue and pink flow channel, in which tests for the optimization of the interaction between hull and screw propeller could be performed, forms a striking contrast to the neo-Baroque Charlottenburger Tor and the institutes along Müller-Breslau-Strasse. It wasn't until 1995 that the testing facility became an official part of the Technical University.

Reuleaux-Haus

Electrical testing area and laboratory for machine tools
Fasanenstrasse | 1905–1907 | Ludwig Hoffmann | 1924 conversion and extension

Laboratory for Hydraulic Engineering
Fasanenstrasse | 1912 | Ludwig Hoffmann | 1919 machine hall added

The **Reuleaux-Haus** situated in the midst of the original property, named after the director of the Institute of Trade and later rector of the Technical College Franz Reuleaux, today unites several older laboratory buildings. The eastern section was erected to accommodate electrical engineering and tooling machines, while the western one was created shortly thereafter as a laboratory for hydraulic engineering. In a further development of the brick aesthetic typical for the Technical College, although orange and not yellow in this instance, practical spaces for labs and offices were created here, which would later be used by various departments. Today, one notices the railroad tracks lying directly in front of the Reuleaux-Haus and the switch-testing tower's signal installation, as well as the ruin-like remains of the Borsig iron foundry (→254) or the Reuleaux memorial stone. Objects like these as well as a series of old columns and statues turned the little campus into an open-air museum for visual instruction.

Testing Laboratory for Heating and Ventilation Systems

power station and apparatus engineering

Fasanenstrasse 1 | 1906–1907 (as replacement for the first testing hall from 1887) | Hermann Rietschel | 1912–1913 extended by Karl Brabbée | until 1953 reconstruction after damage during the war | 1965 move to the north grounds (→133) | 1992–1993 eastern block expanded by Planungskollektiv 1

As a replacement for a simple structure that preceded it – similar to that of the **Laboratory for Mechanical Testing** – an approximately 120-meter long, narrow building running alongside Fasanenstrasse was realized for the Testing Laboratory for Heating and Ventilation Systems. However, it was only accessible from the side of the grounds, in addition to being repeatedly remodeled, rebuilt, and having floors added.

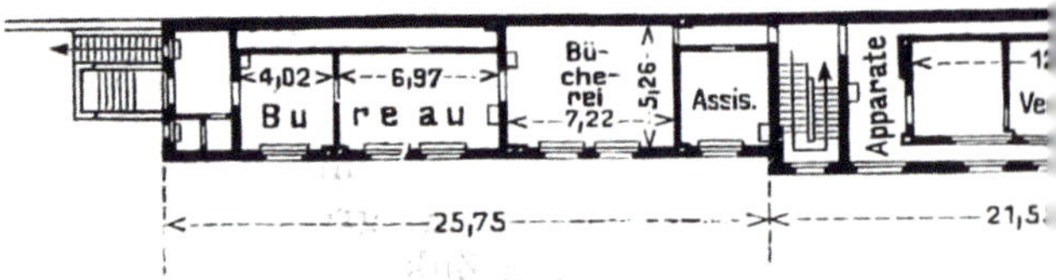

Circulating Tank II after renovation, 2017

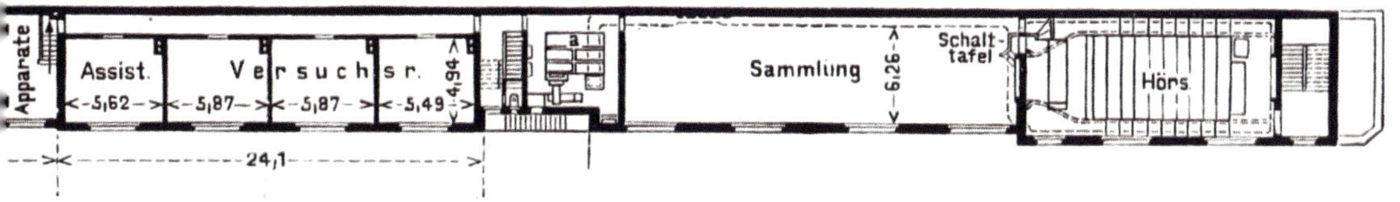

Testing Laboratory for Heating and Ventilation Systems, first floor

Between Laboratory for Mechanical Testing and Testing Laboratory for Heating and Ventilation Systems with a view to the extension of the Chemical Laboratory

Reuleaux-Haus with test signal box

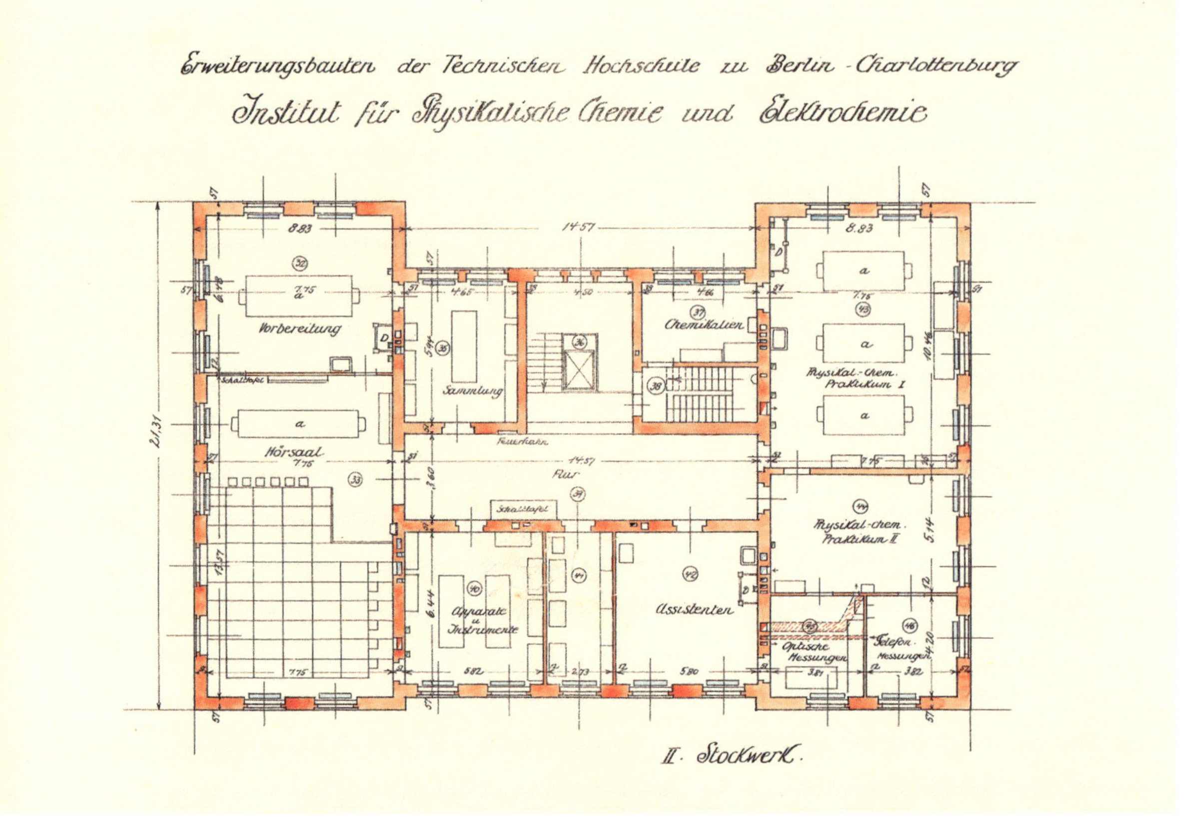
Erweiterungsbauten der Technischen Hochschule zu Berlin-Charlottenburg
Institut für Physikalische Chemie und Elektrochemie
Vorbereitung
Sammlung
Chemikalien
Physikal.-chem. Praktikum I
Hörsaal
Flur
Physikal.-chem. Praktikum II
Apparate u. Instrumente
Assistenten
Optische Messungen
Telefon-Messungen
II. Stockwerk.

Since 1993, the old building has disappeared behind a modern transom added on towards the street side, which took in a chemistry library, among other things, and today houses the areas of power plant and apparatus engineering. From a scientific perspective, the testing facility bears witness to Berlin's turn-of-the-century construction boom, with its new public and residential buildings, in which new heating systems replaced tiled stoves, a novel technology that needed to be mastered and perfected.

Physical chemistry and electrochemistry

Max Volmer Institute (for Biophysical, Electro and Physical Chemistry)

Fasanenstrasse | from 1913 | J. N. Raikebrandt | 1962 addition of one upper floor, Albrecht Sandow

Chemistry had blossomed since the opening of the Technical College, and following the collective exhibition and the addition of side wings to the Institute of Chemistry, the area of **physical chemistry and electrochemistry** received its own building in 1913 – following on the heels of the Kaiser Wilhelm Society, which had opened an institute of the same name a year earlier. It was designed to fit in with the surrounding testing facilities, and its purpose-built structure paled in comparison with the architectural quality of the Institute of Chemistry. The only new development here was the innovative system for supplying fresh air from a tiny ventilation building in the courtyard. Later, the building would be almost entirely ignored, due to remodeling work and its concealed position.

Cranzbau

of the Military Technical Academy, laboratory building Kurfürstenallee, part of the Institute for Federal Real Estate

Hertzallee, formerly Kurfürstenallee | 1904–1905 | Karl Weisenberg | ballistics laboratory | 1920 put at the disposal of the Technical College by army treasury | until 2010 in use by TU

Like the Testing Facility for Shipbuilding and Hydraulic Engineering, the Kurfürstenallee laboratory building of the Military Technical Academy – also known succinctly as the **Cranzbau** – went a long time before being made an official part of the college. The efforts of its personnel, however, the teaching activities and fruitful research performed in this instructional facility, were without a doubt part of the university. Carl Cranz is a good example for the military research conducted at the Technical College, which pushed back against any moves towards incorporation within a military technical academy. From the artillery and engineering school of 1878, which traditionally educated army engineers, there arose at the beginning of the twentieth century the Military Technical Academy, to which Cranz was appointed and tasked with establishing a laboratory for ballistics. However, soon he was also able to teach at the TH as a private lecturer, and the future artillery engineers were able to attend courses there. Following World War I and the subsequent ban on military research, the work in the Cranzbau, renamed the "Institute of Applied Physics" of the TH, was carried on for the most part, and Cranz himself was appointed to a professorship at the TH. After 1933, the so-called Military Technical College was created from this under the direction of Cranz's pupil Karl Becker and was first set up on the former Siemens site on Franklinstrasse, before its building would become the germ cell of the Nazi university city-within-the-city at Heerstrasse (→ 149). The Cranzbau stands as a symbol of the college's entanglements in armaments research, though it has hardly left a trace in the institutional memory of today's TU, despite the fact that it housed one of the Institutes for Mechanics up to the completion of the new physics building and was used by the TU until around 2010.

LARGE INSTITUTES AND ENORMOUS PLANS

Physics Building

Ernst Ruska Building

Hardenbergstrasse 39 | 1929–1931 | Otto Weißgerber, Fritz Schirner | post-war modifications | 2019 restoration of the lecture hall by Kebe + Schoberth Architekten

Seen from the outside, with its long, smooth, unadorned shell limestone facade, the **Physics Building**, completed in 1931, appears to anticipate the monumental architecture of the Nazi era, while its interior represents a rare example of the New Objectivity on the campus. Although at the time of the building's creation leading architects such as Hans Poelzig or Bruno Taut were actively involved at the Technical College, the assignment was given to lesser-known candidates from the outside – not without objections. The positioning of the building at a remove from Hardenbergstrasse was another testament to the need to keep vibrations from traffic to an absolute bare minimum. As was already the case with the first natural science institutes in Berlin (→47), extraordinary buildings stand as evidence of the fact that a coveted, especially renowned expert representative of a certain field could not have been successfully recruited for a professorship in Berlin without luring them with the prospect of a new building. In this case, the objective was to entice Gustav Hertz, a 1925 Nobel Prize winner, to leave Halle for Berlin. On one hand, the intent was to gain a highly visible practitioner of experimental physics to teach the subject, which was indispensable as a foundation for many technical fields of study, and it was clear that these activities could only be housed in the main building in an inadequate manner. Since the Technical College also played a role in teacher training in the natural sciences, a lecture hall with seating for 1,000 students was necessary, along with a great number of specialized laboratory and course rooms, workshops, or the eastern section of the building known as the "doctoral center". On the other hand, with Hertz, research into atomic and nuclear physics came to the university as well. In this way, scientific modernity met architectural modernity within the institute, which at the time was designed with each floor featuring different colors. However, the blossoming of modern physics at the Technical College proved short-lived, as Hertz was branded a "second-degree Jewish half-breed" and stripped of his duties in 1935, in spite of his decorated service in World War I.

Student House
old cafeteria

Hardenbergstrasse 34 | 1935–1936 | Hubert Lütcke | 1965 demolition of the gatehouse

As this phase continued, several structures followed which were intended to promote the students' national-socialist education or were suited to symbolizing a new political era with their over-dimensioned forms. From the outside, only the hipped roof of the largely preserved **Student House** of plastered masonry evokes echoes of the "Heimatschutz" style propagated by the Nazis, while on the inside traditional social halls were meant to make the building useable as a "fellowship house" in addition to its function as a cafeteria. Further, there was a barracks-like residential wing attached to the physics building, to be extended vertically later, and a gatehouse with a pillared gallery dubbed the "Brandenburger Gate", which extended all the way to the art academy, thus completing the campus while at the same time giving it a monumental entrance. The Student House survived the war and became the site of the 1946 re-establishment of the Technical College as the Technical University. The gate construction was torn down in 1965 to make way for the new cafeteria (→ 125).

Ernst-Reuter-Haus
administrative building for municipal authorities

Strasse des 17. Juni 112 | 1938–1942 | Walter Schlempp | 1960–1984 partial use of the middle section by the TU

The architectural influence of the Third Reich remained minimal, and perhaps the redesign of the forecourt of the main building into a square for military parades is most emblematic of the changes that did occur. The green entrance with driveway and park complex was transformed into an empty space, divided into squares in front of a new entrance staircase, which is still recognizable today. This was part of the expansion of the Charlottenburger Chaussee into an east-west axis, which was completed in time for Hitler's fiftieth birthday in 1939 and which the Speerian street lanterns still call to mind today. Corresponding architecturally to a certain extent to a "House of German Doctors" planned for the site across from the main building, which would have represented the creation of a sort of university square on the east-west axis, the **Ernst-Reuter-Haus** conveys a sense of what a national-socialist campus design would have looked like.

State visit, 1939

NEW BEGINNINGS AND COMING TO TERMS WITH THE PAST

Concert hall of the College of Arts

Hardenbergstrasse 33 | 1952–1954 | Paul G. R. Baumgarten | 1963–1975 modern reconstruction of theater and rehearsal halls

Early on in the post-war period, in 1949, a competition was announced for a modern reconstruction of the **concert hall of the College of Arts** destroyed during the war – and five years later an understated, uniformly structured glass front formed the new entrance to the musical arts. In a not uncontroversial departure from the style of representative facades, a democratic view from the outside to the inside was now granted. The comparatively small and light doors now also opened themselves to broader segments of society. Via a simple staircase in the new enclosure constructed with a reinforced concrete skeleton, one makes one's way into the concert hall with its venerable layout, which was resurrected in alignment with the preserved foundation walls. Following the re-opening as the Technical University in 1946 and the addition of a Faculty of Humanities, established in 1950, to the technical subjects, the architectural starting point for the new university was not the damaged main building but the building for Institute of **Mining and Metallurgy**. Erected right at Ernst-Reuter-Platz square, it instantly became a central part of this site symbolizing the new, liberated Berlin. The young architect Willy Kreuer – himself a member of the Technical University faculty – created a work for "coal, iron, and steel", whose aluminum-clad main columns fix blue glass elements in place as the building virtually floats above the floor in its square structure. The modern building now blocked Hertzallee (as Kurfürstenallee had been renamed) and with it the view of the old. However, underground a 40-meter-long replica of a mining tunnel connected the new institute with the old test mine in the extension building, integrated into the old Institute of Metallurgy just like the building itself.

Mining and Metallurgy

Ernst-Reuter-Platz 1 | 1955–1959 | Willy Kreuer

Civil engineering building

Hardenbergstrasse 40 | 1960–1961 | Karl-Heinrich Schwennicke

The **civil engineering building** was constructed between the Kreuer Building and the Institute of Physics a short time later; its facade design featuring window strips, steel partitions, and mounted balustrade panels seems more like a trial run for the new facade of the main building than a successful attempt to match the aesthetic quality of the mining institute.

Telefunken-Hochhaus

Ernst-Reuter-Platz 7 | 1958–1960 | Paul Schwebes, Hans Schoszberger | office building, since 1968 used almost exclusively by the TU

Pepper-Haus

Ernst-Reuter-Platz 9–10 | 1960–1963 | Franz Heinrich Sobotka, Gustav Müller | commercial complex, later used by the UdK | low-rise building under discussion as potential cafeteria for a time

At Ernst-Reuter-Platz, special touches are added to the cityscape by two further buildings, which were created as office blocks, and not university structures, but later used by the Technical University and University of Arts and more or less identified as university buildings. The **Telefunken-Hochhaus**, originally built as a company headquarters, is based on a plan by architecture professor Bernhard Hermkes from the Technical University and is the most visible element on the square thanks to its placement almost exactly on the east-west street axis. By contrast, the so-called **Pepper-Haus**, housing a radio wholesaler, is less spectacular from an architectural perspective, although it temporarily served as the office of the president and the administrative arm of the College of Arts.

Institute of Mining and Metallurgy, test tunnel

Around Ernst-Reuter-Platz (clockwise): Telefunken-Hochhaus, Pepper-Haus with AEG lettering, Institute of Architecture, Institute of Mining and Metallurgy, in the background also Physikalisch-Technische Bundesanstalt and Heinrich Hertz Institute

North wing, model, 1958

Compaction of the TU site: Mining and Metallurgy, new physics building, cafeteria along the Hardenbergstrasse, in the background main building with north wing and north grounds

Mensa

The war's bombs had rendered roughly half of the main building of the former Technical College unusable, with the damage to the inside even worse than that to the outside. There was heated debate for quite some time when it came to the subject of reconstruction, while the damaged street-facing side would determine the appearance of the Technical University for fifteen more years. So it was that the new **north wing of the main building**, a ten-story high-rise building section built above a single-story foyer with lecture halls, managed to negate this formerly determining factor that much more drastically through its sheer endless bands of dark windows and white cladding. The architectural differences could hardly have been greater, and it might even seem as if no value was placed on a harmonious interaction between the old and new constructions on purpose, so that the north wing would be perceived as a separate building in its own right.

North wing of main building

Strasse des 17. Juni 135 | 1963–1968 | Kurt Dübbers, Karl-Heinrich Schwennicke

Over on Hardenbergstrasse too, a break was first made with a remnant of pre-war architecture after some time had passed. The gatehouse from the Nazi era, which still had to be passed through in order get to the main grounds, was first replaced by a **mensa** twenty years after war's end. As with the north wing before, horizontal strips of windows dominated, combined here with smooth plaster surfaces. The Technical University had sealed itself off from the outside world on its main grounds – a problem it has continued to struggle with to this day.

Mensa

Hardenbergstrasse 34 | 1965–1967 | Werner Düttmann | 1988 conversion of the interior

At the same time, within the scope of the innovation competition "Optimization in University Construction", and thus under the auspices of the TU's expansion into a university for the masses, a **new physics building** was also conceived, which was to fill up the last unoccupied space between the cafeteria and the Institute of Church Music. A seven-to-ten-story main structure looms parallel to the old physics building, although it is concealed on the Hardenbergstrasse side by a four-floor low-rise building that doesn't exceed the eaves height of the surrounding and neighboring buildings.

New physics building
Eugene Paul Wigner building

Hardenbergstrasse 36 | 1978–1984 | Bruno Lambart, Dieter Hundertmark (competition in 1967)

THE EXPANSION OF THE TECHNICAL UNIVERSITY TO THE NORTH

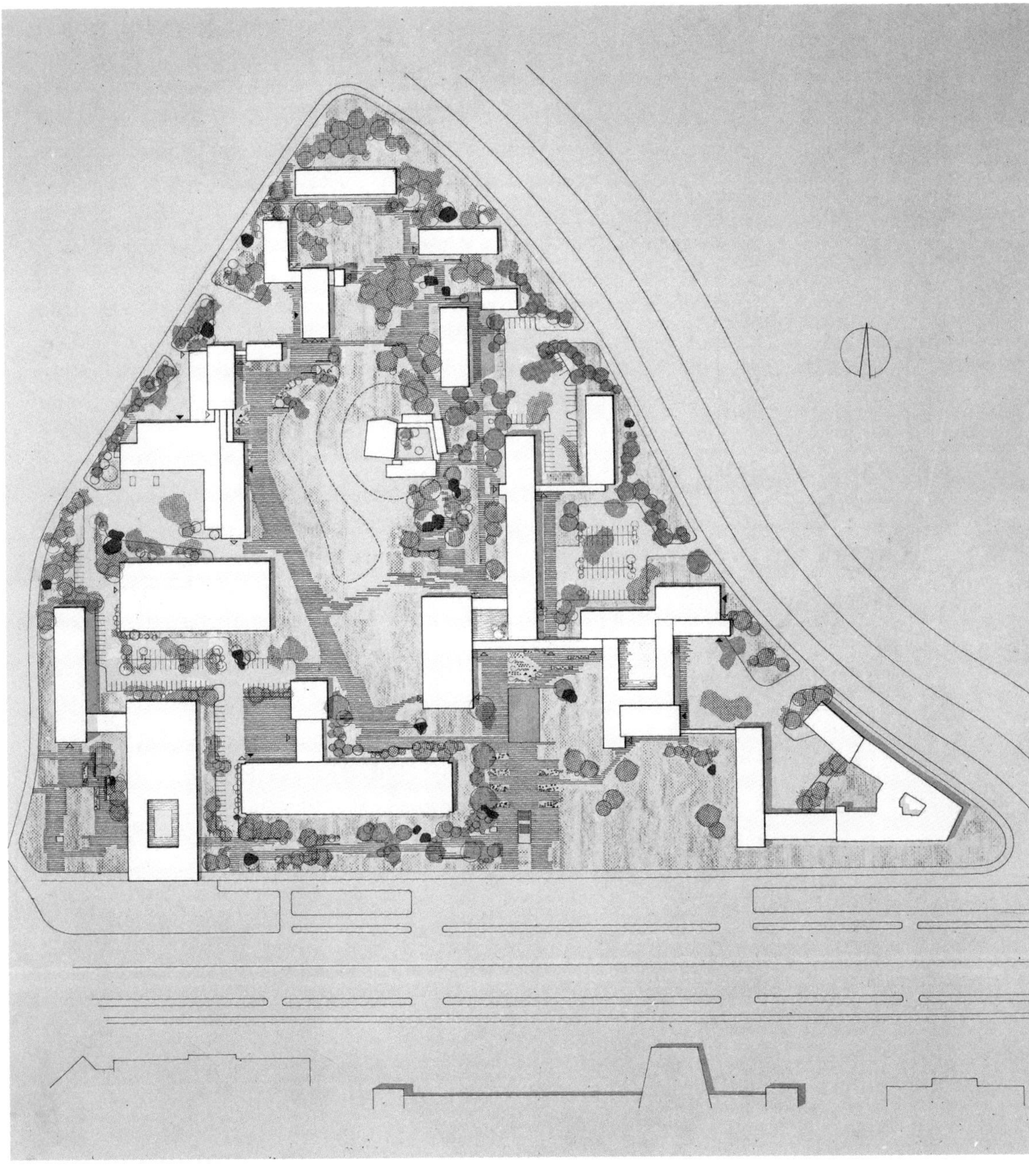

North grounds

Campus Nord

1957 planning stage | corner-stone laid on July 21, 1958 | demonstrative use of a stone taken from the ruins of the Reichstag building | inspired by US-American campus models with interior green area and church (later left unrealized)

Over the course of reconstruction and the architectural expansion which played out in parallel, the space originally made available for the Technical University upon the renamed institution's reopening in 1946 very soon proved no longer sufficient. Just a short distance to the north via Berliner Strasse – or, after its rechristening in 1953, Strasse des 17. Juni – lay the promise of a chance to expand. The north grounds, situated on the opposite side of the street and framed by the Landwehr Canal, Marchstrasse, and Ernst-Reuter-Platz, facilitated connection to the larger neighboring company branch offices, thus strengthening the position of the West Berlin location. A host of institutional and financial circumstances would combine to give the north grounds an extremely multifaceted appearance instead of a uniform one, although all of the buildings were personally realized by architects from the Technical University, making it possible to intepret the story of the north campus as an account of the architectonic evolution of the Institute of Architecture as well.

On the property also referred to today as the north campus, one encounters a series of spots that provide remarkable views and reveal a whole patchwork of architectural history and urban development: modernistic aligned blocks, villas dating from the early days of industrial expansion decked out with post-modern balconies, reserved, clearly minimalist facade designs, special and newly employed materials, such as slate or PVC, overhanging, converted, and mounted structural elements, as well as a rich variety of plants and trees. On its western edge, the north campus comes to a pronounced end facing the development around Ernst-Reuter-Platz, especially with the **Institute of Architecture**, consisting of two building segments, which apparently once included an adjacent "test garden" as well. Bernhard Hermkes's 1955 urban development plan for Ernst-Reuter-Platz proclaimed – in a politically charged manner – that a truly democratic mode of construction must feature a fluid approach to traffic and casually distributed rows of buildings that would open up the square.

Institute of Architecture

Strasse des 17. Juni 152 | main building 1963–1968 | Bernhard Hermkes | low-rise building 1962–1979 | Hans Scharoun | landscaping design by Herta Hammerbacher

Hermkes joined the faculty at the Technical University's Institute of Architecture as a professor for building and industrial construction in 1955, and would design a new building for the institute only a short time later. The facility's north-south orientation had already been stipulated by urban planners, which limited the possibilities for setting up drafting rooms with good access to natural light. However, by placing individual facade elements at an angle, Hermkes managed to capture as much sunlight as possible. On the whole, the building possesses its own distinct architecture, through the alternating arrangement of seminar rooms and offices, the slanted facade elements, different floor heights that were cleverly swapped on the narrow sides, support elements with varying degrees of visibility, as well as the reserved color scheme (with the exception of the orange blinds) and the choice of materials. This self-contained, meticulously thought-out architecture can also be observed within the building's interior, with its generously proportioned stairwell.

Institute for Architecture, northern exterior, in the background Hermann Rietschel Institute

Hermkes wing, view from west

Scharoun wing, view from east

Draft for the panel design in front of the Institute for Architecture by Herta Hammerbacher

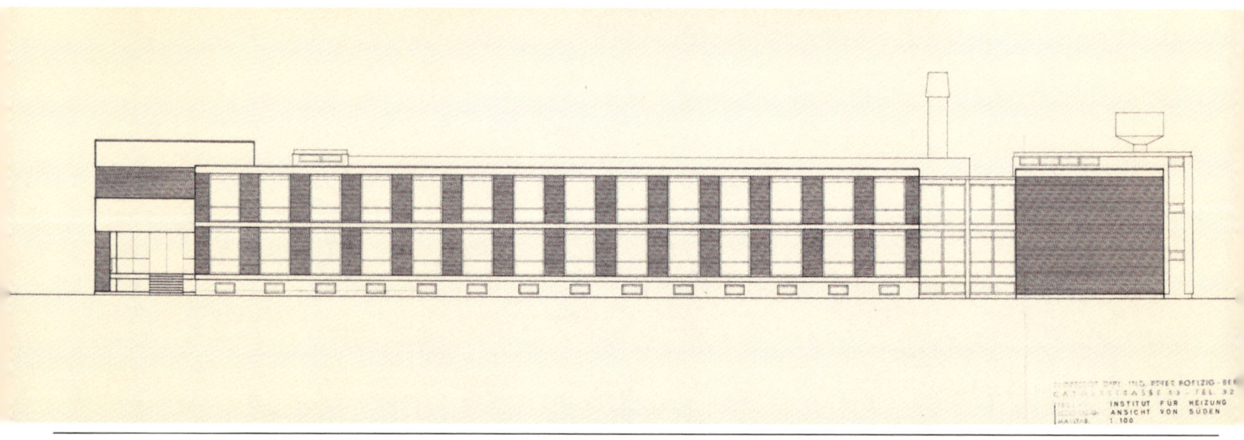

Institute of Hydraulic Engineering and Water Management, Hermann Rietschel Institute of Heating and Air-Conditioning Engineering

former Villa Stilke

Marchstrasse 6, formerly Sophienstrasse 8, formerly Bellstrasse 16 | 1904–1905 | Kayser, Karl von Großheim

former Villa Holtz

Marchstrasse 8, formerly Sophienstrasse 9, formerly Bellstrasse 20 | 1904–1905 | Otto March | 1970s conversion and extension of rear section| Inken and Hinrich Baller

Hans Scharoun had also taught at the Technical University as a professor from 1947 to 1958; although he was already retired with emeritus status by this point, he still managed to realize plans for a low-rise building for the areas of urban development, garden design, and landscape architecture. Thus, the thematic profile of each of the two buildings matched the teaching field of the respective responsible architect. In this regard, Hermkes's nested lecture halls represent the point where the two backgrounds intersected in a certain sense. The Scharoun building is a double-winged facility, in which differing floor heights are again combined with one another deftly and the side facing the courtyard consists almost entirely of glass. Characteristic here is the use of slate to clad the load-bearing walls, a material that the university managed to source from (East German) Thuringia in spite of the difficult political climate. The garden, enclosed by the wings of the building, plays with the contrast between planted areas and terraces composed of poured concrete.

The north grounds was the location of the March Pottery Factory from 1835 to the turn of the century. Ernst March's company became a leading producer of ceramic goods, as well as excelling in the prefabrication of architectonic elements, among other things. In the beginning of the twentieth century, the area was approved for villa construction, similar to developments in Dahlem. Of those built, only the former **Villa Stilke** and **Villa Holtz** remain.

Institute of Hydraulic Engineering and Water Management

Strasse des 17. Juni 144, 144a | 1958–1959 | Helmut Bressler | 1960–1961 addition of the model construction hall on the southern side

The development of the north grounds began right across from the main building as it lay in ruins. On the spot where Nazi plans for an "east-west axis" had called for a monumental "House of German Doctors", a new building was created for the **Institute of Hydraulic Engineering and Water Management**, which had previously been housed in today's Reuleaux-Haus (→111). There is not a single reverberation of representation to be found in the elongated new building, which is situated at a distance from the road for optimum noise protection, with its rear side facing the street. The choice of high-set windows and a plain, almost off-putting, monotonously structured facade conceals the laboratory for hydraulic engineering, which required that the building possess a certain length. As a laboratory, the building was modern and pioneering, and went on to set an example on the international scene as a result. The institute's director Heinrich Press and architect Helmut Bressler, who had held the chair for design and building construction at the Institute of Architecture since 1950, worked together on developing the building. Press stressed that hydraulic engineering models were intended to help make processes visible and to facilitate the taking of measurements – unlike architectural models, which exist for contemplation. An institute building and a connecting workshop building are arranged at right angles facing north.

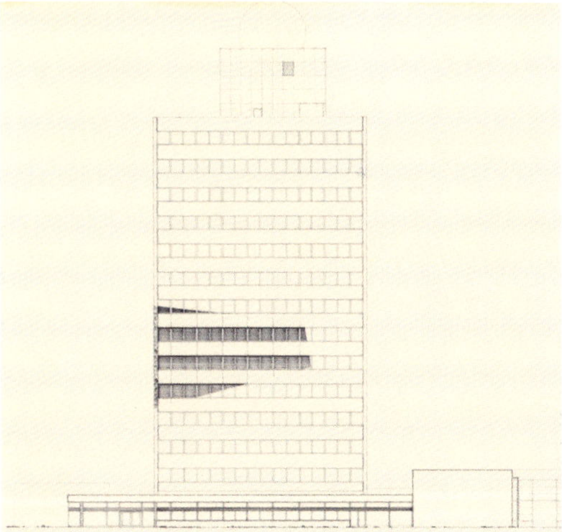

Institute of Energy Engineering, Institute of Aviation and Aerospace Engineering, HHI together with the Institute of Engineering Acoustics

Hermann Rietschel Institute of Heating and Air-Conditioning Engineering

Marchstrasse 4 | 1962–1966 | Peter Poelzig

Institute of Aviation and Aerospace Engineering

Marchstrasse 12–14 | 1959–1961 | Helmut Bressler | 1960 new hall building added | 1986 extension, conversion by Günter Wittemeyer

A path between the buildings for architecture and hydraulic engineering leads to the south side of the **Hermann Rietschel Institute of Heating and Air-Conditioning Engineering**, whose lucid form and design recall architectures of the 1920s. As was the case with its predecessor building on the main grounds (→ 111), which was furnished by professor and developer of the ribbed radiator Hermann Rietschel, individual focal points of the curriculum such as heated flooring are exhibited transparently within the building. For instance, the functions of the ventilation and heating systems for the lecture hall are also illustrated visually.

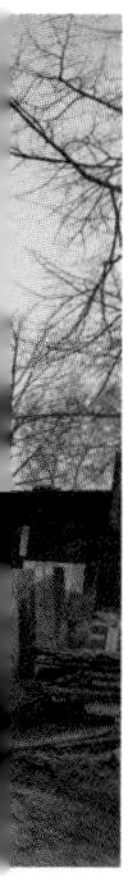

The **Institute of Aviation and Aerospace Engineering** directly adjacent to the north was founded in 1955 following the suspension of the 1945 ban on aviation research. This field had already been represented prominently in Berlin since the early twentieth century: with the Zeppelin and Parseval airships, which ascended from the airfield at Johannisthal in 1909, aviation engineering had also become a subject at the Technical College, and August von Parseval was appointed to be the first chair for airship construction in April 1912.

The institute building planned by Helmut Bressler was supplemented by a test hall for aircraft engineering, equipped with a heat and cold blasting unit, a wind tunnel, and a special section for strength testing, as well as a further windowless hall building. Due to remodeling, the originally white clinker brick facing with its striking blue facade design is barely visible any more. Beyond that, test halls for flight simulation have also been added to the institute.

Institute of Energy Engineering

former Institute of General and Nuclear Processing, Nuclear Technology

Marchstrasse 18, 18a | 1959–1961 | Wolf Sand | 1966 extension building, K. W. Werner

Heinrich Hertz Institute for Telecommunications

HHI

Einsteinufer 37 | 1964–1968 | Karl-Heinrich Schwennicke

The **Institute of Energy Engineering**, a three-part building complex consisting of a two-story building, a hall, and a test tower, was also erected on the northwest side of the north campus. Its architect, Wolf Sand, was also professor of room construction, where he taught introductions to architectural conception.

The **Heinrich Hertz Institute for Telecommunications** forms a conspicuous endpoint in the north. It owes its creation to the introduction of German radio in the 1920s and served from 1928 on – in those days still on the opposite side of the Landwehr Canal – for research into electrical and high frequency engineering, which formed the basis of radio technology. Initially, it was not a direct part of the college, but an affiliated institute instead, one boasting two endowed chairs, however. In the post-war period, it belonged officially to the Technical University, although its new home was already planned for an intended spin-off. Still, the building remained an unmistakable part of the north grounds, not only from an architectural standpoint, but also due to its continued incorporation within the teaching activities of the Technical University. The architect Karl-Heinrich Schwennicke had come to the university in 1951 as an associate professor for interior design. The fourteen-floor, H-shaped high-rise – which one can interpret as an allusion

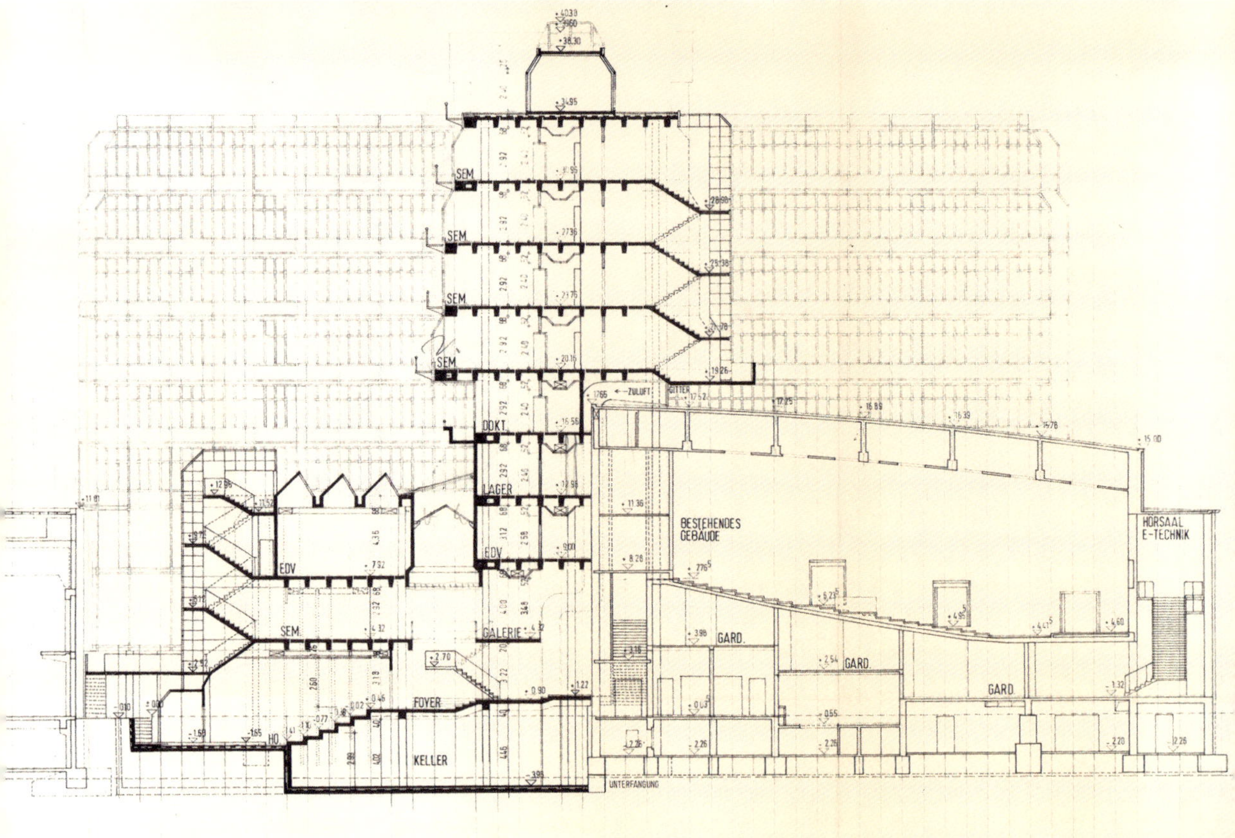

Institutes of Electrical Engineering, plan and new building

Institute of Mechanics

to its name – shapes the visual identity of the northern end of the grounds not least of all through the radiation dome on its roof, no longer operational though illuminated in the meantime, which was originally used to study the effect of atmospheric conditions on radio transmisions.

Institute of Engineering Acoustics
Werner von Siemens Building, formerly Institute of Technical Acoustics, Telecommunications Engineering, and High Frequency Technology

Einsteinufer 25–27 | 1962–1966 | Werner March

Institutes of Electrical Engineering
with electrical machines, high voltage engineering, and lecture hall building for electrical engineering

Einsteinufer 11, 15, 19, Strasse des 17. Juni 134 | 1959–1962 and 1960–1963 | Karl Wilhelm Ochs

New building of the Institute of Electrical Engineering
extension building for the laboratories of the high voltage division

Einsteinufer 17 | 1982–1987 | Peter Bayerer, Gerd Fesel, Hans-Dieter Hecker, Roland Ostertag

Institute of Mechanics

Einsteinufer 5–7 | 1928 | Ernst Schmid-Meiningen | sustained heavy damage during the war | 1951 bought by Oetker company | 1963 acquired by Federal State of Berlin | 1963–1965 conversion and addition of new testing hall, Werner Hammersen, Heinz Mecke

Institute of Technical Chemistry
former Franz Fischer Building

Strasse des 17. Juni 124 | 1963–1968/1969 | Willy Kreuer

The Werner von Siemens Building, which houses the **Institute of Engineering Acoustics**, lies adjacent at Einsteinufer. The three-part building stands out above all in the entrance and transit area due to its glass covered middle section, with its high-grade construction. Werner March was already a professor emeritus. Previously, between 1953 and 1960, he had been the department chair for urban and housing development. March, who like Peter Poelzig had been a member of the Nazi Party, is best known as the architect of Berlin's Olympic Stadium.

Already due to their sheer volume, but also through their significance for industry, the **Institutes of Electrical Engineering** take up a large area with their buildings from the 1960s and 1980s. The architect, Karl Wilhelm Ochs, was appointed to the chair for practical and building design in 1952. His trio of building complexes forms a unified whole, due to their elegant use of materials. The conspicuously elongated form of the northern block is rooted in a request by the lighting engineers that the basement be equipped with a photometric bench in order to be able to take various measurements for spotlights. The building's placement at a remove from Strasse des 17. Juni was chosen for noise protection reasons. The travelling wave room for instance required structural safety measures such as Faraday cages and the grounding of all metal components. In the high voltage hall, experiments featuring up to two million volts are possible. The lecture hall stood on its own for almost twenty years and was first integrated into the mathematics building in the course of expansion plans. Ochs alludes to his proposed design for the Berliner Philharmonie, which garnered him a third place showing in the corresponding competition.

The new building of the **Institute of Electrical Engineering** emphasizes its proximity to the Landwehr Canal and delivers strict sequences and seriality in its facade. In the **Institute of Mechanics**, on the southeast end of the property, the existing former office building of the Hinz und Küster coffee roasting house was expanded with an add-on institute building and a testing hall.

In the 1960s, the **Institute of Technical Chemistry** received a large institute building situated right on Strasse des 17. Juni, doubtless due to the economic significance. The work of Willy Kreuer, who had already been active at the TU since 1949,

Institute of Technical Chemistry

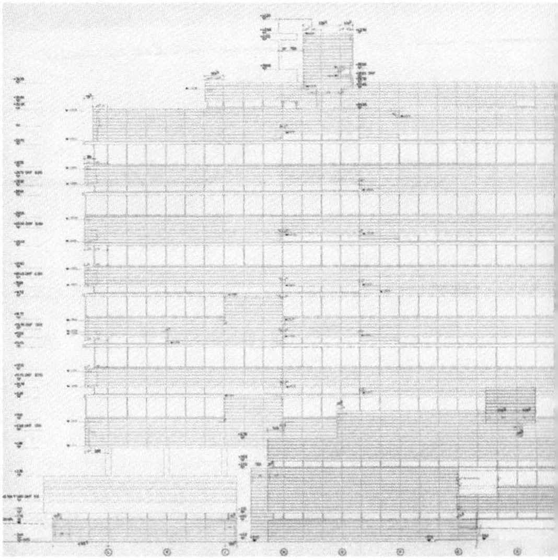

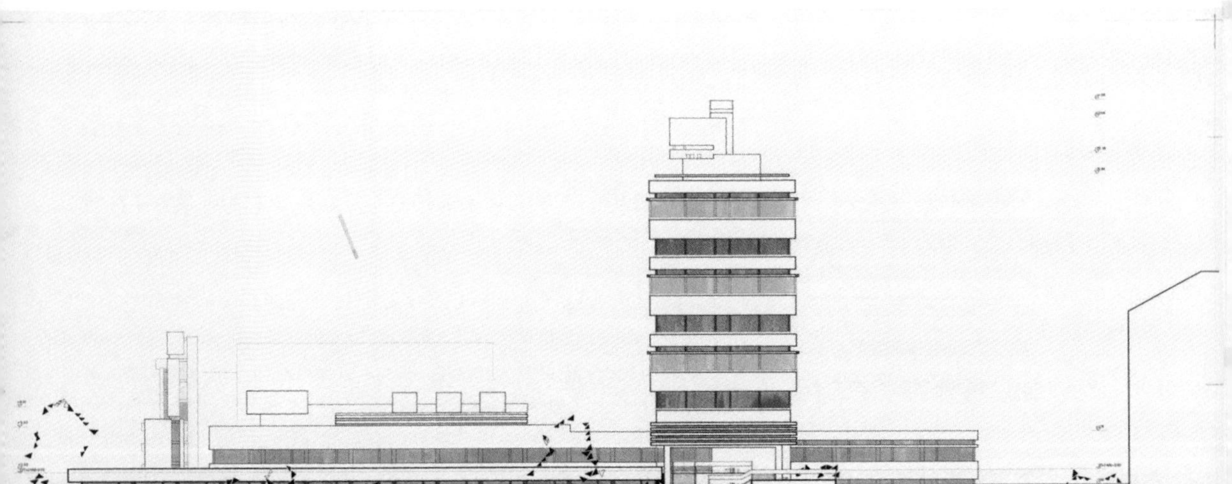

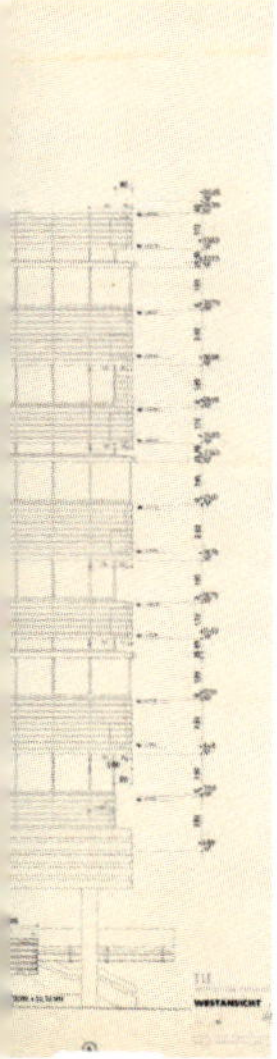

becoming a professor for building design in 1951, is characterized by a great stylistic range and an especially high level of variety concerning the materials used. The low-rise building of the institute is intended for research and engineering, while the high-rise block with its narrow side facing the street is reserved for instruction. Here the inner use of the building is directly reflected in the facade design: the center-to-center spacing of the windows and the spacing of the load-bearing supports correspond to the proportions of a standard laboratory table. The individual floors are divided in an L shape into measurement and laboratory areas, whereby the latter exhibit a greater floor height. From floor to floor, the areas are rotated diagonally, so that vertical and horizontal fluctuations running across the facade due to differences in height create the appearance of dynamic interaction. The employed facade panels are made of PVC, the use of which was still considered experimental at the beginning of the 1960s, an allusion to the research conducted at the institute.

Although they experienced a brief decline after the Berlin Wall went up in 1961, assistance measures and relaxed admissions criteria led to a drastic increase in enrollment figures throughout the 1960s. The TU had become an institution for the masses and urgently needed more space. In the wake of an open competition soliciting ideas for a structural master plan for the main grounds of the university in 1967, a planning commission was established consisting of the six prizewinners. However, a direct implementation of the resulting master plan was impeded by financing issues caused by the Federal University Construction Act of 1969, by the heavily protested evolution from a professor-dominated university into a third-party organization, and by the differing priorities of the Berlin Senate and the university concerning the embedding in the cityscape and the availability of technical facilities. Nevertheless, the young second-place-winning architects Georg Kohlmaier and Barna von Sartory received a commission for the construction of a **mathematics building**. The two had received attention for their "backpack toilets", plastic WC capsules to be mounted on the outside of old buildings in order to save them from being torn down, as well as for visionary ideas regarding mobility in the big city. The building was realized starting in 1975, against the backdrop of the energy crisis (→221). While the incorporation of Ochs's electrical engineering lecture hall within the new building was already included in the call for proposals, a planned pedestrian bridge spanning the Strasse des 17. Juni to the main building on the other side failed to receive the required permit due to fears that it would block the line of sight.

Additionally, a low, reserved new structure has rested within the north campus since 2011: the **electron microscope building**. Inside, a ten-meter-deep and one-meter-thick base plate dampens all vibrations (→17). Due to the fact that the use of modern transmission electron microscopes requires that room-climatic conditions vary as little as possible, the air conditioning system takes up nearly half of the building, while the outward appearance of the elaborate research facility is restrained in its form. The TU is in addition using the Marchstrasse office building, which was also constructed by Nöfer Architekten as a three-wing complex.

Mathematics building

Strasse des 17. Juni 136 | 1967–1983 | construction period: 1973–1983 | Georg Kohlmaier, Barna von Sartory

---

Electron microscopy building

Marchstrasse 10 | 2009–2011 | Nöfer Architekten

Mathematics building, Electron microscopy building, and the north grounds

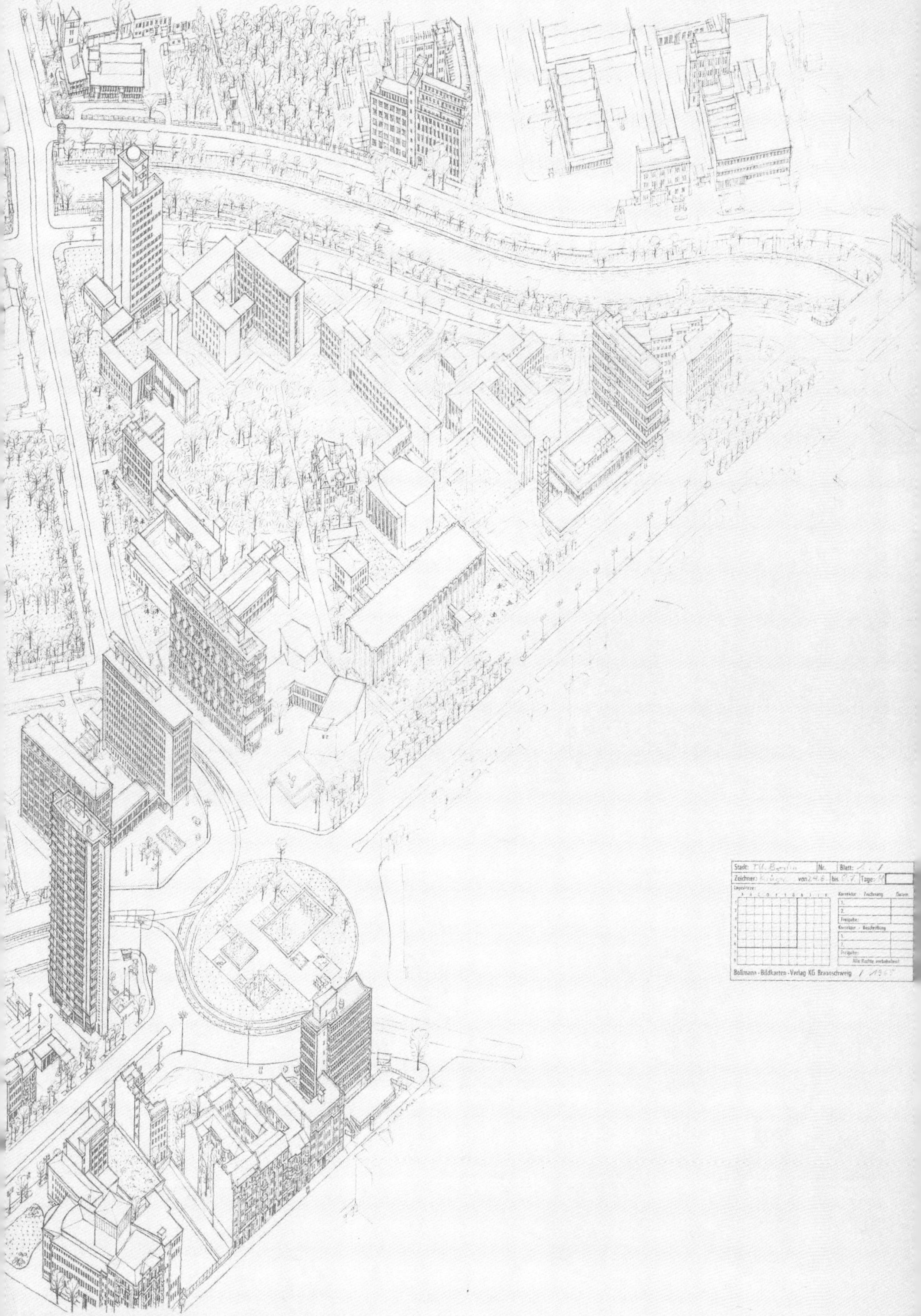
Stadt: TU Berlin
Nr.
Blatt:
Zeichner:
von 24.6
bis
Tage:
Lageskizze:
Korrektur · Zeichnung
Datum
Freigabe:
Korrektur · Beschriftung
Freigabe:
Alle Rechte vorbehalten!
Bollmann-Bildkarten-Verlag KG Braunschweig

RENEWAL OF THE EASTERN GROUNDS

Institute of Fluid Dynamics and Institute of Food Chemistry, Institute of Machine Tools, and Institute of Combustion Engines and Motors

As a first step towards reestablishing research and teaching operations, in the post-war period the main grounds of the former Technical College were extended to the east, beyond Fasanenstrasse. After the former royal riding arena located there had been used in the interwar period as an athletics facility by the Technical College, following World War II it became the site of a rubble recycling company. Originally, an industrial estate was supposed to be created on the property next, until finally permission was granted for a proposal from the senator for construction and housing to create sorely needed space for the Technical University there instead.

In the early 1950s, five institute buildings were erected in a practical and timesaving pre-fab construction style between Fasanenstrasse, Gartenufer (today Müller-Breslau-Strasse), and the Testing Facility for Shipbuilding and Hydraulic Engineering on the sluice island (→111). The new institute buildings can be divided into teaching and administrative structures and are directly connected to a large-scale glazed testing hall. Although time and budget factors played a decisive role both in the creation of an architectural plan and elaboration of an overall concept and in the structural realization, in their serial arrangement, reduced form, and the use of narrow bands of color in the clinker brick cladding, the facade designs still made clear reference to the aesthetics of interwar modernism. Though the areas for theory and practice were separated within the buildings, an attempt was still made to create a unity of research and teaching. The **Institute of Food Chemistry,** the **Institute of Machine Tools and Manufacturing Technology,** the **Institute of Fluid Dynamics and Technical Acoustics**, the **Institute of Fuel Technology**, as well as the **Institute of Combustion Engines and Motors** all arose in this form.

former Institute of Food Chemistry

inorganic and analytical chemistry, Institute of Environmental Technology

Müller-Breslau-Strasse 10 | 1954–1955 | construction department, Bruno Grimmek (director), Erich Schuppe (design)

Institute of Machine Tools and Manufacturing Technology

Fasanenstrasse 90 | 1954–1955 | construction department, Bruno Grimmek (director), Erich Schuppe (design) | 2019 demolition

Institute of Fluid Dynamics and Technical Acoustics

former Hermann Föttinger Institute, Institute of Fluid Engineering

Müller-Breslau-Strasse 8 | construction department, Bruno Grimmek (director), Erich Schuppe (design) | extension building added in the late 1960s

Institute of Fuel Technology

Rudolf Drawe Institute

Fasanenstrasse 89 | 1955–1957 | construction department, Bruno Grimmek (director), Erich Schuppe (design) | 2019 torn down due to planned new mathematics building

Institute of Combustion Engines and Motors

Fasanenstrasse | construction department, Bruno Grimmek (director), Erich Schuppe (design) | copy of the former Institute of Machine Tools and Manufacturing Technology | 1997 torn down to make way for planned new library building

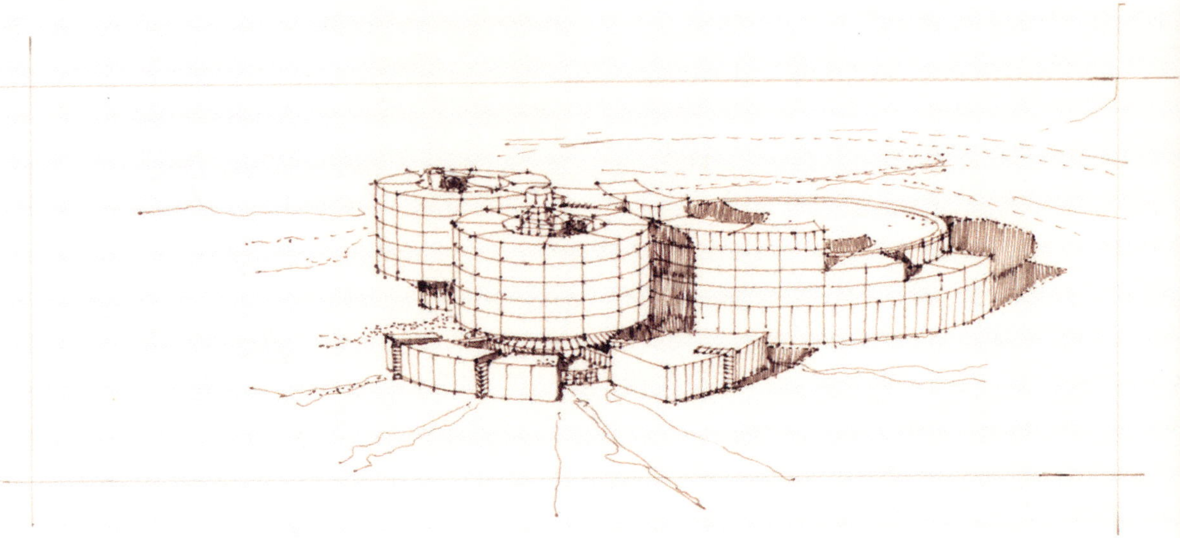

VOLKSWAGEN UNIVERSITÄTSBIBLIOTHEK

The building of the **Center for Production Engineering** constructed further to the north thirty years later, which the Technical University operates together with the Fraunhofer Society, represents another solution for the linking of practical research and university teaching. The rooms for practical research work are housed in a rotunda, which is encircled by an additional two-winged administrative and teaching building. The result is a concavely nesting structure flooded with light, which blends into the urban area around it and flows with the course of the river.

Center for Production Engineering

double Institute of Machine Tools and Factory Management (TU) and Fraunhofer Institute for Production Systems and Design Technology (IPK)

Pascalstrasse 8–9 | 1983–1986 | Peter Bayerer, Gerd Fesel, Hans-Dieter Hecker, Roland Ostertag

Library of the TU and the UdK

Volkswagen University Library, University Library in Volkswagen House

Fasanenstrasse 88 | 2002–2004 | Walter Arno Noebel

At the start of the twenty-first century, with the joint **library of the Technical University** and the **University of the Arts** (→ 199), a new connection of both institutions was created east of Fasanenstrasse for the time being. The elongated, rectangular structure offers space for the collections of the Technical University on three floors, while the holdings of the University of the Arts are located on the fifth upper floor. In the building's interior, open access areas and workstations are arranged around three atria and open staircases. On the outside, the simple, reddish facade facing Fasanenstrasse gains added charm through illuminated glass cases affixed to the front, which serve to ventilate the stacks. Although it is true that the architecture's austerity, functionality, and reserved nature have been the object of criticism, without a doubt the university library forms a hub in Charlottenburg's university network, as well as representing a prelude to the expansion of the area as a renewed location for science.

There is scant potential for further development on the north grounds – for reasons of space and historic preservation. The TU has noticeably chosen to refocus its attention on the eastern grounds when it comes to the further development and architectural consolidation of the Charlottenburg campus.

Institute of Mathematics and Interdisciplinary Center for Modeling and Simulation (IMoS)

Fasanenstrasse | currently in planning phase | Code Unique | expected completion date: early-2020s

A master plan drafted in 2011 calls for the successive use of a large portion of the grounds between Müller-Breslau-Strasse and Hertzallee for the extension of the Technical University. In a first phase of construction, begun in June 2019, the winning proposal of the competition announced by the senate in 2017 will be realized: namely, for the **Institute of Mathematics and the Interdisciplinary Center for Modeling and Simulation**. Together they form a twin center, which consists of two rectangular blocks with courtyards. With its seminar rooms, lecture halls, library, and cafeteria, the Institute of Mathematics will serve as a place for instruction, knowledge exchange, and encounters. The IMoS is reserved for research purposes. The close proximity of research and teaching will also be retained in this construction project. (MW)

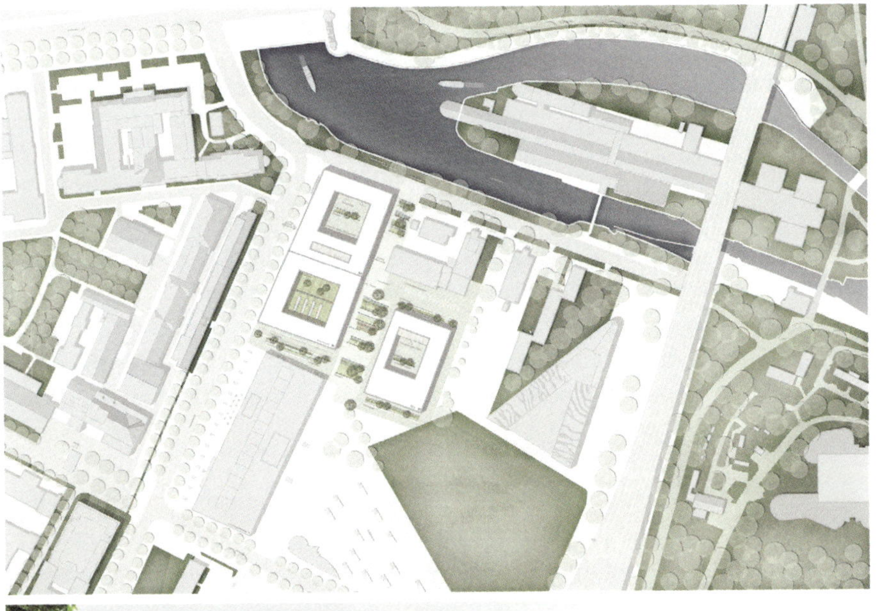

The Campus Idea in Berlin

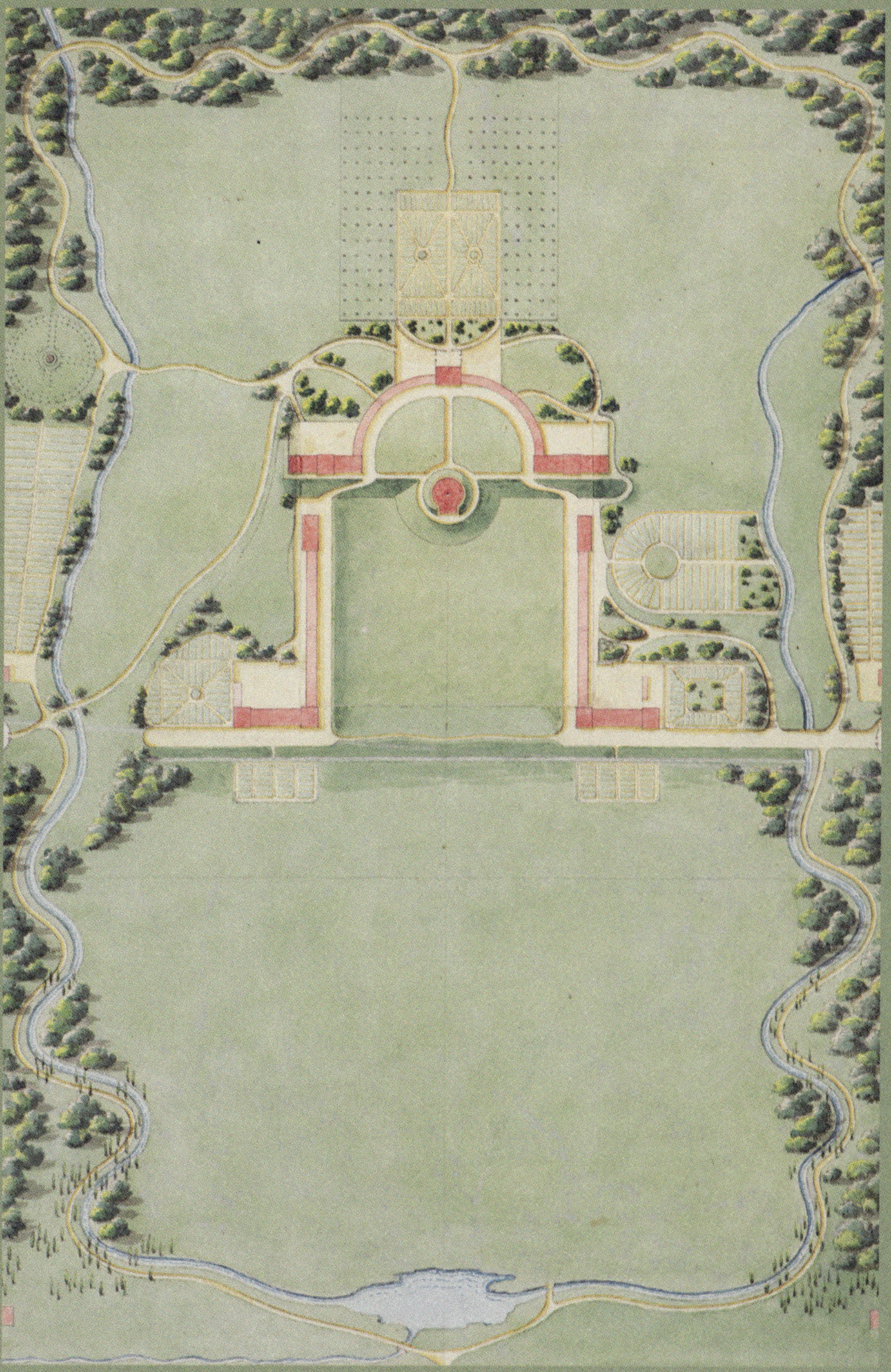

145

The concept of the campus university had already taken root in the United States by the beginning of the nineteenth century. It combined the spatial considerations and specific interests of the emerging modern academic disciplines with their pedagogical ambitions. The practical requirement for realizing such a concept was that a college owned enough land to actually build the campus buildings. The idea was first realized in 1774 at the site of the College of New Jersey, which is now Princeton University. Later on – while the Berliner Universität, renowned as a reform university, began moving into courtly style buildings and thus moving in an antithetical direction to the campus ideal – Joseph Ramée designed a symmetrical, archetypal university embedded in the landscape for Union College in Schenectady, New York state (→ 145). Around the same time, Thomas Jefferson established an "academical village" for the University of Virginia which he had founded some time earlier.

In contrast to Berlin's Prinz Heinrich Palais, which compelled the university to adapt to the given architectural conditions, the main idea of the campus was to distribute university buildings over a site according to their function and to engage with the landscape. This approach was subsequently implemented in grand style in Berkeley, California (1868).
In Germany, this model was first adopted about 150 years later – though not conforming with the archetype, but rather pursuing the basic idea of locating university buildings in a concentrated community on the outskirts of a town or city. This was the model adopted by the newly established universities in Bochum (1962), Düsseldorf (1965) and Bielefeld (1969). The Freie Universität actually began construction on a Campus in Berlin-Dahlem as early as 1948. Conceived as a reform university based on its American antecedents, the Freie Universität also demonstrated an innovative approach to architecture. In contrast to other universities up to that time, it rejected the idea of a grand main building in the city center, and instead opted to make a new beginning in the suburban district of Dahlem. In this new location, it had recourse to an existing stock of buildings: namely the institute building of the former Kaiser-Wilhelm-Gesellschaft (→ 162) and a number of Gründerzeit mansions in the neighborhood. As it expanded to a high-volume university in the 1960s, the demand for space grew rapidly. The campus was extended considerably as a consequence and further sites were added to it. When one observes the establishment and development of the Freie Universität campus, it becomes clear how closely the history of Berlin's academic institutions is bound up with the history of the city. Born out of necessity in a city divided after World War II, the Freie Universität in Dahlem first had to integrate into its location and was frequently forced to improvise.

University planners in Berlin were never able to develop their ideas as they wished due to recurring spatial and political restrictions. This applied to any plans of building a campus university too. There had been thoughts of moving the Berliner Universität to the outlying areas of the city since the nineteenth century, and around the turn of the century there were concrete discussions of relocating the Friedrich-Wilhelms-Universität, the precursor of the modern Humboldt-Universität, to Dahlem. In 1910 and again in 1925 there were proposals to relocate it to a site near the River Havel, and in 1937 the National Socialists demarcated an area on Heerstrasse as a site for the "University Town Berlin". In 1961 the Humboldt-Universität even formally announced its relocation from Unter den Linden in Berlin-Mitte to Blumberg, a village north-east of Berlin. However, like all the other plans, this idea was never to be realized.
The dream of a university campus that was not limited by the existing buildings on a site was always able to create excitement, but it was ultimately never realized in this form in Berlin. Nonetheless, it is worth taking a closer look at these extensive plans: not only do they reflect the academic discussion of the time, they often served as models for subsequent realizations, even if in some altered form. The rapidly developing city and also the profound political changes demanded new forms of architectural expression, which is evident in the visions they are based on and in their pragmatic designs.

An Academic Campus in Dahlem

As early as the 1890s it had become evident that there was a shortage of suitable sites for attractive academic institutions in the center of the city; yet such sites would be essential in order to lure renowned academics to Berlin. The Prussian Ministry of Culture consequently put forward the idea of relocating the entire university to Dahlem, in the south-west of Berlin. The plan was to establish a new, modern site which would integrate the academic disciplines. And although this ambitious goal was to prove unattainable at the time, the Freie Universität today corresponds to the floor plans that were envisaged at the turn of the century (→156).
The plans drawn up in 1888 to relocate inner-city academic institutions were initially only partly realized – with the relocation of the botanical garden (opened in 1904, →169) and the pharmaceutical institute (1902, →173). Friedrich Althoff, who had been the head of the Prussian Tuition and Higher Education Authority since 1897, encouraged the relocation of additional institutions of the university and the Charité to Dahlem. His motivation was in part inspired by Columbia University's move from inner-city New York to a site by the Hudson River. But in Berlin, Althoff's ideas were at first received with little enthusiasm. However, in 1901 when work began on the reallocation of land at the Domäne Dahlem, a former royal estate, new opportunities emerged. The academic senate and the principal of the university began requesting additional and larger spaces for teaching and research. In 1904 they repeated their request and pointed out the imminent shortage of space if women were to be admitted to study there as well (which indeed happened in 1908). However, at the time their main concern was actually the academic collection and the Berlin Observatory, as well as other subjects with a relatively low number of students.
These ambitions initially remained unfulfilled, partly because the German Reich had other priorities at the time, such as building up its naval fleet. In 1906, a group of prominent professors – among them the acclaimed chemists Emil Fischer and Walther Nernst – made a direct appeal to Kaiser Wilhelm II, who was unaware that they had deliberated with Althoff beforehand. They again raised the issue of the increasing need for more space at the university and specifically pointed out that the growing tendency towards

academic specialization made the need for new, larger research institutes all the more urgent. This applied both to the number of university staff and the rooms for teaching. And they were ultimately to have success with the latter request.

Even after his retirement Althoff remained the driving force for this undertaking, and in March 1908 he compiled an impressive (and impressively precise) list of new institutes which he felt could be realized in Dahlem. He campaigned for his ideas right up until his death on October 20, 1908. In March 1909, his successor, Friedrich Schmidt-Ott, developed from these plans a memorandum which highlighted Althoff's conviction that it was essential for academic institutions to be consolidated into "[a] colony, a German Oxford", as he had once put it. The Kaiser was impressed with Althoff's plans, describing them to the Prussian Ministry of State as "a collection of highly commendable proposals and suggestions".

However, the notion of a campus university was only to gain mainstream acceptance in Germany in the mid-twentieth century, which makes the plans of 1908 all the more remarkable. Not only was a location outside the inner city consistently envisaged; convenient access was prioritized above the requirement of suitable premises. This is also evident in the plan to relocate centrally located collections to the outskirts of the city.

Whereas Althoff's concept was greeted with enthusiasm by the Kaiser, several government ministries expressed their reservations. The Interior Ministry objected on the grounds that the development of the "Villenkolonie" (mansion development) at the intended site was already too far advanced. The Ministries of Agriculture, Forestry and Finance complained that a long-term reservation of the site for academic purposes was not economical and that it would deprive the treasury of considerable potential income from the sale of the land plots. Interior Minister Friedrich von Moltke pointed out that Berlin's prominent reputation was in part attributable to the "great educational institutions that enjoy international renown in the arts and academia" in the inner city. He added that this center would be "threatened if, in accordance with Althoff's plans, a second city center were to be systematically established out there in Dahlem".

In the face of such heavy criticism, it is not surprising that the Ministry of State only approved certain parts of Althoff's posthumously released plans: it considered his claims that more space was needed an exaggeration and it rejected the merging of the institutes concerned in order to avoid creating "an almost uninhabited area". Nonetheless, some of Althoff's ideas were realized when the Kaiser-Wilhelm-Gesellschaft zur Förderung der Wissenschaften was founded in 1910: new research facilities were established in Dahlem which soon became some of the best in their respective fields. They were funded in part by the state, but primarily by private industry.

It was only after World War II and Germany's defeat, and after the Soviet occupying forces and the SED party took control of the Universität Unter den Linden that Althoff's plans experienced a renaissance – as did the 1911 concept by the urban planner Hermann Jansen, in which he presented his vision of a mixture of residential housing and academic institutions which today characterizes the Dahlem district.

A Campus University by the River Havel

Friedrich Althoff and Hermann Jansen were not the only ones who had planned a large-scale relocation of the university: in the years 1908 to 1910 there was an international planning competition for "greater Berlin" – a large-scale concept to incorporate the outlying communities around Berlin. However, this extensive urban area, which has existed almost unchanged to the present day, was first established in 1920.

Havestadt & Contag, university town on the river Havel, 1910

Around the turn of the century, Berlin had already developed beyond its own city borders into a large metropolitan area. Along with plans to create a unified urban development concept for the inner city and the outskirts, technical plans for specific sectors was also submitted. The civil engineers Christian Havestadt and Max Contag garnered attention with their plan for a large campus university by the River Havel between the villages of Gatow and Kladow, which is today the most southerly part of the Spandau district. They envisaged a campus in a "tranquil and secluded setting in convenient reach of the city center". Their vision of a campus university included the construction of imposing buildings on a site north of the River Havel which would be connected to the inner city by a railroad bridge. This "new academic center of Berlin" was to be a university "to equal the modern English and especially the American campuses". This plan, like the majority of the other "greater Berlin" concepts was never pursued with any conviction. But the idea was revived during the Weimar Republic, when the architecture critic Karl Scheffler made a renewed appeal: "Students do not belong in a furnished room in Linienstrasse, but in attractive colleges with gardens and playing fields, close to forests and lakes where they can take part in sports."

The National Socialist University Plan

After World War I, the campus university concept gained new popularity in Europe. While this concept served the academic goal of having all the faculties in one location, the campus idea also offered Fascist regimes the opportunity to shape the development of these sites in accordance with their own political ideas. Between 1928 and 1936, the Ciudad universitaria in Madrid was established based on plans by the dictator Primo de Rivera; it was subsequently developed further by Francisco Franco for his own ends. Between 1930 and 1935 the Città universitaria was constructed in Rome under the aegis of Benito Mussolini. Although also discussed in the Weimar Republic, such plans were first reconsidered in Germany at quite a late stage; after the Nazis had seized power. And of course the National Socialist planners wanted to outdo the other fascist countries with their own prestigious buildings.

The construction of a monumental university was a central element in the radical redesign of Berlin planned by Adolf Hitler and his "chief architect" Albert Speer. At a site on the northern edge of Grunewald forest, they planned to bring together all the academic disciplines of the Berliner Universität and the Technical College in Charlottenburg with all the associated academic institutions. The announcement for the 1937 competition to restructure Berlin stated that the "University Town Berlin" should form the "doorway to the capital city of the Reich".

Competition for Nazi Hochschulstadt project, 1937

The competition itself served as a test to establish whether suitable architects could be recruited, though there was no winner of the competition. In accordance with the guidelines of the competition, the participating architects had to base their plans on straight-line axes com plemented with triumphal arches, towers, monumental squares and prestigious building elements. The buildings were not only expected to "fulfill their immediate function"; they should also be "testimony to a great past" in subsequent centuries. The decisive factor in this undertaking was to create the most impressive effect upon the viewer.

In 1937, the construction of the "University Town Berlin" began. The first building was intended for the so-called Military-Technical Faculty, which underlined the primacy of research for war purposes. The building was designed by Hans Malwitz, but due to wartime interruptions only the carcass was ever completed. In his speech at the cornerstone ceremony on November 27, 1937, Hitler emphasized the importance of the project for the greater plan, namely to redesign the whole of Berlin as the capital of the "Third Reich": "On this day, a new era of construction and development begins in Berlin which will profoundly transform the image and [...] the character of this city".

After the war ended, the structure was not torn down but was instead used by the West Berlin Postal Service. During the Berlin Blockade of 1948, two 40-meter antennas were installed to ensure a radio link to the West and telecommunications technicians moved into some of the rooms. In the 1950s, the Nazi building was declared a ruin and was plundered for building materials. It gradually disappeared under the rubble and the hill that resulted from this pile of bricks and stone is now known as the "Teufelsberg" (Devil's Mountain).

The Blumberg Plan in the GDR

At the end of World War II, the buildings of the Friedrich-Wilhelm-Universität (from 1947 the Humboldt-Universität) lay in ruins. Out of 172 structures, over half had been either completely destroyed or were no longer fit for use. The division of the city – and with it the university – also had an effect on the available space. Consequently, the newly founded Freie Universität acquired a further 31 buildings; a dozen of the other remaining buildings were no longer used for university purposes. As a result of the prevailing political circumstances, specifically the partition of Berlin into four sectors, the fragmentation of the university continued. Indeed, even traditional locations which were largely untouched by the conflict between East and West fell victim to political pressure whenever they were affected by the urban planning ideas of the SED Party, which aimed to transform Berlin into a "socialist capital".

The universities had a hard time competing with other state institutions in this struggle for funding and sites. Since this "fragmentation and dispersal" had led to an "inadequate urban planning situation", the municipal planning and construction office advocated the relocation of all the "practical sciences" from the center to the outskirts of the city in 1958.

In early 1961 the university and the city authorities discussed how a unification of the institutes and the respective disciplines could be achieved. Robert Havemann, a winner of the GDR National Prize and at the time Director of the Institut für Physikalische Chemie (he was later to fall into disgrace), demanded the establishment of a "university town", in which he gained the support of the Natural Sciences Institute, which had been severely compromised due to war damage and loss of buildings. However, the Agricultural Faculty also advocated a relocation to the outskirts with the goal of providing a better working environment. Whereas the Humanities departments were to remain in the center of the city, relocating the other disciplines to the outer districts was considered a logical step: this meant the Medical Department would go to Berlin-Buch, the Natural Sciences to Adlershof and Veterinary and Agricultural Sciences would go to Marzahn.

This idea developed into the more extensive notion of relocating the entire university instead of just certain departments, and thus creating a new academic satellite town in the outlying village of Blumberg. Opinions about this ambitious plan were divided in the university: members of the Medical Department expressed their skepticism because, unlike the Natural Sciences Department, they were obliged to consider the practicalities of caring for patients. The majority of the Humanities staff rejected the plans, as they feared they would lose their close proximity to libraries and cultural institutions. Therefore the discussion of an all-inclusive campus was in part defined by the respective requirements and geographic placement of the various academic disciplines.

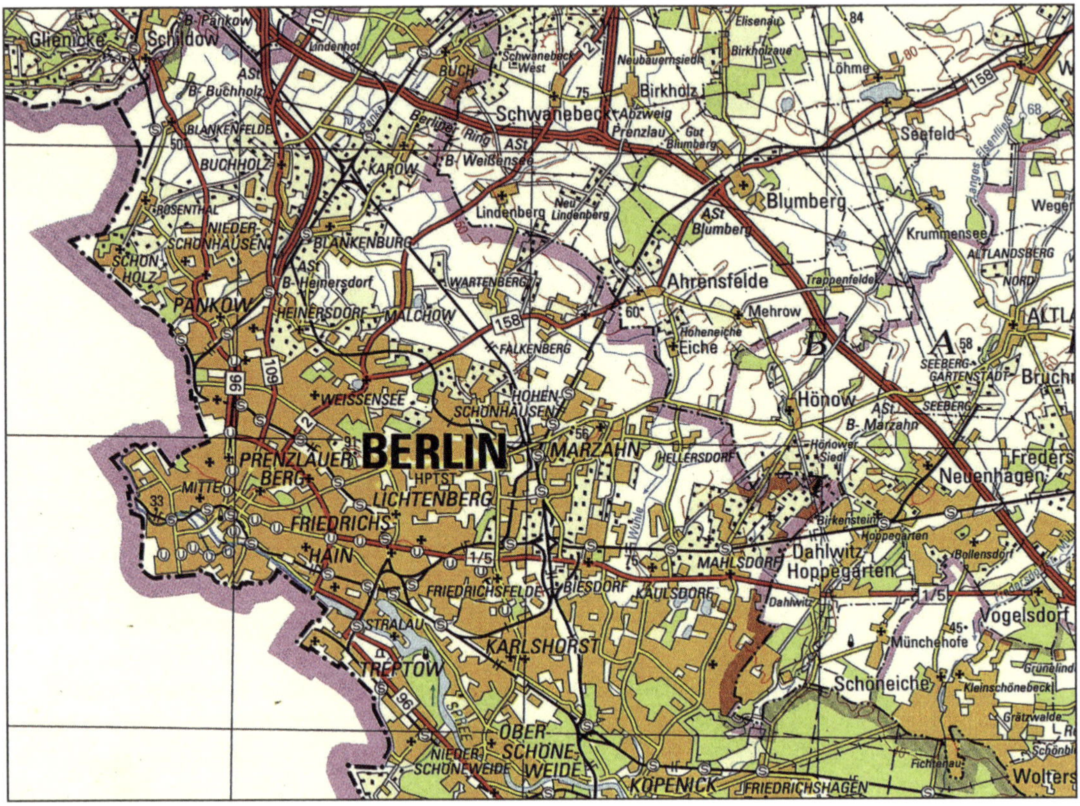

GDR city map for Berlin with Blumberg in the northeast

Despite a number of protests, in June 1961, the Senate approved the relocation of the university to Blumberg, after the SED politburo had given its approval. The planned site in Blumberg was originally part of the parkland belonging to Friedrich Ludwig von Arnim's manor house, which was destroyed in 1945 – and was perfectly suited to the ideals of the SED program to turn former aristocrats' lands into areas to "serve the needs of the workers" (and in this case: the intelligentsia).

However, things were to turn out differently: After the Berlin Wall was erected in August 1961 and just a short time after the resolution of the university senate, the SED was no longer willing to support the project. The prestige value of a Socialist university in the heart of the city outweighed the practicalities of a suburban campus. In reality, however, this prestigious new status of the university did not help solve any of its problems: on the one hand, large development projects like the Blumberg campus were no longer pursued, yet on the other hand, that project itself was used an an excuse to withhold funding for the maintenance of existing university buildings or the construction of new buildings in the city center. As a result, the urgently needed site development of the Humboldt-Universität was blocked for many years.

At the end of 1963 the university came up with its own plan to change the situation. The Humanities Department was to retain its location in the vicinity of the main building on Unter den Linden, while the natural sciences were to be clustered together in an area around the Natural History Museum. It was only several years later in 1981 that the large building at 110 Invalidenstrasse (→85) was finally built for the Institute of Physics and Electronics. The aim of bringing the natural sciences together in one geographical area was only to be realized after the fall of the Berlin Wall: between 1998 and 2003, the Institute of Chemistry and Physics, together with the departments of Geography, Computer Science, Mathematics and Psychology began establishing a university site on the south-eastern edge of the city at the new Adlershof Campus. Today, institutes of the Humboldt-Universität, external research facilities, spin-off projects and startups all cooperate in Adlershof. The Biology Department, along with various Life Sciences departments, have remained at Campus Nord, occupying some of the university's oldest and newest buildings (→73). There, they are able to interact with the Medical and Humanities Departments such as the Berlin School of Mind and Brain.

The campus university in Berlin has a long and complex history punctuated by ambitious plans and far-reaching visions which were always affected by political uncertainty and the obduracy of institutions. Whereas in Berlin the academic district north of the Humboldt-Universität main building and the Charité hospital ensemble paved the way for an expansion of the sciences in the inner-city early on, the campus as an alternative model remained the central subject of discussion: the Dahlem question in particular remained topical. The Technical College (from 1946 called the Technische Universität) Berlin chose a different route. It was founded in 1879 in Charlottenburg, which became the seat of power for Prussian kings in the eighteenth century and a bustling city next to Berlin 100 years later. It was only in 1920 that Charlottenburg actually became a district of Berlin. Its palatial main building – comparable to the Prinz Heinrich Palais – was intended to underline the idea of a unified university for the engineering sciences as well. Initially the site in Charlottenburg was anything but certain, since plans for a location on Invalidenstrasse were already at an advanced stage. However, the extensive area north of the Tiergarten Park was considered more suitable in view of the space required by the emergent engineering sciences – and it was decided to reject the site in the center of Berlin.

Dahlem and Adlershof represented, or represent, two academic locations which, in theory at least, approach the ideals of the campus university. However, these ideals could not be fully realized at either location due to their existing historical buildings and far-flung locations. Thus, the notion of integrating students as residents of the respective campuses – which is typical in North American colleges and universities – never really took hold in Berlin. And although Dorotheenstadt, a neighborhood close to the main building on Unter den Linden, was explicitly specified as students' area when the university was founded, it was soon to be dominated by hotels and business premises. Moreover, university institutions themselves began to move into the area and thus compete with the students for residential space. With the exception of this disparity, which runs contrary to the original campus idea, it is evident today that the Humboldt-Universität's "Campus Nord" has come closest to realizing this ideal. With its park-like grounds featuring numerous historic buildings, the campus seems quite idyllic, while its modern buildings give it a sense of architectural daring. And while it exhibits traces of Jefferson's historical "academical village", it is fully integrated into a large modern city. (NE)

DAHLEM

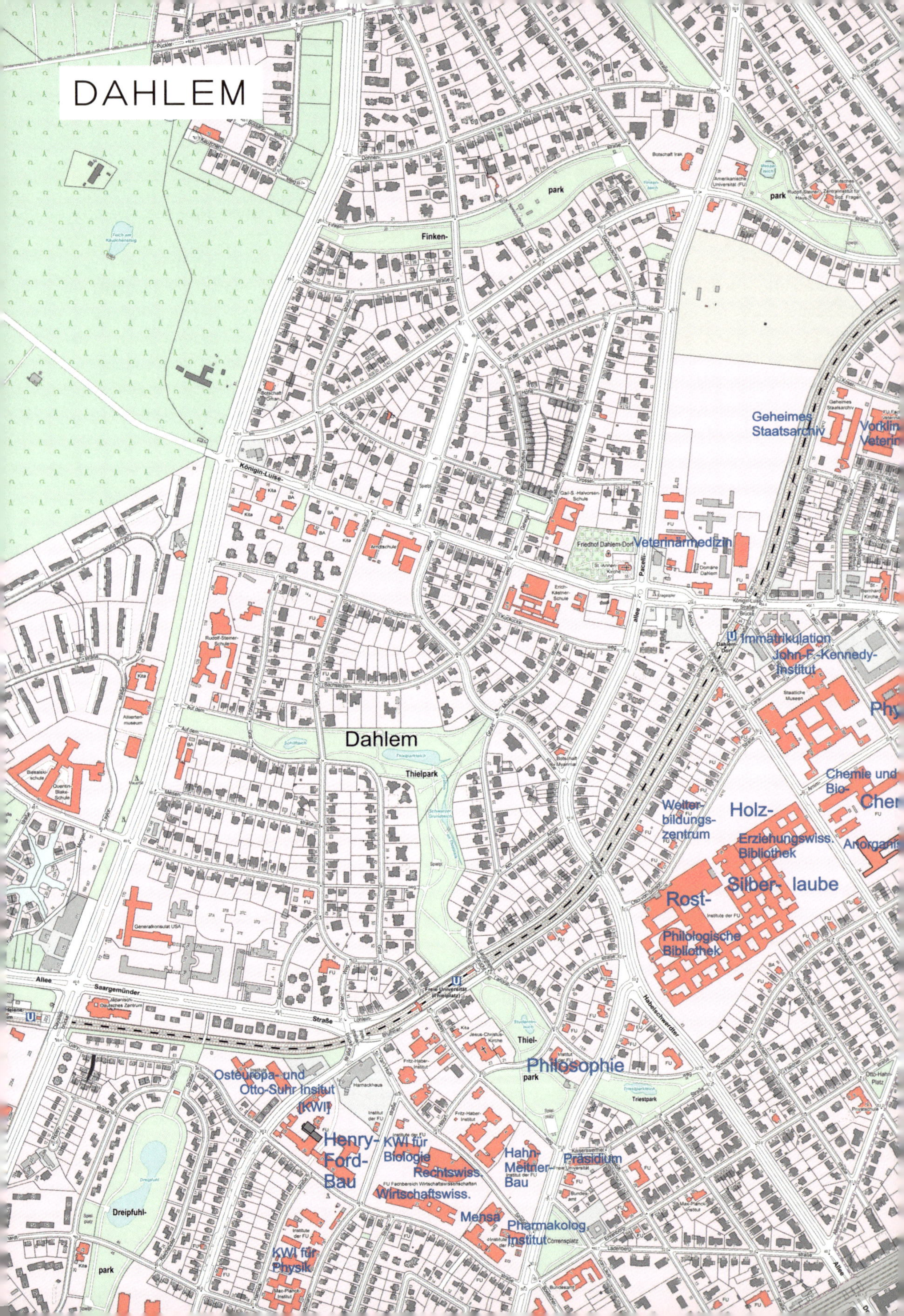
Finken-
park
Geheimes
Staatsarchiv
Veterinärmedizin
Immatrikulation
John-F.-Kennedy-
Institut
Dahlem
Thielpark
Chemie und
Bio-
Holz-
Weiter-
bildungs-
zentrum
Erziehungswiss.
Bibliothek
Silber- laube
Rost-
Philologische
Bibliothek
Thiel-
park
Philosophie
Osteuropa- und
Otto-Suhr-Institut
(KWI)
Henry-
Ford-
Bau
KWI für
Biologie
Rechtswiss.
Wirtschaftswiss.
Hahn-
Meitner-
Bau
Präsidium
Mensa
Pharmakolog.
Institut
KWI für
Physik
Dreipfuhl-
park

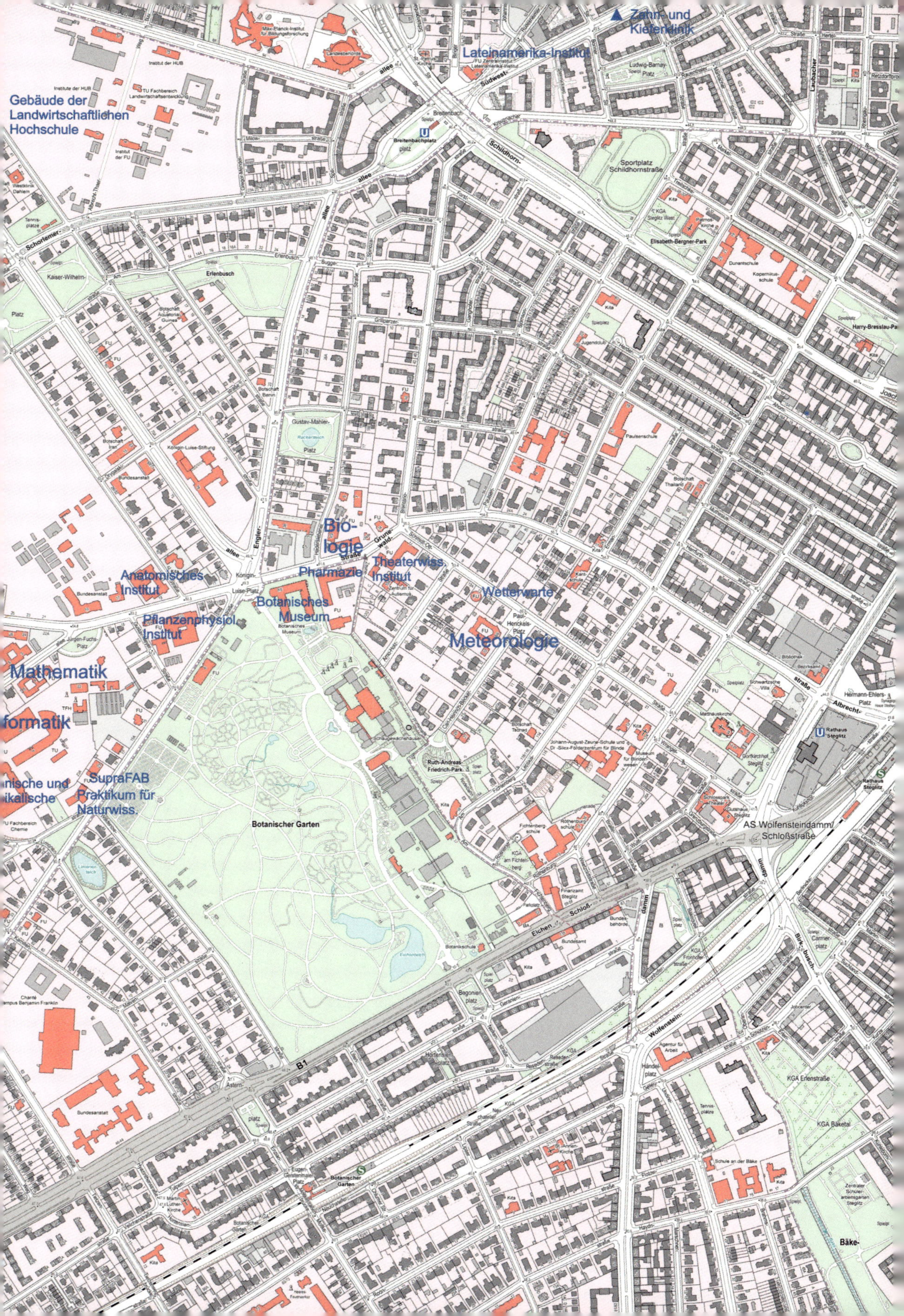

Zahn- und
Kieferklinik
Lateinamerika-Institut
Gebäude der
Landwirtschaftlichen
Hochschule
Breitenbachplatz
Sportplatz
Schildhornstraße
Elisabeth-Bergner-Park
Erlenbusch
Gustav-Mahler-Platz
Bio-
logie
Theaterwiss.
Institut
Pharmazie
Anatomisches
Institut
Wetterwarte
Botanisches
Museum
Pflanzenphysiol.
Institut
Meteorologie
Mathematik
formatik
SupraFAB
Praktikum für
Naturwiss.
Botanischer Garten
Ruth-Andreas-
Friedrich-Park
AS Wolfensteindamm/
Schloßstraße
Rathaus
Steglitz
Hermann-Ehlers-
Platz
KGA Erlenstraße
KGA Bäketal
Schule an der Bäke
B1

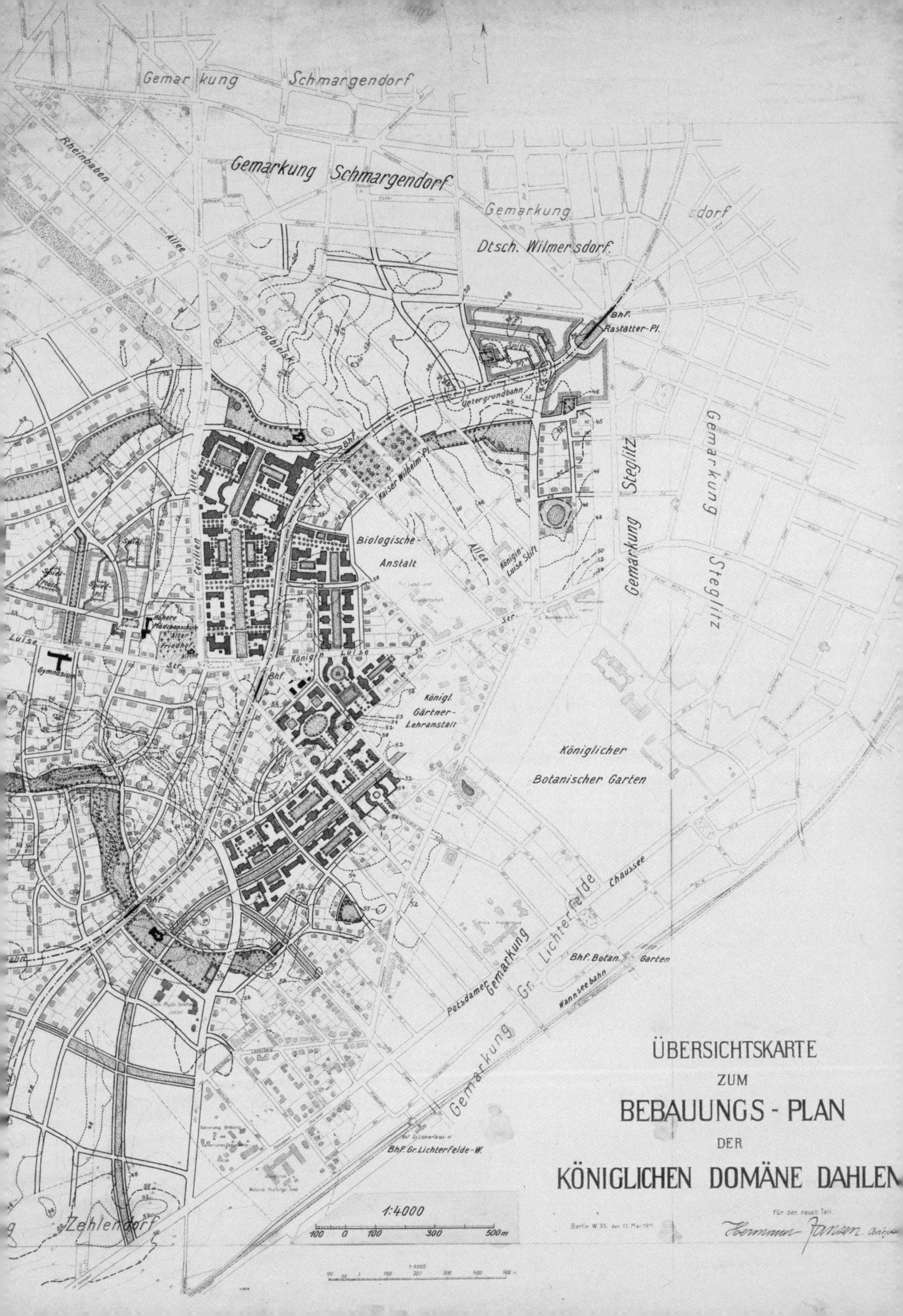

Gemarkung Schmargendorf
Gemarkung Schmargendorf
Rheinbaben Allee
Podbielski Allee
Gemarkung Dtsch. Wilmersdorf
Bhf. Rastatter-Pl.
Untergrundbahn
Bhf. Kaiser Wilhelm-Pl.
Cecilien Allee
Biologische-Anstalt
Königin-Luise Stift
Gemarkung Steglitz
Gemarkung Steglitz
Höhere Mädchenschule
Alter Friedhof
Luise Str.
Königin Luise Str.
Gymnasium
Bhf.
Königl. Gärtner-Lehranstalt
Königlicher Botanischer Garten
Chaussee
Gemarkung Gr. Lichterfelde
Potsdamer
Bhf. Botan. Garten
Wannsee bahn
Bhf. Gr. Lichterfelde-W.
Gemarkung
Zehlendorf
1:4000
100 0 100 300 500m
ÜBERSICHTSKARTE
ZUM
BEBAUUNGS - PLAN
DER
KÖNIGLICHEN DOMÄNE DAHLEM
Für den neuen Teil:
Berlin W. 35. den 12. Mai 1911.
Hermann Jansen

DAHLEM

In the nineteenth century, from what had once been the Dahlem feudal estate, there emerged a state-owned domain set aside for agricultural and forestry use, which, unlike Steglitz, became an expansion area to be absorbed by the rapidly growing metropolis only at the turn of the century. The imperial treasury had waited until lucrative land prices made parceling off an area for villas an attractive proposition, an area for which first Walter Kyllmann and then Hermann Jansen designed a road network. The most crucial step taken in Dahlem's development was its connection to Berlin's transportation system: initially reachable from the southern periphery via the Wannsee local rail line departing from Bahnhof Lichterfelde-West, the tram via Königin-Luise-Strasse and the subway from Wilmersdorf led right through the new district, starting in 1905 and 1913 respectively. When Friedrich Althoff, the powerful department head in the Prussian Ministry of Culture, appeared on the scene, his influence immediately meant competition for the villa district concept and thus concrete opposition to the maximization of profit for state coffers as prime motivation. Althoff ultimately managed to reclaim no less than one hundred hectares for science. In the downtown area, there was hardly any space left for attractive institutes capable of enticing particularly researchers to Berlin, and, aside from that, the venerable experts already situated there were not supposed to wear themselves out teaching either, but were instead meant to receive generous new research facilities in order not to fall behind in international competition. To this end, Althoff developed an initiative for the "founding of a distinguished colony characterized by outstanding scientific institutions, a German Oxford", producing a concrete sketch for his vision shortly before his death in 1908. This proposal was not particularly concerned with relocating the English university to Prussia – instead, it advocated bringing the renown (today we would say the excellence) of an Oxford or Cambridge to Berlin. These ideas took on an enduring form thanks in particular to Hermann Jansen, whose 1911 plan would inscribe "reservations" for science – that is, for the university, but also for non-academic institutes, as well as museums and archives – into Dahlem's topography. These grand plans, which originally even envisioned the relocation of the entire university from Berlin-Mitte to the area of today's Domäne Dahlem, did not, however, become visible at the beginning of the twentieth century, but instead first at the conclusion of World War II, as the new, "free" university was realized within the "reservations" delineated by Jansen.

AT THE HENRY-FORD-BAU

Dahlem's actual history as a university location begins in 1948 with the Freie Universität, which conceived of itself as an institution founded to make up for the "lost" university at Unter den Linden in the eastern sector of the city. The university used the newly available buildings of the former Institutes of Biology, Chemistry, Physics, and Biochemistry (which continued to exist under the aegis of the newly founded Max Planck Society in Tübingen, Munich, and Mainz) as well as the Institute of Anthropology, Human Heredity Studies, and Eugenics, which had been complicit in the crimes of the Nazi regime. The new buildings created here would pursue in particular elements of German pre-war modernism and American university architecture.
Therefore, around the Henry-Ford-Bau, different approaches to educational architecture collided with one another, a collision which would define the character of the new university from the very beginning: while on the one hand both the research institutes of the Kaiser Wilhelm Society and the old villas that were used for the sciences by the FU radiated proud tradition, on the other hand new science buildings and an infrastructure embodying a contemporary, 1950s, take on modernism emerged. Between Van't-Hoff-Strasse, Thielallee, Garystrasse, and the trenches of the subway line, a new epicenter of the area, also referred to as South Campus, was born.

Henry-Ford-Bau and University Library

Garystrasse 35, 37, 39, Boltzmannstrasse 6–8, Ihnestrasse 26, 28 | 1952–1954 | Franz Heinrich Sobotka, Gustav Müller | 2005–2007 renovation, Technical Department of FU

Together with the university library, the **Henry-Ford-Bau**, inaugurated on June 19, 1954, forms the center of Freie Universität. Accessible from three sides, it remained the university's most important representational building – even after the enormous expansion with what are colloquially known as the Rostlaube, Silberlaube, and Holzlaube complexes ("Laube" translates roughly to "lodge" here, for their low, modular design, featuring rust, silver, and wood colored exteriors, hence their full nicknames) – while at the same time breaking with traditional conceptions of representation. The corresponding competition in 1951 called for a building which would provide space for lecture halls, the main auditorium, a university library, a studio theater, the senate chamber, as well as seminar and administrative rooms. As the center of South Campus, the Henry-Ford-Bau represents a connecting link to all of the far-flung former research institutes used by the FU. The winning design envisages low building wings with courtyards and thus extends the urban space taken up by the building towards the outside. The building ensemble combines a roughly H-shaped lecture hall building with an L-shaped university library consisting of two cuboid segments. Large glass-covered areas allow one to observe architectural elements both inside and out. The makers abstained from using a hierarchical main facade, and the two building fronts facing Garystrasse and Boltzmannstrasse respectively each feature a different design. The aesthetic, typical of the era, and the construction possibilities of the 1950s find their expression in the transparent entrance hall, the narrow bands of windows extending to the floor, and the seemingly floating galleries and stairwells, as well as in the choice of materials. As such, the building creates a new species of university building: low to the ground, interconnected, solid, and transparent, where pioneering stylistic elements combine with one another, for instance from Frank Lloyd Wright and Dessau's Bauhaus building by Walter Gropius. The university library running along Garystrasse houses seminar and administrative rooms (towards the western end) and reading rooms (on the north side). The repository tower is set back from the street and eschews dominance and visibility. A closed passage above Harnackstrasse connects the two sections of the building.

Mensa, west view, approx. 1959

KWI for Biology, approx. 1930

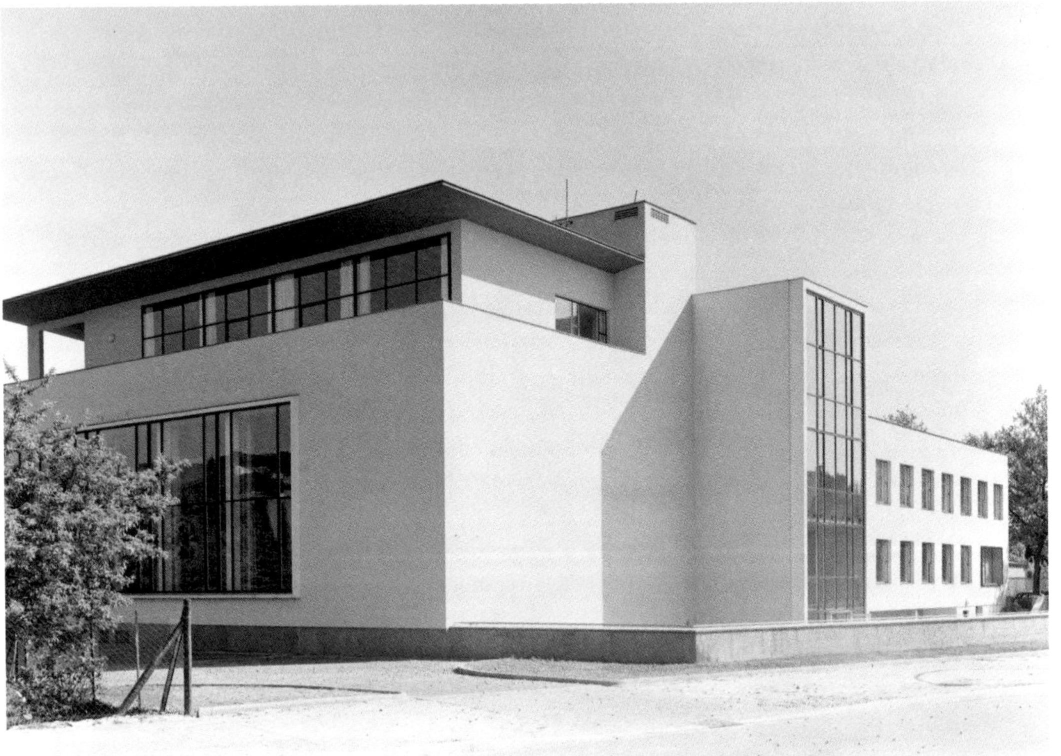

Dental and Maxillary Clinic, 1957

In the first building that Freie Universität was able to use (situated today on Boltzmannstrasse across from the Henry-Ford-Bau), expectations and requirements for a science building were still entirely different. The last of the in total three Kaiser Wilhelm Institutes built by Ernst von Ihne, the **Kaiser Wilhelm Institute for Biology** (today the Law Library), was completed in the second year of World War I, 1915, and features a modest design. In close collaboration, von Ihne and the founding director of the institute, Carl Correns, planned the laboratory building as well as the director's villa, the staff accommodation, breeding facilities for ducks and bees, aquariums, greenhouses, and numerous areas for cultivating plants. The fact that the institute director had a say in the matter too can be traced back to the theologian and first president of the Kaiser Wilhelm Society, Adolf von Harnack, and was a testament to the strong position held by the directors within the society – often referred to as the "Harnack principle". The western facade of the L-shaped institute building was kept comparatively simple, due no doubt to the ongoing war at the time. A middle corridor provides access to smaller rooms intended for flexible use. The building initially served as a main building for Freie Universität for a short period, before becoming the home of the Faculty of Philosophy and the enrollment office.

former Kaiser Wilhlem Institute for Biology
Department of Law

Boltzmannstrasse 3 | 1914–1915 | Ernst Eberhard von Ihne, Max Guth (technical and financial direction) | 1948 first main building of FU Berlin (together with the building diagonally opposite at Boltzmannstrasse 4, the former construction department of the KWG)

In the post-war period, meals for students were originally prepared and served inside a barracks that had remained undamaged during the war, directly adjacent to Ihne's building on the southern side. Next, the **Mensa** would be the first new building to be erected on the South Campus, in 1951, opening in March 1953. The structure's execution as a steel frame construction made an almost entirely glass-paneled western facade possible, thus opening up a view to an extensive green area from within, known as the student meadow.

Mensa
Mensa I, vegetarian cafeteria

Van't-Hoff-Strasse 6 | 1951–1953 | Hermann Fehling, Peter Pfankuch | 1975 extension, Hermann Fehling, Daniel Gogel

The facade design for the **Dental and Maxillary Clinic**, also commissioned by the FU in the early 1950s, though realized in Wilmersdorf between Heidelberger and Rüdesheimer Platz directly on the subway line, speaks a similar modern-organic architectural language.

Dental and Maxillary Clinic

Assmannshauser Strasse 4–6 | 1955–1956 | Rudolf Ullrich, Erich Neubarth | 1981–1982 extension by Rainer Gerhard Rümmler

The first Kaiser Wilhelm Institutes for Chemistry as well as for Physical Chemistry and Electrochemistry with the respective director's villas, 1911

Around the students' meadow (clockwise): Hahn-Meitner-Bau, Mensa, Economics Department, Henry-Ford-Bau, KWI for Biology, Faculty of Law, Fritz Haber Institute, backed by library tower, Otto-Suhr-Institute, Eastern Europe-Institute

University Library

Cafeteria, west facade and extension wing

Department of Law, view from the students' meadow and reading room

Pharmacological Practicum building

View from the cafeteria terrace to the Economics Department

Hahn-Meitner-Bau
former KWI for Chemistry, 1956 Otto Hahn Building, 2010 Hahn-Meitner-Bau

Thielallee 63 | 1911–1912 | Ernst von Ihne, Max Guth | February 1944 partially destroyed by aerial bombardment | 1950 chemical institutes of FU, since 1980 biochemistry | 1953–1955 reconstruction | 1982–1984, 1991–1993 renovation and conversion | 1997 addition of seminar rooms, Grässler and Stolt

Institute of Pharmacology
former KWI for Experimental Therapy and Biochemistry

Thielallee 69–73 | 1913 | Ernst Eberhard von Ihne, Max Guth | from 1948/1950 Institute of Pharmacology of FU | renovation, Carola Schäfers | 2003–2014 Charité university medical department Berlin | since 2014 affiliated with FU

Pharmacological Practicum building

Thielallee 71 | 1966–1968 | building construction department

School of Business and Economics
former Faculty of Economics and Social Sciences

Garystrasse 21, Boltzmannstrasse 9 | 1957–1958 | Geber & Risse | 2003 conversion of the cafeteria, Carola Schäfers

Department of Law
former Faculty of Law

Van't-Hoff-Strasse 8 | 1957–1959 | Hans Geber, Otto Risse

In marked contrast to its architectural neighbors – stylistically, politically, and conceptually, as well as from a technical standpoint – the cafeteria building stands on the western edge of the South Campus between the **Hahn-Meitner-Bau** (the former KWI for Chemistry) to the north and the **Institute of Pharmacology** (the former KWI for Experimental Therapy and Biochemistry) to the south. These two buildings were completed before the end of World War I, and their facade ornamentation and detailed execution testify to the research institutes' desire to project a certain image. It wasn't until 2010 that the building's name was expanded to add Lise Meitner's name to that of Otto Hahn. Together with Fritz Strassmann, both individuals conducted research in this building on nuclear fission, which had been discovered here in December 1938 by Hahn and Strassmann. Lise Meitner, who had been driven from Germany in mid-1938, was responsible for the physical interpretation of the results that made it possible to ultimately understand the phenomenon.

Also situated to the south, the **Pharmacological Practicum building** has been underlining this buildings for the oppositional exhibition all the more forcefully since the late 1960s: in a virtually post-modern manner, it seizes upon elements of the cafeteria building, transforming them, and establishing a contrast to the residential office villas of the old institute buildings by featuring curved corners, portholes, window strips, and an indented first floor. The floor plan on the inside is almost completely variable, enabling the building to be flexibly adapted to the changing spatial needs of scientific work.

Between the cafeteria and the Henry-Ford-Bau, the students' meadow is enclosed in a curved shape by two low buildings: the **School of Business and Economics** is housed in a three-wing, elongated low-rise building running along Garystrasse to the south; along Van't-Hoff-Strasse to the north, one finds the **Department of Law**. Embedded with care in the facilities of the campus, both buildings offer space for lecture halls, seminar rooms, and administrative wings. The Law Library features a curving row of several large-scale glass-fronted reading rooms facing the garden side. Though the design realized here only took second place in a 1954 competition (first place went to Paul Baumgarten), alas, a revised version of the ensemble structure featuring the embedding of the students' meadow ultimately managed to win over the authorities at the university.

Institute for East European Studies and Otto-Suhr-Institut

Garystrasse 55, Ihnestrasse 21 | 1959–1962 | Werner Klenke (building construction department of the Senator for Building and Housing) | 1990–1992 extension, Mario Maedebach, Werner Redeleit | great stylistic similarity to main building of the former Pedagogic Academy, built 1960–1964 by Bruno Grimmek (Malteserstrasse 74–100) at today's Geocampus Lankwitz

former Kaiser Wilhelm Institute of Anthropology, Human Heredity, and Eugenics

Ihnestrasse 22–24 | 1926–1927 | Carl Sattler | 1948 Faculty of Law and Economics of FU | 1959 part of Otto-Suhr-Institut

former Kaiser Wilhelm Institute of Physics

Boltzmannstrasse 16–20 | 1935–1937 | Carl Sattler | 1949–1982 Institutes of the FU for Experimental and Theoretical Physics | 1983 partially occupied by Department of Economics | 1998 storeroom of the archive of the Max Planck Society in high-voltage tower

University Executive Council Headquarters

former administrative building of the Association of Public Fire Insurance Institutions in Germany

Kaiserswerther Strasse 16–18 | 1927 | Heinrich Straumer | 1945–1990 Allied Kommandatura | since 1994 occupied by university direction

With two low, rectangular buildings clearly subdivided by large strips of windows, the **Institute for East European Studies** and the **Otto-Suhr-Institut** form the western endpoint of the campus along Garystrasse and Ihnestrasse. They stand in contrast to the **former Kaiser Wilhelm Institute of Anthropology, Human Heredity, and Eugenics**, located alongside Ihnestrasse to the east, which Carl Sattler completed in 1927, still influenced by upper-class villa construction, a building also used today by the Otto-Suhr-Institut. Since 1988, a commemorative plaque has served as a reminder of the institute's involvement in Nazi race policies and experiments on human subjects, as well as of the absence of efforts to confront this history in the post-war period.

The urban planning and architectural development of Freie Universität in Dahlem was influenced both by the abandoned institutes of the Kaiser Wilhelm Society and the newly founded facilities of the Max Planck Society, such as the Max Planck Institute for Human Development from 1961 (Lentzeallee 94, Hermann Fehling and Daniel Gogel) for instance. At the end of Ihnestrasse, next to the Freie Universität subway station (formerly Thielplatz), one finds the Harnack-Haus, an important place for encounters and conferences for the Max Planck Society. Under the society's possession, the building returned to the science world in 1994, after having served for many years as an Allied officers' mess in the post-war period. Further Max Planck institutes can be found today to the north of Van't-Hoff-Strasse and across from the law institutes, such as the Fritz Haber Institute or, on Boltzmannstrasse, the MPI for the History of Science, right next door to the **former Kaiser Wilhelm Institute of Physics**. Hidden behind this building, one finds two architectural witnesses to physics history, the "lightning tower" for high-voltage experiments (today used as an archive) and a barracks, in which the German atomic project led by Werner Heisenberg during World War II attempted to get the first "uranium machine" up and running. To the east of the South Campus, situated opposite the Hahn-Meitner-Bau, stands a remarkable modernist building that has been used by the FU as a **headquarters for the university executive council** since 1994. The structure is a massive, expressively designed ashlar building with a shell limestone base and red clinker brick facing, from whose midst a monumental entrance area springs forth.

AT KÖNIGIN-LUISE-PLATZ

In the immediate vicinity of the Botanical Garden, research facilities and university buildings also took root in the area around Königin-Luise-Platz square. Although it is true that Friedrich Althoff was unable to realize his plans for a large-scale relocation of university disciplines from Berlin-Mitte to Dahlem, nevertheless two institutes of what was then Friedrich Wilhelm University ultimately resettled here: the Institute of Pharmacy and the Institute of Plant Physiology (today the Institute of Biology). In divided Cold-War Berlin, both of the institutes, actually affiliated with Linden University in the eastern sector, were turned over to Freie Universität by the American military government in the blockade year of 1949.

Institute of Anatomy

Königin-Luise-Strasse 15, Peter-Lenné-Strasse 43 | 1949–1950 | Johann Huntemüller | 1953–1955 | Günter Kalesky | 1976 new build for the dissection hall wing | 1983 floor added to one wing | 1987 planning for lecture hall and seminar building, winning design by Paul Ziegert was not realized | late 1990s abandoned in favor of Charité | since 2008 building unused

The structure erected to house the **Institute of Anatomy** was the very first new building commissioned by Freie Universität. That construction would be initiated at this site in 1951, and not, for instance, at South Campus, can be explained by the fact that the Royal Prussian Biological Bureau for Agricultural and Forest Management, located on Königin-Luise-Strasse since 1905 was already being used as a building for instruction in anatomy, physiology, and physiological chemistry from 1949 on (also known from 1949 on as the Central Institute for Botany, today the Julius Kühn Institute – Federal Research Center for cultivated Plants). Due to its training of medical students, the new institution for higher education was granted full university status. However, this also made more space necessary, as 400 doctors-to-be were already enrolled here in the pre-clinical stage in 1949. Functionality would be the priority when it came to the design of this new building. The greatest importance was placed on meeting hygiene standards, providing easy access, and keeping distances between constituent parts as short as possible. High windows in the dissecting room also provided for copious daylight, a boon in the early years, with their widespread power shortages.

Institute of Plant Physiology

Königin-Luise-Strasse 12–16a | 1962–1970 | Wassili Luckhardt, Peter Bormann | mosaic image in interior courtyard by Hedja Luckhardt-Fresse

The main building of the Institute of **Plant Physiology** across from the Institute of Anatomy rewards a closer look: parallel to Königin-Luise-Strasse rises a glazed research wing perched atop stilts and divided both horizontally and vertically, through which a low building reserved for teaching purposes is interjected at a right angle. This arrangement allows the two working areas within the building to be connected by short routes. In the large glazed entrance area, one finds a free-floating stairwell with a sculpture-like form. The basement of the low-rise structure houses refrigerated rooms and the area for electron microscopy, protected from outside vibration in accordance with technical requirements. The portion of the research wing exposed to direct sunlight is allotted for offices and administration. The windowless interior is home to climatic chambers, areas with consistent temperature conditions, refrigerated rooms, dark spaces, photo laboratories, irradiation facilities, and rooms for cultivating plant cultures.

Botanical Garden and the Botanical Museum

Königin-Luise-Strasse 6–8 | 1903–1906 | Alfred Koerner | main tropical greenhouse also Alfred Koerner, Heinrich Müller-Breslau was responsible for the construction | 1983–1987 new construction of the east wing, Rainer Gerhard Rümmler | since 1995 faculty-independent central facility of FU | 2006–2009 complete renovation of main tropical greenhouse, Haas Architekten

The history of the **Botanical Garden** and the **Botanical Museum** can be traced back to the year 1679, when the pleasure gardener Michael Hanff created a hop garden in Schöneberg, which was integrated into the newly founded University of Berlin in 1908 on the initiative of botanist Carl Ludwig Willdenow and subsequently developed into a botanical garden. Though

Institute of Plant Physiology, south facade and foyer

Botanical Garden, main tropical greenhouse, in the background Botanical Museum and Pharmaceutical Institute

Previous and new building of the Pharmaceutical Institute

Institute of Zoology

an expansion had become necessary towards the end of the nineteenth century, it proved to be no longer possible in Schöneberg, due to lack of space and excessively high building property prices, while air pollution and a lowering of the water table had also resulted in damage to the plants. In 1895, Adolf Engler, one of the era's leading experts on plants and since 1889 a professor of systematic botany at Friedrich Wilhelm University (and in this role simultaneously the director of the Royal Botanical Garden in Schöneberg), and architect Alfred Koerner put together a plan for the construction of a new building. A number of remarkable collections are united within the Botanical Garden and the Botanical Museum: the Herbarium has its roots in the eighteenth century and is protected by thick concrete walls on the basement floor of the museum reconstructed in the wake of heavy damage during the war. With its 22,000 different plant species, the garden is the third largest of its kind in the world.

The **Institute of Pharmacy** was built new two decades after World War II, as the west wing of the predecessor building on the same spot was partially destroyed by aerial bombardment in 1943 and erecting a completely new building appeared to be the more cost-effective solution in the early 1960s. In the 1950s, over 300 laboratory workplaces had already been created within this institute affiliated with Freie Universität. The previous building had been home to Friedrich Wilhelm University's Pharmaceutical Institute and was the first of its type in Prussia. The new building, laid out in an L-shape, features laboratory and seminar rooms, as well as integrated greenhouses. Its proximity to the Otto-Suhr-Institut and the Institute for East European Studies of the same period and, in whose planning architect Rainer Gerhard Rümmler was also involved, is evident in the style (→ 167).

Institute of Pharmacy

new build on site of former Pharmaceutical Institute of Friedrich Wilhelm University

Königin-Luise-Strasse 2–4 | 1960–1966 | Rainer Gerhard Rümmler | due to lack of space, parts of the institute were relocated to Steglitz: Kelchstrasse 31, 1926–1927, Fritz Höger, extension 1987–1989 by Bernd Halbach, since 1971 used by FU (pharmacy, psychology until 1984, as well as central print shop)

Institute of Biology

former Institute of Plant Physiology of Friedrich Wilhelm University

Königin-Luise-Strasse 1–3 | 1912–1913 | Georg Thür, Alfred Koerner (director of construction) | after 1945 school and canteen of the US Air Force | with the founding of the FU in 1948 Institutes of Zoology and Botany | 1970–1971 added wing: Institute of Zoology (accessible via Haderslebener Strasse 9)

Also what is today the **Institute of Biology** initially belonged to Friedrich Wilhelm University. In 1910, plant physiologist Gottlieb Haberland was appointed to teach in Berlin. Haberland quickly advocated for relocating the Botanical Institute from its then site in the city center to Dahlem, and thus in proximity to the Botanical Garden, the Botanical Museum, the Central Institute for Botany, the School for Horticulture, as well as the Pharmaceutical Institute. To this end, a generous facility featuring a director's villa was built right across from the Pharmaceutical Institute. The Institute of Zoology can be found in an add-on building bordering on Haderslebener Strasse.

House of Research, 1940

Institute for Meteorology, courtyard and extension building

Next to the Institute of Pharmacy lies the home of the **Institute of Theater Studies** in the former "House of Research". This was the initial location of the Emergency Association of German Science founded in 1919, the forerunner organization of today's German Research Foundation (DFG). In the wake of enforced conformity to the party agenda under the Nazi regime, the association was transformed in 1934 into the "German Association for the Support and Advancement of Scientific Research", with its headquarters in Matthäikirchstrasse, although it soon had to clear the way for Albert Speer's urban development plans. So it came to pass that a new representative building was constructed in Steglitz. In 1942, the Uranverein, which played a consulting role on the feasibility of the development of atomic weapons, convened here. An **add-on building** from the 1950s manages to clearly distance itself architecturally from the older, representative, symmetric building section through levity, seriality, and the inclusion of subtle irregularities.

At sixty-eight meters, Fichtenberg mountain behind the Institute of Theater Studies is the highest point of elevation in southwestern Berlin. The forty-meter-tall **water tower** perched atop the hill was a very suitable place for taking weather measurements, which led to the settlement of the **Institute of Meteorology** in a simply and quickly built utilitarian structure next door, which stood out from the existing development of the Fichtenberg colony due to its industrial fabrication. Later on, a grass-roots movement pushed back against the planned expansion of the Institute of Meteorology, which led to delays in the development schedule extending beyond the 1980s. When finally completed, the extension section placed an S-shaped, curved new building in front of the three-part U-shaped existing building, thus creating the space urgently needed for offices, seminar rooms, and a library, as well as for a further measuring tower. The passage and the design on the street-facing side are now completely new. Already renowned for other buildings conceived for Freie Universität, as well as for further scientific facilities, the architects here once again demonstrated their feel for material, form, design, and setting.

Institute of Theater Studies
former House of Research

Grunewaldstrasse 35 | 1938–1940 | Hans Th. Lehmann | 1938–1945 headquarters of the German Association for the Support and Advancement of Scientific Research | 1946–1958 headquarters of the US-American military government, then the seat of Berlin's administrative court for several years | 1956 **add-on building**, Hans Schoszberger, commissioned by Berlin's administrative court | since 1958 used by FU: Institutes of Geography, Psychology, Organic Chemistry, Systematic Botany, Plant Geography | until 1963 cafeteria in basement | 1973 officially acquired by FU

Water tower with meteorological observatory of FU

Schmidt-Ott-Strasse 13 | 1886 | Otto Techow

Institute of Meteorology

Carl-Heinrich-Becker-Weg 6–10 | 1974–1975 Hochtief, concrete component construction style | 1978–1991 extension, Daniel Gogel, Hermann Fehling | until 1983 also Institute of Psychology

AN ORGANIC GRID OF RUST, SILVER, AND WOOD

"LODGES LAID OUT UPON AN ORCHARD"

In light of rapidly rising enrollment figures, in 1963 Freie Universität planned an expansion on a site that had already been earmarked for science use at the beginning of the century. The area had been used by the Technical University as a fruit plantation since World War II. The university's aim was to build structures here that would enable productive interdisciplinary connections and overcome the traditional isolation of individual institute buildings. Building for the sciences now became a research enterprise in and of itself, resulting in a laboratory-like situation for urban construction. On the property between Habelschwerdter Allee and Fabeckstrasse, a winning architectural proposal that had caused as much excitement as it had controversy was realized in two phases of construction. The resulting spatial assemblage followed an entirely new approach to the structuring and organization of academic units. A structuring carpet-like development was laid over the former orchard: the Rostlaube and Silberlaube (or Rust and Silver Lodges) were created – named after the visual appearance of their facades.

The "Idea Competition for the Expansion of Freie Universität" first announced on March 1, 1963, was won by the Paris-based architectural firm of George Candilis, Alexis Josic, and Shadrach Woods. In their statement, the jury explained: "The order here is not one in search of false representation, instead it corresponds in its moderate restraint with the idea of the university in the best possible sense." The building is low and expansive, and extendable in all directions, like a carpet pattern (→15). Although its height conforms to its still sparsely developed surroundings, its novel internal and external appearance makes no compromises. The construction, designed for flexibility and shifting uses, is structured horizontally; the impression it leaves breaks with conventional viewing habits. The steel composite construction is based on a measuring system known as Modulor developed by Le Corbusier, a scale of proportions that takes a general human body size of 183 centimeters as its departure point. The shell construction system, developed together with renowned steel construction engineer and furniture designer Jean Prouvé, was intended to provide the greatest possible freedom of design through the option of dismantling partition walls in an uncomplicated manner. This possibility was of great practical use when changes were to be made and free spaces created, which proved particularly beneficial for the new building of the **Philological Library.**

Rostlaube and Silberlaube
institutes for the humanities

Habelschwerdter Allee 45, Thielallee 38, Otto-von-Simson-Strasse 26 | 1967–1973 Rostlaube, first construction phase, facade material: corten steel, rust patina not stable as planned, replaced by bronze sheeting over the course of renovation work | 1975–1979 Silberlaube, second construction phase, external shell: aluminum | Georges Candilis, Alexis Josic, Shadrach Woods, Manfred Schiedhelm with Jean Prouvé | 1999–2007 renovation, Norman Foster

Mensa II cafeteria building
1977–1982 | Rainer Gerhard Rümmler | 2006–2007 conversion of the foyer, Carola Schäfers Architekten

parking level
1981–1985 | Manfred Schiedhelm

Philological Library

Habelschwerdter Allee 45 | 2001–2005 | Norman Foster

Silberlaube, courtyard

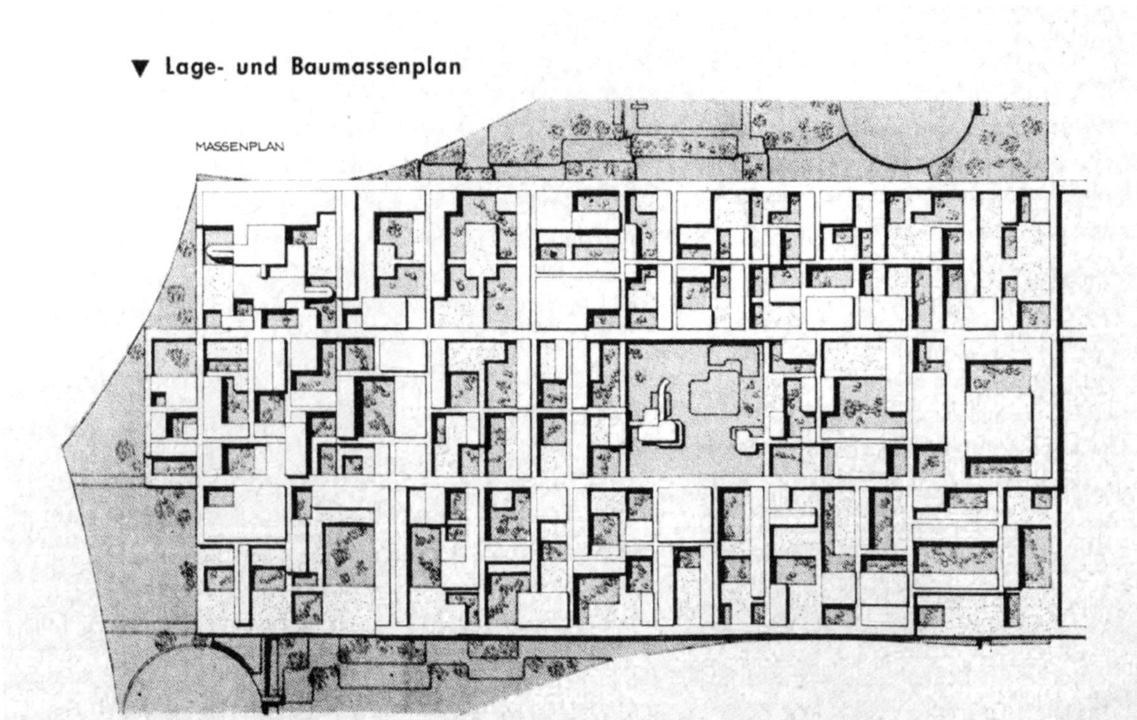

Competition draft, Rostlaube and Silberlaube, site and construction plan

Rostlaube

Philological Library

Opened in the middle of the Rostlaube complex in 2005, the library is located in a biomorphic rotunda, whose four dynamically curved floors feature an arrangement of bookshelves and workplaces. The team of architects led by Norman Foster developed a solution for the library and its 800,000-volume collection that blends into the structures of the Rostlaube as a solitary building. The orange-yellow accents in the entranceway and in the construction of the double-walled outer shell refer back to the color scheme for the carpets and awnings throughout the whole building complex.

Running along the "main roads" J, K and L of the Rostlaube and Silberlaube buildings – the fact that letters from the middle of the alphabet were chosen here is a further reminder of the original inclusion of a possibility for expansion in both directions – one finds the heavily frequented rooms, such as lecture halls, seminar rooms, and assembly rooms. Located at a right angle to these main paths in numbered "side streets" arranged around several atria, one finds the quieter areas, such as the libraries, or offices for professors, assistants, and doctoral students. As intended by the architects, structured in this way, the fabric of the buildings recalls urban entities such as the Quartier Latin in Paris or traditional residential districts like the Old City in Casablanca. The floors are accessed via ramps located in the main streets. In this connection, an architectonic motif of Le Corbusier was borrowed from the Villa Savoye in Poissy. Contrary to the original plans, the Rostlaube and Silberlaube are home exclusively to institutes for the humanities.

Integrated into the Silberlaube complex, though independent and separately planned, the **Education Library** followed new, ecologically influenced concepts for spatial design, such as flat roofs with lush greenery, trellises on the outside, as well as fountains and flora on the inside. The **Mensa II** cafeteria building was realized almost simultaneously, though it breaks with the complex's strict grid for practical reasons.

The Rostlaube and Silberlaube were most recently joined by the **Holzlaube** (or "Wood Lodge" building complex) inaugurated in 2014. Three lecture halls, twelve seminar rooms, 220 offices and work rooms, in addition to reading and working areas, extend organically the concepts behind the Rostlaube and Silberlaube: a one-to-three-story building landscape is arranged around small courtyards.

Education Library

Fabeckstrasse 23–25, Otto-von-Simson-Strasse 16 | 1980–1984 | Manfred Schiedhelm

---

Holzlaube with Campus Library

Fabeckstrasse 23–25 | 2012–2014 | facade cedar | Florian Nagler

Institute of Philosophy

Habelschwerdter Allee 30 | 1981–1983 |
Hinrich and Inken Baller

Further Education Center
planned as "House of the Student Body"

Otto-von-Simson-Strasse 13–15 | 1995–1998 |
Thomas Wolf and Adolf Doerfler

The Holzlaube complex brings together the so-called "smaller subjects", which throughout the decades had been housed in primarily crowded quarters in various villas in the surrounding area. In particular, the jointly used, integrated **Campus Library**, which also absorbed the Education Library, is meant to serve for better interconnectedness between the "smaller subjects".

The **Institute of Philosophy** was already built as a conscious renunciation of the trend towards megastructure architecture back in the early 1980s. Instead, the building took up the Dahlem villa style and altered it in a post-modern manner. The interleaved, irregularly folded concrete roof supported atop twin pillars is particularly striking. The entirely glazed facade, with its turquoise network of steel mullions, is multifaceted and rich in structural detail, and approximates the external appearances of villa architecture, admittedly not through the choice of materials, but instead through the forms of their arrangement. The visible side on Habelschwerdter Allee presents itself as a one-story building, yet seen from the lower-lying garden side, which extends all the way to Triestpark, two floors become visible, and inside there are even three. Open, curved staircases, once again decorated in turquoise, are conceived as nodes for social encounters in the middle of the irregular structure.

The **Further Education Center** is a special postmodernist architectural example. Originally planned as a "House of the Student Body", the structure attracts the eye through its eccentric colorfulness and its jutting, curved shape. As early as 1979, the creation of a bespoke building for the General Students' Committee (AStA) was supposed to acknowledge the organization's significance. The university chose to forego a competition and after unsuccessfully soliciting the services of Frank Gehry, the university turned to architects Thomas Wolf and Adolf Doerfler to design a place for students that would take the villa structure of the surrounding area into account. The final result was an inverted truncated pyramid with nesting cuboid and conical formations and a curved, cantilevered roof in opaque blue and green that can be used in multiple ways and blends in well with the sloping terrain. However, funding problems led to the university giving priority to the accommodation of the Further Education Center instead of permitting AStA to move in upon completion.

INSTITUTES FOR THE NATURAL SCIENCES

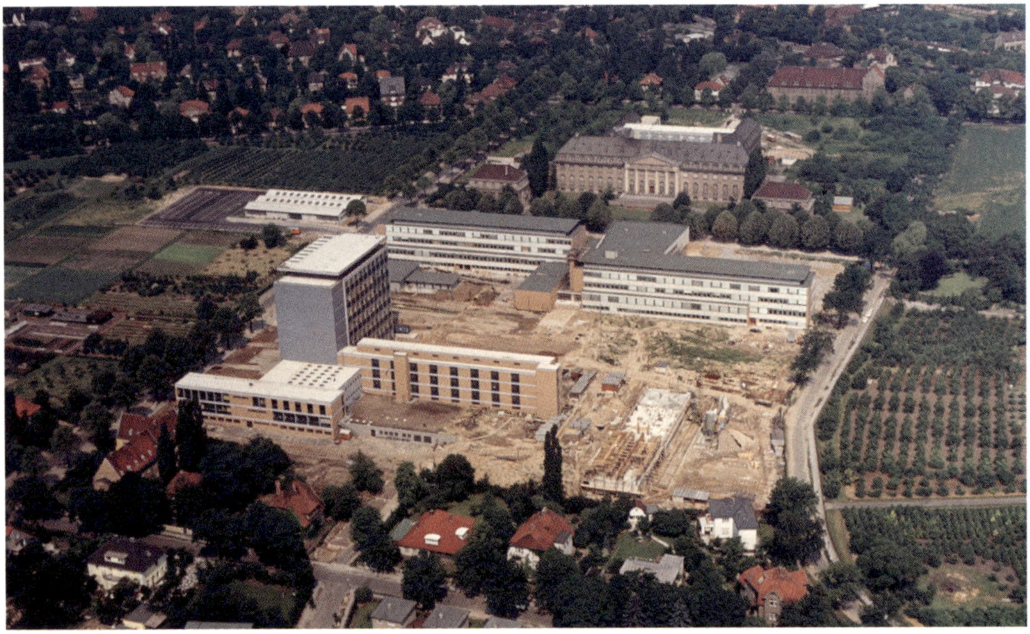

Institute for Inorganic Chemistry, together with pre-clinic, in the background the Dahlem museums

Institute of Physics, library and facade

The natural science institutes of the FU are located on a tract of land between Fabeckstrasse and Takustrasse, as well as alongside the perpendicular-running Arnimallee across from the Dahlem museum complex. Megastructures from the 1970s extend the belt of the Rostlaube and Silberlaube towards the northeast.

Institute of Inorganic Chemistry

Fabeckstrasse 34–36 | 1960–1963 | Hans Geber, Otto Risse | 1979–1980 redesign of the facade with solar energy system, Gerd Hänska

Building for chemistry and biochemistry

pre-clinic

Arnimallee 22 | 1961–1963 | formerly Institutes of Physiology and Molecular Biology, as well as for Human Medicine | 2014–2019 renovation, Friedhelm Nussbaum, Carpus + Partner AG

Institute of Physics

Arnimallee 14 | 1973–1982 | Henning Larsen | 2008 installation of one of the largest photovoltaic systems in Berlin

The construction of the **Institute of Inorganic Chemistry** at the beginning of the 1960s represented the birth of an area for the natural sciences. Research, teaching, and administration activities are clearly divided in a three-winged, asymmetrical facility. This conception bears a strong resemblance to Walter Gropius's Bauhaus building in Dessau. With a height of 38.5 meters, the seven-story building section devoted to instruction towers above the entire surrounding development, thus rendering it a unique specimen in Dahlem's urban fabric. The elongated pre-clinic also completed in 1963 has since been used in various ways as a **building for chemistry and biochemistry**.

Alongside Arnimallee and Takustrasse, very near the Institute of Inorganic Chemistry, the Institute of Physics and the Institute of Organic and Physical Chemistry were built to expand the first institution. In two building phases, they took up Henning Larsen's plan as already developed in 1963, which had taken second place in the "Idea Competition for the Expansion of Freie Universität" (the Rostlaube and Silberlaube). Larsen arranged the **Institute of Physics** in two square units capable of being extended on all sides. The interior gridding yields four inner courtyards, which provide for a sufficient amount of sunlight. Two pedestrian bridges connect the different segments beyond Arnimallee. The exposed pipes and the red steel framework recall the Centre Georges Pompidou in Paris, which also wears its structure, function, and construction on the outside while accentuating them through the use of color. The specialist library on the north side ruptures the closed symmetry with a glass facade tilted at a fifty-degree angle and creates an opening into the greenery of the villa gardens.

Institute of Organic and Physical Chemistry

Institute of Computer Science, courtyard

SupraFAB, visualization of design planning

Institute of Organic and Physical Chemistry

Takustrasse 3 | 1975–1978 | Manfred Kiemle, Hermann Kreidt, Dietrich Garski, Günter Saleh Dybe, Otto Herrenkind | since 1999 also administrative branch of the Departments of Biology, Chemistry, and Pharmacy | under renovation until 2025

New research building: SupraFAB

Supramolecular Functional Architectures at Biological Interfaces

Altensteinstrasse 23a | 2016–2020 | Benjamin Rämmler, Nickl & Partner Architekten

Institute of Mathematics

Arnimallee 2–4 | 1974 | technical department of the FU

Institute of Computer Science

Takustrasse 9 | 1991–1993 | Klaus Baesler, Bernhard Schmidt | overall concept for the development of the block interior already formulated in 1987

Natural Science Practicum building

Institutes of Biology, Didactics in Biology, Medieval Latin Philology

Schwendenerstrasse 1, Altensteinstrasse 23 | 1986–1989 | Peter Beller

In direct proximity, a building was erected especially for the **Institute of Organic and Physical Chemistry**. Special laboratories, workshops, lecture halls, and workrooms are laid out in a square with four wings. Strict horizontal window strips and the facade raster are juxtaposed with gold clinker brick clad utility shafts that extend vertically beyond the height of the rest of the building. To the south, one finds today's Institute for Animal Behavior, Genetics, and Neurophysiology (Takustrasse 6). To the north, a new building, the **SupraFAB**, is slated to extend the site.

The area between Takustrasse and Arnimallee has been the object of constant extension and expansion: today the **Institute of Mathematics**, the **Institute of Computer Science**, and the non-university-affiliated Zuse Institute Berlin are located here. As early as the 1960s, computer science was already being taught as a sub-discipline of mathematics; in 1985, a separate course of study was devoted to it at Freie Universität. Since accommodation in already existing buildings was no longer possible, and the properties facing the street had also already been developed, a continued development in the interior of the block was planned. With translucency and openness, two courtyards featuring glass ceilings and bamboo plants shape the character of the rectangular building, which extends the northwest alignment of the physics building. The facade facing the inner courtyard is structured with large windows and columns, crowned by small, round windows that provide for ventilation. The still adjacent Department of Food Technology and Food Chemistry of the Technical University at Königin-Luise-Strasse 22 testifies to the previous use for gardening purposes by the Royal School for Horticulture (→257).

A new tone in the language of architecture was set in the mid-1980s with the **Natural Science Practicum building**. As with the Institute of Philosophy (→183), one is dealing with an example of post-modern architecture here, which blends into the lay of the street in its dimensions and adapts itself to the surrounding development, while taking up stylistic elements from diverse epochs and altering them. While it is true that the practicum building was conceived as a place to learn practical skills for the natural sciences, shortly following its completion Medieval Latin philology was also given a new home in the building.

BETWEEN DAHLEM-DORF AND BREITENBACHPLATZ

The various research centers of Freie Universität are concentrated around the Henry-Ford-Bau, at the Botanical Garden, alongside the Rostlaube, and in the area of the natural science institutes. Additionally, a further group of institutes can be found within a broad band between the subway stations Dahlem-Dorf and Breitenbachplatz. This band has been shaped by both the subway line, already inaugurated in 1913, and the move of some institutes of the Agricultural College to Dahlem in the 1920s. At the endpoints the Max Planck Institute for Educational Research was erected in the early 1960s and in 1990 the Admissions Office opened, which was conceived to serve as a sort of "front door" to the area.

College of Agriculture, competition design by Heinrich Straumer

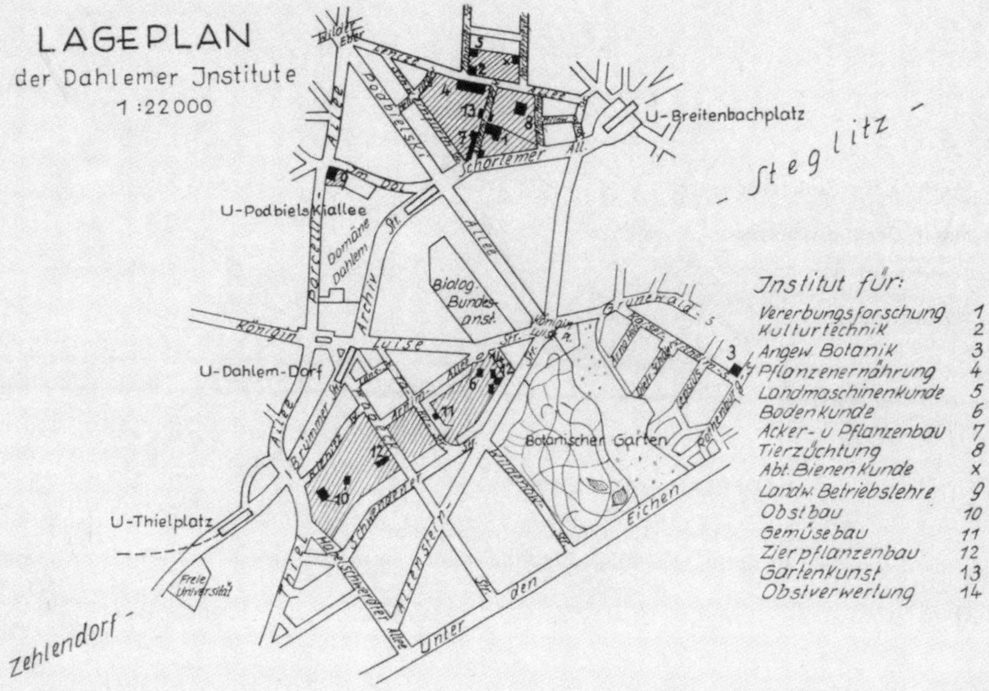

Bauplan der Landwirtschaftlichen Hochschule in Dahlem nach dem 1. Weltkrieg

Roof of Admission Office

John-F.-Kennedy-Institute

Admissions Office

Iltisstrasse 1–5 | 1994–1996 | Doris and Ralph Thut

Student Services Center

Iltisstrasse 4 | 2013–2014 | braun.busse.architekten

John-F.-Kennedy-Institute

Lansstrasse 7–9 | 1904–1905 | Otto Stahn | elementary school in the scope of city expansion | 1928 extension, Erich Schwiertz | 2007–2008 remodeling of the library, Geier Maass Architekten

Institutes for Veterinary Medicine

research area for dog keeping, Institute of Animal Nutrition

Königin-Luise-Strasse 49 | 2006–2007 | Geier Maass Architekten | not accessible to the general public

Right next to the Dahlem-Dorf subway station stands the surprisingly tiny building of the **Admissions Office** of Freie Universität, as it has since 1996, with an overhanging red roof signaling the way to the campus. The creation of this new building was a reaction on the part of the university to the lack of space in the former admissions office on Boltzmannstrasse. In 2014, the office was joined by the **Student Services Center**, which lies kitty-corner.

In the direct vicinity, one finds the **John-F.-Kennedy-Institute** for North American Studies, which has been housed in a former schoolhouse since 1965. The institute library was set up in the former gymnasium.

The station building at the Dahlem-Dorf stop, which was constructed in the style of a northern-German manor at the personal behest of Kaiser Wilhelm II, unmistakably underlines the stylized, rural character of the place. This former feudal estate in front of the gates of Berlin was used for agriculture for centuries. In 1841, it passed into the possession of the Prussian state. The resulting state domain was ultimately divided up for further use of the land sixty years later. On the opposite side, north of Königin-Luise-Strasse, one finds the entrance to a remnant of the Dahlem estate. Today, a foundation, the Stiftung Domäne Dahlem, operates an open-air museum for agricultural and food culture in the site. Since 1951, the domain has also been home to diverse **Institutes for Veterinary Medicine** of Freie Universität, which also maintains the Equine Center in Bad Saarow and the Veterinary Clinic Düppel in Berlin-Zehlendorf, far from its main site. On the site of the former domain, is to be found the former Düppel distillery (built around 1838/1839), whose area was used for agriculture after 1875, before becoming part of the Department of Veterinary Medicine of Freie Universität in 1951, as well as the Library of Veterinary Medicine Düppel (1996–1998), installed in the former riding arena at Oertzenweg 19b.

Buildings of Agricultural College

Institutes for Farming and Plant Cultivation, Genetics Research (Erwin Baur) and Apiology | residential houses for professors

Albrecht-Thaer-Weg | 1921–1926 | Heinrich Straumer | for the Agricultural College →77

Alongside Albrecht-Thaer-Weg, one finds buildings of the **Agricultural College**. Together with those on the Invalidenstrasse they were affiliated with the university in Mitte in 1934 and passed on to the Technical University after World War II as a "Faculty of Farming". Today the grounds, a protected site since 1993, are used by all three of Berlin's larger universities. Long-term agricultural field experiments are still being conducted in this institute originally planned by Heinrich Straumer. In 1919, a resolution was passed to relocate the Agricultural College in its entirety from Invalidenstrasse to Dahlem, in this way providing it with larger cultivation areas for the first time. To this end, a competition for the development of the tract of land between Lentzeallee and Schorlemerallee was already announced in 1920. Though parts of the winning design had already been realized by 1926, due to funding difficulties the facility would remain uncompleted and the headquarters of the Agricultural College remained in Mitte.

Geheimes Staatsarchiv

Secret State Archives Prussian Cultural Heritage

Archivstrasse 12–14 | 1915–1924 | Eduard Fürstenau

former Pre-clinic for Veterinary Medicine

Institute for Veterinary Anatomy, Pharmacology, and Toxicology, as well as Friedrich Meinecke Institute and Institute of Art History

Koserstrasse 20 | 1963–1968 | Wassili Luckhardt, Hans Joachim Wandelt | 1990–1998 closed for renovation work | 1993–1998 remodeling, Betz Architekten

On Koserstrasse south of Podbielskiallee, in the 1960s the department of veterinary medicine was allotted a solitary building, set perpendicular to the **Geheimes Staatsarchiv** and standing out sharply from its surroundings. The impressive building, initially the site of the **former Pre-clinic for Veterinary Medicine**, consists of a six-story high-rise slab that is supplemented by several low-rise buildings in the background positioned around four courtyards. A range of renovation measures was made necessary by asbestos contamination and a change in the use of the building (following the veterinary pre-clinic, institutes for art history, history, veterinary anatomy, pharmacology, and toxicology moved in): namely, a new entrance, a two-story library, and newly laid out administrative wings with windowless utility units on the inside. In spite of drastic alterations, such as the placement of an embankment and staircase facing the glazed main entranceway, the rigorously structured facade remains striking and virtually monumental.

Institute for Latin American Studies

former administrative building of the Reichsknappschaft workers' welfare organization

Rüdesheimer Strasse 54–56 | competition 1928, realization 1929–1930 | Max Taut, Franz Hoffmann | also headquarters of technical department of FU

Today, the **Institute for Latin American Studies** is no longer located in Dahlem, but instead in neighboring Berlin-Wilmersdorf, in its position behind Breitenbachplatz. Home for the institute is a structure completed in 1930 as an administrative building for the Reichsknappschaft, a health insurance and social security agency with roots in the mining industry. Executed in a steel skeleton structure approach, the building met modern, functional administrative needs with its short routes between units and interior design featuring glass partitioning walls and flexible, sunlight flooded offices. Leased by Freie Universität from 1970 on, the building became the official property of the institution in 1986 and was subsequently renovated with great care. (MW)

Meeting Places and

Interspaces

Although Berlin's universities have expanded and spread considerably over the last two centuries, it has always been the main buildings that primarily project their image to the outside world.
Along with individual academic institutions, that is, the places of daily work, education and research, there are other meeting places that have influenced the relationship between the academic community and the city and also the interactions between those who use these institutions: students of academies use the branch libraries of other universities; a students' working group mainly meets in the cafeteria; the PhD student carries out his studies in a Stadtteilbibliothek; the research assistant is most creative in the Scharoun Building at the **Staatsbibliothek**, and student dormitories shape the atmosphere of entire city blocks.
Researching and studying in Berlin require us to accept an apparent disorderliness, as well as the noise and aesthetic of the big city; and yet despite several attempts, the insular life of a campus university is nowhere to be found here. And because of this, Berlin's dense mix of university institutions, non-university research centers as well as academies, foundations, museums, archives, scientific associations, and memorials provides an extraordinarily rich educational infrastructure.
This multitude of institutions was partly a consequence of the partition of Berlin after World War II – which explains why the Staatsbibliothek occupies two separate buildings: one of these can be found in the former East Berlin on Unter den Linden, and another more recent building was constructed in the West within sight of the Berlin Wall near the Alte Potsdamer Strasse. The building lies south-west of the Potsdamer Platz across from the Kulturforum, which itself was originally intended to form a counterpart to the Museumsinsel in the East. In fact, the tendering procedure for the design was carried out before the Berlin Wall was built.
After World War II, the major part of the book inventory from Berlin's libraries was stored in areas controlled by the Western Allies, and was correspondingly handed back to West Berlin. This explains why the planning for a new library

began at a relatively early stage. Due to the new route of the Potsdamer Strasse (which was redirected after the Wall was built), city planners decided to depart from the original concept by Albert Speer and make a new start. There had also been a plan to construct a highway to the east of the library, with the administrative wing of the new Staatsbibliothek acting as a traffic noise barrier for the Kulturforum.

The new Staatsbibliothek was the largest building to be realized by renowned architect Hans Scharoun, who is famed for his organic, ship-like designs. The immense central reading room could easily accommodate the Berliner Philharmonie, which Scharoun had previously built just across the street. Although some individual elements of the main building are of vast dimensions, the building on the redirected Potsdamer Strasse possesses a light, airy character. Constructed with nested trapezoid forms layered like steps, this "ship of books" comprises a reading landscape formed from several terraces which are oriented towards the Kulturforum. Round openings in the sawtooth roof provide the large room with daylight. In the early 2000s, the capacity of the "Stabi-West" reading room was regularly exceeded, and the situation was only alleviated with the opening of the new library at the Technische Universität (together with the Universität der Künste), the Philologischen Bibliothek, the Erwin-Schrödinger-Zentrum and the Grimm-Zentrum.

The second site of the **Staatsbibliothek**, which is also a few decades older, has its roots in a totally different historical context. This imposing structure beside the main building of the Humboldt-Universität occupies an entire city block. It was commissioned by Kaiser Wilhelm II in 1903. It replaced the Academy of Science which had formerly stood on the site, and housed the inventory of the Königliche Bibliothek (→33) on the other side of the street – a collection that had grown so dramatically during the nineteenth century that the

---

Staatsbibliothek
building Potsdamer Strasse, Stabi, Stabi West, Stabi 2

Potsdamer Strasse 33 | 1967–1978 | Hans Scharoun, Edgar Wisniewski | Scharoun died in 1972, his students and his colleague Wisniewski completed the building | 1991 refurbishment underground car park, 2001 conversion for electronic research, since 2006 asbestos removal and retrofitting of air conditioning | research library with modern stock

---

Preußische Staatsbibliothek
building Unter den Linden, Stabi 1, Stabi Ost

Unter den Linden 8 | 1903–1914 | Ernst von Ihne | 1941 war damage, destruction of the dome reading room | 1955 temporary roof over the dome reading room | 1977 demolition of the dome- and univeristy reading room, construction of repository towers | 2005–2019 refurbishment and renovation | 2013 opening of the new reading rooms | research library with modern stock

Staatsbibliothek, building Unter den Linden, reading room and court of honor

original rooms were bursting at the seams. The central reading room of the building, a three-storey neo-Baroque structure, was originally covered by a dome with a diameter of 38 meters; six meters larger than the famous Berlin Cathedral dome. A cour d'honneur precedes six parallel inner courtyards which provide structure and access to the massive building. The interior features wood-paneled offices, well-lit staircases, and ostentatious banquet halls in accordance with the specific usage and function of the rooms at that time.
In 1905, the theologian, church historian and science organizer Adolf von Harnack took on the additional role of General Director at the library – a post he held until 1921. After it was founded in 1911, Harnack also took on the post of President of the Kaiser-Wilhelm-Gesellschaft, in which capacity he supervised the establishment of new academic institutes in Dahlem until 1930. As director of the library, Harnack managed to double the acquisition budget, increasing the size of the inventory by around 40 percent. In addition, he simplified the inter-library lending procedure and compiled a catalog documenting the stock of all Prussian academic libraries. The building, part of the ensemble dedicated to academic learning (→40), originally provided – aside from its rooms for the Staatsbibliothek – space for Universitätsbibliothek and the Academy of Sciences. The latter is still housed within the building, along with the Akademiebibliothek. At the time of its opening, the Staatsbibliothek on Unter den Linden was the largest and most modern library in Europe and featured an innovative new shelving system. Although now housed in two buildings, it remains the largest academic university library in the German-speaking countries.

The Jacob-und-Wilhelm-Grimm-Zentrum (→41), which opened in 2009, was the Humboldt-Universität's first self-contained post-war library. Located beside the S-Bahn train line, the building is a seven-story cube characterized by very tall, narrow rectangular windows and a two-storey drop in height on the northern side. The expansive reading room, composed of terraces over five storeys, dominates the building's interior. The bookshelves and additional study cubicles are arranged around its perimeter. Since its opening, the daily number of visitors has increased threefold.

Library of the TU in the main building

Strasse des 17. Juni 135 | 1950–1951 | Willy Kreuer | second floor, south-west wing

Amerika-Gedenk-Bibliothek

Blücherplatz 1 | 1952–1954 | Willy Kreuer, Fritz Bornemann | consolidated with the Zentral- und Landesbibliothek together with the Berliner Stadtbibliothek since 1995

FU Sports Center

"Schlachtschiff"

planing between 1962 and 1980 | 1976 Senate Building Authority design | 1978–1979 public tender, winning design: Peter Beller

Another building that dates from the early twenty-first century is the shared Zentralbibliothek of the Technische Universität and the Universität der Künste (→ 143). The Universitätsbibliothek at the Technische Universität was also augmented by the university archive and the TU Berlin University Press, as well as the Architekturmuseum and the Sondersammlung Gartenbau (Horticultural Collection).

Before its relocation, the **library of the Technical University** was in the main building. After World War II, it was remodeled according to a design by the architect Willy Kreuer. The elegant and discreet interior design of the 1950s is particularly notable for it light-flooded reading room, open plan stairs and the use of materials such as steel tubing and wood.

Kreuer was also responsible for the **Amerika-Gedenk-Bibliothek**, which remains an imposing architectural landmark at the Hallesches Tor. The building's austere character is relieved by a gentle curve in its form, and a mainly glazed flat-roofed structure intersects the six-storey block, providing space for a lecture hall. The interior continues this transparent, open-plan concept.

The Freie Universität and the Pedagogical College – which was annexed by the former in 1980 – jointly pursued a plan for several decades to establish a large **sports center**. As early as 1962, the Berlin Senate had allocated part of the Domäne Dahlem estate for the project. It took ten years before the Freie Universität presented a utilization concept. However, after local residents rejected the design put forward by the Senate Building Authority, problems with the location and financing could not be satisfactorily resolved. Progress was hindered by long delays and the planned large-scale complex, consisting of institute buildings and sports halls, was ultimately shelved on the grounds of it being unsuitable for the location.

Library of the TU in the main building

Amerika-Gedenk-Bibliothek

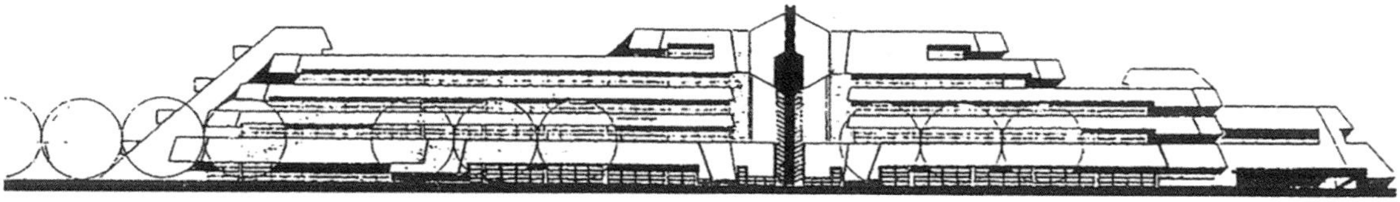

Planned sports center, FU

Alte Mensa Nord

Studentenwohnheim Biesdorf

Oberfeldstrasse dormitory (Victor Jara)

Oberfeldstrasse 111–132 | 1952–1954 | Kurt Ehrlich, Kurt Lässig | 1994–1997 refurbishment

Studentendorf Eichkamp

International student dormitories Eichkamp

Berlin-Westend | 1959, 1966–1967 second construction phase | Ludwig Leo with Georg Heinrichs and Hans C. Müller

Studentendorf Schlachtensee

1957–1964 | Hermann Fehling, Daniel Gogel, Peter Pfankuch, landscape design by Hermann Mattern | 1976–1978 extension and densification | 1991 historic monument and landscape monument | 2006 national cultural monument | 2006–2022 refurbishment, Autzen and Reimers

Alte Mensa Nord

Reinhardtstrasse, Schumannstrasse |
1974–1975 | Ulf Zimmermann | 2006–2007
demolished

In the east part of the city, the main focus of redevelopment was on social housing. A notable building of this type and an outstanding example of East European Modernism was the **Alte Mensa Nord** (old northern cafeteria), which was situated in a park bordering the Reinhardtstrasse on the site of a former barracks. A square, two-storey building housed the canteen kitchen and provided space for dining halls with 1000 seats in total. Although the Mensa Nord was not conceived as an archetype, its construction led to its design being adopted for cafeterias in Halle, Merseburg, Leipzig and Dresden.

Apart from the provision of meals, accommodation was the most urgent issue for Berlin's students. The **Studentenwohnheim Biesdorf** (Biesdorf Student Dormitories), which opened in 1954, was originally planned as a university community which would comprise over 1,625 students. The long, narrow neoclassical building on the Oberfeldstrasse was complemented by a central cafeteria and seminar building, an indoor swimming pool, and a library. The outlying location was a result of the changing realities of available urban space and the new location distribution plans of the young Humboldt-Universität (→150).

The architecture of dormitories in the West was more individual, more compartmentalized, and purportedly more democratic. During his studies, the architect and college tutor Ludwig Leo lived in the **Studentendorf Eichkamp** (Eichkamp student village), which was built in the post-war years by students of the Hochschule für Bildende Künste (former Academy of the Arts 1945–1975). Established in 1947 as a work camp for the clearance of wartime rubble, by the late 1950s, Leo added new buildings to the existing structures in Eichkamp.
The next, significantly larger dormitory project was the **Studentendorf Schlachtensee** (Schlachtensee student village). Architecturally imposing, it comprises 28 apartment houses that were realized with the aim of encouraging a sense of democracy and personal responsibility. The cubic, rectangular and z-shaped building elements were inspired by Hans Scharoun's notion of the urban landscape and an organic urban building style as well as an ensemble around a "village green".
The communal spaces were created using extensive glass surfaces and other materials corresponding to Ludwig Mies van der Rohe's concept of free-flowing spaces. As in Eichkamp, the architects considered it essential to provide meeting places and private spaces of retreat.

The Studentendorf Schlachtensee was built in the same years as the buildings for the 1957 Interbau exhibition and the Haus der Kulturen der Welt (then called the Kongresshalle). It was inspired by the modern western International Style. In Biesdorf there are evident associations with the Karl-Marx-Allee and its role models in Moscow architecture. (MW)

ADLERSHOF
ehemaliges Flugfeld
Johannisthal
Physik
IRIS
Chemie
Motorenprüfstand
Trudelturm
Windkanal
Erwin-Schrödinger-Zentrum
Zentrum für Photonik und Optik I
II
LINSE
Mathematik und Informatik
Institut für Kosmosforschung
BESSY II
HAFEN RUDOW OST
Teltowkanalbrücke
Rudower
Forum
Akademieplatz
Inliner-bahn

Adlershof
Fernsehzentrum
Kugellabore
Umwelttechnologie
und
Wirtschaftsstandort
Adlershof
B96a
Studio Berlin Adlershof
MEDIENSTADT
Adlershof
Chaussee
Dörpfeld-
Platz der Befreiung
Marktplatz
Heide-Schule
Sporthalle
Sportplatz
Anna-Seghers-Schule
Verklärungskirche
Christus-König-Kirche
Bibliothek/Artothek
FFW
Ehrliche Arbeit
KGA
Brandenburgische TU Cottbus
Bundesamt
Tennisplätze
Kleingartenanlage
Teltowkanal III
Glienicker
Köpenicker
Ufer
Altglienicker Brücke
Berufsbildungszentrum
Fachschule
Musikschule
Forschungsgeb.
Havestadtplatz
Lunapark II
Kleingartenanlage

Rudower Chaussee with Institute of Geography and Psychology and Institute of Mathematics and Computer Science, left Aerodynamic Park with Großer Windkanal, Trudelturm, and engine testing chamber, top Institute of Physics, right Erwin Schrödinger Center

FROM ZEPPELINS TO START-UPS

A railway embankment for the S-Bahn divides the district of Adlershof into two halves with entirely different appearances. Separated from the old residential areas in the northeast of the city, in southwestern Berlin – alongside Rudower Chaussee – a location for science, business, and media was created following reunification, the WISTA Science and Technology Park (Wissenschafts- und Wirtschaftsstandort Adlershof). It has in the meantime grown to be the largest and most modern one of its kind in Germany, and it also encompasses Humboldt-Universität's campus for the natural sciences. Prior to 1990, the research institutes of the Academy of Sciences of the GDR were to be found here, although the development of this site had already begun as early as 1909, with the German Laboratory for Aviation Testing (DVL) and the Johannisthal airfield bordering in the north. Thus, Adlershof can look back on an over 100-year tradition as a location for science and technology.

Drawn to the area by the recently opened airfield, enterprises settled here quickly. During World War I, the site was used above all for airplane manufacturing, then, afterwards, primarily for the civil airmail service. Under the National-Socialists, large airplane manufacturers were based in Adlershof, where they conducted intensive research into new aviation technology - while using the forced labor of prisoners of war and concentration camp inmates on the production side. During World War II, one of Berlin's largest forced labor camps was located not far from Aviation Testing Laboratory and the Johannisthal airfield.

In the immediate post-war period, the site did not initially play a role as a place of research any longer. A barracks complex for the guard regiment of the GDR Ministry for State Security was set up near the airfield in 1954. However, the Academy of Sciences, founded in 1946, had already built more than a dozen institutes along Rudower Chaussee by the end of the 1950s.

Großer Windkanal

Brook-Taylor-Strasse 1 | 1932–1934 |
Hermann Brenner,
Werner Deutschmann

Engine testing chamber

Newtonstrasse 16 | 1933–1935 |
Hermann Brenner,
Werner Deutschmann

Trudelturm

Brook-Taylor-Strasse 2 | 1934–1936 |
Hermann Brenner,
Werner Deutschmann

The secret rearmament of the German armed forces in the 1930s left visible traces in Adlershof, in particular in the form of the numerous structures on the grounds of the German Laboratory for Aviation. The DVL's house architects Hermann Brenner and Werner Deutschmann conceived the design plans for all of these buildings. Among other works, they created the unusual research buildings that are listed as historical monuments today and grouped under the name Aerodynamic Park. The first to be completed was the **Großer Windkanal** (Large Wind Tunnel) for testing airplane components. Exposed to an air current generated by a giant propeller, the aerodynamic qualities of the parts could be measured. The technical fittings have since been removed from the Windkanal, and today one section of the measurement halls serves as a student laboratory for Humboldt-Universität's Institute of Physics.
In the soundproof **engine testing chamber**, the performance and durability of airplane motors were tested. Due to the chamber's construction style and internal wood cladding, the acoustic insulation was exceedingly effective. Today students of Humboldt-Universität use the former testing chamber as a café and meeting place.
In the **Trudelturm** (Tailspin Tower) on the other hand, a twenty-meter-high concrete tower, scientists studied the effects that a tailspin had on airplanes with the aid of a vertical air tunnel. Further DVL buildings designed by Hermann Brenner and Werner Deutschmann in the same era include the main workshop, a facility for testing the effects of increased altitude on motors, and the institute building. The listed airplane factory halls are now integrated into the new building constructed for the Erwin Schrödinger Center (→217).

Kugellabore, telescope, and Institute of Cosmos Research

Following the founding of the Academy of Sciences of the GDR in 1946, the search began in war-ravaged Berlin for spaces to house the academy's research facilities. Locations with an existing scientific tradition were favored. In Berlin-Buch, the new Institute of Medicine and Biology was able to move into the buildings of the former Kaiser Wilhelm Institute for Brain Research (→245), and in Adlershof the buildings of the former DVL were available. In 1950, the first institutes were able to move into the buildings, which had been renovated in the meantime. Within a very brief period of time, further research facilities would follow, attracting researchers from former Kaiser Wilhelm Institutes or from research institutions in West Berlin. Although the academy institutes were conceived as non-university-affiliated institutions, there were still manifold connections to the East Berlin-based university. For example, physicist and science organizer Robert Rompe simultaneously occupied the position of director at the Humboldt-Universität's 2nd Institute of Physics on Mohrenstrasse and at the Academy Institute for Radiation Sources in Adlershof.

Central Institute for Physical Chemistry

Rudower Chaussee, Am Studio | 1959–1961 | Horst Welser, Peter Adolf Thiessen (scientific concept) | demolition

Kugellabore
"Academy Bosom"

Rudower Chaussee 5, Am Studio 1 | 1959–1961 | Horst Welser, Peter Adolf Thiessen

When the former buildings of the DVL became increasingly unable to satisfy the evolving standards for research structures, from 1960 on more new buildings were to be built for the institutes that had settled in the area. The expansion projects were for the most part laboratory buildings that could be used universally, conceived to be easily adapted to changing research tasks. The new building for the **Central Institute for Physical Chemistry** from 1961 was considered a prototype for this sort of structure. Joining these flexible structures were special buildings for specific research tasks, such as for instance the thermo-constant **Kugellabore** (Spherical Laboratories). With the passage of time, the "Academy Bosom", as the laboratory is also known colloquially, is now surrounded by other new buildings erected after 1990, whose presence, however, does not obstruct the view of the characteristic spheres. Originally, the isothermal laboratories were supposed to host experiments related to metallurgy, in the service of aerospace research. Due to the fact that such experiments require constant temperatures, and as such only fluctuations of maximum 0.01 degrees Celsius can be tolerated, the external walls consist of ten-centimeter-thick reinforced concrete.
A further special building and at the same the visible emblem of the Adlershof site was a radio telescope with a diameter of thirty-six meters, which went into operation in 1958. In its day the second largest telescope of its kind in Europe, it had already fallen behind in international competition with far larger telescopes fifteen years later, leading to its dismantling. A further expansion of Adlershof's science center fell through for financial reasons during this period. As such, the desired new buildings could only be realized for a handful of institutes. More frequently, the institutions had to make do with simple shacks or structures featuring lightweight designs.

Institute of Cosmos Research

1978–1982 | Joachim Hahn and collective | from 1973 Institute of Electronics | from 1981 Institute of Cosmos Research | 1991 integration into the Deutsche Zentrum für Luft- und Raumfahrt (DLR)

In the early 1980s, the **Institute of Cosmos Research** was able to move into a new building for theoretical and experimental research. To keep costs down, the seven-story building featured a reinforced concrete skeleton and was constructed from standardized and pre-fabricated building components. By 1989, 17 scientific facilities with a total of 5,000 employees spread over an area of 76 hectares were ultimately based in Adlershof, making the district the largest site for Academy of Sciences research facilities in the GDR.

Television center

Rudower Chaussee, Agastrasse, Moriz-Seeler-Strasse and Franz-Ehrlich-Strasse | 1949–1957 | Franz Ehrlich, Wolfgang Wunsch

However, the Academy of Sciences was not the only institution that chose to settle in Adlershof: East German television also came to be based here. Deutsche Fernsehfunk (the DFF, or German Television Broadcasting – though East German in origin of course) took to the airwaves for the first time in 1952. By the mid-1950s, a **television center** had been built, consisting of several buildings. It was assumed until the end of the twentieth century that the plans were drawn up by Franz Ehrlich. In fact, however, it was architect Wolfgang Wunsch who designed the core of the building complex, while Ehrlich was only responsible for a small section running along Agastrasse. Upon completion of the full site in the early 1960s, Adlershof evolved into the main location for East German television broadcasting; indeed, programming for two full television stations would be entirely produced from this site up until reunification.

The combination of research facilities, industry, and business concerns made Adlershof the central location for applied, technology-oriented industrial research in the GDR. On top of that, the television center made Adlershof into a hub for media. While the latter was able to survive the systemic change of the late 1980s and early 1990s without any great difficulty, the reunification agreement called for the total liquidation of the academy institutes. Employees were laid off and the buildings were left to stand empty. The re-establishment of Adlershof as a place for science and business became one of Berlin's most important projects in the 1990s – driven by the intention of using the old building stock to create a new structure that would bring university-based and non-university-based research together with commercial enterprises.
The first significant construction project was **BESSY II**, an electron storage ring for the production of synchrotron radiation in the x-ray range. The ring, which became operational in 1998, serves the purpose of material analysis. The design for the building is by Jürgen Brenner, the son of Hermann Brenner, who himself had already realized construction projects in Adlershof for DVL in the 1930s. The storage ring, with a diameter of 120 meters, is located directly adjacent to an affiliated administrative and laboratory building.

BESSY II

Albert-Einstein-Strasse 15 | 1992–1997 | Jürgen Brenner and Partner

Center for Photonics and Optics I

Institute of Mathematics and Computer Science

Around roughly the same time, the new buildings of the so-called innovation and technology centers were also completed. As no real spatial connection exists between these disparate centers, a true ensemble character consequently failed to manifest here, unlike the case for instance with the university buildings in Adlershof or the Aerodynamic Park. Nevertheless, together they represent a focal point for Adlershof as a site for science.

Center for Environmental Technology

Volmerstrasse 9 | 1996–1998 |
Eisele, Fritz and Bott

Center for Photonics and Optics I

Carl-Scheele-Strasse 16 | 1996–1998 |
Sauerbruch Hutton

Center for Photonics and Optics II

Schwarzschildstrasse 10 | 1996–1998 |
Ortner & Ortner BAUKUNST

The buildings adhere to an overarching ecological concept that takes both urban development requirements and flexible usage possibilities for tenants into account.
The Center for Environmental Technology puts these requirements into practice with the aid of suspended ceilings, which allow for the quick conversion of office spaces into laboratories (and vice-versa), while serving as part of the building's cooling system. The over 200-meter-long structure is divided into two units, which are connected to one another via bridges. Thanks to the materials employed and its horizontal arrangement, the building harmonizes well with the character of the urban development outside the center and in the surrounding area.
The story of the multi-part Center for Photonics and Optics is a different one altogether. Several buildings were integrated together into a listed ensemble made up of former academy buildings. The **Center for Photonics and Optics** I consists of two buildings whose design plans are remarkable for their curved and fluid external facades. The organic construction alludes to the form of an amoeba, which is why the buildings are also colloquially referred to as such. In spite of their unusual shape, the buildings are designed with an emphasis on functionality and can be adapted to meet various requirements for use. In particular, special attention has been devoted to the research subject of light in the architecture here. For instance, the facades of both buildings consist of glass in diverse colors; the impression they make is reinforced by sunlight shining through the equally colorful Venetian blinds. By contrast, the **Center for Photonics and Optics II** is based on a cuboid building shape and as such blends in well with the historical academy buildings. Entirely glazed facade sections alternate with irregularly distributed window surfaces on perforated facades. Nonetheless, the irregular facades hint at the flexible usage inherent in the design of the building's interior – an aspect that is of great significance for all innovation centers.

Contemporaneous with the settlement of these centers in Adlershof, institutes of natural science from Humboldt-Universität also made their homes here, forming around Rudower Chaussee the so-called Adlershof Campus, with the Aerodynamic Park in turn lying at its center. This spatial composition gave birth to a shared public space.

Erwin Schrödinger-Zentrum

Institute of Mathematics and Computer Science
Johann von Neumann House

Rudower Chaussee 25 | 1996–1997 | Dörr Ludolf Wimmer Architekten

Institute of Chemistry
Emil Fischer House

Brook-Taylor-Strasse 2 | 1998–2002 | Volker Staab

Institute of Physics
Lise Meitner House

Newtonstrasse 15 | 1999–2003 | augustinundfrankarchitekten

Erwin Schrödinger Center

Rudower Chaussee 26 | 1999–2002 | Gössler, Kinz, Kerber, Kreienbaum Architekten

The **Institute of Mathematics and Computer Science** was able to move into a new building in 1997, one originally planned not for these departments, but as a simple office building instead. However, the heavily used Rudower Chaussee cuts the institute off from the other new university buildings, which effectively divides the envisaged common public space. The building is arranged in a classic comb structure, which one encounters often in Adlershof. Glazed inner courtyards connect the individual parts of the building while muffling traffic noise and lending the building a closed block structure on the side facing the street.

Another university building in Adlershof also exhibits a similar structure: namely, the **Institute of Chemistry**, which stands in the immediate vicinity of Aerodynamic Park and abuts it in the north. The building is characterized by the two-story foyer, which extends across the entire transverse section. The **Institute of Physics** presents itself in a very different light. Although it was also built in very close proximity to Aerodynamic Park, its most characteristic structural component is however its exterior facade. On the one hand, it ensures that sufficient sunlight always penetrates into the building, while on the other hand its construction combines various energy concepts with ecological approaches to research (→220). The choice of the rectangular building form is a conscious attempt to blend in with the surrounding street grid. As previously the case with the technology center buildings, great attention was also paid here to having a flexibly configurable interior suitable for various use scenarios. For instance, individual walls are made of wood and easily repositioned.

The **Erwin Schrödinger Center** lies to the southeast of Aerodynamic Park on Rudower Chaussee. With its inauguration in 2003, the individual branch libraries of the natural science departments, up to that point all housed separately, could be disbanded and brought together in one central library for the natural sciences. The previous system of organization, with separate facilities, was both cost and personnel intensive and unsuitable for the university's future orientation. With the amalgamation of the library stocks in the Erwin Schrödinger Center, a modern and user-oriented library was born. The desire to integrate the historical core of the protected manufacturing halls from the 1930s into the new design was already explicitly formulated in the competition brief and was ultimately implemented as a result. On the inside, the reading room provides for easy orientation with its square layout. This is further supported by a lowered working area in the middle of the room. In addition, the Erwin Schrödinger Center also features lecture halls and serves as the home base for Humboldt-Universität's computer and media service.

Institute of Geography and of Psychology
Alfred Rühl House,
Wolfgang Köhler House

Rudower Chaussee 16 | 2001–2004 | Benedict Tonon, nhp-Architekten

IRIS Adlershof
Integrative Research Institute for the Sciences

Zum großen Windkanal 6 | 2014–2019 | Nickl & Partner

Further university buildings in Adlershof include the **Institute of Geography** and the **Institute of Psychology**. Two of the few remaining preserved GDR barracks buildings were extended with cube-like new structures to this end. The case is similar for the building of **IRIS Adlershof**, which also combines two former barracks buildings with one another via a modern middle section. In this manner, the architecture reflects a web of interconnections that is also present in the work performed at IRIS Adlershof, where diverse fields in the natural sciences pursue research on new projects and ideas together. (SM)

Sustainability and Ecology

219

Climate change and sustainability are issues that have gained increasing public focus over the last few years. In response to this, architectural concepts to reduce energy have been applied in the construction of many new academic buildings in Berlin.

The pioneering "Adlershof 2020+" project in the Berlin district of Adlershof sets new standards for this development in the city. Participants in competitions held by the innovation centers in Adlershof were expected to present an explicitly ecological overall concept, rather than the more usual notion of individual ecological measures. The competition submissions demonstrated an increased adoption of sustainable building materials such as timber, and the installation of photovoltaic units on rooftops, which can be found not only on the technology centers, but on the roofs of numerous new buildings in Adlershof. The solution found at the Institut für Physik at Humboldt-Universität (→215), in which research on the construction of buildings is carried out in a research building at the same time, is particularly noteworthy. In a pilot project for urban ecology supervised by the Technical University, the Humboldt-Universität and the Neubrandenburg University of Applied Sciences, the focus is on the sustainable use of water and energy and also the reduction of construction and operating costs. This approach will provide useful experience for future construction projects. Several different sustainability concepts have been brought together in this building: Rainwater usage, the greening of buildings, and a cooling system that conserves resources.
Rainwater from the roof is collected in several large cisterns and is used for irrigating the green facades. This water is also used for building's cooling system and, too, as an ancillary supply for flushing the toilets. Since the building is not connected to the main drainage system, a possibility had to be created to direct excess water to a pond where it can evaporate. All of the rooftops have been "greened" – or covered with vegetation – to generate evaporative cooling powered by solar energy in the summer, which in turn is used to cool the building. The green facade also contributes to the cooling, though it also plays an aesthetic role by creating a characteristic appearance to the facade while also providing shade during the summer months. The choice of plants was a particularly challenging task: the available plant containers provided barely sufficient space for large roots to grow, and the only provision for climbing plants was the steel girders on the building's facade and additional boat ropes that were strung between them.
The combination of these three sustainability concepts has allowed the energy needs and operating costs of the building to be reduced to a minimum.
However, ecological considerations in the architecture of Berlin's academic buildings go much further back than the Adlershof energy project. The 1973 oil crisis in particular proved to be a catalyst for a discourse on sustainable and ecological construction. As a result, the increasingly emphatic demands for meaningful ecological concepts have influenced architecture since the 1970s.

One of the first university buildings in Berlin to be designed on the basis of an ecological concept was the Institute of Mathematics at Berlin's Technische Universität (→137). Architects Georg Kohlmaier and Barna von Sartory presented an experimental design, and Kohlmaier himself claims that the realization of the project was primarily a response to the student movement, which demanded a modern and future-oriented university. The design incorporated the principle of a greenhouse – though it is actually a hybrid of a greenhouse, a factory, and a skyscraper. At the same time, it is considered a prototype since it is one of the first buildings in Germany

to be based on such an ecological concept, although it was not yet known at the time if this idea would actually work.
The building is characterized by large glass panels that make optimal use of available natural light. Sunshades fitted to the building's exterior function as a second skin, regulating the temperature inside – however, their maintenance has proved to be problematic. The distance between the glass panels and the sunshade is optimized so that a sufficient quantity of warm air can rise upwards and thus prevent the glass from heating up. In addition, the panels are triple glazed. Unlike the other building at the site, the interior walls do not use a drywall construction but are composed of open-pore Bredero concrete blocks that function as thermal accumulators. In order to release the stored heat when needed, thermostats and room sensors would be required, but for reasons of cost these were not included in the final construction. As a result, the energy saving concept is more reliant on the active involvement of the users: during the summer, the windows have to be opened in the evening to facilitate night cooling, and in winter the exterior blinds should not be used for shade. But the concept ultimately failed in practice since it required that the users adapt their behavior, and it was thus not possible to achieve the energy saving targets. A new building is currently being constructed for the Technische Universität's Institute of Mathematics on the eastern area of the site (→144). The future of the Kohlmaier-Sartory building is therefore uncertain. However, as a result of modern technical improvements, the climate concept of the older mathematics building has been widely adopted in northern Europe.

The construction of the Erziehungswissenschaftlichen Bibliothek at the Freie Universität (→180) also incorporated a concept combining energy saving with flexible room usage that allows for a relocation or extension of individual library areas.
The building is constructed using cavity walls with a layer of insulation in between. On the outside, the facades are fitted with a trellis framework for climbing plants, similar to the new building of the Institut für Physik at Humboldt-Universität. Roses, ivy, and vines provide shade during the summer months and in winter when some of the plants lose their leaves, sunlight can pass through unobstructed and thus contribute to heating the building. The flat roofs of the building are covered with a 30 cm layer of soil and planted with wild grasses. The layer of soil absorbs the sun's rays in summertime, which prevents a rapid heating of the building: in winter it provides insulation and stores heat inside the building for longer. Due to this natural climatic regulation, it was not necessary to install an air conditioning system. The underfloor heating is operated using raw water, which also saves energy since no process water must be fed into the system.
A fountain and numerous plants in the atrium help regulate the humidity. Due to cost limitations, it was not possible to install the originally planned sunshades on the glazed gable roof during the construction phase, and as a result the building heats up considerably in the summer.

At the Philologische Bibliothek at the FU (→177), the cavity wall construction is likewise used in combination with two concrete service cores that serve as heat conductors and accumulators.
The outer skin is made of aluminum panels and glass which scatter the natural light, and on the inside there are single-piece fabric blinds. The free space between is used to regulate the climate inside the building: when there is enough wind, individual panels can be opened for thermal balance. Fresh air enters the building via openings at floor level. Concrete core activation has been incorporated into the two service cores in which a system of pipes carrying water is

integrated into the cores. The two-way system can be used to provide stored heat on demand, or conversely it can provide cooling. This makes it possible to regulate the climate within the library in a more natural way. Yet this outer skin has also turned out to be the building's greatest flaw: for some time it has been shown to leak during rain showers, although the cause of this defect does not lie in the architectural design, but in the way it was built. In the Jacob and Wilhelm Grimm Center at the Humboldt-Universität the architects also opted to implement concrete core activation to provide cooling in the summer and heating in the winter.

As part of the extensive renovation of the main tropical greenhouse (→ 169) in the Botanic Garden in Berlin, planners set out to reduce energy costs. As in the case of the Philologischen Bibliothek, the outer skin of the building also proved to be the weak point of the structure. Instead of using glass panes in the reconstruction after World War II, it was decided that Plexiglas should be used. Over time both small and large cracks developed in the acrylic material, reducing the transmission of sunlight and allowing heat to escape. The Plexiglas was later replaced with a new type of insulated glazing which improved UV permeability while reducing heat loss. One of the key elements of the heating system is the air conditioning-ventilation units underneath the main hall. These provide air circulation, and the silica sand granulate contained within the units either binds the airborne water or releases it: this allows precise control of humidity. Two ventilation towers disguised as tropical trees provide auxiliary air circulation by drawing in warm air at the top and blowing it out at the bottom with the help of powerful fans. This simple system has resulted in a considerable reduction of energy costs. The plants are irrigated using mainly rainwater.

The construction of the Holzlaube (wooden pergola) at the Freie Universität (→ 180) was based on a totally different concept of sustainability: the use of a regenerative – and eponymous – building material for the facade cladding that complemented the existing facade structure and materials used in the Rost- und Silberlaube. Cedar wood from North America was used for the structure, sourced from sustainable forests and certified in accordance with the PEFC. This type of wood has a high dimensional stability, making it a good choice for facade cladding. Ultimately, however, the contractor chose not to implement any of the technical innovations in terms of the building technology.

In collaboration with the Leibniz-Institute of Freshwater Ecology and Inland Fisheries, a new building dedicated to biodiversity is to be completed by 2021 on the grounds of the Freie Universität. The building is scheduled to fulfill the strict guidelines of energy-optimized and sustainable construction.

All these buildings and their ecological concepts reflect contemporary architectural efforts to reduce energy requirements and thus the running costs of modern structures, while making efficient use of regenerative energy sources. The fact that some of the concepts were not able to achieve the desired targets was at times due to incorrect implementation during construction, and other times due to the unwillingness of the users to operate the buildings in accordance with recommendations, and also due to cost-cutting measures during construction. (SM)

Institute of Mathematics, TU

Institute of Physics, HU

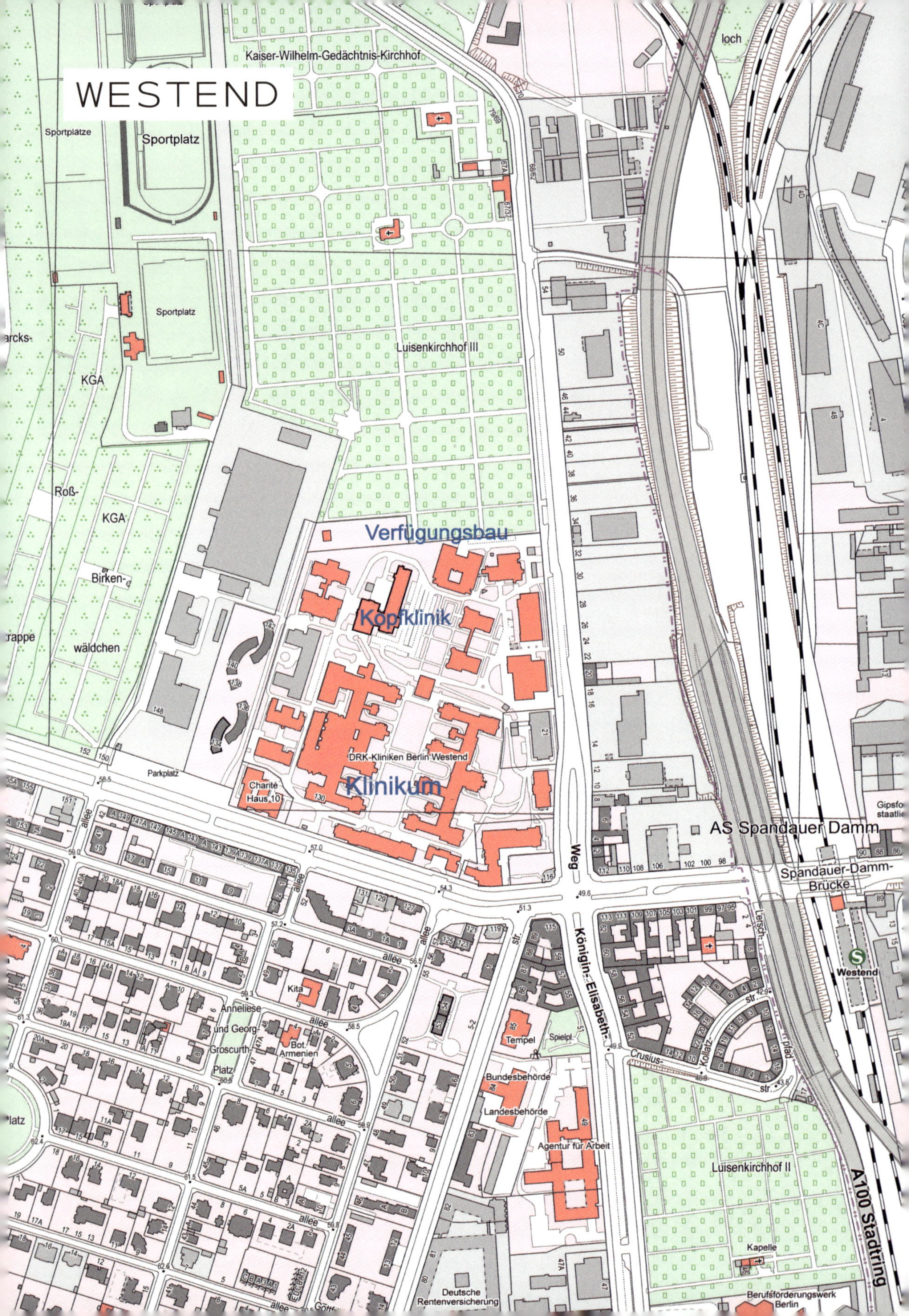
WESTEND
Kaiser-Wilhelm-Gedächtnis-Kirchhof
Sportplätze
Sportplatz
Sportplatz
Luisenkirchhof III
KGA
Roß-
KGA
Birken-
wäldchen
Verfügungsbau
Kopfklinik
DRK-Kliniken Berlin Westend
Klinikum
Charité Haus 10
Parkplatz
AS Spandauer Damm
Spandauer-Damm-Brücke
Westend
Königin-Elisabeth-
Weg
Kita
Anneliese und Georg-Groscurth-Platz
Bot. Armenien
Tempel
Spielpl.
Bundesbehörde
Landesbehörde
Agentur für Arbeit
Crusius-
Kollatz-
str.
Luisenkirchhof II
Kapelle
A100 Stadtring
Deutsche Rentenversicherung
Berufsförderungswerk Berlin
loch
Gipsfo staatlic

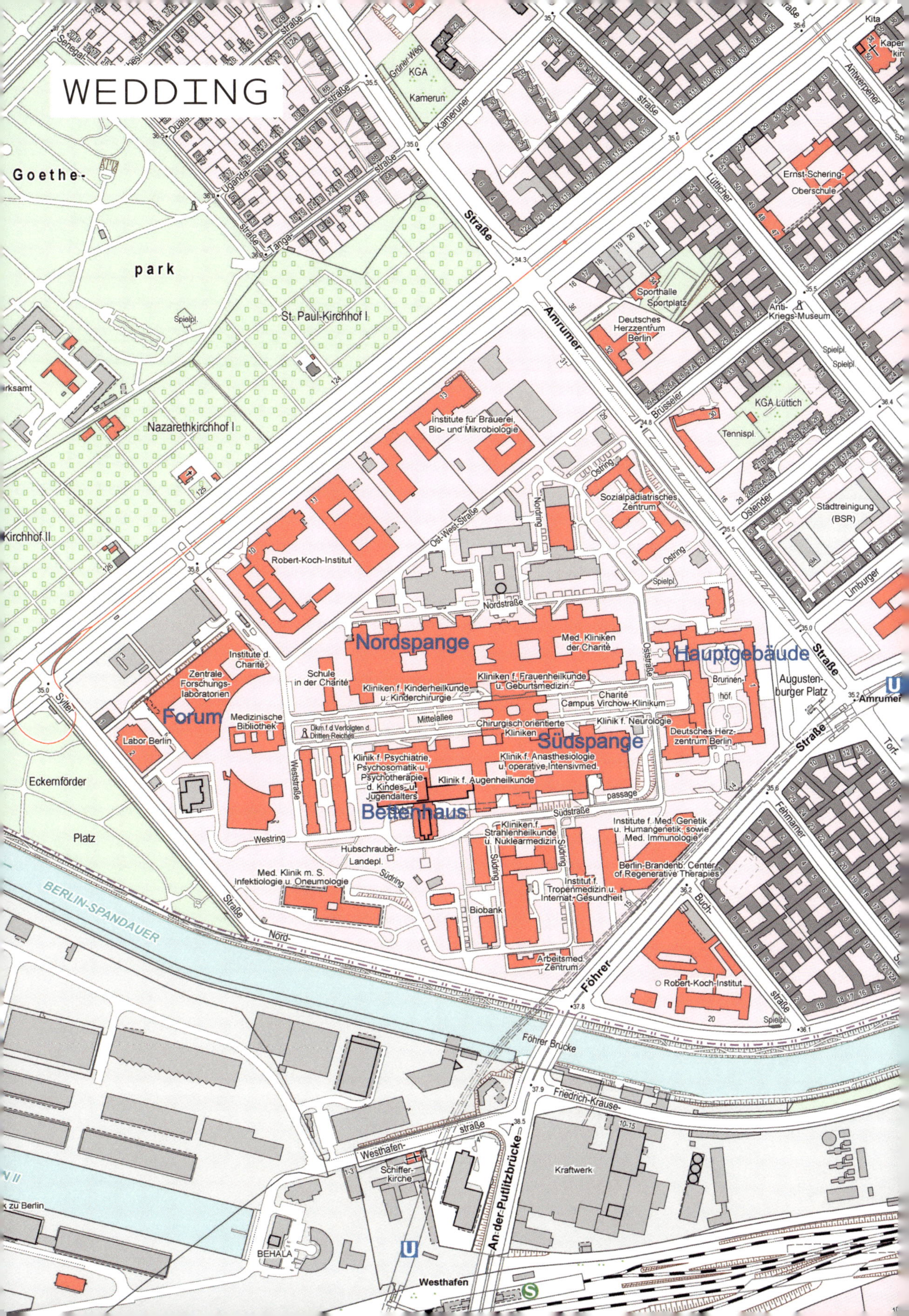
WEDDING
Goethe-
park
St. Paul-Kirchhof I
Nazarethkirchhof I
Kirchhof II
Spielpl.
KGA
Kamerun
Grüner Weg
Kameruner
Straße
Dualastr.
Ugandastr.
Tangastraße
Senegalstr.
Amrumer
Straße
Lütticher
Brüsseler
Ostender
Limburger
Ernst-Schering-Oberschule
Sporthalle
Sportplatz
Deutsches Herzzentrum Berlin
Anti-Kriegs-Museum
KGA Lüttich
Tennispl.
Stadtreinigung (BSR)
Kita
Antwerpener
Institute für Brauerei, Bio- und Mikrobiologie
Robert-Koch-Institut
Ost-West-Straße
Nordring
Ostring
Sozialpädiatrisches Zentrum
Nordstraße
Nordspange
Med. Kliniken der Charité
Hauptgebäude
Institute d. Charité
Zentrale Forschungslaboratorien
Forum
Medizinische Bibliothek
Labor Berlin
Schule in der Charité
Kliniken f. Kinderheilkunde u. Kinderchirurgie
Kliniken f. Frauenheilkunde u. Geburtsmedizin
Charité Campus Virchow-Klinikum
Mittelallee
Chirurgisch orientierte Kliniken
Klinik f. Neurologie
Brunnenhof
Deutsches Herzzentrum Berlin
Südspange
Dkm. f. d. Verfolgten d. Dritten Reiches
Klinik f. Psychiatrie, Psychosomatik u. Psychotherapie d. Kindes- u. Jugendalters
Klinik f. Anästhesiologie u. operative Intensivmed.
Klinik f. Augenheilkunde
passage
Bettenhaus
Weststraße
Westring
Südstraße
Ostrstraße
Augustenburger Platz
Amrumer
Eckernförder
Platz
Sylter
Hubschrauber-Landepl.
Südring
Kliniken f. Strahlenheilkunde u. Nuklearmedizin
Institute f. Med. Genetik u. Humangenetik sowie Med. Immunologie
Berlin-Brandenb. Center of Regenerative Therapies
Institut f. Tropenmedizin u. Internat. Gesundheit
Med. Klinik m. S. Infektiologie u. Pneumologie
Biobank
Arbeitsmed. Zentrum
Robert-Koch-Institut
Föhrer
Straße
Buch-
Fehmarner
Torf-
Nord-
BERLIN-SPANDAUER
Föhrer Brücke
Friedrich-Krause-
Westhafen-
straße
Schifferkirche
Kraftwerk
An der Putlitzbrücke
BEHALA
Westhafen
zu Berlin

LICHTERFELDE
Agentur für Arbeit
KGA Erlenstraße
KGA Bäketal
Schule an der Bäke
Kita
Zentraler Schüler-arbeitsgarten Steglitz
Bäke-
park
Bäketeich
Spielplatz
Friedhof Lichterfelde Moltkestraße
Klingsor-platz
Ludwig-Beck-Platz
Parkplatz
HAFEN STEGLITZ
TELTOWKANAL
Kronachschule
Charité Campus Benjamin Franklin
Universitäts-klinikum
Promenadenteich
BSR-Betriebshof
BWB Betriebshof
KGA Steglitzer Hafen
Schlosspark Lichterfelde
Stadion Lichterfelde
Anna-Essinger-Schule
Institut für Hygiene und Umweltmedizin
FU
Pauluskirche
Dorfkirche Lichterfelde
Sportplätze
„Mäusebunker“
Lilienthalschule
Tennisplätze
Willi-Graf-Schule
Botschaft Äthiopien
Bäkebrücke
Siemens-damm

BUCH
Gemeinde Panketal
Neue Heimstätte für Brustkranke
ZI Herz- und Kreislaufforschung
Krankenanstalten („IV. Irrenanstalt")
Regierungs-krankenhaus I
Spezial-krankenhaus I
Heimstätte für Brustkranke
Alte-Leute-Heim
Buch
Krankenanstalten („III. Irrenanstalt")
Helios-Klinikum
Biobank
Hirn-forschung
Neubau [ZI Krebsforschung]
Genomforschung
MDC

CHARITÉ, NEW SITES

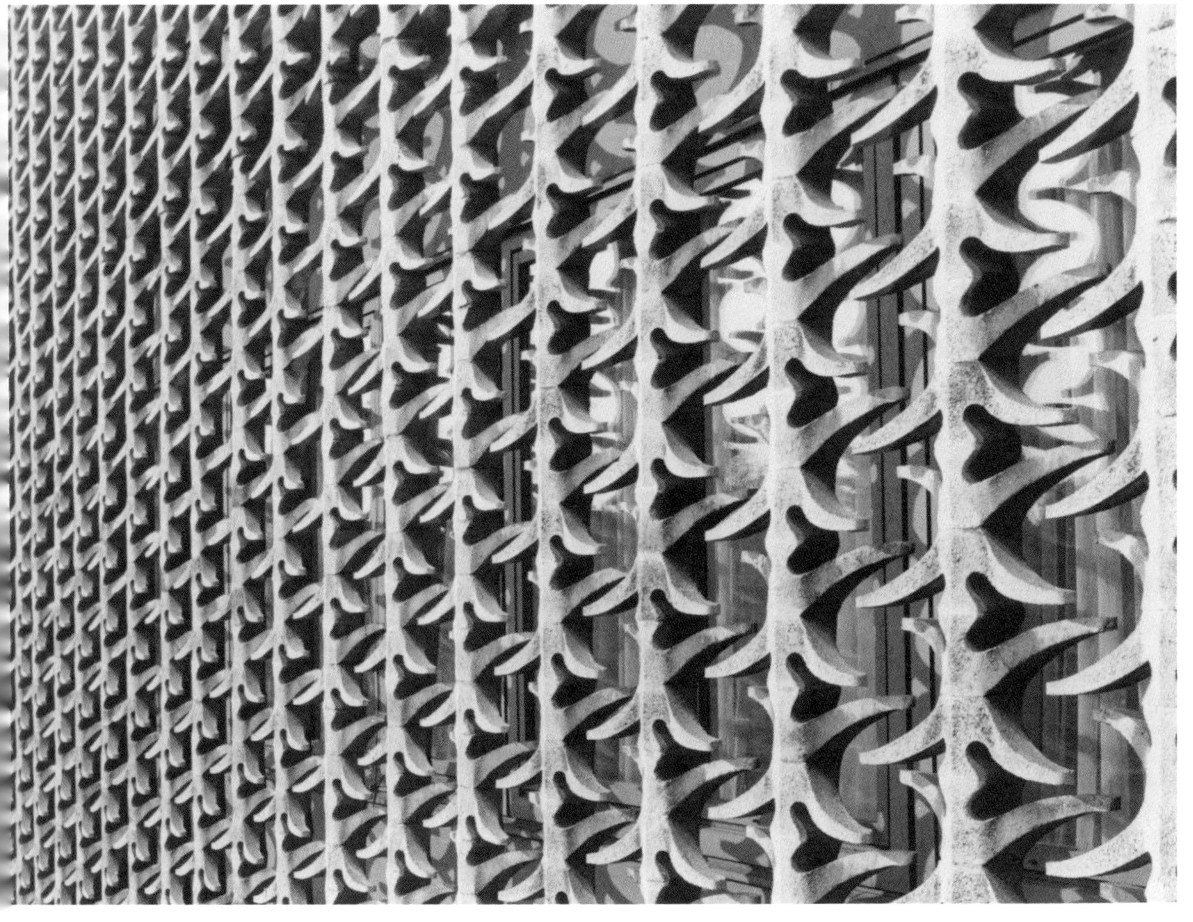

As the largest university clinic in Europe, today Charité is spread out over four different locations in Berlin. Its center lies in Mitte, where it has been providing care for patients without pause since the early eighteenth century, as well as pursuing medical research and training doctors. The Virchow-Klinikum in Wedding, created in the early twentieth century, represents the second oldest part. Specializing in biomedical research, Campus Buch in the north of the city originated from the non-university research facilities that settled in the district in the 1920s as well as from the sanatoriums located there. Campus Benjamin Franklin is the most recent addition, dating back to the post-war period.

The history of university medicine in Berlin has been profoundly shaped by external political influences. The Cold War and the division of the city had a direct impact on the evolution of the sites. The consolidation into Charité University Medicine Berlin was on the other hand entirely due to the conclusion of the Cold War and the transcendence of the aforementioned division.

The consequences of science policy already proved to have a sustained influence on the institution prior to World War I. So it is that one can still recognize to a significant extent the mark left on the present form of Charité Campus Mitte by the influential Prussian science manager Friedrich Althoff, who led efforts to completely redesign the site in the early twentieth century.
In the architectures of the university medical division, one can observe how medical knowledge and the practical approaches of doctors and care personnel have undergone fundamental changes over the centuries. This is already quite evident in the designs of the respective clinics and the external organization of the buildings: whereas the early clinics were preferably housed in a shared building, the pavilion approach prevailed in the second half of the nineteenth century. The first hospital of this kind to appear in Berlin was the City Hospital at Friedrichshain; the Westend Clinic in Charlottenburg followed in the early twentieth century. Architects Martin Gropius and Heino Schmieden virtually specialized in this type of construction. Not only did they design of these two clinics, they were also responsible for the university clinics for surgery, ophthalmology, and gynecology and obstetrics on Ziegelstrasse (→ 53). Compared with the traditional corridor building style, the pavilions had the advantage that they could be better ventilated. Sophisticated building technology was employed here, in a manner that would become a model for many more clinics to come.
It was not only technical advantages that tipped the scale in favor of this building type: the separate-standing buildings (or, as in the case of the Virchow-Klinikum, separate, but linked via passageways) also gave expression to the increasing differentiation and specialization in the field of human medicine. As a function of this evolution, the needs of the various specialties were different when it came to clinical buildings. While surgeons, for instance, required operating theaters with the best possible lighting conditions, other disciplines were concerned above all with having efficiently arranged laboratory spaces. Enrollment figures for medicine were growing, and so larger teaching spaces, namely lecture halls, had to be made available. Collections and libraries supported instruction and research and thus also had to be housed adequately. Significant advancements were being made in the nursing and care of patients, which led to a shift away from large hospital wards towards rooms featuring one, two, or (at most) four beds. Hygiene standards were evolving due to increasing knowledge about the origins of infections. The fact that reformist ideas regarding the optimal approach to caring for the sick exerted an influence on planning especially at the turn of the twentieth century can still be observed today in the park-like facilities in which the clinic buildings were embedded.
The representative function of the buildings for medicine had clearly taken a back seat to growing technical demands. Whereas the earlier clinic buildings had also always been conceived to symbolically emphasize the significance of the work performed within their walls, today utilitarian structures are given priority when it comes to housing facilities for high-tech medicine – which is doubtless to the benefit of patients as well.

KLINIKUM WESTEND, CHARLOTTENBURG

Hospital complex with head clinic and annex building at the upper left edge of the picture

Clinic

Klinikum Westend

Spandauer Damm 130 | 1901–1904, 1905–1907 | Heino Schmieden, Julius Boethke | extensions 1912–1916 by Heinrich Seeling, Wilhelm Winkler, Richard Ermisch | 1913 creation of the hospital garden | Erwin Barth

Towards the end of the nineteenth century, the then still independent city of Charlottenburg found itself in a phase of strong population growth. Along with the population, the number of sick individuals who needed care was also growing. As a consequence, planning for a large-scale hospital featuring 600 beds on the grounds of the former horse market at Spandauer Damm was begun in 1895. The complex Heino Schmieden designed in co-operation with physician Fritz Karl Bessel-Hagen, who became the first director of the **Clinic**, consisted of an ensemble of red brick buildings in the style of the German Renaissance, from which the four-story administrative building protruded with its middle gable and elevated central section. The remaining structures, which were grouped in a horseshoe shape, were realized in pavilion form, the preferred style for clinic buildings in this period. Patients were accommodated within them, and a bathing and an operation house were added for good measure. Bessel-Hagen made sure that the latest advances in hygiene and microbiology were taken into account in the planning, and thus the clinic, above all due to its separate septic and aseptic operation areas, became a model for hospital construction in this era. The grounds were steadily expanded in the years that followed. The doctor and poet Gottfried Benn worked in the spacious pathology hall around 1912 for more than a year. Due to the clinic's slightly elevated location and the associated improvement in atmospheric conditions over other parts of Charlottenburg, the emphasis in the early years lay on the care of tuberculosis sufferers.

In World War II, all of the buildings were either heavily damaged or destroyed, although a large portion is still preserved today. The reconstruction that took place from 1946 on was combined with a modernization of the clinic. It was here that the first successful open heart surgery performed in Germany took place in 1954, and 1963 marked the occasion of the first kidney transplant.

Dedicated rooms for teaching and research like lecture halls and laboratories were created, particularly as the clinic functioned as a research and teaching facility for Freie Universität for the training of its medical students starting in 1948. In 1961, Klinikum Westend officially became a university clinic, and in 1971 it became a university medical center of the FU through the assignment of further clinics; the FU continued to operate it for some time in parallel to the Klinikum Benjamin Franklin in Steglitz, before giving it up in the 1980s in favor of the Virchow-Klinikum. Since 1991, the hospital has been run by the German Red Cross, though it remains a Charité teaching hospital.

Head Clinic

Spandauer Damm 130 | 1963–1969 | Peter Poelzig, Josef Paul Kleihues | 1998–2001 renovation by Pawlik + Partner

Building for general use

building 31 | 1977–1980 | Peter Poelzig, Cornelius Hertling

The most striking new building to be added after the war was the so-called **Head Clinic**, a ten-story structure consisting of two connected building sections. While the high-rise wing contains rooms for patients, the perpendicular block features treatment and operating rooms. A modern **building for general use** was erected in the late 1970s. The surgery and urology facilities were expanded in the 1980s by Günter Saleh Debye.

CAMPUS VIRCHOW-KLINIKUM, WEDDING

The Charité Campus Virchow-Klinikum in Wedding was built as a city hospital between the years 1899 and 1906. Rudolf Virchow, the hospital's namesake, was involved in the planning until his death in 1902. The new clinic combined the most up-to-date medical techniques and large-scale care for the sick – the facility boasted no fewer than 2,000 beds – with an urban development complex that recalled a garden city. The **main building** at Augustenburger Platz, whose exterior form plays on the architecture of a Baroque palace complex, has served as the entrance to the complex up to the present day. Like its historical reference point, the main building also possesses a forecourt. Also connected to the gatehouse in the main building to this day is a 500-meter-long, tree-lined boulevard on whose sides approximately twenty-five pavilions once stood, arranged symmetrically. Further pavilions were distributed over the grounds behind them. Alongside the boulevard, the individual specialist clinics took up their positions, strictly divided according to the patients' sex. In the southern section of the complex, and thus on the north bank of the Spandau ship canal, stood separate pavilions that served as isolation wars for those suffering infectious diseases. On the opposite side (today a road running east to west), were to be found the buildings housing the technical systems, including a high water tower. The Institute of Anatomy and Pathology marked the western end of Mittelallee.

Main building

Augustenburger Platz 1 | 1898–1906 | Ludwig Hoffmann | 1984–1985 expanded for the German Heart Center, Helmut von Werz, Johann Christoph Ottow, Erhard Bachmann, Michel Marx

The chief architect, Ludwig Hoffmann, had envisioned a hospital complex on a human scale, a "city for the sick", as Kaiser Wilhelm II referred to it at the inauguration ceremony – a hospital town surrounded by greenery as in Berlin-Buch too (→243), for the sprawling park complex was an integral part of the concept. The main building was the only structure featuring significant representative ornamentation – the copper clad clock tower on the roof and the visual allusion to the stairwell on the facade stand out in particular; in contrast the buildings were kept rather plain.

The fact that Robert Koch's Prussian Institute for Infectious Diseases (previously in Mitte) had taken up quarters right across the way in 1901 may have played a part in the choice of this location. The institute moved onto the Virchow grounds in 1906 and was soon absorbed by the clinic. The experimental department was carved out again later as the Robert Koch Institute, while the clinical department is still in operation here today.

Bettenhaus, 1962

Forum, new construction of research building and teaching building

Bettenhaus

Westring | 1957–1962 | Peter Poelzig | surgery | used today as an administrative building

"Südspange" building

Mittelallee (south) | 1979–1991 | Helmut von Werz, Johann Christoph Ottow, Erhard Bachmann, Michel Marx

"Nordspange" building

Mittelallee (north) | 1988–1996 | Johann Christoph Ottow, Erhard Bachmann, Michel Marx, Georg Brechensbauer

Forum

Sylter Strasse | 1990–1994 | Deubzer & KönigMarx, Brechensbauer

Like almost all of Berlin's hospitals, the Virchow-Klinikum also suffered serious damage from aerial bombardment during World War II. Hardly anything remains of the original pavilion array, due in particular to the fact that additional major alterations were also made to the historical building stock in the scope of post-war reconstruction. The **Bettenhaus**, a high-rise building for patient accommodation, grafted onto the ensemble, accompanied by an adjoining low-rise building as a treatment wing for the surgery department, already managed to rupture the original structure of the pavilion complex.

In 1974, a competition for a redesign of the site was announced. In its wake, the campus would be fundamentally altered. To the south of Mittelallee, new buildings were erected for the surgical departments with the **Südspange**, or "South Brace", while on the north side with the **Nordspange**, or "North Brace", the departments of internal medicine, gynecology, and pediatrics received new structures. The pavilions had to make way for a two-story block development, whose individual components are all connected underground with the central radiology department located on the historical transverse axis.

These remodeling efforts went hand in hand with a change in status for the clinic, which was known from 1986/87 on as the University Clinic Rudolf Virchow, instead of the Westend Clinics. Briefly affiliated to Humboldt-Universität starting in 1995, the hospital merged in 1997 with Charité to become the Medical Faculty Charité of Humboldt-Universität, and then in 2003 with the Clinic Steglitz (Benjamin Franklin) becoming Charité University Medical Center Berlin. The resulting increased significance of research and teaching would soon also be acknowledged with new architectural development. The so-called **Forum** was created on the western end of Mittelallee, a semi-circular structure that is built around the old pathology building. The matter-of-fact, cuboid shaped building houses rooms for academic instruction as well as clinical and research laboratories.

Only very few traces remain of Ludwig Hoffmann's "city for the sick" today. The former Institute of Pathology at the end of Mittelallee is used today as a library, and along Föhrer Strasse one can still observe former quarantine pavilions. The former pavilions for the treatment of skin and venereal diseases are also still present, as well as buildings from the former business wing, including the nearly fifty-meter-tall water tower, still visible from afar. (GM)

CAMPUS BENJAMIN FRANKLIN, LICHTERFELDE

Enormous concrete formwork, ramps, floating building sections, remarkable facades, and unusual designs set the three most striking buildings of Campus Benjamin Franklin radically apart from their environment. In their choice of materials and execution, they pay homage to medical progress, to urban automobile circulation, to technology, to architectonic possibilities, and to the natural sciences.

University Clinic Benjamin Franklin

former Clinic Steglitz, FU

Hindenburgdamm 30 | Curtis Davis, Franz Mocken (executive architect) | 1994 University Clinic

In 1960, Berlin's House of Representatives passed a resolution to build the Clinic Steglitz, today's **University Clinic Benjamin Franklin**. There had been calls to establish a hospital in Berlin's former American sector since the 1950s; now this vision could be realized with the support of the Benjamin Franklin Foundation and became Germany's first large hospital. Following the US-American example, and as already put to the test by the Berlin university medical center on Ziegelstrasse, care for the sick, research, and instruction were to be brought together in one location. The cleverly nested structure of the individual slices of the building and the elaborate facade cladding – a suspended concrete grid facade that calls to mind spinal column structures – provide for the most efficient processes possible in everyday clinic operations, as well as for sufficient sunlight protection and privacy.

Institute of Hygiene and Environmental Medicine

former Institute of Hygiene and Medical Microbiology

Hindenburgdamm 27, Krahmerstrasse 1 | 1968–1974 (planning from 1964) | Fehling + Gogel, contributors: Jürgen Kümmel, Manfred Walz

A location in direct proximity, between Hindenburgdamm and Teltow Canal, was chosen for today's **Institute of Hygiene and Environmental Medicine**. Embedded between the neo-Gothic Pauluskirche church from 1900, the old Lichterfelde village green, and the small Carstenn castle from the late eighteenth century with its accompanying park, the extraordinary concrete structure is, in its approach to material and form, a shining example of Brutalism, an architectural style that reveals its own construction and material aspect as openly as possible

University Clinic Benjamin Franklin

Institute of Hygiene and Environmental Medicine

and prefers to make use of exposed concrete. The name is derived from "béton brut", the French expression for raw concrete. By staggering building sections and moving the main entrance to Krahmerstrasse, an attempt was made to integrate the building into the fabric of the urban landscape around it. The stairwells, which tower above like chimneys, the curvaceous, fluid forms, and porthole windows all take up the expressive architectural vocabulary of modernist masters such as Le Corbusier or Hans Scharoun. Clearly divided according to function, the building areas are separated into sections for teaching, administration, and research – an arrangement that also recalls the conception of the Institute of Inorganic Chemistry (→ 185), which is itself inspired in turn by the Bauhaus Building in Dessau. Admittedly, there was definitely a significant amount of debate regarding more open structures, as evidenced in particular in the consolidation plans for the former faculties of the humanities and natural sciences in the Rostlaube and Silberlaube complexes. Alas, clear and strict requirements for everyday teaching and research practices ruled out the use of diaphanous forms such as these. In particular for an institute conducting experiments with a high risk of infection and bacteriological-serological studies, it was only logical in the end that parts of the building instead be realized within what effectively amounts to a high-security wing.

Mäusebunker
former central animal laboratories of the FU

Krahmerstrasse 6–12 | 1971–1974, 1978–1980 | Gerd Hänska, Kurt Schmersow (contributor)

The neighboring building known as the **Mäusebunker** (or "Mice Bunker"), which houses Freie Universität's central animal laboratories, possesses, whether in spite or precisely because of its extreme functionality, an impressive, virtually chilling architecture, which evokes associations with steam or space ships. There are but few windows here – the air intake and exhaust are conducted via a complex system of pipes. Clad with concrete plating and isolated so as to ensure hygiene and security, the walls and roof overlap. The four operational floors are separated by additional utility floors. It remains uncertain whether the Mäusebunker will also be placed under a preservation order as has already occurred for the Institute of Hygiene and Environmental Medicine. (MW)

CAMPUS BERLIN-BUCH

Hospital Facilities Berlin-Buch

Heimstätte für Brustkranke
Alt-Buch 74 | 1900–1905 | Ludwig Hoffmann | from 1963 Medical Area IV, additionally referred to as "Waldhaus"

III. Irrenanstalt
Karower Strasse 11 | 1900–1906 | Ludwig Hoffmann | from 1945 Hufeland Hospital, from 1963 Medical Area II, additionally referred to as "Christoph Wilhelm Hufeland"

Alte-Leute-Heim
Zepernicker Strasse 1 | 1905–1908 | Ludwig Hoffmann | from 1963 Medical Area III, additionally referred to as "Ludwig Hoffmann"

IV. Irrenanstalt (planned name)
Wiltbergstrasse 50 | 1909–1914 | Ludwig Hoffmann | from 1914 reserve military hospital | from 1940 city hospital | from 1963 Medical Area

Neue Heimstätte für Brustkranke
Hobrechtsfelder Chaussee 150 | 1914–1916 | Ludwig Hoffmann | 1927–1929 completion by Martin Wagner | 1963 Medical Area V or Ernst Ludwig Home

Far removed from Berlin's other science buildings, towards the end of the nineteenth and at the beginning of the twentieth century the first care facilities – initially nursing homes and sanatoria – were created in the district of Buch. Prior to 1920, Buch did not yet belong to Berlin, although the city used large swaths of land located there as sewage farms. The care facilities were spread out over the entire settlement area in Buch and together represented Europe's largest "hospital city", with over 5,000 beds. Berlin's head of city planning Ludwig Hoffmann was in charge of planning and realizing the buildings. All in all, thirteen hospital facilities were built in Berlin-Buch, in five separate complexes: the Home for Tuberculosis Sufferers, the III. Irrenanstalt (3rd Mental Asylum), the Alte-Leute-Heim (Home for the Elderly), the IV. Irrenanstalt (4th Mental Asylum), and the Neue Heimstätte für Brustkranke (New Home for Tuberculosis Sufferers).

Beyond merely building simple hospitals, Hoffmann, a product of the late-period Schinkel school of architecture, wanted instead to create total architectonic works through the inclusion of generous park complexes and inner courtyards. For his buildings in Buch, he combined diverse architectural styles. Due to the imposing spatial design of the main building and the vastness of the park grounds, several complexes resemble a Baroque palace complex more than a medical facility. By contrast, Hoffmann's last building in Buch, the New Home for Tuberculosis Sufferers, differentiated itself clearly from its predecessors in its external appearance, as the individual buildings were realized as modest stucco structures whose spatial design was also kept very simple. Hoffmann's creations left an indelible mark on Buch's urban landscape, and with them the cornerstone had been laid for further development and expansion in the medical field.

Institute for Brain Research with former roofed corridor to the research clinic (part of the Robert Rössle Clinic), background right Cemetery chapel (demolished in 1951)

Institute for Brain Research

Oskar and Cécile Vogt House

Robert-Rössle-Strasse 10 | 1929–1931 | Carl Sattler | from 1947 laboratories of the Institute of Medicine and Biology | 1996–1998 conversion measures for Innovation and Incubation Center for Biotechnology Companies

Starting in the late 1920s, the Kaiser Wilhelm Society (KWG) was on the lookout for a new location for the **Institute for Brain Research** run by Oskar Vogt. Buch, now officially part of Berlin, lent itself to this objective particularly well due to its already existent health care infrastructure. A site that was originally earmarked for a cemetery but had proven unsuitable for the purpose was available for development. Vogt argued that the close proximity of the research institute to the 3rd Mental Asylum would open up new possibilities for scientific collaboration, the likes of which Europe had never before seen.

Carl Sattler designed the institute building in close collaboration with Oskar Vogt in the style of the New Objectivity. Due to its east-west alignment, the elongated six-story structure provided enough sunlight for laboratory work and was able to accommodate the various scientific departments – including special rooms and areas for keeping monkeys and dogs as test subjects. Like the preserved buildings in Dahlem, the institute building inaugurated in 1930 in Buch stands as an architectonic representation of German cutting-edge research, although unlike the case in the imperial era, the institute architecture of the Weimar Republic dared to embrace modernism. In 1932, the complex was extended with a research clinic featuring forty beds and accessible via a passageway. The KWI for Brain Research was an especially important place of work for the scientist Nikolai Wladimirovich Timoféeff-Ressovsky, who played a crucial role in establishing the institute's department of genetics. In 1935, together with Max Delbrück and Karl Zimmer he described the physical structure of genes, thus founding the field of modern molecular genetics.
Oskar Vogt, who studied "extraordinary brains" together with his wife Cécile and was permitted to travel to Moscow in 1925 in order to dissect Lenin's brain into thousands of slices there, ran afoul of political enemies and was replaced as institute director in 1937. In the aftermath, a reorientation took place, in particular towards a stronger affiliation with the "race research" pursued under National Socialism. New military structures at the institute favored an inclusion in the Nazis' euthanasia program, and from 1940 to 1945 several hundred brains belonging to victims of the mass murder of the mentally ill or handicapped were examined there.

With the conclusion of the war, the Soviet Army took over control of Berlin-Buch and the medical facilities located there. The city hospital became the central military hospital of the Red Army and would remain occupied until 1950. The 1950s were characterized by numerous new openings of clinics and individual departments. For the most part, these took up quarters in vacant buildings of Ludwig Hoffmann's former hospital complex.

The most extensive restructuring of the medical facilities in Buch took place at the beginning of 1963. The individual hospitals were amalgamated into the City Clinic Berlin-Buch, now with nearly 5,000 beds the largest hospital in the GDR and indeed all of Europe. The merger gave birth to a hospital capable of offering much wider care, in which individual medical disciplines were able to co-operate with one another better and more cost-effectively. Due to the size of the city clinic and its large number of clinical disciplines, Buch was also incorporated into the teaching curriculum for students at Humboldt-Universität's Faculty of Medicine.

In the 1970s, two new hospital buildings were erected in restricted areas under military guard that were not accessible to the general public. The **Governmental Hospital I** was built from 1973 to 1976. This six-story building was laid out in a T shape. The clinic featured 110 beds and diverse clinical departments, in addition to being exceptionally well equipped from a technical point of view. In case of war, the basement floor of the special pavilion was designed to serve as a protective structure.

A **Special Hospital** was built right next to the Government Hospital starting in 1976: the so-called Stasi Hospital (for the East German state security service). As large swaths of the Bucher Forst woods had to be cleared for the construction, the local population reacted in protest to the project. Upon its completion in 1980, the hospital boasted seven stories and 260 beds. With their striking simplicity, both facilities stood out sharply in their architectonic design from the typical new Berlin hospital buildings realized as pre-fab high-rise blocks, while in both choice of materials and facade design they resembled contemporary Western architecture.

Governmental Hospital I
Special Clinic of the Ministerial Council
Berlin-Buch

Wiltbergstrasse, on the corner of
Hobrechtsfelder Chaussee | 1973–1976 |
Roland Korn and Joachim Härter

Special Hospital
Stasi Hospital

Hobrechtsfelder Chaussee 96 |
1976–1980

Robert Rössle Clinic, park view and main entrance

The KWI for Brain Research was also under Soviet control following World War II. In 1947, the building was handed over to the Academy of Sciences of Berlin and renamed the Institute of Medicine and Biology. This marked the genesis of the second generation of medical-biological research in Berlin-Buch. In the years to come, the existing institute grew to include further research departments and employees. In a manner analogous to that of the new clinics springing up at the same time, these new additions occupied already existent buildings of Ludwig Hoffmann's former hospital complexes. In 1961, the first restructuring of the institute took place with the carving out of several departments, and in 1965 the Institute for Cardiovascular Research received a building of its own on Lindenberger Weg. With the academy reform plan of 1972, three central institutes or CI's were founded.

CI for Cardiovascular Research
Franz Volhard Clinic

Wiltbergstrasse 50 | 1956–1957 | Franz Ehrlich, Bauhaus pupil | from 1958 Institute for Cortico-Visceral Pathology and Therapy | from 1992 Franz Volhard Clinic

CI for Cancer Research
Robert Rössle Clinic

Lindenberger Weg 80 | 1961–1968 | new construction of the operating building, designed by Roland Jaenisch and a collective | from 1949 Clinic for Oncological Diseases | from 1960 Robert Rössle Clinic | 2018 demolition for new building (→252)

The **CI for Cardiovascular Research** took up quarters in the already existing Franz Volhard Clinic, a building realized in accordance with the principles of organic construction of the 1920s and among the most important creations of Franz Ehrlich. As with the KWI for Brain Research before it, the design process was carried out in close collaboration with the clinic director. Featuring rooms arranged by function equipped with floor-to-ceiling windows and doors and soundproof rooms aligned along a garden courtyard, the completed structure gained recognition around the world – especially due to the fact that the sleep clinic was without any international precedent. The **CI for Cancer Research** found a home in the Robert Rössle Clinic on Lindenberger Weg. The two-story structure added on to the operating building documents the shift from a rudimentarily existent individual construction approach to an industrial one.

The structure of the central institutes of the GDR's Academy of Sciences – which also included a CI for Molecular Biology with a laboratory buiding erected between 1974 and 1980 that became the Max-Delbrück-Haus of the MDC – would continue to exist until the end of 1991, before these would ultimately be shut down in accordance with the terms of the reunification agreement.

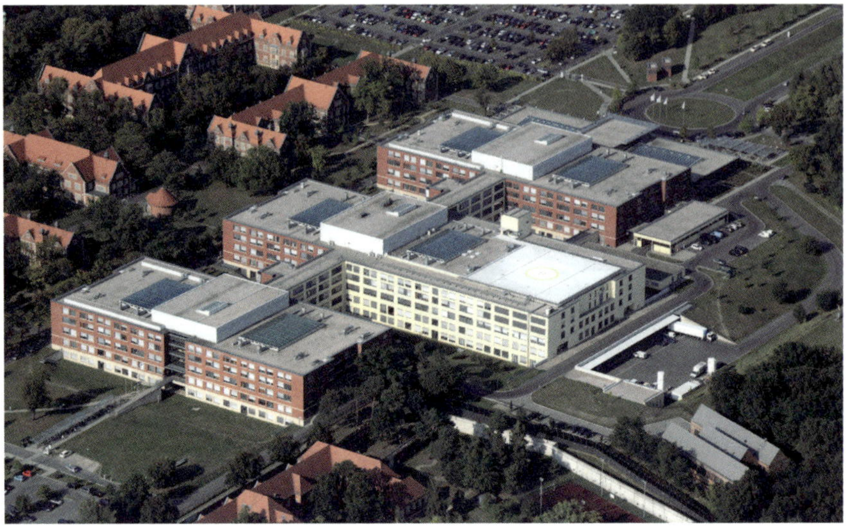

Helios Hospital

Schwanebecker Chaussee 50 | 2004–2007 | TMK Architekten.Ingenieure

Laboratory Building for Genome Research
Timoféeff-Ressovsky-Haus

Robert-Rössle-Strasse 10 | 2006 | Volker Staab

After reunification, the future of the hospital and the three former central institutes was more than uncertain. With the founding of the Campus Berlin-Buch as a science and technology park in 1990, a first step was taken towards preservation. The Max Delbrück Center for Molecular Medicine (MDC) founded on the Campus Berlin-Buch in 1992 continued the legacy of biomedical research in Berlin-Buch. At the same time, the MDC also initiated the third generation of research. Due to funding difficulties, the Robert Rössle Clinic and Franz Volhard Clinic could not be merged with the MDC, but were instead initially attached to Freie Universität's Virchow Clinic, before finally becoming part of Charité University Medical Center in 1997.

In 2001 on the other hand, the private Helios Clinic Group took over ownership of the two clinics, purchasing the former Buch City Hospital in addition the same year. The acquisition resulted in various restructuring measures and the closing of entire clinical departments. From 2004 to 2007, a new building was constructed for the **Helios Hospital**, situated to the south of the old buildings of the former Hufeland Hospital (previously the 3rd City Mental Asylum). With its triple-row construction arrangement, the new structure established an architectural connection with Ludwig Hoffmann's old three-section complex for the 3rd Mental Asylum facility. The complex's historical old buildings were restored little by little and thus made available for use by various private clinics and medical institutions.

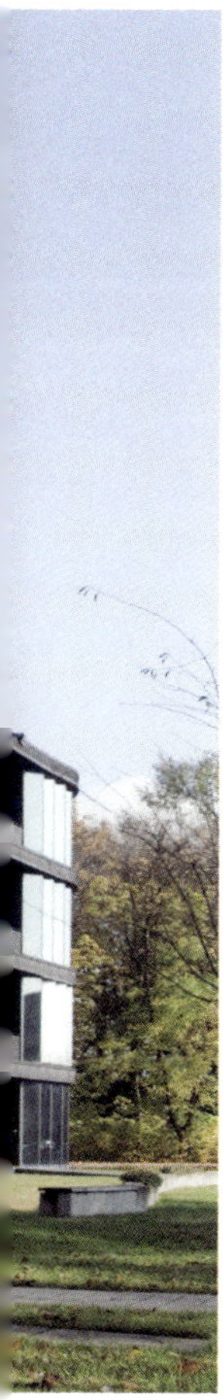

From the mid 1990s, the Campus Berlin-Buch was successively expanded with the addition of new buildings, without losing its historic core in the process. The buildings of the former KWI for Brain Research underwent renovation and modernization following the relevant guidelines for listed structures, and were integrated into the campus just as the earlier buildings of Ludwig Hoffmann and those from the GDR era had been previously. Since the dawn of the new millennium, further new buildings have carefully extended the existing inventory of buildings while preserving the ensemble structure. In this regard for instance, the new construction for a **Laboratory Building for Genome Research**, realized according to plans by Volker Staab, also adds a new impulse to the Campus Berlin-Buch. The curvaceous building form takes up the contours of the adjoining forest and extends them. At the same time, the corner of the building that houses the main entrance is shifted into the campus's primary axis and thus forms a sort of end point. A laboratory lies at the heart of the building, around which individual office wings are arranged.

In 2016, a new building for a **Biobank** was created on the campus right next to the Laboratory Building for Genome Research. The single-story construction, small in comparison to the other buildings here, manages to impress with its compact structure, which can be expanded if need be. In spite of its minimal size, the research building serves well as a place to meet up and communicate – an outdoor bench around the perimeter invites passers-by to stop and stay a while.

Biobank of the Max Delbrück Center

Robert-Rössle-Strasse 10 | 2014–2016 |
Heide & von Beckerath

New building for research space at the Robert Rössle Institute

Käthe Beutler House

Lindenberger Weg 80 | 2016–2020 |
kleyer.koblitz.letzel.freivogel.architekten

The **new building for research space at the Robert Rössle Institute** is being erected at the location of the CI for Cancer Research and is supposed to be distinguished by clear architecture and flexible options for use, and thus also expand on the existing structures in a meaningful manner.

Today, some 3,000 people work in over fifty companies on the grounds of Campus Berlin-Buch. Berlin's universities are also increasingly taking advantage of the special possibilities for collaboration offered by the location in Buch. This co-operation between the city's universities and medical facilities dates all the way back to the Weimar Republic. The first dissertation by a student of the Friedrich Wilhelm University of Berlin to be supervised in Buch was already published in 1930, for instance. As was already the case back in the GDR era, several of the clinics serve as teaching hospitals of the Charité University Medical Center Berlin, and nearly 400 doctoral candidates from the Berlin partner universities TU, FU, and HU are currently pursuing research at the Max Delbrück Center.

In 2013, the MDC and Charité founded a joint center for clinical research in Buch, the Berlin Institute of Health (BIH). The center's mission is to reduce the period of time it takes for results from fundamental research to be applied in the treatment of patients. Since 2019, the MDC has also been represented by a new structure in Berlin-Mitte. The building of the Berlin Institute for Medical Systems Biology (BIMSB) is located on Humboldt-Universität's North Campus on Hannoversche Strasse 28. This site is the first extension of the MDC outside of Berlin-Buch, and thus underscores the intense co-operation among Berlin's academic institutions for the study of medicine. (SM)

Percent for Art, Monuments, and the City

253

Art that is associated with architecture, formally known as "percent for art", is regulated and defined by official guidelines: A certain portion of the total construction costs, usually 1 percent, is allocated for such art and public or semi-public tenders are invited from applicants. Historic monuments are protected by law, classified, listed, and placed in categories. Every German federal state classifies its monuments as building monuments, cultural monuments, industrial monuments or landscape monuments.
Percent for art can evade our perception, it can inspire and confuse us, but it only works in association with architecture if the external space, the architecture, the facade, and the artwork itself have a relation to one another. However, percent for art has the potential to sharpen our senses, to create an atmosphere and a sense of space, to give structure to a square, to establish associations, and in special cases to deepen our knowledge and promote concentration. The interplay between art and academic architecture generates a broad spectrum of effects and impressions.
This selection of recent works, chosen from the wealth of existing monuments, artworks, and installations, encompasses those which are casually familiar, perhaps generally unnoticed, or newly installed creations by predominantly younger artists. The main focus is on the interplay between the city, its architecture, its protagonists and the space in which they live and work.

Many of the university ensembles in Berlin are richly adorned with sculptural works. There are memorials and monuments, statues, commemorative sites, and artistically creative memorial plaques that are dedicated to people or historic events. Works of art make clear reference to individual architectures or their urban context. Interventions can only be apprehended by walking through them, around them or interacting with their multi-faceted dimensions.

Some works perform multiple roles within a setting: as formal design elements, as an eye-catching decoration, or for educational purposes. In the rear-facing green space of the Technische Universität main building stands an Ionic column between the laboratories and workshop buildings. The structure, built by Karl Friedrich Schinkel, once formed part of the portal of the church – which was demolished in 1893 – that stood on the current site of the Berlin Dom.
There is also a pair of doric columns by August Stüler which between 1857 and 1907 adorned the customs house of the Charlottenburg Bridge.
These are complemented by three Tuscan column shafts and a delicately styled **arcade**.

Arcade

Ruin, former arched hall

Strasse des 17. Juni, Fasanenstrasse (previously junction of Chausseestrasse, Oranienburger Tor) | 1858–1860 | Johann Heinrich Strack | 1886 closure | 1887 demolition | 1901 reconstruction in the gardens of the former Technical College by Carl Vohl, commisioned by Julius Kohtes

Königliche Gärtnerlehranstalt

Specialty food technology and materials science, TU Berlin

Königin-Luise-Strasse 22 | 1902–1903 | Theodor Echtermeyer (overall plan), Preller (architecture) | augmented in the 1950s and 1960s | 1983 refurbishment and reconstruction, Eberhard Fink | used by the TU Berlin and the Königliche Gartenakademie | 2012–2014 restoration

In its original location, the arcade formed the street-facing frontage of the Borsig-Werke and served as an attractive visual barrier to the machine engineering facility behind. Generations of architecture students have made detailed sketches here.

In those city districts where university departments have a strong presence, one often finds natural and landscape monuments: the ginkgo tree in the inner courtyard of the Humboldt-Universität main building, the yew tree in front of the Freie Universität's Institute of Biology at Königin-Luise-Platz, the grounds of the Technische Universität's Institute of Architecture at Ernst-Reuter-Platz, which itself is a garden monument, and also the garden courtyard of the Staatsbibliothek and the front garden of the Museum für Naturkunde.

Located on the corner of Königin-Luise-Strasse and Arnimallee in Berlin-Dahlem one finds the former **Königliche Gärtnerlehranstalt** (Royal Gardening School). Like the ensemble of the former Landwirtschaftlichen Hochschule (→ 77), the Gardening School is also included in the list drawn up by the Berlin Monument Authority. Founded in 1823 by the Court Garden Director Peter Joseph Lenné, the Royal Gardening School was at first based in the Wildpark near Potsdam. Since it was not possible to expand with the growing demands of the school, around the turn of the century it was decided to relocate the school and a large-scale site dedicated to research and study was planned. The main building and pergola form an axial relationship and incorporate further buildings, an ornamental and educational garden and an arboretum. Since the 1970s, the original green spaces have been drastically reduced by new buildings: to the west, the Institut der Freien Universität für Organische Chemie (→ 187), für Physik (→ 185) and für Informatik (→ 187) and in the mid-1990s, the Konrad-Zuse-Zentrum für Informationstechnik.

Back in 1984, Jean Christophe Ammann, the long-term head of the Frankfurt Museum of Modern Art, demanded that – in view of the extensive discussions about percent for art – new solutions should be found in order to speed up the "pedestrian pace of enhancement processes". He wanted that "artworks in public spaces should be imbued with a social, communicative and aesthetic meaning" – an approach that Hans Scharoun had pursued by setting aside areas for artworks in collaboration with designers and artists during the planning phase of his construction projects. In the Staatsbibliothek (building Potsdamer Strasse)

this is expressed by the integration of glass blocks in a work by Alexander Camaro, the floral-geometric lamps by Günter Ssymmank and in the creative floor design of the foyer by Erich Fritz Reuter. The latter was Professor of Plastic Arts at the Technische Universität from 1952 to 1966, during which time he realized the installations *Gespräch* (1953), *Universitas Aeterna*, which was originally presented in the catalog room of the University Library (1956/1958, → 214), and *Gegensätzliche Strukturen* (1964) in the main building.

Scraps of paper, newspaper clippings, notes, color images, familiar things, inklings, ancient scripts, new typographies... The floating sculpture ***Noch Fragen?*** (Still questions?), which resembles an ephemeral cloud of ideas, unites seemingly diverse analog media that are scrunched together, and gives us in inkling of contentual fragments or leaves us in the dark. The chaos that is conveyed by the sculpture, density and the difficulty of penetrating thoughts, hangs over the austere aesthetic of the newly built reading room in the Staatsbibliothek.

In front of the Universitätsbibliothek der Humboldt-Universität, the work titled ***Esc-Enter*** underlines the effect and appeal of the forecourt by subtly giving structure to the space. The flat, almost inconspicuous execution raises the central significance of text characters as an expression of language and human communication. The individual keypad legends of a computer keyboard, which are set into stone paving slabs, accentuate the narrow square between the S-Bahn train track and the library entrance. The use of tones and forms in the foyer of the Grimm-Zentrum subtly and almost decoratively refers to the history of the urban environment: a series of photographs by Arun Kuplas titled ***Bullet Holes*** is set into the wall; the images are close-ups of World War II artillery holes. They show the columns of the arcade outside the Alte Nationalgalerie and also facade details of 1, Dorotheenstrasse, the building where the university library administration was formerly housed.

To mark the 200-year anniversary of the Humboldt-Universität, in 2009 a restricted competition was held for an art intervention in the foyer of the main building. The competition focused on an artistic contextualization of the Karl Marx quote that occupies a prominent position on the wall of the main stairway. The result of an interplay between the Marx quote and the work ***Vorsicht, Stufe*** (Mind the Step) links the historical site with contemporary installation art. The jury ultimately selected the British concept artist Ceal Floyer,

Noch Fragen?
Olaf Metzel (Berlin 1952)

2011 | double-sided print on sheet aluminium | 6.8 x 5.2 x 3.4 meters | reading room, Staatsbibliothek Berlin, building Unter den Linden

Esc-Enter
Rolf Wicker (Ravensburg 1965)

2010 | 104 stone slabs | square in front of the Jacob-und-Wilhelm-Grimm-Zentrum, 1–3 Geschwister-Scholl-Strasse

Bullet Holes
Arun Kuplas (Chandigarh 1967)

2009 | photography | foyer of the Jacob-und-Wilhelm-Grimm-Zentrums, 1–3, Geschwister-Scholl-Strasse

Vorsicht Stufe!
Ceal Floyer (Karachi 1968)

2006/2009 | 56 brass warning signs | main building of the HU, Unter den Linden 6

whose 56 warning signs (one for each stair) repeat the advice "mind the step!" This exaggerated repetition undermines the warning; indeed, it reverses its effect and causes our thoughts to stumble and falter.

The shiny surface of the warning signs makes reference to the golden letters of the quote from the eleventh of Karl Marx's "Theses on Feuerbach". Marx, like Ludwig Feuerbach a student of the university, accused the latter of falling prey to idealism: "Philosophers have merely interpreted the world in various ways; the point, however, is to change it." For the published version, Friedrich Engels added the "however" and replaced the first comma with a semicolon. The quote was put up by the SED (East German Communist Party) after World War II, and in the 1990s a controversy erupted about whether or not it should be removed. The university council proposed replacing the text with a quote by Wilhelm von Humboldt. The debate centered around the self-image and the (new) orientation of the university as well as the issue of historic monument conservation.

In the 1950s, renovation work was carried out to repair war damage in the foyer. The wall cladding of knotted lime stone made it one of the more lavish interior designs of GDR building from that period. The foyer was subsequently given protected status after German reunification, though

gewidmet
Lorna
Lorna in Liebe

in excerpere
für Erich M. von Hornbostel

Ruth Tesmar (Potsdam 1951)

2003 | script design for the Musicological Seminar, HU, Am Kupfergraben 5

Realität in den Regalen: Fußnote, Vermerk, Widmung

Elsbeth Arlt (Kiel 1948–2015 Flensburg)

2004 | text installation: "19 Cf.: Hans Arp, Unsern täglichen Traum, p. 23.", "All rights reserved. No part of this book may be reproduced, in any form or by any means, without written permission from the publisher.", "Lorna in Liebe gewidmet" | Library of the TU and the UdK, in the three atria, Fasanenstrasse 88

a bust of Karl Marx was removed. The university management planned to redesign the entrance hall in a more open style, with proposals ranging from limited modernization while retaining the cladding to an extensive rebuild which would have included the removal of the Marx quote. Amid accusations that the university was seeking to suppress its East German past, it was ultimately decided that a moderate refurbishment was the best course of action.

Another notable art intervention at the Humboldt-Universität was created by the artist and college professor Ruth Tesmar. At the Musikwissenschaftliche Institut (Department of Musicology) she provided a script installation titled ***in excerpere für Erich M. von Hornbostel***. The essay „Die Einheit der Sinne" (1925) by musicologist Erich M. von Hornbostel has been reproduced by hand. It links the inner courtyard with the entrance area and the elevator. Ruth Tesmar has been the director of the Seminar für künstlerisch-ästhetische Praxis in the east wing of the building, called the "Menzel-Dach", since it was founded in 1993. The Seminar (department), which in terms of it concept is unique in Germany, focuses on practical instruction in drawing and printing techniques, and also on the associated knowledge structures between theoretical development and practical conspicuities.

Like Ruth Tesmar, Elsbeth Arlt is fascinated by script, literature, books, the art of printing and their associated haptic. Arlt won the percent for art competition for the new joint University Libraries of the Technischen Universität and the Universität der Künste (→ 143). A student of Franz Erhard Walther, Arlt's oeuvre captivates its audience with its condensed interrelations between script and images, metaphors and jokes, texts and ideas, fabrics and haptics. The artist chose three different text modules for the library's three inner courtyards, which she names in the work's title: ***Realität in den Regalen: Fußnote,***

Vermerk, Widmung (Reality on the shelves: footnote, note, dedication). The differing height, color and font of the individually designed letters highlight the materiality of the work and the architecture. The contentual references draw on central themes of working in a library.

In front of the entrance to the massive main building of the Technische Universität (→125), which was augmented by a ten-storey block after World War II, one can find the kinetic sculpture ***Flügeltor*** (Winged gate) by the German-Norwegian artist Reinhard Haverkamp. The fragile intricacy and changing form of the wind sculpture creates a strong contrast to the massive, two-part main building. A few meters westward, directly at the Ernst-Reuter-Platz and the entrance to the U-Bahn train station, one encounters *Wachsende Flügel (Kristalline Form)*, literally Growing wings (crystalline form), a sculpture by Karl Hartung. The heavy bronze sculpture expresses an ambivalence between the natural form and mathematical rigor, and suggests no immediate association with the clear lines of the facade of the Institut für Bergbau und Hüttenwesen (→121). On the students' meadow at the Freie Universität, which also contains a sculpture by Karl Hartung, the filigree sculpture ***Kore (Torso)*** engages in a cautious, quiet dialog with the park grounds.

The winning percent for art design for the recently unveiled Holzlaube at the Freie Universität (→180) by sculptor and installation artist Robert Patz links the campus library, the forecourt, and the six stairwells accessing the institute's "small subjects" which are gathered here. The three-part installation ***Tricksters Plan*** visualizes production and the limits of knowledge with its mischievousness, as the director of the library Martin Lee pronounced, in a yet endearing way. Patz himself calls it the "fundamental unsecuredness of knowledge", which he illustrates in an exuberant diagram at the entrance to the library, a simultaneous visualization and fragmentation which is continued in six vertical columns in the stairwells. The linking figure of a coyote, which

Flügeltor

Reinhard Haverkamp (Reichenbach 1954)

1993 | steel | in front of the TU main building, Strasse des 17. Juni 135

Kore (Torso)

Karl Hartung (Hamburg 1908–1967 Berlin)

1953 | bronze | 204 centimeters high, approx. 180 kilogramms | student's meadow at the FU Berlin between Garys-trasse and Van't-Hoff-Strasse

Tricksters Plan

Robert Patz (Magdeburg 1981)

2018 | three-part interior and exterior installation | digitally printed, durable wallpaper, bent aluminium, oak (realized by wood sculptor Sebastian Hertrich) | Holzlaube, FU, Fabeckstrasse 23–25

constantly reappears in the drawings, would give form to manifold associations as a wooden sculpture underneath a walnut tree: Joseph Beuys and Hermann Hesse, Meso- and North American cultures, metaphors by the philosopher of science Donna Haraway. The coyote, as an ambiguous object of projection, embodies the shift of perspective as a condition for the acquisition of knowledge. (MW)

Tricksters Plan, three-part interior and exterior installation

Register

(Aaa–Zyy)

BUILDINGS AND STREETS

Buildings

The directory collects all building names and names of institutions associated with specific buildings. The latter are sorted alphabetically according to disciplines and sub-disciplines and within a subject in historical order. The differentiation between universities is made according to today's names, i.e. HU, TU, FU, UdK, and for the Charité facilities outside Mitte according to the location abbreviations CBF, CVK, Westend, and Buch.

Streets

SCIENTISTS, ORGANIZERS, SPONSORS

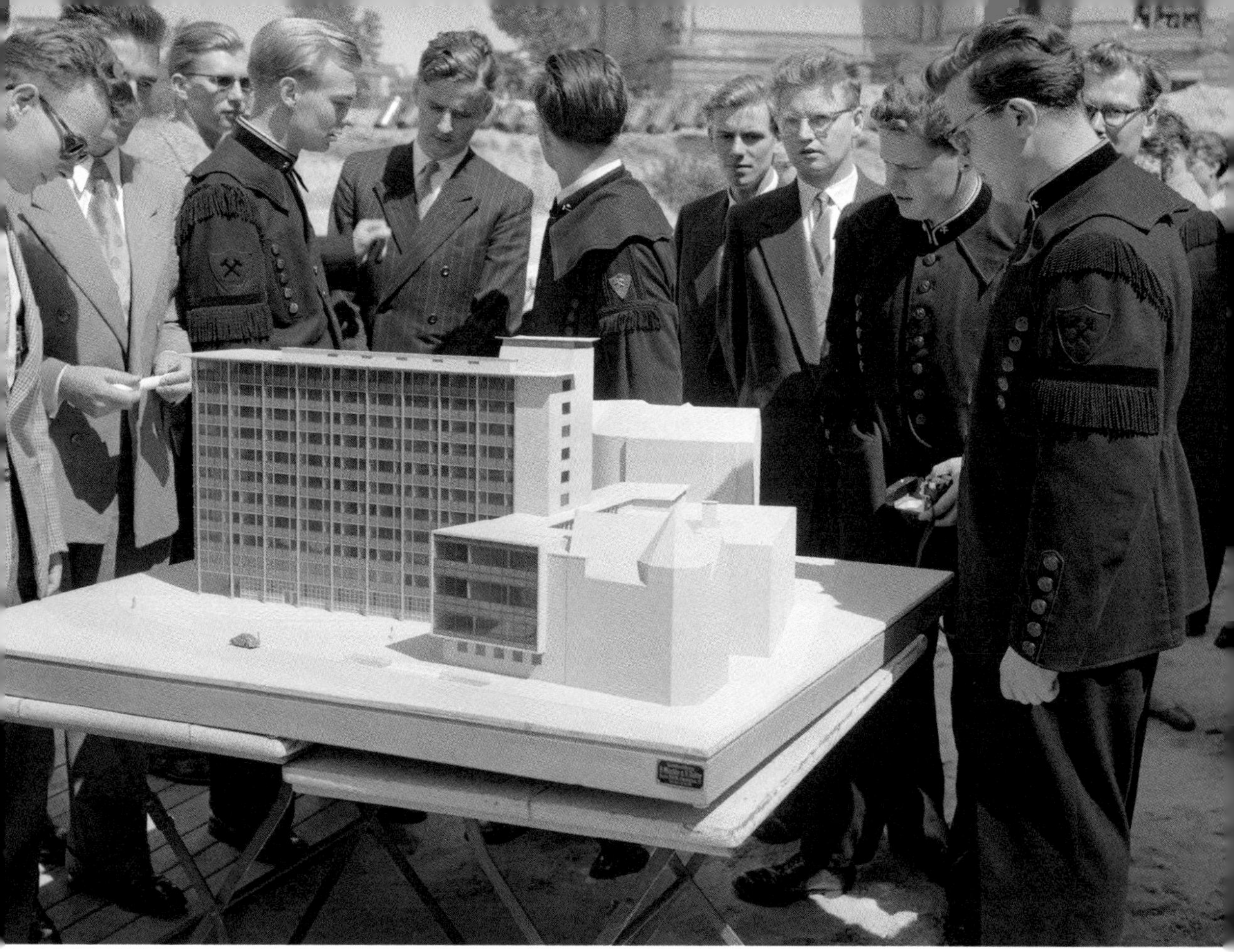

ARCHITECTS, BUILDERS, CONSTRUCTION MANAGERS

The following catalog does not make any claims to completeness or uniformity. It is primarily concerned with university buildings in Berlin and aims to indicate special correlations, historic associations and personal relationships. In this way, biographical information can be provided in addition to certain ideas, plans, projects, as well as structures that have in the meantime been demolished.
The institutes are attributed to the respective universities in accordance with their contemporary designation: HU (Humboldt-Universität zu Berlin) also refers to the Berliner Universität and the Friedrich-Wilhelms-Universität, TU (Technical University Berlin) stands for both the Technical College and UdK (Universität der Künste) and includes the College of Fine Arts and the College of Music. Illustrations were not given captions, but reference is made by underlined text. (Concept MW)

A

Adams, Anton (Saarburg 1856–1915 Berlin) | **33 107**
Anton Adams was a civil servant and building officer. Together with Paul Mebes he designed the new Institute of Church Music (1902–1903) in Hardenbergstrasse. He also realized the Institut für Zuckerindustrie (1901–1903) in Amrumer Strasse.

Assmann Salomon und Scheidt (ASS) | 191
Frank Assmann, Peter Salomon, Hermann Scheidt | Library of the Veterinary Clinic Düppel, FU, 1996–1998 | Architecture firm from 1987 to 1999

augustinundfrankarchitekten | 217
In 1986 Georg Augustin and Ute Frank founded an architecture firm which gained fame as a result of many widely publicized competitions. They designed the new Institut für Physik at the HU, known as the Lise-Meitner-Haus (2000–2002). For many years, Georg Augustin was a professor and Head of Architectural Design at the University of Kassel. Ute Frank was a professor in the specialist field of Design and Building Construction at the TU Berlin.

B

Baesler Schmidt und Partner (BSP) | 187
Klaus Baesler, Bernhard Schmidt | Institute of Computer Science, FU, 1991–1993 | Architecture firm from 1979 to 2000

Baller, Inken (Tondern 1942) | and
Baller, Hinrich (Stargard 1936) | **131 183**
Inken Baller and her husband Hinrich realized the Institute of Philosophy (FU, 1981–1984). In the context of the 1987 International Building Exhibition, the two architects also created the characteristic appearance of the residential houses at the Admiralsbrücke (Admiral's Bridge, Fraenkelufer) by the use of turquoise-colored, delicately floral curved steel braces. In the 1970s they reconstructed the two surviving town mansions at the TU Nordcampus.

Baumgarten, Paul G. R. (Tilsit 1900–1984 Berlin) | **121 165**
Paul Baumgarten was in his early years employed by Paul Mebes. From 1943 onward he held the post of lecturer and from 1949 of professor at the College of Fine Arts. During this period he designed the concert hall of the College of Music (1953–1955), which is today part of the UdK. In 1954 he submitted the winning design in the competition for new buildings at the Departmente of Law and the School of Business and Economics of the FU. However, his design was never realized.

Peter Bayerer, Gerd Fesel, Hans-Dieter Hecker, Roland Ostertag (Architektengemeinschaft) | 135 143

Center for Production Engineering, TU, 1983–1986 | New building of the Institute of Electrical Engineering, TU, 1982–1987

Behrens, Peter (Hamburg 1868–1940 Berlin)

Since 2003 the TU Institute for Civil Engineering has used the "Peter-Behrens-Halle" as a testing hall. The assembly hangar was built by Peter Behrens in 1912 as part of the development of the AEG industrial site (1905–1925). It is an outstanding example of modern industrial architecture. Other TU departments are situated around the former AEG factory grounds – today called the Technologie- und Informationszentrum – as well as departments of the Fraunhofer Gesellschaft and the Berliner Innovations- und Gründerzentrum.

Peter Behrens was an autodidact: first a painter, then an architect and designer. His extensive oeuvre in Berlin includes AEG Turbine Hall (1908–1909), planning for the AEG site south of Humboldthain Park, several family homes and apartment houses and also the Berolinahaus and the Alexanderhaus. Behrens realized an enormous number of buildings and applied himself to the fields of book art, the industrial arts, interior design and typography. His interest in industrial design, functionality and serial production had a profound influence on his work. Behrens was ahead of his time in creating a corporate design for the AEG company. He was active as a teacher and was seen as a role model: his students included Ludwig Mies van der Rohe, Le Corbusier and Walter Gropius.

Beller, Peter (1943) | **187 199**

Internship in the natural sciences, FU, 1986–1989 | Cafeteria for the Veterinary Clinic Düppel, FU, 1991 | Winning design submission for a sports center, FU, not realized

Berndt, Kurt (Berlin 1863–1925 Berlin) | **83**

Office building, Neue Schönhauser Strasse 20, 1906–1907, collaboration with August Endell | Office building and factory premises Kurt Berndt Courtyards, HU, 1911–1912, subsequently Department of Food Production and Technology of the HU, now located in the Goethe-Institut Berlin

Betz Architekten | 193

Remodeling of the Pre-clinic for Veterinary Medicine, FU, 1993–1998

Blunck, Erich (Heide 1872–1950 Berlin) | **43**

Erich Blunck was a professor at the TU Berlin from 1916 to 1937 and from 1947 to 1950. He was active as an architect, author and monument conservationist. In addition to several residential houses, mansions and churches, he also designed the office building at 3b, Universitätsstrasse, which is today used by the HU as the Institute of Social Science.

Bodamer Faber Architekten | 69 73

In 2002, Achim Bodamer and his brother Hansjörg Bodamer founded their own architecture firm in Stuttgart. Since 2013, Alexander Faber has been part of the management team. Bodamer Faber Architekten realized the Rhoda-Erdmann-Haus, Institute of Biology, HU (2013–2016).

Boethke, Julius (Konitz 1864–1917 Berlin) **| 231**
Design of the Royal Artillery Barracks, 1898–1901, today the Institute of Educational Sciences at the HU

Böhme, Martin Heinrich (Augsburg 1676–1725 Berlin) **| 29**
Gewerbeinstitut, 1712–1717, first built as the Royal Technical Institute in the Palais Creutz-Haake, later the Königliches Gewerbe-Institut, then the Königliche Gewerbeakademie.

Böttger, Paul (1852–1933) **| 65**
2nd Anatomical Institute, HU, 1892–1893, in collaboration with Karl Friedrich Endell

Boumann Sr., Johann (Amsterdam 1706–1776 Berlin) **| 25 35**
From 1732 on, Johann Boumann worked under the aegis of Georg Wenzeslaus von Knobelsdorff in Potsdam. In 1748 he was appointed the Royal Prussian Chief Building Director in Berlin where he played a leading role in realizing the prestigious Forum Fridericianum for Friedrich II. As site manager for the ensemble, he supervised the building of the Sankt-Hedwigs-Kirche (1747–1773) and the Prinz Heinrich Palais (1748–1753), which is today the main building of the HU. He based his work here on plans by Friedrich II and Georg Wenzeslaus, and his son Georg Friedrich was later to add further buildings to complete the forum.

Boumann Jr., Georg Friedrich (Potsdam 1737–1812/1817 Berlin) **| 33 37**
Georg Friedrich, son and student of Johann Boumann Sr. – not to be confused with his brother, the architect Michael Philipp Daniel Boumann (who built Bellevue Palace) – held the post of Royal Councilor of Works in Berlin. Like his father before him, Georg Friedrich worked on the Forum Fridericianum, where he built the Königliche Bibliothek (now the Law Department of the HU), based on plans by Georg Christian Ungers (1775–1781). He also built the Magnus-Haus.

braun.busse.architekten. | 191
Hugo Braun, Adriane Busse | Students' Service Center, FU, 2013–2014

Brenner, Hermann (Stuttgart 1899–1969) **| 209 213**
Together with Werner Deutschmann, Brenner was an exponent of National Socialist industrial functionalism | Large wind tunnel, 1932–1934 | Soundproof engine test bed, 1933–1935 | Trudelturm, 1934–1936 | Other new buildings in the grounds of the German Laboratory for Aviation Testing, 1933–1939

Bressler, Helmut (1907– unknown) **| 131 133**
Institute of Hydraulic Engineering and Water Management, TU, 1958–1959 | Institute of Aviation and Aerospace Engineering, TU, 1959–1961

Brinkert, Peter (Essen 1936–2014 Berlin)
Institute for Glass, Ceramics and Binders, TU, 1970–1971, brick facade with orange tiles, former location: Englische Strasse 20, demolished after 2014

Bürde, Georg Heinrich (Berlin 1796–1865 Berlin) **| 29**
Georg Heinrich Bürde worked on several high-profile by Karl Friedrich Schinkel, among them the Bauakademie, the Schauspielhaus, the Altes Museum and the Artillery and Engineering School (1822–1823).

C

Candilis, Georges (Baku 1913–1995 Paris) | **177**
Georges Candilis studied in Athens, took part in the 1933 Congrès Internationaux d'Architecture Moderne (CIAM) in Athens, and worked with André Lurçat and Le Corbusier after World War II. His social housing projects and the urban themes dealt with by Team X remain the most important part of his oeuvre. Candilis founded Team X together with Alexis Josic, Shadrach Woods, the British architects Alison and Peter Smithson, the Dutch architects Jacob Bakema and Aldo van Eyck, the Italian Giancarlo De Carlo and the German architect Stephan Wewerka. The stated goal of this group of young architects was to turn away from the modernist dogma of Le Corbusier, which advocated the division of housing, work, transport and the supply of goods, and to reintroduce linking elements and densification to urban planning. After the 9th CIAM congress, Team X was given responsibility for organizing the 10th event – which explains the group's name. In 1954 Candilis founded a joint company with Woods and Josic. Woods and Candilis had already worked on social housing projects in North Africa in the early 1950s. In Berlin he realized the Rost- und Silberlaube (1967–1973 and 1975–1979); from 1961 he drew up plans for the satellite town of Toulouse-Le-Mirail. Between 1967 and 1975 a new building was added to the university which was inspired by plans for the Rost- und Silberlaube.

Carola Schäfers Architekten | 165 177
Remodeling of the cafeteria in the former Department of Economics and Social Sciences, FU, 2003 | Redesign of the canteen foyer in the Rost- und Silberlaube, FU, 2006–2007

Carpus+Partner | 185
Friedhelm Nussbaum (contact architect) | Refurbishment of the Building for chemistry and biochemistry, FU, 2014–2019

Code Unique Architekten | 144
Martin Boden-Peroche and Volker Giezek founded a joint architecture company in 1998 which has since made a name for itself with its university buildings in Dresden and Hamburg. The company is currently planning the new Institute of Mathematics and the Interdisciplinary Center for Modeling and Simulation (IMoS) at the TU.

Cohen, Michiel (Haarlem 1946)
Innovation center for Computer Science, Adlershof, 1996–1998

Cremer, Albert (Aachen 1824–1891 Wiesbaden) | **39 63**
After graduating, Albert Cremer became a civil servant and joined the Berlin Bauakademie in 1855. After a short period in Koblenz, in 1859 he was summoned to the Berlin Ministerial Building Commission where he designed the 1st Anatomical Institute (1863–1865) and the Chemische Laboratorium of the Friedrich-Wilhelms-Universität (1865–1867). From 1869 until his death he worked in the privy council for construction in Wiesbaden.

Cremer, Wilhelm (Cologne 1845–1919 Berlin) | **43 45**

Wilhelm Cremer worked with Julius Raschdorff in Cologne until 1867, after which he began his studies at the Berlin Bauakademie. In addition to his subsequent profession as a freelance architect in Berlin he often taught at the Kunstschule and the Kunstgewerbemuseum, and from 1883 he also tutored at the Technical College in Charlottenburg. In 1882 Cremer founded the Cremer & Wolffenstein company together with Richard Wolffenstein. His works include the School of Commerce (1905–1906) – subsequently the Faculty of Economics of the HU, the Kaiser-Wilhelm-Akademie (1905–1910) and the Chamber of Commerce Berlin (1903–1904), which is today the main office of the School of Library and Information Science (IBI) at the HU.

Curtis & Davids | 237

Nathaniel Cortlandt Jr. Curtis, Arthur Quentin Davis, Clinic Steglitz, 1959–1968

D

Deubzer König Architekten | 235

Virchow-Clinic Campus Wedding, Forum, 1996 | Remodeling and refurbishment of the Clinic for Small Pets, FU, 2009 | Max Planck Institute for Infection Biology and German Rheumatism Research Center, 2000

Deutschmann, Werner | 209

Together with Hermann Brenner, Deutschmann was an exponent of National Socialist industrial functionalism | Large wind tunnel, 1932–1934 | Soundproof engine test bed, 1933–1935 | Trudelturm, 1934–1936 | Other new buildings in the grounds of the German Laboratory for Aviation Testing, 1933–1939

Diener & Diener | 79

Reconstruction of the east wing of the Museum für Naturkunde, 2008–2010

Diestel, Georg (Königsberg 1862–1946 Dresden) | **59 61 63**

Collaborated on the Institute of Pathology, HU, 1896–1898 | Psychiatric and Neurological Clinic, 1899–1905 | Administration buildings of the Charité 1898–1901 | Pediatric Clinic 1901–1904 | Surgical 1901–1904 | 1st and 2nd Medical Clinics1910–1914

Doerfler, Adolf (Bromberg 1941–2015) | **183**

House of the Student Body, in collaboration with Thomas Wolf, FU, 1995–1998

Dörr Ludolf Wimmer Architekten | 215

Joachim Dörr, Axel Ludolf, Josef Wimmer | Institute of Mathematics, HU, 1996–1997

Dübbers, Kurt (Düsseldorf 1905–1987 Düsseldorf) | **125 127**

From 1942 until his retirement in 1971 (when he became a professor emeritus) Kurt Dübbers taught at the TH and the TU Berlin. In collaboration with Karl-Heinrich Schwennicke he built the north wing of the TU main building and was involved in the planning for the northern area (1957) of the TU, for which he proposed an overall plan and a design for the Institute of Hydraulic Engineering and Water Management

(1958–1959) which was subsequently developed further and realized by Helmut Bressler.

Dudler, Max (Altenrhein 1949) | **41 75**
Jacob-und-Wilhelm-Grimm-Zentrum, HU, 2006–2009 | Refurbishment of the State Geological Institution and the Mining Academy, today the German Federal Ministry of Transport, Construction and Housing, 1996–2000 and also the new annex building on Schwarzen Weg, 1997–2004

Düttmann, Werner (Berlin 1921–1983 Berlin) | **125**
After completing his studies, Werner Düttmann worked with Hans Scharoun, designing Berlin's College of Arts (1958–1960) and the new cafeteria of the TU (1965–1967) in Hardenbergstrasse. He also built the Brücke-Museum (1964–1967), the Kirche St. Agnes (1964–1967) and the Ku'Damm-Eck (1969–1972) which was torn down in 1998. He was involved in the planning for the Märkisches Viertel and worked for Hugh Strubbins as a contact architect in the realization of the Haus der Kulturen der Welt. From 1964 until 1970 he worked as a professor at the TU, and between 1960 and 1970 he held the post of Senate Building Director.

Dybe, Günter Saleh | **187**
Institute of Organic and Physical Chemistry, FU, 1975–1978 | Extension of the Surgical and the Urologic, Klinikum Westend, 1980s

E

Eggert, Hermann (Burg 1844–1920 Weimar) | **109**
Annex building, 1899–1902

Ehrlich, Franz (Leipzig 1907–1984 Bernburg) | **213 249**
Franz Ehrlich studied at the Bauhaus in Dessau and worked in the studios of Mies van der Rohe, Hans Poelzig and Walter Gropius. He spent the Nazi years in jail and in a penal battalion. In the GDR he realized the Rundfunkzentrum in Nalepastrasse, the CI for Cardiovascular Research (1956–1957) and sections of the television center in Adlershof (1949–1957).

Eisele, Fritz und Bott | **215**
Johann Eisele, Nicolas Fritz, Helmut Bott, in collaboration with Rainer Hilka and Gerd Begemann | Center for Environmental Technology, Adlershof, 1996–1998

Emmerich, Julius (Trier 1834–1917 Zehlendorf) | **69**
Extension to the Equine Clinic, HU, 1874–1877 | Autopsy room of the Tieranatomische Theater, 1874

Endell, Karl Friedrich (Szczecin 1843–1891 Berlin) | **65**
From 1871, Karl Friedrich Endell worked as an architect for the city of Berlin and co-founded several architecture magazines. In collaboration with Paul Böttger he built the 2nd Anatomical Institute (1891–1892) for the Friedrich-Wilhelms-Universität. He also built the staff quarters (1892–1893) and stables for the Tierärztliche Hochschule (1893).

F

Fehling, Hermann (Hyères 1909–1996 Berlin) | **161 167 175 237**
Hermann Fehling studied architecture in Hamburg and worked variously with Hans Scharoun, Erich Mendelsohn and Alfred Issel. He also spent a brief time sharing an office

with Heinrich Sobotka and Gustav Müller. In 1949 he founded his own architecture company in Berlin. Peter Pfankuch and Daniel Gogel were his partners from 1955 on, though Peter Pfankuch dropped out in 1960. The company was responsible for the Mensa I (1951–1953, FU), the Studentendorf Schlachtensee (1956–1959), the Institute of Hygiene and Medical Microbiology (1971–1974, FU, in collaboration with Jürgen Kümmel and Manfred Walz), the annex of the Institute of Meteorology (1978–1991, FU) and also the Max Planck Institute for Educational Research (1971–1974). Continuing the ideas formulated by Scharoun, Fehling's works emphasize their origins in organic, holistic construction, although the designs and realized buildings are expanded by a polygonal, geometrical approach. Prominent works in Berlin include St. Norbert Church and Paul Gerhardt Church in Schöneberg and the Berlin Pavillon in the Hansaviertel. Between 1963 and 1971 Fehling was Deputy Director of the Architecture Section at the Akademie der Künste; in the early 1970s he was a professor at the TU Berlin, and following Scharoun's death he was an artistic adviser during the completion of the Staatsbibliothek Berlin.

Foster, Norman (Manchester 1935) **| 177 180**
Philological Library, FU, 2001–2005 | Refurbishment of the Rost- und Silberlaube, FU, 1999–2007 | Reichstag dome, 1995–1999

G

Garski, Dietrich (Potsdam 1931) **| 187**
Institute of Organic and Physical Chemistry, FU, 1975–1978

Geber & Risse | 165 185
In 1951, Hans Geber and Otto Risse founded an architecture firm. They realized administration buildings, offices and community halls as well as modern churches. Among the company's academic buildings are the Department for Economics and Social Sciences (1957–1958, FU), the Law Department (1957–1959, FU), the Institute of Inorganic Chemistry (1960–1963, FU) and the extension of the Institute of Electron Microscopy at the Fritz-Haber-Institut of the MPG (1957 and 1963).

Gebert & Söhne | 45

Apartment house and factory building, Sophienstrasse 22, HU, 1899, now the Berlin-Brandenburg Center for Jewish Studies

Geier Maass Architekten | 191

Almut Geier, Enno Maass | Library building at the John-F.-Kennedy-Institut in a former elementary school, FU, 2007–2009 | Research area for dog keeping, Institute of Animal Nutrition, FU, 2006–2007

Gentz, Johann Heinrich (Wrocław 1766–1811 Berlin) **| 29**

Gentz was born in Wrocław and first came to Berlin in 1779 when his father was appointed General Director of the mint. In Berlin he was to later realize the Alte Münze (old mint) at Werderscher Markt (1798–1800), which housed part of the Prussian Mint (torn down in 1886). From 1783 to 1790, Gentz trained as an architect at the Berliner Kunstakademie under the tutelage of Carl von Gontard. He subsequently spent five years in Rome and Sicily, where he made studies based on the remains of ancient buildings. Upon his return to Berlin, Gentz took up a post at the Royal Building Office and also worked at the Akademie der Künste from 1796 on. In 1799 he co-founded the Berliner Bauakademie, where he became Professor for Urban Design. On the insistence of Johann Wolfgang von Goethe, in 1801 Gentz was released from his duties in Berlin and moved to Weimar. There, he worked for Duke Carl August on the Residenzschloss (Royal Palace) and other court buildings. He returned to Berlin in 1803 and became a member of the Senate of the Kunstakademie. In 1810, in his capacity as Royal Officer of Works, he was appointed the first Director of the Berlin Palace Building commission. In the same year, the Berliner Universität was founded and moved into the Prinz Heinrich Palais, for which Gentz, Wilhelm von Humboldt and Aloys Hirt were responsible.

Gisske, Erhardt (Schönstedt 1924–1993 Berlin) **| 65**

Erhardt Gisske studied to be a construction engineer, and held several leading ministerial posts in the early years of the GDR before becoming the Director of Urban Planning in (East) Berlin from 1958 to 1963. From 1974 to 1989 he was the General Director of the Building Department of the Berlin Ministry of Construction and as Director of the Special Planning Department he realized several large, prestigious projects: the refurbishment of the Nikolaiviertel (1980–1987); the Friedrichstrasse and the Friedrichstadtpalast (1981–1984); the Surgical Center of the Charité (Bettenhochhaus, 1976–1982), the Palast der Republik (1973–1976, demolished from 2006) and the Zeiss Planetarium (1987).

Gogel, Daniel (Berlin 1927–1997 Berlin) **| 161 167 175 237**

As a partner of the Fehling, Pfankuch und Gogel office collective (also Fehling + Gogel), Daniel Gogel was involved in various projects: The Mensa I (1951–1953, FU) and its subsequent extension (1975); the Institute of Hygiene and Medical Microbiology (1971–1974, FU, in collaboration with Jürgen Kümmel and Manfred Walz); the annex of the Institute of Meteorology (1978–1991, FU); the Studentendorf Schlachtensee (1956–1959, 1962–1964, FU) and also the Max Planck Institute for Educational Research (1971–1974). He influenced the signature style of the office collective with his focus on simple materials, clarity of construction, and his intricate geometric designs for university buildings, sacred buildings and residential housing.

Gontard, Karl von (Mannheim 1731–1791 Wrocław) | **33 59**

Karl von Gontard was trained in Paris. After stays in Bayreuth and Potsdam, in 1779 he took up the post of Royal Building Director in Berlin. Nine years later he became a teacher at the Akademie der Künste, a post he held until his death. One of the many works supervised by Gontard was the interior of the Königliche Bibliothek.

Gössler, Kinz, Kerber, Kreienbaum Architekten | 217

Bernhard Gössler, Daniel Kinz, Arndt Kerber, Martin Kreienbaum | Erwin Schrödinger-Zentrum, HU, 1999–2002

Grimmek, Bruno (Berlin 1902–1969 Berlin) | **141 167**

In the 1920s, the trained mason and graduate of the Berlin Baugewerbeschule studied under exponents of the Neues Bauen (New Objectivity) movement such as Hans Poelzig and Bruno Ahrends. From 1928 onward he was employed by the Berlin Building Authority and was thus exempted from military service during World War II. After 1945 he played a significant role in the rebuilding of West Berlin, primarily focusing on public buildings. He realized the Amerika Haus (1956–1957) and built several U-Bahn train stations including Westhafen, Turmstrasse and Hansaplatz (with Werner Klenke). In the field of university buildings, he also designed the main building of the former Pedagogical College (1960–1964, today the FU-Geocampus) in Berlin-Lankwitz, the Institute of Fuel Technology (1955–1957, TU-Nordgelände) and was site manager during the construction of the Institute for East European Studies and the Otto-Suhr-Institut.

Gropius, Martin (Berlin 1824–1880 Berlin) | **53, 229**

During his youth, Martin Gropius already began admiring Karl Friedrich Schinkel as a role model. He went on to study at the Königliches Gewerbeinstitut in Berlin with the aim of becoming a master builder like his idol. After passing his field surveyor's exams in 1847, he began attending the Berlin Bauakademie where he acquired practical experience under Heinrich Strack. In 1855 he graduated as a master builder and subsequently worked under Karl Bötticher as an assistant teacher. In 1865 he founded the Sozietät Gropius & Schmieden together with Heino Schmieden. In 1867 Gropius became head of the Education Department of the Berlin Gewerbemuseum, and two years later he was appointed Director of the Königlichen Kunst- und Gewerbeschule, which meant that he was also a member of the Senate of the Akademie der Künste.
In the course of his work with Karl Bötticher, Gropius became familiar with the formal concepts of the ancient Greeks and went on to use these concepts in a modified form in his own buildings. At first he designed residential houses, mansions and country manors, most of which in the style of Schinkel and Classicism. His most prestigious buildings were also designed in this style. The Surgical Clinic (1878–1883) and the Gynecological Clinic (1880–1882) in the Ziegelstrasse – both in collaboration with Heino Schmieden – were inspired by the Bauakademie in their use of reddish-yellow clinker brick for the facades.

His last major work, the Königliche Kunstgewerbemuseum Berlin (1875–1883), which since 1980 bears the name Martin-Gropius-Bau, was a collaboration with Heino Schmieden in the Italian Renaissance style.

Gropius, Walter (Berlin 1886–1969 Boston) **| 159 185**

Although he built several great works in Berlin, in particular residential buildings, there are no academic buildings by Walter Gropius in the city except his design for the Bauhaus-Archiv. The founding father of the Bauhaus, Gropius had an enormous influence on modern architecture as both an architect and teacher. His most famous works include the Fagus-Werk in Alfeld (1911–1914), the Haus Sommerfeld in Berlin (1921) and the Bauhaus building in Dessau (1925–1926). In 1934 Gropius emigrated to Britain, and from 1937 he held the post of Professor of Architecture at Harvard University.

Guth, Max (Danzig 1859–1925) **| 43 81 161 165**

Together with Ernst von Ihne, Guth was a contract architect at the Kaiser-Wilhelm-Gesellschaft until 1914 | Chemical Laboratory, HU, 1899–1900, with Georg Thür | Kaiser Wilhelm Institute of Chemistry, 1911–1912 | Kaiser Wilhelm Institute of Biology, 1914–1915 | Kaiser Wilhelm Institute for Experimental Therapy, 1913 | Institute of Hygiene and Institute of Physiology, HU, 1903–1905 | Dental Institute, HU, 1911–1912, with Georg Thür

H

Haas Architekten | 169

Friedhelm Haas, Silke Gehner-Haas | Research greenhouse, HU, 2014 | Refurbishment of the large tropical greenhouse at the Botanical Garden, FU, 2009

Haesecke, Eduard | 53

Annex of the Surgical Clinic, HU, 1891–1893

Hahn, Joachim (1923) **| 211**

Institute of Cosmos Research, Adlershof, 1978–1982

Hammerbacher, Herta (Munich 1900–1985 Niederpöcking) **| 127**

The landscape architect Herta Hammerbacher taught at the Institute of Architecture at the TU Berlin for over two decades. She created the design for the green spaces at the northern area, the so-called test garden of the Architecture building (1963–1967, TU) and from 1946 to 1969 she was Associate Professor for Landscape and Garden Design.

Hammersen, Werner | 135

Institute of Mechanics, TU, remodeling and new test hall, 1963–1965

Hänska, Gerd (Berlin 1927–1996 Berlin) | **185 241**

Gerd Hänska mainly designed social housing, schools and higher education buildings. In the 1970s he realized the former central animal laboratories (1971–1974, 1978–1980, FU, in collaboration with Kurt Schmersow) and was responsible for the remodeling of the tower block facade at the Institute of Inorganic Chemistry (1979–1980, FU). Another FU project, in collaboration with Bernd Johae, was the extension of the Institute of Botany at Altensteinstrasse 6 between 1984 and 1986. The BESSY electron storage ring in Berlin-Schmargendorf was built between 1978 and 1981 in accordance with Hänska's plans. Its successor, BESSY II was built by Jürgen Brenner and is located in Adlershof.

Heide & von Beckerath | 252

Tim Heide, Verena von Beckerath | Biobank at the Max Delbrück Center | 2014–2016

Heinrichs, Georg (Berlin 1926) | **203**

Studentendorf Eichkamp, 1958–1959 and also 1967, in collaboration with Ludwig Leo | Märkisches Viertel, overall urban planning with Hans Christian Müller and Werner Düttmann, 1960–1970, and housing development on the Senftenberger Ring, 1963–1974 | Highway above building complex Schlangenbader Strasse with Gerhard and Klaus Krebs, 1967–1981 | "Forum Steglitz" shopping mall in the Schlossstrasse with Finn Bartels and Christoph Schmidt-Ott, 1967–1970 | Evangelical consistory in the Hansaviertel, with Hans-Christian Müller, 1968–1971, demolished in 2011

Hermkes, Bernhard (Simmern 1903–1995 Hamburg) | **121 127 131**

Bernhard Hermkes initially studied architecture at the Technical University of Munich, later attending the Technical College in Charlottenburg. In 1926 he completed his diploma thesis under Paul Bonatz at the Technical University of Stuttgart.
As a result of his interest in the modern architectural philosophy of Neues Bauen he left Stuttgart, which was primarily famed for its traditionalist handicrafts school. Hermkes took up a post in the Frankfurt Urban Planning Office, where Ernst May had been in charge of the planning and realization of the "New Frankfurt" project since 1925. Hermkes managed the department of industrial buildings, which garnered attention and acclaim for its distinctive concrete constructions.
In 1927, upon receiving a commission for a residential home for working women, Hermkes set up his own company. He drew up functional, minimalist designs and gained renown as an exponent of the Neues Bauen movement.
During the Nazi era he was involved in the construction of the Heinkel-Werke weapons factory in Oranienburg. Due to the growing demand for armaments, industrial buildings were given significant state support during that time. Hermkes was also involved in the construction of the Messerschmidt factory in Regensburg, later moving to Hamburg as the site manager of the MAN Engine Works. Hermkes worked on this project and other wartime commissions until 1944 when he was drafted for military service.
After his release from an American POW camp, Hermkes returned to Hamburg and set up a new architecture company. Thanks to his reputation as an exponent of modern architecture, Hermkes quickly established himself; he was also categorized as "politically untarnished". His residential projects in particular express the ideal of a decentralized and structured city. An outstanding example of this can be found at the Ernst-Reuter-Platz in West-Berlin. Hermkes' design won the competition for this project which – like the

contemporaneous Hansa-Viertel development – was considered a response to the architectural style of the Stalin Allee in the east of the city. Hermkes himself was to design two buildings at the Ernst-Reuter-Platz: the Osram-Haus and the Institute of Architecture at the TU (1963–1967) – where he subsequently worked as a professor of Building Construction and Industrial Architecture from 1955 to 1969. Hermkes placed particular emphasis on the constructive formation of the structures, which he described as a "formed construction", which also influenced his teaching at the TU. His preferred material was concrete, which played a key role in his designs due to its plasticity – as illustrated by the Audimax at Hamburg University (1957–1958).

Hertling, Cornelius (Berlin 1928–2002 Berlin) | **231**
Building for general use (Klinikum Westend, in collaboration with Peter Poelzig), 1977–1980

Hesse, Carl Johann Paul (1827–1895)
Lindenstrasse Observatory, Königliches Statistisches Büro und Meteorological Institute, 1867–1868

Hesse, Ludwig Ferdinand (Bialogard 1795–1876 Berlin) | **59 69**
Ludwig Ferdinand Hesse held several courtly posts (from 1832 Court Building Inspector, 1865 Chief Privy Councilor for Buildings). In 1863 he was appointed Director of the Palace Construction Commission and was thus in charge of the existing palaces and future royal buildings. In 1866 he became a member of the Senate of the Akademie der Künste. From 1824 to 1839 he realized the Friedrich-Werderschen Kirche based on a design by Karl Friedrich Schinkel, and from 1831 to 1834 he built the New Charité hospital – which was torn down in 1905. He also designed the University of Veterinary Medicine, which was built between 1839 and 1840.

Hilmer Sattler Architekten | 45
Berlin Palace - Humboldt Forum, reconstruction and new building 2009–2019, Franco Stella Humboldt-Forum Projektgemeinschaft | Museum Barbarini, reconstruction of the Palais Barbarini am Alten Markt, 2013–2017 | railway station Potsdamer Platz, 1995–2006 | Gemäldegalerie Berlin 1986–1998

Hitzig, Georg Friedrich Heinrich (Berlin 1811–1881 Berlin) | **97 101 103**
Having started out as an employee of Karl Friedrich Schinkel, in 1837 Georg Friedrich Hitzig set up his own architecture firm. In addition to several residential houses and mansions, Hitzig also designed the Reichsbank building. One of the most outstanding examples of his architectural talent is his work at Technical College Charlottenburg: In collaboration with Richard Lucae and Julius Raschdorff he designed the vast main building of the university (1878–1884) and complemented it with the nearby Chemical Laboratory (1881–1884). Hitzig also held the post of President of the Akademie der Künste between 1875 and 1881.

Hoffmann, Franz (Charlottenburg 1884–1951 Berlin) | **194**
Former administration buildings of the Reichsknappschaft, FU, 1929–1930, in collaboration with Max Taut

Hoffmann, Ludwig (Darmstadt 1852–1932 Berlin) | **25 111 233 235 243 247 251**
Ludwig Hoffmann studied architecture at the Berlin Bauakademie and was a student of Richard Lucae, Johann Heinrich Strack, Friedrich Adler and Julius Raschdorff. In 1896 he was appointed Head of Municipal Planning in Berlin, a post he held for 28 years. During

this time he was responsible for almost 150 public building projects which would leave a lasting impression on the Berlin cityscape. Among these were almost 70 school buildings, and he was largely responsible for the planning and execution of the hospital complex in Berlin-Buch (1900–1929). He also planned the extension of the HU main building (1913–1920) with its distinctive H-shaped layout. Hoffmann also designed the Rudolf-Virchow-Krankenhaus (1899–1907), the Märkisches Museum (1901–1907) and the Altes Stadthaus (1902–1910). His final project in Berlin was the construction of the Pergamon Museum (1910–1930).

Höger, Fritz (Bekenreihe 1877–1949 Bad Segeberg) | **173**

After completing his studies in Berlin, Fritz Höger worked mainly in Hamburg, where he designed the Chilehaus (1922–1924). However, he also left traces on the urban landscape of Berlin: he designed the Scherk perfume factory in Steglitz (1926–1927, extended by Bernd Halbach, 1987–1989) which later housed the Institute of Psychology of the FU. Höger was a member of the Deutsche Werkbund and was a professor at the Nordische Kunstschule in Bremen from 1933 to 1936.

Hundertmark, Dieter (Inzell 1937–2016 Inzell) | **125**

New physics building, TU, 1978–1984

Huntemüller, Johann (approx. 1875–1950) | **169**

Institute of Anatomy, FU, 1949–1950, first construction phase | Gatehouses at the Grosser Stern, 1939–1941

I

Ihne, Ernst von (Elberfeld 1848–1917 Berlin) | **23 41 161 165 197**

Ernst Ihne, named "von Ihne" since joining the nobility in 1906, is considered a representative of the Wilhelmian Neo-Baroque style. He was the Royal Prussian Court Architect during the reigns of Friedrich III and Wilhelm II. He studied at the Building Department of the Technische Hochschule in Karlsruhe, the Berlin Bauakademie and at the École des Beaux-Arts in Paris. In 1877 he and Paul Stegmüller founded the Büro für Architektur + Kunstgewerbe, which mainly designed country houses and furniture. Von Ihne was also one of the founding members of the Berlin Architects' Association. Although his work was initially oriented towards the German Renaissance with French influences, his major works in Berlin are in the Neo-Baroque style.
Among his first commissions were the new Hummelshain hunting lodge (1880–1885) and the design of the officers' mess of the Leib-Garde-Husaren Regiment in Potsdam (1888). That same year he was appointed Court Architect by Kaiser Friedrich III, which helped his meteoric rise. Meanwhile, he had parted ways with Stegmüller. In 1888 he was also commissioned by Friedrich's widow Victoria to build Friedrichshof Palace in Kronberg im Taunus. In 1894 he worked on the extension of the Palais Schaumburg in Bonn, which later became the seat of the German Chancellery.

Beginning in 1888, von Ihne began planning the extension to the royal apartment in Berlin's City Palace on a commission by Wilhelm II. His Neuer Marstall (new stables) building (1897–1900) has survived to the present day, as has the Kaiser Friedrich Museum (1898–1904, now the Bode Museum). His oeuvre also includes the extension of the Palais Arnim when it housed the Akademie der Künste (1905–1907). The exhibition building has survived, though the Palais itself was destroyed in 1945. His extensive architectural works under Kaiser Wilhelm II illustrate a self-confident use of the dominant building forms of the time, though he did not create his own distinctive architectural style.
In Berlin, especially in the Mitte district, von Ihne designed several academic buildings that left a lasting impression on the cityscape – and one can also see the grand style representative of the monarchy at the time. These buildings include the Staatsbibliothek on Unter den Linden (1908–1914), the Kaiserin-Friedrich-Haus for the Continuing Education in Medicine (1904–1906) and also the first institutes of the Kaiser-Wilhelm-Gesellschaft in Berlin-Dahlem: the Institute for Chemistry, now called the Otto-Meitner-Bau (1911–1912) of the FU, the Institute of Biology, now the Law Library and administration of the FU (1914–1915), and the Institute for Experimental Therapy (1913).

J

Jaenisch, Roland (Ulbersdorf 1928–2018) | **249**
Roland Jaenisch worked at the GDR Institute for Technology of Medical Buildings from 1961 to 1990. From 1969 to 1992 he was Honorary Professor of Public Building Construction at the Technische Universität Dresden. In Berlin-Buch he realized (Jaenisch und Kollektiv) a new surgery building for the Robert Rössle Clinic (1961–1968).

Jansen, Hermann (Aachen 1869–1945 Berlin) | **148 157**
Architect, urban planner and professor | Founded an architecture firm in 1899 with William Müller | Professor at the TH Berlin 1923–1938

Josic, Alexis (Stari Becej 1921–2011) | **177**
Alexis Josic studied painting and architecture in Belgrade. As part of the Candilis, Josic and Woods collective he realized numerous residential projects in North Africa and also the Rost- und Silberlaube (1967–1973, 1975–1979, FU) and parts of the university in Toulouse-le-Mirail. Like his partners and other European architects he was a member of Team X, a group of young architects that focused on the linking elements of urban planning and rejected the separation of residential and working areas.

Josse, Emil (Darmstadt 1866–1940 Berlin) | **105**
Mechanical Laboratory, TH, 1896

Jürgen Brenner und Partner | 213
Jürgen Brenner (son of Hermann Brenner), Nils Krause, Markus Hammes | BESSY II electron storage ring synchrotron in Adlershof, 1992–2001

K

Kalesky, Günter | 169
Institute of Anatomy, FU, 1953–1955, second construction phase

Kalusche, Fritz | 85
Departmental building for physics and electronics, HU, 1982–1984, in collaboration with Karl-Ernst Swora | Participated in the master plan for northern section of Friedrichstrasse in the early 1980s

Kebe + Schoberth Architekten | 109
Felicitas Schoberth, Ehrenfried Kebe | Refurbishment of the Institute of Metallurgy, TU, 2005 | Labor Bascat, TU, 2014 | Refurbishment of the Director's Villa at the Botanical Garden (formerly the Villa Engler), FU, 2018 | Refurbishment of the Physics building (Ernst-Ruska Building), TU, 2019

Kieschke, Paul (Szczecin 1851–1905 Baden-Baden)
Worked for Martin Gropius and H. Schmieden and in the civil sector | Prussian State Bank, 1901–1902 | Berlin-Brandenburgische Akademie der Wissenschaften, 1901–1903 | Prussian Ministry of Culture, 1901–1903

Kleihues, Josef Paul (Rheine 1933–2004 Berlin) | **231**
Head Clinic (Klinikum Westend), 1963–1969

Kleinwächter, Friedrich (1847–1898) | **47**
Institute of Hygiene in the Klosterstrasse, HU, 1885 | Worked under Paul Emmanuel Spieker at the Institute of Physiology, HU, 1873–1877

Klenke, Werner (1926–1978) | **167**
Institute for East European Studies and Otto-Suhr-Institut, FU, 1959–1962

kleyer.koblitz.letzel.freivogel.architekten | 252
New building for research spaces at the Robert Rössle Institute, Käthe-Beutler-Haus, 2016–2020

Knobelsdorff, Georg Wenzeslaus von (Gut Kuckädel 1699–1753 Berlin) | **29**
Forum Fridericianum, collaborative planning with Friedrich II of Prussia, who was a close acquaintance. Von Knobelsdorff designed and supervised the construction of the Staatsoper and Sankt-Hedwigs-Kirche.

Koerner, Alfred (Rangsdorf 1849–1926 Berlin) | **169 173**
Buildings in the Botanical Garden: Administration and finance building (1899–1903), large tropical greenhouse (1900), coolhouse for subtropical plants (1903–1906), Botanical Museum (1903–1906) (east wing destroyed) | Former Astronomisches Recheninstitut der of the Royal Observatory, FU, 1911–1912

Kohlmaier, Georg (Graz 1937) | **137 220 221**
Mathematics building, TU, 1967–1983

Korn, Roland (Saalfeld 1930) | **247**
Berlin's "Chief Architect", 1973–1989 | Head of the Urban Planning Office, especially during the preparations for Berlin's 750-year anniversary in 1987 | Government Hospital I, 1973–1976, collaboration with Joachim Härter | State Council Building, 1961–1964 | Interhotel Stadt Berlin, 1968–1971, today the Park Inn Berlin-Alexanderplatz | Haus des Reisens, 1968–1971

Korneli, Peter (Wüstegiersdorf 1930) | **65**
The leading expert for hospital construction in the GDR. Surgical Center at the Charité (Bettenhochhaus), 1977–1982, in collaboration with Karl-Ernst Swora

Kötteritzsch, Werner | 33
Reconstruction of the Alte Bibliothek, HU, 1963–1969

Kraemer, Pfennig, Sieverts | 203
Friedrich Wilhelm Kraemer, Günter Pfennig, Ernst Sieverts | Expansion of the Studentendorf Schlachtensee, 1977–1978

Kreuer, Willy (Cologne 1910–1984 Berlin) **| 121 135 137 199**
From 1938 onward, Kreuer worked for Werner March in Berlin. After World War II he set up his own business and in 1949 he began teaching at the TU Berlin. In 1951 he became an associate professor at the TU Berlin, and between 1968 and 1976 he was Director of the Institute for Housing Construction at the TU. In collaboration with Fritz Bornemann, Gerhard Jobst and Hartmut Wille he realized the Amerika-Gedenkbibliothek (1952–1954) and was responsible for stylistically diverse projects at the TU Berlin including the Institute for Mining and Metallurgy (1955–1959), the Institute of Technical Chemistry (1963–1968/1965–1970) and the library in the main building of the TU (1950–1953).

L

Lambart, Bruno (Düsseldorf 1924–2014 Ratingen) **| 125**
New physics building, TU, 1978–1984

Langhans, Carl Gotthard (Landeshut 1732–1808 Grüneiche near Wrocław) **| 45 67 69**
In the 1750s, Carl Gotthard Langhans studied law, mathematics and languages in Halle. Even at this early stage he began private studies of architecture, reading ancient texts by the Roman architecture theorist Vitruvius and works by Johann Joachim Winckelmann.
He made his breakthrough as an architect in 1764 with a design for the "Schifflein Christi" Protestant church in Glogau. He took up a post as building inspector for Prince Franz Philipp von Hatzfeld-Gleichen-Trachenberg and drew up plans to rebuild the city palace in Wrocław (1766–1774). Like his colleagues Karl Friedrich Schinkel and Heinrich Gentz, Langhans' works were influenced by his travels in Italy (1768–1769). He would later travel to England, the Netherlands, Belgium and France. Upon the endorsement of Prince von Hatzfeld he was to achieve renown in the Berlin court as well. Until the mid-1780s, Langhans was primarily engaged in Silesia, after which he went to Berlin.
It was in Berlin that he began to flourish as an architect. In 1786 he became an honorary member of the Akademie der Künste, and two years later he was appointed Director of the Royal Office of Works by Friedrich Wilhelm II. Although he did not develop his own architectural style, his combination of ancient elements with Baroque and Classical forms was highly innovative. He would often refer to the sketches he made during his travels, and form them – combining different styles – into his own designs. Langhans was responsible for the interior design of the Potsdam Marmorpalais (Marble Palace), and redesigned some of the rooms in the Berlin City Palace. He also built the Schlosstheater (Palace Theater) and Belvedere in Charlottenburg. In addition to the "Mohrenkolonnaden" (up to 1787) he also designed the Tierarzneischule (1787–1789), which draws heavily on Andrea Palladio's villa architecture. Langhans is mainly famed for his design of the Brandenburg Gate (1789–1791).

His last major work was the Schauspielhaus on Gendarmenmarkt (1800–1802, burned down in 1817).

Langhans, Carl Ferdinand (Wrocław 1782–1869 Berlin) | **35**
Son of the architect Carl Gotthard Langhans | Altes Palais, 1834–1837 | Rebuild of the Staatsoper (Royal Opera House) after the fire of 1843, opened in 1844

Larsen, Henning (Videbæk 1925–2013 Copenhagen) | **185**
Institute of Physics, FU, 1973–1982 | Second place in the competition for the extension of the FU

Laske, Fritz (Königsberg 1854–1918 Berlin) | **75**
State Geological Institution and Mining Academy, extension by August Tiede, HU, 1890–1892

Lehmann, Hans Th. | **175**
House of Research, FU, 1938–1940

Leo, Ludwig (Rostock 1924–2012 Berlin) | **111 203**
Studentendorf Eichkamp, TU, 1947–1967 | Kindergarten in the Loschmidtstrasse, 1958–1959 | Sports hall Charlottenburg, 1960 | Circulation tank II at the Testing Facility for Shipbuilding and Hydraulic Engineering (VWS), 1969–1972 | Teaching and research facility of the German Lifesaving Association (DLRG) in Berlin-Spandau, 1967 | Designs for the Bielefeld Laboratory School, 1971

Lucae, Richard (Berlin 1829–1877 Berlin) | **97 103**
Teacher at the Bauakademie from 1859, Director from 1873 | Remodeling of the Bauakademie, 1874–1875 | Designs for the TH Charlottenburg, 1876–1877, altered realization

by Friedrich Hitzig and Julius Raschdorff, 1878–1884

Luckhardt, Wassili (Berlin 1889–1972 Berlin) and **Luckhardt, Hans** (Berlin 1890–1954 Bad Wiessee) | **169 193**
The Luckhardt brothers studied as architects in Berlin, Dresden and Karlsruhe and began working together in 1921. Between 1924 and 1934 Alfons Anker was also a member of their architecture firm. Both brothers were members of the Arbeitsrat für Kunst (from 1919), the November Group (from 1919) and "Der Ring" architects' collective (from 1926). After the death of his brother Hans, Wassili Luckhardt continued to work as an independent architect, realizing the Institute of Plant Physiology (FU) (1962–1970, with Peter Bormann) and the Pre-clinic for Veterinary Medicine (1963–1968, with Hans Joachim Wandelt). Between 1956 and 1959 he was Deputy Director of the

Architecture Department of the Akademie der Künste in Berlin.

Lütcke, Hubert | 118
Students' dorm, TU, 1935–1936

M

Malwitz, Hans (Seckenburg 1891–1987 Münster) **| 150**
Military-Technical Faculty, 1938. After World War II, Hans Malwitz designed a number of buildings for the University of Münster including the law school building.

Manfred Kiemle, Herman Kreidt und Partner | 187
Institute of Organic and Physical Chemistry, FU, 1975–1978, in collaboration with Dietrich Garski, Günter Saleh Dybe, and Otto Herrenkind

March, Otto (Charlottenburg 1845–1913 Charlottenburg) **| 131**
Father of Werner and Walter March | Holtz residential house in the former Bellstrasse, 1904–1905, now part of the northern area of the TU

March, Werner (Charlottenburg 1894–1976 Berlin) **| 135**
Son of the architect Otto March and grandson of the building ceramics manufacturer Ernst March | Nazi Party member from 1933 | 1936 title of professor conferred by Wilhelm Frick and Adolf Hitler | Head of the National Socialist League of the Reich for Physical Exercise | 1938 rejected an appointment at the TH Berlin | 1953–1960 Professor of Urban Planning and Settlement at the TU | Olympiastadion, 1934–1936 | Werner-von-Siemens-Bau, TU, 1963–1966

Mattern, Herrmann (Hofgeismar 1902–1971 Greimharting) **| 203**
Landscape architect | Studentendorf Schlachtensee, FU, 1956–1959 and 1962–1964

Mebes, Paul (Magdeburg 1872–1938 Berlin) **| 107**
Institute of Church Music, 1902–1903 | associate of his brother-in-law Paul Emmerich 1911–1938 (Mebes & Emmerich Co.) | 1912 member of the Deutsche Werkbund | 1919–1933 Member of the Akademie der Künste

Mecke, Heinz | 135
Institute of Mechanics, TU, remodeling and new test hall, 1963–1965

Mocken, Franz (1913–1973) **| 237**
Contact architect for Davids und Curtis, former Clinic Steglitz, FU, 1959/1961–1968 | Kongresshalle, today called Haus der Kulturen der Welt, contact architect for Hugh Strubbins, in collaboration with Werner Düttmann

Müller, Gustav | 125 159
Collaboration with Franz-Heinrich Sobotka: Henry-Ford-Bau, FU, 1952–1954 | House of the Chamber of Commerce and Industry, 1945–1955, currently the Center for Metropolitan Studies | Pepper-Haus at the Ernst-Reuter-Platz, 1960–1963

Müller, Hans Christian (Berlin 1921–2010 Itzehoe) **| 203**
Studentendorf Eichkamp, TU, 1958–1959 and 1967 | Märkisches Viertel, Berlin, 1962–1967 | Evangelical consistory in the Hansaviertel, with Hans-Christian Müller, 1968–1971, demolished in 2011

N

O

P

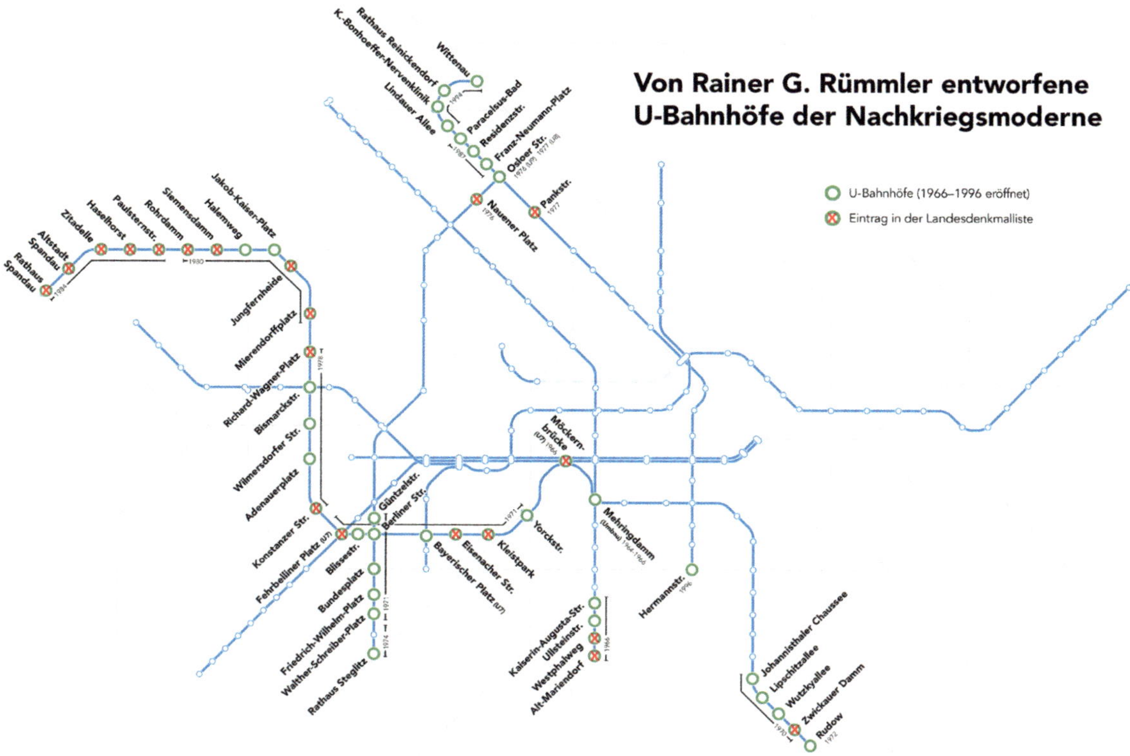

Institute of Architecture at the TH Berlin in the 1920s. Peter Poelzig studied in Berlin and Stuttgart, became a Nazi Party member in 1938, and was City Building Councilor in Münster until 1945. From 1954 onward he was Professor for Hospital Construction at the TU Berlin and was Director of the Institute for Hospital Construction at the IfA until being granted emeritus status in 1976. His works in Berlin include the Hermann Rietschel Institute of Heating and Air-Conditioning (1963–1964, TU); the Clinic Am Urban (1963–1970); the Bettenhaus in Westend (1957–1962); the Head Clinic (collaboration with Josef Paul Kleihues, 1963–1969) and the Building for general use (collaboration with Cornelius Hertling, 1977–1980).

Poetsch, Otto (1848–1915) | **71**
Institute of Hygiene, HU, 1899–1900, now the Institute of Pharmacology at the Charité | Institute of Veterinary Anatomy, HU, 1899–1902, now the Institute of Biology

Prouvé, Jean (Paris 1901–1984 Nancy) | **177**
Metalworker and designer | Rost- und Silberlaube, FU, 1967–1973 and 1975–1979

R

Rackebrandt, J. N. | **109 115**
Institute of Physical Chemistry and Electrochemistry, TH, 1913 | Institute of Metallurgy, TH, 1913–1916 | Inorganic Chemistry Laboratory, TH, 1912–1914 | Government master builder as a university subject

Raschdorff, Julius Carl (Pleß 1823–1914 Waldsieversdorf) | **97 101 103**
1878–1911 Teacher at the TH Charlottenburg | Main building of the TU, 1878–1884, in collaboration with Friedrich Hitzig and Richard Lucae | Chemical Laboratory, TU, 1881–1884 | Testing Laboratory for Heating and Ventilation Systems, TU, 1883–1884 | Berliner Dom, 1884–1905

Richter, Otto | 43
Institute of Social Science, HU, 1903–1904, collaboration with Erich Blunck, built as a commercial building

Rümmler, Rainer Gerhard (Möckern 1929–2004 Berlin) **| 161 169 173 177**
After World War II, Rainer Rümmler studied at the TU Berlin under Willy Kreuer and Hans Scharoun et al. He graduated in 1954, though he had already begun working in the civil engineering department at Berlin-Spandau in 1953. In 1964 he succeeded Bruno Grimmek as head of design at the Senate Building Department. His designs for numerous U-Bahn subway stations gave the underground train network in West Berlin its characteristic, colorful appearance. The planning and execution of the pedestrian passage to the Internationales Congress Centrum were also based on a design by Rümmler. He also designed the Western Allies' Checkpoint Bravo (now Dreilinden rest stop) and several fire stations and administration buildings. His academic buildings include the new Pharmaceutical Institute (1960–1966, FU, collaboration with Horst Kretschmer and Cuno Ratsch), the annex of the Dental and Maxillary Clinic (1981–1982, originally from 1955–1956, FU), the new building of the Botanical Museum (1983–1987) and the Mensa II in the Rost- und Silberlaube (1977–1982, FU).

Rüthnick Architekten | 45
Elisabeth Rüthnick, Wolfgang Planitzer, Malte Looff | "Pergamon Palais", HU, 2009–2011 | Refurbishment of main building, HU, 2005–2011 | Refurbishment of the morgue, 2012–2014 | Restoration of the Palais am Festungsgraben, 2018–2022, since 2019 HU

S

SAA Schweger Architekten | 65
Bettenhochhaus, remodeling of the facade, 2014–2016

Sand, Wolf (1904–unknown) **| 133**
Institute of Energy Engineering, TU, 1959–1961

Sandow, Albrecht | 115
Remodeling of the Institute of Physical Chemistry and Electrochemistry (from 1913), TU, 1962

Sartory, Barna von (Pécs 1927–2000 Berlin) **| 137 220 221**
Mathematics building, TU, 1967–1983

Sattler, Carl (Florenz 1877–1966 Munich) **| 167 245**
The last contract architect at the Kaiser-Wilhelm-Gesellschaft, successor of Ernst von Ihne | Kaiser Wilhelm Institute of Physics, FU, 1935–1937 | KWI of Anthropology, Human Heredity, and Eugenics, FU, 1926–1927 | Institute for Brain Research, Berlin-Buch, 1929–1930 | Harnack-Haus, 1928–1929 | Institute for Cell Physiology, KWG, 1929–1931

Sauerbruch Hutton | 215
Since 1989, Louisa Hutton and Matthias Sauerbruch have run a company specializing in architecture, urban planning and design. Their work has made its mark on cities including Berlin, Munich and recently Heilbronn. Their Center for Photonics in Adlershof, built between 1996 and 1998, has enhanced the academic landscape of Berlin. Matthias Sauerbruch is the Director of the Architecture Section at the Akademie der Künste Berlin

Scharoun, Hans (Bremen 1893–1972 Berlin) | **127 131 196 197 203 241 256**

Hans Scharoun studied architecture at the TH Berlin but never completed his studies. He subsequently worked as an architect in Wrocław, where he became a professor at the Akademie für Kunst und Kunstgewerbe. In the late 1920s he was responsible for the building plan for the large Siemensstadt development in Berlin. In 1945 he became City Building Councilor in Berlin, a post he held briefly until 1947. That same year, the TH Berlin appointed him Professor for Urban Planning. Parallel to this, he was head of the East Berlin Institut für Bauwesen until 1950. During this time he drew up various ideas for the urban planning of Berlin. From 1955 until 1968 he was President of the Akademie der Künste, in which period he also designed the flat-roofed building at the Institute of Architecture at the TU (1962–1970) and the new Staatsbibliothek in Potsdamer Strasse in collaboration with Edgar Wisniewski (1966–1978). Just across the street from the Staatsbibliothek is the Berliner Philharmonie (1957–1963) which Scharoun also designed.

Schiedhelm, Manfred (Worms 1934–2011 Berlin) | **177 180**

Following his architecture studies in Darmstadt, Schiedhelm stayed in the city to work for a time before moving to Paris. In 1961 he joined Candilis, Josic and Woods in a collective that won the tender for the extension of the FU; in 1966 he formally became a partner of the group. He was a member of Team X, a group of young architects that organized the tenth CIAM congress and rejected the division of work and housing in urban planning. He left his mark on the FU with his collaboration on the Rost- und Silberlaube (1967–1973, 1975–1979, FU) and the adjacent Education Library (1980–1984, FU). Between 1988 and 2004 he was in charge of the refurbishment of the chemistry building at the TU, which was extended to include an underground chemical storage facility (1991–1994). Schiedhelm opened his own office in Berlin 1968 – together with Karen Axelrad-Schiedhelm from 1978 onward – which he ran until his death in 2011. He taught in Braunschweig as Professor of Building Construction, and was a guest professor in Boston, Los Angeles, Vienna, Budapest and Glasgow.

Schinkel, Karl Friedrich (Neuruppin 1781–1841 Berlin) | **17 23 29 35 69 96 101 254**

The list of Karl Friedrich Schinkel's activities is a long one: as a master builder, architect, urban planner, graphic designer, painter, medalist, stage designer, Schinkel's work had a huge influence on the Neoclassicist and Historicist movements in Prussia.
After attending an exhibition of drawings by Friedrich Gilly, Schinkel made up his mind to become a master builder. He was later to become Gilly's student, enrolling at the newly founded Berliner Bauakademie in 1799. He attended lectures at the Akademie der Schönen Künste and was one of the first

graduates to pass the exams as a civil servant. Following the death of Friedrich Gilly, who by then had become a good friend, Schinkel continued his mentor's building projects.
In 1803 he made his first trip to Italy, which was to have a lasting influence on his artistic career. While in Rome he befriended Wilhelm von Humboldt, and after extended stays in France, Frankfurt and Weimar he returned to Berlin in 1805. Wilhelm von Humboldt recommended Schinkel for the post of Head of Artistic Affairs, which he took up in 1810. He was later to become Privy Chief Building Assessor of the Berlin Building Commission. He designed the interior of Queen Luise's chambers in Berlin Palace. Following the death of Paul Ludwig Simon in 1815, Schinkel took over his post as Privy Upper Building Councilor, in which capacity he made definitive contributions to the urban landscape of Berlin as the prestigious capital city of Pussia. Schinkel realized several famous state buildings including the Königswache (Guard House) and the Altes Museum. After the Royal National Theater by Carl Gotthard Langhans was almost completely destroyed by fire in 1817, it was rebuilt based on plans by Schinkel.
While working as Professor of Architecture, between 1822 and 1837 Schinkel (with Peter Beuth) published "Vorbilder für Fabrikanten und Handwerker" (Models for Manufacturers and Craftsmen), a comprehensive collection with illustrations of forms and patterns intended to provide orientation for ideas for vocational schools. In 1824 he was commissioned to travel to Italy to gather ideas for the foundation of museums and collections in Berlin. He made a further trip with Beuth across France to England and Scotland in order to study the advanced developments in engineering there. During the years 1827 to 1829 he realized the annex of Beuth's Gewerbeakademie. In 1836 Schinkel moved

into an official residence in the Bauakademie building, which he realized between 1832 and 1836. Upon being appointed Chief Building Director in 1838 and thus the Royal Architect, he reached the high point of his career. He built an observatory for the university in 1835, though it was torn down in 1913. In addition, Schinkel designed an alternative building for the Alte Palais and planned a library behind the HU.

Schlempp, Walter | 118

Ernst-Reuter-Haus, administration building for the council of communities, 1938–1942

Schlüter, Andreas (Danzig 1659/1660–1714 Sankt Petersburg) **| 23**

Fasade and courtyard of the Berlin Palace um 1699

Schmid-Meiningen, Ernst | 135

Institute of Mechanics, TU, 1928

Schmieden, Heino (Soldin 1835–1913 Berlin) **| 53 229 231**

Heino Schmieden began studying at the Berlin Bauakademie in 1854, and following his Building Authorities traineeship he passed his exams to become a State Master Builder in 1866. He realized plans for museums, hospitals, monuments, and mansions, and also designed numerous residential homes and commercial buildings. Up until the death of Martin Gropius, he was a partner in Sozietät Gropius & Schmieden, which was one of the largest and most successful architecture firms in Berlin. Victor von Weltzien was a partner in the firm until 1888, and Rudolph Speer was a partner until 1893. Between 1899 and 1913 Schmieden collaborated with Julius Boethke. After Heino Schmieden died, his son Heinrich took over his share of the company. In 1881 Schmieden became a member of the Prussian Akademie des Bauwesens, and from 1887 a member of the Prussian Akademie der Künste. The Royal Institute of British Architects named him a corresponding member. Among the academic buildings in Berlin that Schieden was involved with were the Surgical Clinic (1878–1883); the Gynecological Clinic (1880–1882); the Clinic for Surgery and Ophthalmology (1873–1883) and the Königliche Kunstschule (completed in 1880).

Schoszberger, Hans (Oderfurt 1907–1997 Berlin) | **121 175**

Extension to the former House of Research, FU, 1956 | Telefunken-Hochhaus, 1958–1960, with Paul Schwebes | Zentrum am Zoo, 1956–1957, with Paul Schwebes (high-rise building at Hardenbergplatz, Zoo Palast, Bikini-Haus, Kleines Hochhaus, parking garage am Zoo)

Schwebes, Paul (Stargard 1902–1978 Berlin) | **121**

Telefunken-Hochhaus, 1958–1960, in collaboration with Hans Schoszberger | Zentrum am Zoo, 1956–1957, collaboration with Schoszberger

Schwechten, Franz (Cologne 1841–1924 Berlin)

Kriegs-Akademie, 1879–1883

Schwennicke, Karl-Heinrich (Berlin 1901–1985 Berlin) | **121 125 133**

Heinrich-Hertz-Institut für Schwingungsforschung, 1964–1968 | North wing of the main building with Kurt Dübbers, TU, 1963–1968

Sobotka, Franz-Heinrich (Vienna 1907–1988 Berlin) | **125 159**

Franz-Heinrich Sobotka studied at the Academy of Applied Arts in Vienna. From 1927 onward he worked in Berlin, in the office of Erich Mendelsohn among others. He designed residential homes and commercial buildings with his own company, which he ran for many years with Gustav Müller | Henry-Ford-Bau, FU, 1952–1954 | House of the Chamber of Commerce and Industry, 1945–1955, Center for Metropolitan Studies at the TU | Pepper-Haus at the Ernst Reuter Platz, 1960–1963

Spieker, Paul Emmanuel (Trarbach 1826–1896 Wiesbaden) | **39 47**

Institute of Physics, HU, 1873–1879 | Institute of Physiology, HU, 1873–1879 | Second Chemical Institute, HU, 1873–1879 | Technological Institute, HU, 1873–1879 | Metronomical Institute (Normal-Aichungs-Kommission), 1871–1873 | Institute of

Pharmacology, HU, 1873–1879 | University Library, HU, 1871–1874 | Theater and lecture hall of the Urania Society, 1888–1889 (Invalidenstrasse 58)

Staab, Volker (Heidelberg 1957) | **217 251**
Institute of Chemistry, HU, 1998–2002 | Laboratory building for medical genome research, Berlin-Buch, 2003–2006

Stahn, Otto (Berlin 1859–1930 Berlin) | **191**
Student of J. C. Raschdorff, from 1913 building officer, built mainly bridges such as the Oberbaumbrücke (1892–1896) | Former elementary school (now the John-F.-Kennedy- Institut), 1904–1905 (Extension by Erich Schwiertz, 1928)

Straumer, Heinrich (Chemnitz 1876–1937 Berlin) | **167 193**
Heinrich Straumer was a student and later employee (from 1887) of the Reichstag architect Paul Wallot. Between 1903 and 1906 he worked for Cremer & Wolffenstein and in 1906 he set up his own architect's firm in Berlin. Together with Hans Hermann, Straumer was the architect of the former Deutsches Entomologischen Museums (1909–1911), which today houses the East Asian Studies of the FU. The former Institut für Vererbungs- und Züchtungsforschung of the Agricultural College (1921–1922) was also designed by Straumer and shows the influences of the English "Cottage Style", of which he was an exponent. Today there are several university institutes along the Albert-Thaer-Weg that are used by the HU, the TU and the FU. A further building designed by Straumer, and which is now part of the FU, is the Haus des Verbandes der öffentlichen Feuerversicherungsanstalten (1926–1927). Since 1994 it has housed the executive board of the FU. Straumer designed several new buildings for the Agricultural College Berlin in Dahlem (1921–1929). He was also involved in the construction of the U-Bahn subway stations at Thielplatz (1912–1913) and the Berlin Funkturm (1924–1926).

Swora, Karl-Ernst (1933–2001 Berlin) | **65 85**
Surgical Center of the Charité (Bettenhochhaus), 1976–1982, collaboration with Peter Korneli | Palast der Republik (with five other architects), 1973–1976, demolished 2006–2008 | Departmental building for physics and electronics, HU, 1982–1984, in collaboration with Fritz Kalusche | Haus der sowjetischen Wissenschaft und Kultur 1981–1984

T

Taut, Max (Königsberg 1884–1967 Berlin) | **117 194**
Former administration buildings of the Reichsknappschaft, 1928–1930, in collaboration with Franz Hoffmann | From 1918 a member of the November Group artists' collective | From 1926 a member of "Der Ring" architects' collective | 1945–1953 professor at the College of Arts Berlin | From 1955 Director of the Architecture Department of the Akademie der Künste Berlin

Techow, Otto (Brandenburg an der Havel 1848–1919 Berlin) | **175**
Water tower with weather station, FU, 1886

Thür, Georg (Berlin 1846–1924 Dortmund) | **33 43 53 81 111 173**
Georg Thür was a state ministry official in Berlin for almost 50 years and was responsible for the administration of the department for the university buildings for over two decades. In Berlin he realized the Chemical Laboratory (HU, 1899–1900), the Institute of Hygiene and the Institute of Physiology (HU, 1903–1905), the

BIBLIOGRAPHY

The following bibliographical references summarize the main sources from which this publication draws for its thematically redesigned presentation. The aim was to offer an easily accessible perspective on the genesis and development of Berlin's scientific architecture. Accordingly, the focus is on the presentation of the connections between mostly established facts rather than on scientific research into novel issues. For this reason, footnotes were omitted in favor of legibility. As an invitation to readers, the following bibliographical references include on the one hand titles which are suitable for researching further information on scientific buildings in Berlin, and on the other hand, publications which the editors consider particularly suitable for further study of the topics of architecture, science and the city. Here, both comprehensive descriptions and exemplary analyses were selected. An exhaustive enumeration of all sources used, especially archival sources, was, however, omitted.

Berlin Architecture

A good starting point for many inquiries about buildings in Berlin is the book series of the Architekten- und Ingenieurverein zu Berlin (AIV), which has been published since 1887. The current third series contains the volumes in particular:

Berlin und seine Bauten, Teil V, Bd. A: Bauten für die Kunst, Berlin/München 1983.

Berlin und seine Bauten, Teil V, Bd. B: Hochschulen, Petersberg 2004.

Berlin und seine Bauten, Teil V, Bd. C: Schulen, Berlin 1991.

Berlin und seine Bauten, Teil VII, Bd. A: Krankenhäuser, Berlin 1997.
Berlin und seine Bauten, Teil VII, Bd. B: Sozialbauten, Berlin 2003.

Berlin und seine Bauten, Teil IX: Industriebauten, Bürohäuser, Berlin 1971.

Berlin und seine Bauten, Teil XI: Gartenwesen, Berlin 1972.

The digitally available historical editions of 1877 and 1896 are also helpful, in some cases with far more detailed descriptions of the (planned) scientific use of the university and academic buildings:

Berlin und seine Bauten. Zwei Bände, Berlin 1877. digital.zlb.de/viewer/metadata/16337858/3

Berlin und seine Bauten. Drei Bände, Berlin 1896. digital.zlb.de/viewer/metadata/16337874/1

More detailed insights are provided by the articles in the following two journals, which can be easily retrieved with the help of the building data given in this volume:

Zentralblatt der Bauverwaltung digital.zlb.de/viewer/metadata/14688302/1/

Zeitschrift für Bauwesen digital.zlb.de/viewer/!metadata/15239363/0/ LOG_0000

For research on individual buildings, the monument database, the monument map and the monument list of the Landesdenkmalamt Berlin are also available:

www.berlin.de/landesdenkmalamt/denkmale/

For a more compact description, see the general architecture guides for Berlin:

Brendgens, Guido; König, Norbert: Berlin Architektur. Ein Architekturführer, Berlin 2003.

Schendel, Dominik: Architekturführer Berlin. Zwölf Touren durch die deutsche Hauptstadt, Berlin 2016.

Schulz, Joachim; Gräbner, Werner: Berlin. Architektur von Pankow bis Köpenick, Berlin 1987.

Wörner, Martin: Architekturführer Berlin, 7. Auflage, Berlin 2013.

On Historical Urban Development

Ribbe, Wolfgang (Hg.): Geschichte Berlins, 2 Bände, 3. erweiterte und aktualisierte Auflage, Berlin 2002.

Schwenk, Herbert: Berliner Stadtentwicklung von A bis Z. Kleines Handbuch zum Werden und Wachsen der deutschen Hauptstadt, 3. erweiterte Auflage, Berlin 2001.

Specific Topics in Berlin's Architectural History

Bernhardt, Christoph: Schönheit versus Funktionalität. Architekten, Ingenieure und der Wandel der Expertenkultur im Städtebau im Kontext des Wettbewerbs Groß-Berlin 1908/10, in: Bodenschatz, Harald; Kress, Celina (Hg.): Kult und Krise des großen Plans im Städtebau, Petersberg 2017, S. 152–159.

Bodenschatz, Harald (Hg.): Städtebau 1908/1968/2008 – Impulse aus der TU (TH), Berlin 2009.

Hoffmann, Utz: Naturforscher. Ein Reiseführer zu Denkmälern und Sammlungen in Berlin und Brandenburg, Berlin 1992.

Kleihues, Josef (Hg.): 750 Jahre Architektur und Städtebau in Berlin. Die Internationale Bauausstellung im Kontext der Baugeschichte Berlins, Stuttgart 1987.

Krohn, Carsten (Hg.): Das ungebaute Berlin. Stadtkonzepte im 20. Jahrhundert, Berlin 2010.

Reichhardt, Hans J.; Schäche, Wolfgang: Von Berlin nach Germania – Über die Zerstörungen der Reichshauptstadt durch Albert Speers Neugestaltungsplanungen, 3. verbesserte und veränderte Auflage, Berlin 1985.

Reuther, Hans, Die große Zerstörung Berlins – Zweihundert Jahre Stadtbaugeschichte, Frankfurt 1985. Schäche, Wolfgang: Architektur und Städtebau in Berlin zwischen 1933 und 1945, Berlin 1991.

Stephan, Hans: Die neue Formgebung im städtebaulichen Bild der Reichshauptstadt, in: Jahrbuch der Reichshauptstadt, Berlin 1939, S. 28–34.

Berlin Universities (and Their Cooperation Partners)

The Technische Universität, the Hochschule der Künste, and the Freie Universität have their own architectural guides, each containing a large number of references to individual plans and buildings:

Ahrens, Rotraud; u. a.: Villen, Rost- und Silberlauben. Baugeschichtliche Spaziergänge über den Campus der Freien Universität, Berlin 1993.

Bollé, Michael (Hg.): Der Campus. Ein Architekturführer durch das Gelände der Hochschule der Künste und der Technischen Universität, Berlin 1994.

Brachmann, Christoph; Suckale, Robert (Hg.): Die Technische Universität Berlin und ihre Bauten. Ein Rundgang durch zwei Jahrhunderte Architektur- und Hochschulgeschichte, Berlin 1999.

Schilling, Martina (Hg.): Freie Universität Berlin – Ein Architekturführer zu den Hochschulbauten, Berlin 2011.

The publications on the individual university histories often deal in varying depth with their academic buildings, the conversion of existing buildings, and also the history of academies and non-university research institutions:

HU

vom Bruch, Rüdiger; Tenorth, Heinz-Elmar (Hg.): Geschichte der Universität Unter den Linden 1810–2010, 6 Bände, Berlin 2010–2012.

Lenz, Max: Die Geschichte der Königlichen Friedrich-Wilhelms-Universität zu Berlin, 4 Bände, Berlin 1910–1918.

TU

Becker, Josef: Von der Bauakademie zur Technischen Universität. 150 Jahre technisches Unterrichtswesen in Berlin, Berlin 1949.

Rürup, Reinhard (Hg.): Wissenschaft und Gesellschaft. Beiträge zur Geschichte der Technischen Universität Berlin, 1879–1979, Berlin 1979.

Schwarz, Karl (Hg.): 1799–1999. Von der Bauakademie zur Technischen Universität Berlin, Berlin 2000.

FU

Hoffmann, Jessica; Seidel, Helena; Baratella, Nils (Hg.): Geschichte der Freien Universität Berlin. Ereignisse – Orte – Personen, Berlin 2008.

Kubicki, Stanislaw Karol; Lönnendonker, Siegward (Hg.): Beiträge zur Wissenschaftsgeschichte der Freien Universität Berlin, 7 Bände, Göttingen 2009–2015.

Akademien

Akademie der Wissenschaften der DDR (Hg.): Die Akademie der Wissenschaften der DDR. Geschichte und Auftrag, Berlin 1987.

Fischer, Wolfram (Hg.): Die Preußische Akademie der Wissenschaften zu Berlin 1914–1945, Berlin 2000.

Kocka, Jürgen (Hg.): Die Königlich Preußische Akademie der Wissenschaften zu Berlin im Kaiserreich, Berlin 1999.

Kocka, Jürgen (Hg.): Die Berliner Akademien der Wissenschaften im geteilten Deutschland 1945–1990, Berlin 2002.

KWG/MPG

vom Brocke, Bernhard; Laitko, Hubert (Hg.): Die Kaiser-Wilhelm-/Max-Planck-Gesellschaft und ihre Institute. Studien zu ihrer Geschichte: Das Harnack-Prinzip, Berlin/New York 1996.

Henning, Eckart; Kazemi, Marion: Handbuch zur Institutsgeschichte der Kaiser-Wilhelm-/Max-Planck-Gesellschaft zur Förderung der Wissenschaften 1911–2011. Daten und Quellen, 2 Teilbände, Berlin 2016.

Vierhaus, Rudolf; vom Brocke Bernhard (Hg.): Forschung im Spannungsfeld von Politik und Gesellschaft. Geschichte und Struktur der Kaiser-Wilhelm-/Max-Planck-Gesellschaft, Stuttgart 1990.

Science and Humanities in Berlin

In 1987, publications from both German states on the 750th anniversary of the city of Berlin placed a special focus on Berlin as a city of science and scholarship. In different ways, Berlin's role in the development of the modern sciences is presented from urban, cultural, and socio-historical perspectives.

Laitko, Hubert (Leiter eines Autorenkollektivs): Wissenschaft in Berlin. Von den Anfängen bis zum Neubeginn nach 1945, Berlin 1987.

Buddensieg, Tilmann; Düwell, Kurt; Sembach, Klaus-Jürgen (Hg.): Wissenschaften in Berlin, 3 Bände (1. Objekte, 2. Disziplinen, 3. Gedanken), Berlin 1987.

Further perspectives on science in Berlin can be found in:

Architekten- und Ingenieur-Verein zu Berlin (Hg.): Schinkel-Wettbewerb 2011. Science City – Die unbedingte Universität, Berlin 2011.

vom Bruch, Rüdiger: Die Stadt als Stätte der Begegnung. Gelehrte Geselligkeit im Berlin des 19. und 20. Jahrhundert, in: Kant, Horst (Hg.): Fixpunkte – Wissenschaft in der Stadt und der Region, Berlin 1996, S. 1–30.

Felt, Ulrike: Die Stadt als verdichteter Raum der Begegnung zwischen Wissenschaft und Öffentlichkeit. Reflexionen zu einem Vergleich der Wissenschaftspopularisierung in Wien und Berlin um die Jahrhundertwende, in: Goschler, Constantin (Hg.): Wissenschaft und Öffentlichkeit in Berlin, 1870–1930, Stuttgart 2000, S. 185–220.

Fischer, Norbert: Wissenschaft und Kunst in Berlin. Ein Führer durch die wissenschaftlichen Anstalten, Vereinigungen, Museen und Sammlungen, Berlin 1934.

Hachtmann, Rüdiger: Wissenschaftsmetropole Berlin, in: Wildt, Michael; Kreutzmüller, Christoph (Hg.): Berlin 1933–1945. Stadt und Gesellschaft im Nationalsozialismus, München 2013, S. 261–277.

Hennig, Jochen; Andraschke, Udo (Hg.): Weltwissen. 300 Jahre Wissenschaften in Berlin, München 2010.

Laitko, Hubert: Friedrich Althoff und die Wissenschaft in Berlin. Konturen einer Strategie, in: Bernhard vom Brocke (Hg.): Wissenschaftsgeschichte und Wissenschaftspolitik im Industriezeitalter. Das System Althoff in historischer Perspektive, Hildesheim 1991, S. 69–85.

Vogt, Annette: Vom Hintereingang zum Hauptportal? Lise Meitner und ihre Kolleginnen an der Berliner Universität und in der Kaiser-Wilhelm- Gesellschaft, Stuttgart 2007.

Zöbl, Dorothea: Siemens in Berlin. Spaziergänge durch die Geschichte der Elektrifizierung, Berlin 2008.

Science, Architecture, City

Ash, Mitchel G.: Räume des Wissens – was und wo sind sie?, Berichte zur Wissenschaftsgeschichte 23 (2000), S. 235–242.

Brake, Klaus; Kress, Celina: „Wissens-Orte" in Berlin: Wahrnehmung, Verständnis und räumliche Repräsentation 1810–2010, Informationen zur modernen Stadtgeschichte (IMS) 1 (2015), S. 99–120.

Dierig, Sven; Lachmund, Jens; Mendelsohn, Andrew: Science and the City, Chicago 2003.

Franz, Peter: Knowledge City Berlin? Potenziale und Risiken einer Stadtentwicklungsstrategie mit dem Fokus Wissenschaft, in: Ulf Matthiesen/ Gerhard Mahnken (Hg.): Das Wissen der Städte, Wiesbaden 2009, S. 95–110. Heßler, Martina: Die kreative Stadt. Zur Neuerfindung eines Topos, Bielefeld 2007.

Heßler, Martina: Science in the City. European Traditions and American Models, in: Hård, Mikael; Misa, Thomas J. (Hg.): Urban Machinery. Inside Modern European Cities, Cambridge, Mass. 2008, S. 211–232.

Hughes, Thomas P.: The City as Creator and Creation, in: Kleihues, Joseph Paul; Rathgeber, Christina (Hg.): Berlin, New York. Like and Unlike. Essays on Architecture and Art from 1870 to the Present, New York 1993, S. 13–32.

Koch, Wilfried: Baustilkunde, 34. Auflage, München 2014.

Kruft, Hanno-Walter: Geschichte der Architekturtheorie. Von der Antike bis zur Gegenwart, 6. ergänzte Auflage, München 2013.

Lampugnani, Vittorio Magnago: Die Stadt von der Neuzeit bis zum 19. Jahrhundert: Urbane Entwürfe in Europa und Nordamerika, Berlin 2017.

Lampugnani, Vittorio Magnago: Die Stadt im 20. Jahrhundert. Visionen, Entwürfe, Gebautes, 2 Bände, Berlin 2010.

Livingstone, David N.: The Spaces of Knowledge. Contributions Towards a Historical Geography of Science, Environment and Planning. Society and Space 13 (1995), S. 5–34.

Livingstone, David N.: Putting Science in Its Place. Geographies of Scientific Knowledge, Oxford 2003.

Livingstone, David N.; Withers, Charles W. J. (Hg.): Geographies of Nineteenth-Century Science, Chicago 2011.

Matthiesen, Ulf (Hg.): Stadtregion und Wissen. Analysen und Plädoyers für eine wissensbasierte Stadtpolitik, Wiesbaden 2004.

Matthiesen, Ulf (Hg.): Das Wissen der Städte. Neue stadtregionale Entwicklungsdynamiken im Kontext von Wissen, Milieus und Governance, Wiesbaden 2009.

Meusburger, Peter: Wissen und Raum – ein subtiles Beziehungsgefecht, in: Kempte, Klaus; Meusburger, Peter (Hg.): Bildung und Wissensgesellschaft, Heidelberg 2006, S. 269–308.

Nägelke, Hans-Dieter: Hochschulbau im Kaiserreich. Historische Architektur im Prozeß bürgerlicher Konsensbildung, Kiel 2000.

Schmidtke, Oliver: Die Architektur der Ruhr-Universität Bochum sowie der Universität. Bielefeld und ihre Entsprechung im technokratischen Deutungsmuster von Wissenschaft, in: Franzmann, Andreas; Wolbring, Barbara (Hg.): Zwischen Idee und Zweckorientierung. Vorbilder und Motive von Hochschulreformen seit 1945, Berlin 2007, S. 137–182.

Schregel, Susanne: Interdisziplinarität im Entwurf. Zur Geschichte einer Denkform des Erkennens in der Bundesrepublik (1955–1975),

NTM. Zeitschrift für Geschichte der Wissenschaften, Technik und Medizin 24 (2016), S. 1–37.

Tietz, Jürgen: Gebaute Bildung. Hochschularchitektur der Nachkriegszeit, Bonn 2012.

Mitte

Akademie der Wissenschaften der DDR (Hg.): Die Entwicklung der Physik in Berlin (Die Entwicklung Berlins als Wissenschaftszentrum 1870–1930, Teil V), Berlin 1984.

Akademie der Wissenschaften der DDR (Hg.): Zur Entwicklung der biologischen Disziplinen in Berlin – insbesondere an der Berliner Universität (Die Entwicklung Berlins als Wissenschaftszentrum 1870–1930, Teil III), Berlin 1982.

Barthel, Manfred (Hg.): Beiträge zur Geschichte des Museums für Naturkunde der Humboldt-Universität zu Berlin und zu seinen aktuellen Forschungs- und Bildungsaufgaben, Wissenschaftliche Zeitschrift der Humboldt-Universität zu Berlin, Math.-Natw. Reihe 38, 4 (1989), S. 277–420.

Bredekamp, Horst: Berlin am Mittelmeer. Kleine Architekturgeschichte der Sehnsucht nach dem Süden, Berlin 2018.

Demps, Laurenz: Die ehemalige königliche Bibliothek. Bau- und Nutzungsgeschichte; in: Oestreich, Axel; Hentschel, Ingrid (Hg.): Kommode. Die Fassadenrestaurierung der ehemaligen Königlichen Bibliothek, Berlin 2011, S. 13–49.

Dierig, Sven: Wissenschaft in der Maschinenstadt. Emil Du Bois-Reymond und sein Laboratorium in Berlin, Göttingen 2006.

Gandert, Klaus-Dietrich: Vom Prinzenpalais zur Humboldt-Universität. Die historische Entwicklung des Universitätsgebäudes in Berlin mit seinen Gartenanlagen und Denkmälern, 3. überarbeitete und erweiterte Auflage 1992, Berlin 1985.

Henning, Hans-Georg; Jugelt, Werner: Zur Geschichte der organischen Chemie an der Berliner Universität, Wissenschaftliche Zeitschrift der Humboldt-Universität zu Berlin, Math.-Natw. Reihe 38, 3 (1989), S. 197–201.

Hoffmann, Dieter: Das Physikalische Institut der Berliner Universität, Physikalische Blätter 55 (1999), S. 55–57.

Hoffmann, Dieter: Physics in Berlin: A Walk Through the Historical City Center, Physics in Perspective 1 (1999), S. 445–454.

Kempf, Jens Oliver: Die Königliche Tierarzneischule in Berlin von Carl Gotthard Langhans. Eine baugeschichtliche Gebäudemonographie, Berlin 2008.

Klein, Helmut (Hg.): Zur Entwicklung der Physik an der Berliner Universität, Wissenschaftliche Zeitschrift der Humboldt-Universität zu Berlin, Math.-Natw. Reihe 32, 5 (1983), S. 549–652.

Meisel, Manfred: Die Chemischen Institute der Berliner Friedrich-Wilhelms-Universität und der Humboldt-Universität zu Berlin, Humboldt-Spektrum 2/3 (2011), S. 18–23.

Paulukat, Inge (Hg.): 100 Jahre Geographisches Institut der Berliner Universität, Wissenschaftliche Zeitschrift der Humboldt-Universität zu Berlin, Math.-Natw. Reihe 36, 3 (1987), S. 173–260.

Sucker, Ulrich; Jahn, Ilse (Hg.): Beiträge zur Entwicklung der Biologie in der Geschichte der

Berliner Universität, Wissenschaftliche Zeitschrift der Humboldt-Universität zu Berlin, Math.-Natw. Reihe 34, 3/4 (1985), S. 187–385.

Urban, Florian: The Invention of the Historic City – Building the Past in East Berlin, Berlin (Dissertation TU Berlin) 2006.

Weischedel, Wilhelm (Hg.): Idee und Wirklichkeit einer Universität – Dokumente zur Geschichte der Friedrichs-Wilhelms-Universität zu Berlin, Berlin 1960.

Charlottenburg

Go, Jeong-Hi: Herta Hammerbacher. Virtuosin der Neuen Landschaftlichkeit – der Garten als Paradigma, Berlin 2006.

Gundlach, Wilhelm: Geschichte der Stadt Charlottenburg, 2 Bände, Berlin 1905.

Hoffmann, Dieter: Physics in Berlin: Walking tours in Charlottenburg and Dahlem and excursions in the vicinity of Berlin, Physics in Perspective 2 (2000), S. 426–445.

Lemmerich, Jost: Zur Geschichte der Physik an der Technischen Hochschule Berlin-Charlottenburg, Berlin 1987.

Wirth, Irmgard (Hg.): Die Bauwerke und Kunstdenkmäler von Berlin/Stadt und Bezirk Charlottenburg, Berlin 1961.

Dahlem

Engel, Michael: Geschichte Dahlems, Berlin 1984. Henning, Eckart (Hg.): Beiträge zur Wissenschaftsgeschichte Dahlems, 2. Auflage, München 2004.

Hnilica, Sonja: Systeme und Strukturen. Universitätsbau in der BRD und das Vertrauen in die Technik, in: Wolkenkuckucksheim 33 (2014), S. 211–233.

Kant, Horst; Reinhardt, Carsten (Hg.): 100 Jahre Kaiser-Wilhelm-/Max-Planck-Institut für Chemie (Otto-Hahn-Institut): Facetten seiner Geschichte Berlin, Berlin: Archiv der Max-Planck-Gesellschaft, Berlin 2012.

Kiem, Karl: Die Freie Universität Berlin (1967–1973) – Hochschulbau, Team-X-Ideale und tektonische Phantasie, Weimar 2008.

Kleilein, Doris: Implantat. Philologische Bibliothek der Freien Universität in Berlin-Dahlem, Die Bauwelt 34 (2005), S. 13–36.

Adlershof

Ahlbrecht, Bernd-Rüdiger; Strunk, Peter; Karlsch, Rainer; Flemming, Thomas; Ciesla, Burghard: 100 Jahre Innovation aus Adlershof. Wiege der deutschen Motorluftfahrt, Berlin 2009.

Graichen, Kurt; Heinzerling, Werner; Seifert, Karl-Dieter; Ahlbrecht, Bernd-Rüdiger: Technische Denkmale der Luftfahrtforschung in Berlin-Adlershof, Berlin 2012.

Günther, Manfred; Weichold, Jochen: Die Akademie der Wissenschaft der DDR in Berlin-Adlershof, Berlin 2000.

Thiessen, Karsten Peter; Welser, Horst: Die kugelförmigen Thermolabore, in: Müller, 307 Mandfred (Hg.), Adlershofer Splitter, Bd. 1. Zur Geschichte von chemischen Forschungsstätten der Akademie der Wissenschaft, Berlin 1996, S. 124–130.

Welser, Horst: Über den Bau der thermokonstanten Kugellabore der Deutschen Akademie der Wissenschaften zu Berlin in Adlershof, in:

Adlershofer Splitter, Bd. 3. Zur Geschichte der Forschungsgemeinschaft der naturwissenschaftlichen, technischen und medizinischen Einrichtungen der Deutschen Akademie der Wissenschaften zu Berlin, Berlin 1997, S. 116–126.

WISTA-Management GmbH (Hg.): 100 Jahre Innovation aus Adlershof. Wiege der deutschen Motorluftfahrt, Berlin 2009.

Charité

Bielka, Heinz: Geschichte der Medizinisch-Biologischen Institute Berlin-Buch, 2. Auflage, Heidelberg 2010.

Bleker, Johanna; Hess, Volker (Hg.): Die Charité. Geschichte(n) eines Krankenhauses, Berlin 2010.

Brinkschulte, Eva; Knuth, Thomas (Hg.): Das medizinische Berlin. Ein Stadtführer durch 300 Jahre Geschichte, Berlin 2010.

Einhäupl, Karl; Ganten, Dieter; Hein, Jakob (Hg.): 300 Jahre Charité. Im Spiegel ihrer Institute, Berlin 2010.

Interessengemeinschaft Bucher Chronik (Hg.): Aus einhundert Jahren Bucher Geschichte 1898–1998, 1. Auflage, Berlin 1998.

Schleiermacher, Sabine; Schagen, Udo (Hg.): Die Charité im Nationalsozialismus. Die Indienstnahme medizinischer Wissenschaft im Nationalsozialismus, Paderborn 2008.

Schmuhl, Hans-Walter: Hirnforschung und Krankenmord. Das Kaiser-Wilhelm-Institut für Hirnforschung 1937–1945, in: Vierteljahreshefte für Zeitgeschichte 4 (2002), S. 559–609.

Streckwall, Ralf (Hg.): 20 Jahre Bauen für die Wissenschaft. Max-Delbrück-Zentrum für molekulare Medizin – Campus Berlin Buch, Berlin 2013.

Wolff, Horst-Peter; Kalinich, Arno: Zur Geschichte der Krankenhausstadt Berlin-Buch, Frankfurt am Main 2008.

Collections: From the Kunstkammer to the Humboldt-Forum

Bredekamp, Horst: Architektur und Sammlungen der Humboldt-Universität zu Berlin (Ein Projekt des Kunstgeschichtliches Seminar), Berlin 1999, online: https://edoc.hu-berlin.de/handle/18452/65

Bredekamp, Horst; Brüning, Jochen; Weber, Cornelia (Hg.): Theater der Natur und Kunst. Theatrum Naturae et Artis, 2 Bände, Berlin 2000, 2001.

Hiller von Gaertringen, Katrin; Hiller von Gaertringen, Hans Georg (Hg.): Eine Geschichte der Berliner Museen in 227 Häusern, Berlin 2014.

Möbius, Hanno (Hg.): Vierhundert Jahre Technische Sammlungen in Berlin. Von der Raritätenkammer der Kurfürsten zum Museum für Verkehr und Technik, Berlin 1983.

The Campus Idea in Berlin

Havestadt, Christian; Contag, Max; Schmitz, Bruno; Blum, Otto: Die Umgestaltung im Stadtbild Berlin, Die Bauwelt 10 (1910), S. 26–28.

Scheffler, Karl: Berlin in 50 Jahren. Perspektiven einer Weltstadt, Uhu 9 (1926), S. 48–56.

Bodenschatz, Harald: Städtebau in Berlin. Schreckbild und Vorbild für Europa, 2. erweiterte Auflage, Berlin 2013.

Thorau, Dagmar; Schaulinski, Gernot (Hg.): Mythos Germania – Vision und Verbrechen, 2., aktualisierte und erweiterte Auflage, Berlin 2016.

Tubbesing, Markus: Der Wettbewerb Groß-Berlin 1910. Die Entstehung einer modernen Disziplin Städtebau, Tübingen, Berlin 2017.
Turner, Paul V.: Campus. An American Planning Tradition, Cambridge, Mass. 1984.

Meeting Places and Interspaces

Barz, Andreas: Die Anmut der Nachkriegsmoderne. Die Erneuerung des Nationalen Kulturdenkmals. Studentendorf Schlachtensee, kunsttexte.de 3 (2008), S. 1–4.

Naumann, Ulrich: Grundsätze des Bibliotheksbaus. Von den „Zehn Geboten" von Harry Faulkner-Brown zu den „Top Ten Qualities" von Andrew McDonald, in: Hauke, Petra; Werner, Klaus Ulrich (Hg.): Bibliotheken bauen und ausstatten, Bad Honnef 2009, S. 14–37.

Preußische Staatsbibliothek (Hg.): Fünfzehn Jahre Königliche und Staatsbibliothek, Berlin 1921.

Zünder, Ralf: Studentendorf Schlachtensee 1959 bis 1989. Eine Dokumentation, Berlin 1989.

Zünder, Ralf: Eichkamp! 60 Jahre Internationales Studentenheim in Berlin 1947–2007, Öhringen 2006.

Klack, Gunnar: Gebaute Landschaften: Fehling + Gogel und die organische Architektur. Landschaft und Bewegung als Natur-Narrative, Bielefeld 2015.

Sustainability and Ecology

Senatsverwaltung für Stadtentwicklung (Hg.): Bausteine der Nachhaltigkeit. Ökologisch Bauen in Berlin, Berlin 2009.

Kohlmaier, Georg; von Satory, Barna: Bürohaus und Ökologie, Berlin 1984.

Percent for Art, Monuments, and the City

Ammann, Jean-Christophe; Schelbert, Catherine: Plädoyer für eine neue Kunst im öffentlichen Raum, Parkett 2 (1984), S. 6–35.

Dickel, Hans; Fleckner, Uwe: Kunst in der Stadt. Skulpturen in Berlin 1980–2000, Berlin 2003.

Johnen, Jörg: Marmor für alle. Zur Kunst im öffentlichen Raum in Berlin, mit einem Gastbeitrag von Jeff Wall, Berlin 2018.

ILLUSTRATIONS

Title top, Henry-Ford-Bau, FU, 2009, Photo: Mila Hacke, Berlin

Title center, Leopold Ahrendts (zugeschrieben), Unter den Linden. Blick vom Opernplatz zur Universität, o. J. [1857], Photo, 16,50 cm x 21,60 cm, IV 69/266 V © Stiftung Stadtmuseum Berlin

Title below, Strasse des 17. Juni, taken from the Telefunkenhochhaus, 1960, Photo: unknown, presumably Willy Pragher or Friedrich Seidenstücker

inside cover, Scan of the map "Berlin um 1910" from the publication: "Städtebauliche Entwicklung Berlins seit 1650 in Karten", Geoportal Berlin / Berlin um 1910, EPSG: 25833 - TIFF, dl-de/by-2-0

9, Carl Daniel Freydanck, Die neue Sternwarte in Berlin, 1838, Oil on canvas, G 18, Stiftung Preußische Schlösser und Gärten Berlin-Brandenburg, KPM-Archiv, Photo: Fotostudio Bartsch

12, Karl Friedrich Schinkel, George Gropius (Publishing house), Entwurf zu der neuen Sternwarte in Berlin, Detail, 1836, Copper engraving on paper, 64 cm x 48 cm, VII 63/1127 w © Stiftung Stadtmuseum Berlin, Photo: Oliver Ziebe, Berlin

13, Photo: Eva-Maria Darge

14, Hermann Rückwardt, Ansicht der Eintrittshalle an der Vorderseite, Hauptgebäude von Friedrich Hitzig, 1885, Collotype on cardboard, 48,7 x 64,2 cm, 45635, Architekturmuseum, TU Berlin

15 top, in: Universität Bielefeld, Gerhard Trott, Bauplanung der Universität Bielefeld. Schriften Zum Aufbau einer Universität, Bd. 7, Bielefeld, 1974, Faltplan

15 top, in: Bauwelt 1964, Heft 6, p. 164

15 top, in: Bauwelt 1964, Heft 6, p. 170

16, in: Albert Guttstadt, Die naturwissenschaftlichen und medicinischen Staatsanstalten Berlins. Festschrift für die 59. Versammlung Deutscher Naturforscher und Ärzte, 1886, p. 267

17 left, in: Albert Guttstadt, Die naturwissenschaftlichen und medicinischen Staatsanstalten Berlins. Festschrift für die 59. Versammlung Deutscher Naturforscher und Ärzte, 1886, p. 271

17 right © Nöfer Architekten, Florian Profitlich

18,19, Senatsverwaltung für Stadtentwicklung und Wohnen

20, 21, Senatsverwaltung für Stadtentwicklung und Wohnen

22, Die Kaiserstadt aus der Vogelschau. Nach der Natur aufgenommen von Adolf Eltzner (old titel), in: Robert Springer: Berlin. Die deutsche Kaiserstadt nebst Potsdam und Charlottenburg mit ihren schönsten Bauwerken und hervorragendsten Monumenten, 1878, p. 2, Wood engraving, F Rep. 250-01 A 176-2, Landesarchiv Berlin, Ansichtensammlung

24 top, Photo: Matthias Heyde

24 below, Georg Wenzelaus von Knobelsdorff, Forum Fridericianum mit Anmerkungen von König Friedrich II., um 1740, 45,5 x 57cm, Drawing, A Pr. Br. Rep. 041 (Karten) 1844, Landesarchiv, Plankammer

26 top, approx. 1935, Photo, 13 x 18 cm, F Rep. 290 (02) Nr. II13119, Landesarchiv Berlin, Photo: unknown

26 below, Humboldt-Universität zu Berlin, 1951, Photo, Bild 183-12230-0006, Bundesarchiv, Photo: Martin Schmidt

28 top, Ludwig Eduard Lütke, Die Königliche Bauakademie in Berlin, Colored lithography, VII 62/574 a-f w © Stiftung Stadtmuseum Berlin

28 left, Andreas Kraska, Treppenhaus der Bauakademie von Karl Friedrich Schinkel, 1905, Watercolor and pencil, 67,5 cm x 99,5 cm, GHZ 69/44 © Stiftung Stadtmuseum Berlin, Photo: Michael Setzpfandt

28 below, Eduard Gaertner, Das königliche Gewerbeinstitut zu Berlin, approx. 1835, Steel engraving, 25 x 31 cm, VII 84/518 a w © Stiftung Stadtmuseum Berlin, Photo: Michael Setzpfandt, Berlin

30, Unbekannter Zeichner mit Einzeichnungen von Friedrich Wilhelm IV. von Preußen, Planungen zu einem Forum Fridericianum, approx. 1840, GK II (1) Berlin, Mappe 152, Stiftung Preußische Schlösser und Gärten Berlin-Brandenburg, Photo: Daniel Lindner 2018

31 top, Ludwig Eduard Lütke, Das Universitätsgebäude in Berlin, approx. 1830, Colored lithography on paper, VII 62/600 a-c w © Stiftung Stadtmuseum Berlin, Photo: Oliver Ziebe, Berlin

31 below, Friedrich August Calau, Baptista Weiss, Berlin (Publishing house), Das Königliche Bibliothek Gebäude zu Berlin, approx. 1810, Colored etching, 12 x 18 cm, GDR 76/57,6, © Stiftung Stadtmuseum Berlin, Photo: Oliver Ziebe

32 top, Rektoratsübergabe 1922, Walther Hermann Nernst © bpk/Bayerische Staatsbibliothek/Archiv Heinrich Hoffmann

32 left, Alte Bibliothek, Wiederaufbau, 1967, Photo, 6 x 6 cm, F Rep. 290-02-23 Nr. 7/1, Landesarchiv Berlin, Photo: Dieter and Vera Breitenborn

32 right, HU Universitätsarchiv, Fotosammlung, Photo 18

34 top © Landesdenkmalamt Berlin

34 left, HU Universitätsarchiv, Fotosammlung, Photo 16

34 below left, Königliche Akademie für Kunst und Wissenschaft (ehem. Marstall) von Johann Arnold Nering, 1902, Photo, 20,6 x 26,8 cm, F 0056, Architekturmuseum, TU Berlin

34 below right, Friedrich Wilhelm Klose, Die alte Sternwarte zwischen Dorotheenstraße und Unter den Linden, approx. 1835, Water color, 18 x 15,50 cm, GHZ 77/8 © Stiftung Stadtmuseum Berlin, Photo: Oliver Ziebe

35, Kaiser Wilhelm I. in seinem Arbeitszimmer im Alten Palais © Landesdenkmalamt Berlin

36, Magnus-Haus, approx. 1921/1923, Photo, 18 x 24 cm, F Rep. 290-01-30 Nr. 69, Landesarchiv Berlin, Photo: Otto Hagemann

38 top, Chemisches Institut von Albert Friedrich Cremer, Ansicht von der Georgenstraße (in: Atlas zur Zeitschrift für Bauwesen, hrsg. v. G. Erbkam, Jg. 17, 1867), 1865–1867, Engraving on paper, 27,2 x 43,7 cm, ZFB 17,003, Architekturmuseum, TU Berlin

38 left, in: Berlin und seine Bauten, Teil V, Bd. B, Hochschulen, p. 24, ill. 36

38 center right, Lesesaal in der Bibliothek von Paul Emanuel Spieker, HU, 1901, Photo, 24 x 30 cm, F Rep. 290 (05) Nr. II4173, Landesarchiv Berlin, Photo: Waldemar Titzenthaler

38 below, Photo: Eva-Maria Darge

40, in: Berlin und seine Bauten, Teil V, Bd. B, Hochschulen, p. 237, ill. 472

41, 1929, 400006590, bpk

42 top, Photo: Matthias Heyde

42 below left © Landesdenkmalamt Berlin

42 below right © Landesdenkmalamt Berlin

43, HU Universitätsarchiv, Fotosammlung, Photo 27

44 top left, HU Universitätsarchiv, Fotosammlung, Photo 26a

44 top right, Ganzfeldanordnung mit Spiralprojektion im ehemaligen Salon der Hohenzollern-Wohnung im Berliner Stadtschloss, Raum 699, 1930, Photo, 00193802 © ullstein bild/Zander & Labisch

44 below left, Photo: Arne Schirrmacher

44 below right, HU Presse

46 top, Publishing house Knackstedt & Näther, Hamburg 267, Ansichtskarte: Marschall-Brücke und Physikalisches Institut, approx. 1900, IV 61/3415 V © Stiftung Stadtmuseum Berlin, Photo: Dorin Alexandru Ionita

46 below, in: Berlin und seine Bauten, Teil V, Bd. B, Hochschulen, p. 39, ill. 65

48, Photos: Arne Schirrmacher

49 left, in: Franz Baltzer, Die Elektrische Stadtbahn in Berlin, Berlin 1897, Tafel 1

49 right, in: F. Baltzer, Die Elektrische Stadtbahn in Berlin, p. 27

50, Liegehalle auf dem Dach des Erweiterungsbaus der Universitäts-Frauenklinik, undated, Photo, 17 x 23 cm, A Pr. Br. Rep. 042 (Fotos) Nr. 2120, Landesarchiv Berlin, Photo: unknown

52 top, in: Albert Guttstadt, Die naturwissenschaftlichen und medicinischen Staatsanstalten Berlins. Festschrift für die 59. Versammlung Deutscher Naturforscher und Ärzte, Berlin 1886, p. 328

52 below, Photo: Arne Schirrmacher

54 top, Bildarchiv des Instituts für Geschichte der Medizin und Ethik in der Medizin, Charité – Universitätsmedizin Berlin

54 below, Erweiterungsbau der Universitäts-Frauenklinik, undated, Photo, 17 x 23 cm, A Pr. Br. Rep. 042 (Fotos) Nr. 2116, Landesarchiv Berlin, Photo: Ernst H. Börner

55, Photo: Arne Schirrmacher

56, Matthaeus Seutter, Blick auf die noch außerhalb der Stadtmauern gelegene Charité, approx. 1740, Colored etching, Wikipedia Commons

58 top, Charité-Krankenhaus © Landesdenkmalamt Berlin

58 below, Friedrich Albert Schwartz, Blick auf die Charite vom alten Hamburger Bahnhof aus, Photo, approx. 1888, Kart. Y 44252 –Blatt 194, SBB PK, Kartenabteilung, Sammlung F. A. Schwartz

60 top, Georg Diestel, Psychiatrische- und Nervenklinik der Charité, Berlin, Lageplan 1:500, Colored lithography on cardbord, 73,1 x 61,3 cm, 29607, Architekturmuseum, TU Berlin

60 below, Verwaltungsgebäude der Charité, Westansicht 1:100, 1899–1903, Colored lithography on paper, 47,8 x 66,4 cm, BZ-H 27,026, Architekturmuseum, TU Berlin

62 top, Photo: Arne Schirrmacher

62 center, Albert Friedrich Cremer, Friedrich-Wilhelms-Universität Berlin, Anatomisches Institut, Vorderansicht (in: Atlas zur Zeitschrift für Bauwesen, hrsg. v. G. Erbkam, Jg. 16, 1866), Etching on paper, 27,9 x 43,9 cm, ZFB 16,022, Architekturmuseum, TU Berlin

62 below, Photo: Arne Schirrmacher

64 top, Photo: Arne Schirrmacher

64 left, Architektur der DDR, title page September 1982

64 right, HU Universitätsarchiv, Fotosammlung, Photo 3

66 top left, Friedrich August Calau, Die Thier-Arzneyschule in Berlin No. 15, (3. Exemplare), 1795, Colored etching, 13,9 x 20 cm, VII 62/586 a-c w © Stiftung Stadtmuseum Berlin, Photo: Oliver Ziebe

66 top right, HU Universitätsarchiv, Fotosammlung, Photo 4

66 below, Johann Friedrich Kluge, Tierarzneischule Berlin (Entwurfszeichnung), 1812, Watercolor pen drawing, 42,7 x 64,7 cm, VII 89/100 W © Stiftung Stadtmuseum Berlin, Photo: Oliver Ziebe

68 Photos: Arne Schirrmacher

70 top, in: Masterplan, Campus Nord der HU, Faltblatt hg. v. TA HU Berlin, Bild und Texte: Prof. Dorothee Dubrau Architektur sowie Stadtplanung/Gast.Leyser LandschaftsArchitekten, Layout: Philipp Dubrau, undated

70 below © Rainer Gollmer

72 top, Photo: Arne Schirrmacher

72 below, Photo: Werner Huthmacher

74 top, Karl Eduard Biermann, Die Borsigsche Maschinenbau-Anstalt, 1847, Oil on canvas, 110 cm × 116,5 cm, Stiftung Stadtmuseum Berlin, Erworben mit Unterstützung der Kunststiftung der Länder, der Ernst von Siemens Kunststiftung, des Vereins der Freunde und Förderer des Stadtmuseums Berlin und weiterer Partner

74 below, © Landesdenkmalamt Berlin

76 top left, approx. 1940 © BGR Hannover

76 top right, in: Zentralblatt der Bauverwaltung, 20.5.1911, p. 250

76 below left, Photo: Matthias Heyde

76 below right, Photo: Arne Schirrmacher

78 top, approx.1960, Photo, 40018444, Photo: Max Ittenbach © bpk/Max Ittenbach

78 below, in: Zentralblatt der Bauverwaltung, 20.5.1911, p. 251

78 below right, Lichthof mit Walskeletten, im Vordergrund Aufsicht auf Dermoplastik und Skelett indischer Elefant, 1893, MfN, HBSB, ZM B III 832, N009 Nr. 212, Historische Bild- und Schriftgutsammlungen, Museum für Naturkunde Berlin

80, H. Gruber, Chemisches Institut, 1900, Print, 81 x 58 cm, H 015, HU Kustodie, Photo: Matthias Heyde

82 top, 40004145, bpk

82 left, Photo: Arne Schirrmacher

82 right, Photo: Eva-Maria Darge

84 top, HU Universitätsarchiv, Fotosammlung, Photo 9

84 left, Photo: Eva-Maria Darge

84 right, in: Wissenschaftliche Zeitschrift der Humboldt-Universität zu Berlin, 32 (1983), p. 643, ill. 4

87, Schwarminstallation des Humboldt Labors der HU Berlin auf dem Kosmografen im Foyer des Humboldt Forums, Photo: David von Becker, Compositing: Ali Hossaini

91, in: Hugo Koch, Die königliche Technische Hochschule zu Berlin, Berlin 1903, ill. 4

91 in: Ludwig Wittmack, Die Königliche Landwirtschaftliche Hochschule in Berlin, Berlin 1906, p. 59

91, Späth-Arboretum, Photo: Daniela Incoronato

91, Winckelmann-Institut der HU, Photo: Antonia Weiße

92, Senatsverwaltung für Stadtentwicklung und Wohnen

94, Gebäudealterkarte von Charlottenburg, 1905, Geschichte der Stadt Charlottenburg, hrsg. Wilhelm Gundlach, Berlin 1905, Stadtverwaltung Charlottenburg

96, Friedrich Hitzig, Hauptgebäude, TU, Aufriss der Hauptfront und Grundriss des Hauptgeschosses, 1878, Watercolor, ink on paper, 72,2 x 106,1 cm, 1854, Architekturmuseum, TU Berlin

98 top, in: Zeitschrift für Bauwesen 1886, Jahrgang XXXVI, Bl. 19

98 below, Richard Lucae, Hauptgebäude Querschnitt, 1877, Watercolour ink, heightened with white on cardboard, 72 x 116 cm, 10766, Architekturmuseum, TU Berlin

99 top, Hermann Rückwardt, Ansicht der Aula, Hauptgebäude von Friedrich Hitzig, 1885, Collotype on cardboard, 48,1 x 64,4 cm, 45639, Architekturmuseum, TU Berlin

99 below, Hermann Rückwardt, Glashof, Hauptgebäude von Friedrich Hitzig, 1885, Photo, 40,7 x 31,1 cm, 45636, Architekturmuseum, TU Berlin

100 top left, Photo: Arne Schirrmacher

100 center, Julius Raschdorff, Chemiegebäude, Fassadendetail, 1881–1884, Ink on cardboard, 100,6 x 70,5 cm, 14900, Architekturmuseum, TU Berlin

100 below left, Hermann Rückwardt, Ansicht der Eintrittshalle, Chemisches Laboratorium von Julius Raschdorff, 1885, Collotype on cardboard, 63,8 x 48,4 cm, 45634, Architekturmuseum, TU Berlin

100 below right, Photo: Eva-Maria Darge

102 top, in: Berlin und seine Bauten, Hochschulen, 1896, p. 288, ill. 278

102 left, Julius Raschdorff, Mechanisch-Technische Versuchsanstalt, Schnitt A-B 1:100 (Erweiterungsbau der MTV), 1894, Watercolor ink on cardboard, Detail, 20277, Architekturmuseum, TU Berlin

102 right, Richard Lucae, Schornstein, 1877, Ink colored, watercolored on paper, Detail, 10769, Architekturmuseum, TU Berlin

104 top, in: Michael Bollé, Der Campus. Ein Architekturführer durch das Gelände der Hochschule der Künste und der Technischen Universität, Berlin 1994, p. 64

104 center, Louis Müller, p. Kuhberg, Sammelausstellung der deutschen chemischen Industrie, Ansicht 1:400, Detail, 20367, Architekturmuseum, TU Berlin

104 below, Hauptgebäude, Rückansicht mit Gewächshaus, TU, 1962, F Rep. 290 (05) Nr. 0081295, Landesarchiv Berlin, Photo: Willi Nitschke

106 top, bpk/Luftbild Berlin GmbH

106 below, W.& H. C. Jogel, Berlin W., Ansichtskarte: Berlin-Charlottenburg. Akademisches Institut für Kirchenmusik, Hardenbergstrasse, IV 61/3609 V © Stiftung Stadtmuseum Berlin

108 top, Hermann Eggert, Erweiterungsbau, Grundriss (Erdgeschoss) 1:100, 1902, Lithography colored on cardboard, 68,8 x 100,3 cm, 29150, Architekturmuseum, TU Berlin

108 below, Erweiterungsbau, TU, 1960, Photo, 9 x 12 cm, F Rep. 290 (05) Nr. 0069438, Landesarchiv Berlin, Photo: Bert Sass

110, Photo: Mila Hacke, Berlin

112 top © Landesdenkmalamt Berlin, Photo: Wolfgang Bittner

112 below © Philipp Lohöfener/Wüstenrot Stiftung

113 top, Photo: Eva-Maria Darge

113 below, Photo: Arne Schirrmacher

114 top, J.N. Rackebrandt, p. Kuhberg (Drawings), Institut für Physikalische Chemie und Elektrochemie, 1923, Watercolored collotype print on paper, Ausschnitt Grundriss 1. OG 1:100, 20315, Architekturmuseum, TU Berlin

114 below, Photo: Arne Schirrmacher

116 top, Ansicht des Physikalischen Instituts von Otto Weißgerber von der Kurfürstenallee, 1932, Photo, F 8105, Architekturmuseum, TU Berlin, Photo: Hugo Schmölz

116 below, Innenansicht des Großen Hörsaals, Physikalisches Institut von Otto Weißgerber, 1932, Photo auf Karton, 61,3 x 81,3 cm, F 8106, Architekturmuseum, TU Berlin, Photo: Hugo Schmölz

119 left, Das Studentenhaus am Steinplatz in Charlottenburg, 40013483 © bpk/Kunstbibliothek, SMB

119 top, Staatsbesuch Prinzregent Pauls von Jugoslawien 2. Juni 1939, Photo, 10 x 15 cm, 50048864 © bpk/Bayerische Staatsbibliothek/Heinrich Hoffmann

119 below, Die Technische Hochschule anläßlich der 700-Jahr-Feier Berlins im Scheinwerferlicht, davor die aufgebauten Tribünen © bpk/Julius Wilcke

120 top, ullstein bild - imageBROKER/Thomas Robbin

120 center, in: Fritz Winckel, Technische Universität Berlin, 1965, p. 469

120 below, Photo: Mila Hacke

122 top, Photo: Markus Hilbich
122 below, Demonstration im "Stollen" des Instituts für Bergbau und Hüttenwesen, 1964, Photo, 6 x 9 cm, F Rep. 290 (05) Nr. 0103328, Landesarchiv Berlin, Photo: Raillon

123, Ernst-Reuter-Platz, 1967, 00045674 © bpk/Rolf Koehler, Photo: Rolf Koehler

124 top, Kurt Dübbers, Karl Heinrich Schwennicke, Hauptgebäude, Modellansicht von Westen mit Audimax, 1958, Photo, 18,6 x 24,4 cm, F 15706, Architekturmuseum, TU Berlin

124 center, TU Hochschularchiv, Photo: unknown
124 below, Photo: Eva-Maria Darge

126, Kurt Dübbers, Lageplan Nordgelände 1:500, 1957, Photo, 24,6 x 18,9 cm, F 15739,1, Architekturmuseum, TU Berlin

128 top left, Herta Hammerbacher, Architekturgebäude, Außenanlagen, Werkstatthof an der Nordseite des Hochhauses, Photo, 7 x 6,5 cm, F 11957, Architekturmuseum, TU Berlin

128 top right, Architekturgebäude der TU von Bernhard Hermkes, 1971, Photo, 9 x 12 cm, F Rep. 290 (05) Nr. 0147623, Landesarchiv Berlin, Photo: Günther Metzner

128 center, Bernhard Hermkes, Hans Scharoun, Herta Hammerbacher, Architekturgebäude. Ansicht von Westen auf Hochhaus und Flachbau 1:200, 1962, Blue print on paper, 48,4 x 112,9 cm, HH 0539,092, Architekturmuseum, TU Berlin

128 below, Architekturgebäude der TU, im Vordergrund Bau von Hans Scharoun, im Hintergrund: Bau von Bernhard Hermkes, 1971, Photo, 9 x 12 cm, F Rep. 290 (05) Nr. 0147622, Landesarchiv Berlin, Photo: Günther Metzner

129 Herta Hammerbacher, Architekturgebäude, Außenanlagen, Ernst-Reuter-Gedenkstätte, Platzgestaltung mit Platten, Ink and pencil on transparent, 67,2 x 66,9 cm, HH 0539,114,03, Architekturmuseum, TU Berlin

130 top, Institut für Wasserbau und Wasserwirtschaft, TU, Wasserrinne mit Wellenmaschine und Modell eines Staudamms für Südwestafrika, 1959, Photo: akg-images/Gert Schütz

130 center, Institut für Wasserbau und Wasserwirtschaft, 1960, Photo, 9 x 12 cm, F Rep. 290 (05) Nr. 0311389, Landesarchiv Berlin, Photo: Willi Huschke

130 below, Herta Hammerbacher, Peter Poelzig, Institut für Heizung und Lüftung, Ansicht von Süden 1:100, 1962, Blue print on paper, 29,5 x 88,5 cm, HH 0543,005, Architekturmuseum, TU Berlin

132 top, Institut für Allgemeine und Kernverfahrenstechnik, 1962, Photo, 9 x 12 cm, F Rep. 290 (05) Nr. 0084402, Landesarchiv Berlin, Photo: Johann Willa

132 center, Institut für Luftfahrt, 1960, Photo, 9 x 12, F Rep. 290 (05) Nr. 0072829, Landesarchiv Berlin, Photo: Johann Willa

132 below, Herta Hammerbacher, Karl Heinrich Schwennicke, Heinrich-Hertz-Institut, Nordansicht 1:100, 1963, Blue print on paper, 78,9 x 88,5 cm, HH 0544,004, Architekturmuseum, TU Berlin

132 below right, Institut für technische Akustik, TU, im Hintergrund Heinrich-Hertz-Institut für Schwingungsforschung, 1972, Photo, 6 x 6 cm, F Rep. 290 (05) Nr. 0006830_C, Landesarchiv Berlin, Photo: Günther Metzner

134 center, Karl Wilhelm Ochs, Elektrotechnische Institute, 2. Bauabschnitt, Schnitt 1:100, Pencil, Blue print on paper, 50,1 x 108,5 cm, 37697, Architekturmuseum, TU Berlin

134 below left, Institut für Elektrotechnik, TU, Photo, 6 x 7 cm, F Rep. 290 (05) Nr. 0271710, Landesarchiv Berlin, Photo: Edmund Kasperski

134 below right, Firma Dr. August Oetker - Nährcenterlfabrik GmbH - Zweigfabrik Berlin, 1962, Photo, 9 x 12 cm, F Rep. 290 (03) Nr. 0079624, Landesarchiv Berlin, Photo: Johann Willa

136 right, Willy Kreuer, Technische Chemie, Westansicht, 1:50, 1964, Ink on transparent, 103,6 x 151 cm, 55527, Architekturmuseum, TU Berlin

136 left, Institut für technische Chemie, TU, 1987, Photo, 6 x 7 cm, F Rep. 290 (05) Nr. 0288747, Landesarchiv Berlin, Photo: Thomas Grenz

136 below, Willy Kreuer, Technische Chemie, Südansicht 1:100, 1962, Tusche auf Transparent mit Folie hinterklebt, 79,2 x 150,5 cm, 55522, Architekturmuseum, TU Berlin

138 top left, Georg Kohlmaier und Barna von Sartory, Ansicht Institut für Mathematik, TU, Silver gelatine on polyester, 29,6 x 21,2 cm, BG-AS 17/2015,2, Berlinische Galerie

138 © Nöfer Architekten, Florian Profitlich

138, Innenbereich, Nordgelände, Photo, 9,1 x 13 cm, F 11960, Architekturmuseum, TU Berlin, Photo: Herta Hammerbacher

139, unbek. Verfasser, Campusplan Nordgelände, Isometrische Ansicht, 1965, Blue print on paper, 99,2 x 85,7 cm, 50015, Architekturmuseum, TU Berlin

140 top, Gesamtansicht der Institute für Strömungstechnik und Lebenscenterlchemie, TU, 1957, Photo, 9 x 12 cm, F Rep. 290 (05) Nr. 0051496, Landesarchiv Berlin, Photo: Willi Nitschke

140 below left, Institut für Fertigungstechnik, TU, 1957, Photo, 9 x 12 cm, F Rep. 290 (05) Nr. 0051497, Landesarchiv Berlin, Photo: Willi Nitschke

140 below right, Institut für Verbrennungs- und Kraftmaschinen, TU, 1957, Photo, 9 x 12 cm, F Rep. 290 (05) Nr. 0054504, Landesarchiv Berlin, Photo: Willi Nitschke

142 top, Peter Bayerer, Doppelinstitut IWF/IPK: Zentrum für Produktionstechnik der Technischen Universität Berlin und der Fraunhofer Gesellschaft, Perspektivische Ansicht, 1980, Felt-tip pen on transparent, 34,3 x 59,2 cm, 46359, Architekturmuseum, TU Berlin

142 center, Photo: Siebrand Rehberg

144 © Code Unique Architekten

144 © Code Unique Architekten

145, Joseph Ramée, Union College in Schenectady, New York, Lageplan, 1813, Colored drawing, 21 x 28,5 cm, Union College Schaffer Library Special Collections

159, in: Wettbewerb Gross-Berlin 1910: die preisgekrönten Entwürfe mit Erläuterungsberichten, Berlin 1911, Teil IV, p. 41, ill. 10

151, Albert Speer, Wettbewerb Hochschulstadt Berlin, Luftbild mit Modellsimulation, in: Broschüre mit Bestimmungen für den öffentlichen und den engen Wettbewerb, 1937, Print on paper, 30,9 x 22,3 cm, 42293, Architekturmuseum, TU Berlin

152, approx. 1988, ZLB

154, Geoportal Berlin/3815811, 3815814, 3555814, 3855811

156, Hermann Jansen, Revision und Ergänzung des Bebauungsplanes der Königlichen Domäne Dahlem, Übersichts- und Parzellierungsplan über Grundkarte 1:4000, 1910, Ink colored over print on cardboard, 114,8 x 99,3 cm, 20577, Architekturmuseum, TU Berlin

158, Photo: Mila Hacke, Berlin

160 top © Archiv der Max-Planck-Gesellschaft, Photo: Irmingard Grashey-Straub

160 center, Blick von der Studentenaue auf die Mensa, 1962, Photo (Negativ), 6 x 9 cm, RF/0107-03, FU Universitätsarchiv, Photo: Reinhard Friedrich

160 below, Zahn- und Kieferklinik, FU, 1957, Photo, F Rep. 290 (05) Nr. 0202446, Landesarchiv Berlin, Photo: Otto Hagemann

162 top © Archiv der Max-Planck-Gesellschaft, Photo: Irmingard Grashey-Straub

162, Luftbildaufnahme vom Campus Dahlem zwischen Garystraße, Thielallee und Clayallee, Juni 1964, Photo (Dia), 24 x 36mm, RF-Dia/031-06, FU Universitätsarchiv, Photo: Reinhard Friedrich

163 top, Photo: Bernd Wannenmacher

163 center, Photo: Bernd Wannenmacher

163 below, Photo: Mila Hacke, Berlin

164, Juristische Fakultät, 1960, Photo (Dia), 24 x 36 mm, RFDia/012-14, FU Universitätsarchiv, Photo: Reinhard Friedrich

164 center left, Bibliothek der Juristischen Fakultät in der Van't-Hoff-Straße 8 (Innenansicht), 1950er–1960er Jahre, Photo, 17,1 x 23cm, Foto/20067, FU Universitätsarchiv, Photo: Erich Raillon

164 below, Baustelle für den Neubau der Wirtschafts- und Sozialwissenschaftlichen Fakultät, 1958, Photo (Dia), 24 x 36mm, RFDIA/003-13, FU Universitätsarchiv, Photo: Reinhard Friedrich

164 below right, Photo: Eva-Maria Darge

166 top, Luftbildaufnahme vom Osteuropa-Institut und dem Otto-Suhr-Institut, Photo,7 x 7,7 cm, RF/0364-06, FU Universitätsarchiv, Photo: Reinhard Friedrich

166 left, Otto-Suhr-Institut, 1962, Photo, 6 x 9 cm, RF/0106-05, FU Universitätsarchiv, Photo: Reinhard Friedrich

166 center top, Ihnestraße 22, Außenansicht, 1949–1953, Photo, 10,5 x 15 cm, FU Universitätsarchiv, Photoarchiv der Deutschen Kinemathek, Photo: Gerd Victor Krau

166 center below, Boltzmannstraße 16-20, Außenansicht, 1949–1953, Photo, 10,5 x 15 cm, FU Universitätsarchiv, Photoarchiv der Deutschen Kinemathek, Photo: Gerd Victor Krau

166 below, Photo: Arne Schirrmacher

168, Anatomisches Institut, 1958, Photo, 24 x 36 mm, RFDia/003-07, FU Universitätsarchiv, Photo: Reinhard Friedrich

170 top, Pflanzenphysiologisches Institut, Photo, 6 x 6 cm, RF/0157-01, FU Universitätsarchiv, Photo: Reinhard Friedrich

170 below, Pflanzenphysiologisches Institut (Innenansicht), Photo, 6 x 6 cm, RF/0157-05, FU Universitätsarchiv, Photo: Reinhard Friedrich

171, Luftbildaufnahme vom Botanischen Garten, 2015, Photo, 15 x 17,7 cm, Foto/20104, FU Universitätsarchiv, Photo: unknown

172 top, Georg Thür, Friedrich-Wilhelms-Universität, Pharmazeutisches Institut in Dahlem, Hinteransicht 1:100, 1901–1902, Colored lithography on cardboard, 40,6 x 85,4 cm, 29137, Architekturmuseum, TU Berlin

172 center, Pharmazeutisches Institut, FU, 1960, Photo, 9 x 12 cm, F Rep. 290 (05) Nr. 0072799, Landesarchiv Berlin, Photo: Johann Willa

172 below left, Photo: Arne Schirrmacher

172 below right, Zoologisches Institut, FU, 1973, Photo, 9 x 12 cm, F Rep. 290 (05) Nr. 0160066, Landesarchiv Berlin, Photo: Günther Metzner

174 top, Haus der Deutschen Forschung, 1940, Photo, 9 x 12 cm, F Rep. 290 (01) Nr. 0173152, Landesarchiv Berlin, Photo: Otto Hagemann

174 center, Institut für Meteorologie, 1980er Jahre, Photo, 16,4 x 21,5cm, Foto/20093, FU Universitätsarchiv, Photo: Günter Schneider

174 below, Photo: Matthias Seidel

176, Ein Student und eine Studentin sitzen in

einem der Innenhöfe der Rostlaube, Photo, 5,7 x 7,2 cm, RF/0182-06, FU Universitätsarchiv, Photo: Reinhard Friedrich

178 left, in: Bauwelt 1964, Heft 6, p. 166

178 top, Silberlaube, 1998, Photo, 17,8 x 23,9 cm, Foto/20096, FU Universitätsarchiv, Photo: Enrico Straub

179 top left, Rostlaube, Innenansicht, Photo, 9 x 12 cm, RF/0175-02, FU Universitätsarchiv, Photo: Reinhard Friedrich

179 top right, Eine Wendeltreppe in der Rostlaube (Innenansicht), Photo, 9 x 12 cm, RF/0175-04, FU Universitätsarchiv, Photo: Reinhard Friedrich

179 below right, Photo: Bernd Wannenmacher

179 below left, Philologische Bibliothek (Innenansicht), Photo, 24,11 x 36,31 cm, Foto/20101, FU Universitätsarchiv, Photo: Peter Himsel

181 top, Erziehungswissenschaftliche Bibliothek, undated, Photo, 12,7 x 17,8 cm, Foto/20100, FU Universitätsarchiv, Photo: unknown

180 center, Photo: Stefan Müller-Naumann

180 below, Photo: Stefan Müller-Naumann

182 left, Büroraum im Institut für Philosophie, Photo (Dia), 5,5 x 6,9 cm, RFDia/049-05, FU Universitätsarchiv, Photo: Reinhard Friedrich

182 right, Institut für Philosophie, Photo (Dia), 24 x 36 mm, RFDia/047-06, FU Universitätsarchiv, Photo: Reinhard Friedrich

182 below, Photo: Bernd Wannenmacher

184 top, Luftbildaufnahme vom Areal zwischen Takustraße, Arnimallee und Fabeckstraße, Photo (Dia), 24 x 36 mm, RFDia/030-14, FU Universitätsarchiv, Photo: Reinhard Friedrich

184 left, Institut für anorganische Chemie (Außenansicht), undated, Photo, 23 x 29,9 cm, Photo/20081, FU Universitätsarchiv, Photo: unknown

184 center, Institut für Physik, Fachbereichsbibliothek, FU, 1982, Photo, 24 x 36 mm, F Rep. 290-02-15 Nr. 0272523, Landesarchiv Berlin, Photo: Günther Schneider

184 center right, Photo: Arne Schirrmacher

184 below right, Fachbereich Physik, 1980er, Photo, 17,8 x 24 cm, Photo/20091, FU Universitätsarchiv, Photo: Inge Kundel-Saro

186 top, Institut für Chemie und Biochemie, 1998, Photo, 17,7x23,8cm, Photo/20090, FU Universitätsarchiv, Photo: Enrico Straub

186 center, Visualisierung der Entwurfsplanung, Forschungsgebäude SupraFAB, FU, Entwurf: Nickl & Partner Architekten

186 below left, Institut für Informatik, 1992, Photo, 17,7x23,9cm, Foto/20092, FU Universitätsarchiv, Photo: Frank Nürnberger

189, in: 75 Jahre Landbaustudium in Berlin, p. 12

190 top, Photo: Eva-Maria Darge

190 below, John-F.-Kennedy-Institut für Nordamerikastudien, undated, Photo, 17,7 x 23,9 cm, Foto/20074, FU Universitätsarchiv, Photo: Enrico Straub

192 top © Landesdenkmalamt Berlin

192 center © Landesdenkmalamt Berlin

192 below, Fachbereich Veterinärmedizin, 1972, Photo,18 x 24 cm, RF/0158-03, FU Universitätsarchiv, Photo: Reinhard Friedrich

194 center, Lateinamerika Institut, approx. 1999, Photo, 17,7 x 23,9 cm, Photo/20077, FU Universitätsarchiv, Photo: Enrico Straub

194 below, Treppe im Lateinamerika Institut, approx. 1990er, Photo, 12,6 x 17,8 cm, Photo/20070, FU Universitätsarchiv, Photo: Karsten Krüger

195, Staatsbibliothek Berlin, Haus Unter den Linden, 2016, Photo: Gunnar Klack CC BY-SA 4.0

196, Staatsbibliothek, Potsdamer Straße, 1979, Photo, 6 x 6 cm, F Rep. 290 (05) Nr. 0218837 Landesarchiv Berlin, Photo: Horst Siegmann

197, Staatsbibliothek, 1981, Kleinbild-Dia, 24 mm x 36 mm, SM 2014-1783,176 © Stiftung Stadtmuseum Berlin – Archiv Rolf Goetze, Photo: Rolf Goetze

198 left, Preußische Staatsbibliothek, Großer Lesesaal, 1937, Photo, 13 x 18 cm, F Rep. 290 (05) Nr. II12955, Landesarchiv Berlin, Photo: Emil Leitner

198 right, Staatsbibliothek, 1979, Kleinbild-Dia, 24 mm x 36 mm, SM 2014-2018,114 © Stiftung Stadtmuseum Berlin – Archiv Rolf Goetze, Photo: Rolf Goetze

200 top, Universitätsbibliothek, Lesesaal, undated, TU Archiv, Photo: unknown

200 left, Universitätsbibliothek, Eingangsbereich, undated, TU Archiv, Photo: unknown

200 center, Amerika-Gedenkbibliothek (Berliner Zentralbibliothek), Freihandsaal, 1954, Photo, 9 x 12 cm, F Rep. 290 (05) Nr. 0036213 Landesarchiv Berlin, Photo: Gert Schütz

200 below right, Zentral- und Landesbibliothek Berlin, Haus AGB, 1954, ZLB Fotoarchiv

201 top, in: Rotraud Ahrens, Villen, Rost- und Silberlauben, Baugeschichtliche Spaziergänge über den Campus der FU, Berlin 1993, p. 51

201 center, HU Universitätsarchiv, Fotosammlung, Photo 15

201 below, HU Universitätsarchiv, Fotosammlung, Photo 19

202 top, in: Deutsche Architektur 5/1955, p. 226

202 center, Internationales Studentenheim Eichkamp, 1961, Photo, 9 x 12 cm, F Rep. 290 (05) Nr. 0073357, Landesarchiv Berlin, Photo: Johann Willa

202 below, Studentendorf Schlachtensee Gemeinschaftshaus. Bauzeitliche Aufnahme, Schweizerisches Architekturmuseum Basel

204, Geoportal Berlin/3975808

206, Technologiepark Adlershof Juni 2015 © WISTA Plan GmbH, Photo: D. Laubner

208 top left, Windkanal Adlershof, undated, Photo, 17,7 x 24 cm, Foto/2007, FU Universitätsarchiv, Photo: Paul Glaser

208 top right, Windkanal, 1935, Foto, 13 x 18 cm, Bild 102-17156, Bundesarchiv, Photo: Georg Pahl

208 right, Windkanal neben Erwin Schrödinger-Zentrum © WISTA Management GmbH

208 below left, Trudelturm, 1935, Photo, 13 x 18 cm, Bild 102-17159, Bundesarchiv, Photo: Georg Pahl

208 right below, Trudelturm im Aerodynamischen Park © WISTA Management GmbH

209 top left, Photo: Heike Zappe, CC BY-SA 3.0 DE

209 top right, Motorenprüfstand, 1935, Photo, 13 x 18 cm, Bild 102-17157, Bundesarchiv, Photo: Georg Pahl

210 top, Photo: Brigitte Dittmar

210 left, in: Wissenschaftlich-technische Gesellschaft Adlershof WITEGA (Hg.), Adlershofer Splitter 2, Das Heinrich-Hertz-Institut in Berlin-Adlershof, 1997, Titelabbildung

210 right, DLR-Standort, Berlin-Adlershof, CC-BY 3.0

212 top, Fernsehfunk, 1960, Photo, Bild 183-79070-0002, Bundesarchiv, Photo: Horst Sturm, Eva Brüggmann

212 below, Luftbild BESSY II am Wilhelm-Conrad-Röntgen Campus des HZB in Berlin Adlershof © HZB/Dirk Laubner

214 top, Zentrum für Photonik und Optische Technologien © WISTA Management GmbH

214 below, Johann-von-Neumann-Haus © WISTA Management GmbH

216 top und below, Photos: Marcus Bredt, Berlin © Marcus Bredt

218 top, Photo: Felix Löchner

218 below, Integrative Research Institute for the Sciences (IRIS), HU, Entwurf: Nickl & Partner Architekten

219, Photo: Dirk Altenkirch, 2009

223 left, Photo: Luise Rellensmann

223 right, Photo: Luise Rellensmann

223 below, Photo: Werner Huthmacher

224 Geoportal Berlin/3815820; 3855820, 3855823

226, Geoportal Berlin/3855811, 3855808; 3975829, 3975832, 3935832

228, Detail der Fassade vom Universitätsklinikum Steglitz, 1978, Photo, 17,7 x 23,9 cm, Photo/20075, FU Universitätsarchiv, Photo: Enrico Straub

230 © euroluftbild.de/Robert Grahn

232 top, Rudolf Virchow-Krankenhaus von Ludwig Hoffmann, Ansicht Hauptgebäude mit Brunnen auf der centerlallee, (in: Neubauten der Stadt Berlin, Bd. VI, 1907), Print on paper, 39,5 x 51,7 cm, B 2376,036, Architekturmuseum, TU Berlin, Photo: Ernst von Brauchitsch

232 below, Ludwig Hoffmann, Rudolf Virchow-Krankenhaus, Ansicht vom Augustenburger Platz, (in: Neubauten der Stadt Berlin, Bd. VI, 1907), 1907, Print on paper, 52,1 x 38,9 cm, B 2376,002, Architekturmuseum, TU Berlin, Photo: Ernst von Brauchitsch

234 top, Bettenhaus des Rudolf-Virchow-Krankenhauses, 1962, Photo, 9 x 12 cm, F Rep. 290 (04) Nr. 0311240, Landesarchiv Berlin, Photo: Willi Huschke

234 below © Deubzer König Architekten

236, Universitätsklinikum Steglitz, 1978, Photografie, 17,7 x 24 cm, Foto/20099, FU Universitätsarchiv, Photo: Enrico Straub

237, Photo: Mila Hacke, Berlin

238 top, Luftbildaufnahme vom Universitätsklinikum Steglitz, 1980er, Photo, 17,6 x 23,8 cm, RF/0000-37, FU Universitätsarchiv, Photo: Reinhard Friedrich

238 below left, Institut für Hygiene und Mikrobiologie, 1974, Photo, 18,1 x 23,8 cm, RF0208-05, FU Universitätsarchiv, Photo: Reinhard Friedrich

238 below right, Schweizerisches Architekturmuseum Basel, Photo: Ullmann

239 top, Schweizerisches Architekturmuseum Basel

239 below, Luftbildaufnahme vom Institut für Hygiene und medizinische Mikrobiologie, 1980er, Photo, 17,6 x 23,8 cm, RF/0000-41, FU Universitätsarchiv, Photo: Reinhard Friedrich

240 top left, Baustelle für die Zentralen Tierlaboratorien, August 1975, Photo (Negativ), 6 x 6 cm, RF/0131-10, FU Universitätsarchiv, Photo: Reinhard Friedrich

240 top right, Luftbildaufnahme vom Institut für Hygiene und medizinische Mikrobiologie und der Baustelle für die Zentralen Tierlaboratorien, 1980, Photo (Dia), 24 x 36 mm, RFDia/045-15, FU Universitätsarchiv, Photo: Reinhard Friedrich

240 below, Zentrale Tierlaboratorien, 1980er, Photo, 17,9 x 24 cm, Foto/20094, FU Universitätsarchiv, Photo: Inge Kundel-Saro

242, Ludwig Hoffmann, Genesungsheim, in: www.l-h-q.de/geschichte-lhq

244 top, Kaiser-Wilhelm-Institut für Hirnforschung, Eingang, Archiv der Max-Planck-Gesellschaft

244 below, Archiv der Max-Planck-Gesellschaft

246, Regierungskrankenhaus I, MfS, HA II, Photo Nr. 307, Bild 20, approx. 1980, Bundesbeauftragte für die Unterlagen des Staatssicherheitsdienstes der ehemaligen DDR

248 top, Institut für Herz-Kreislaufforschung Berlin-Buch von Franz Ehrlich. Außenansicht, 1953/1956, 14,0 x 23,5 cm, Photo, I 12111 F, Stiftung Bauhaus Dessau/© (Ehrlich, Franz) Erbengemeinschaft nach Franz Ehrlich, Photo: G. Draeger

248 left, Robert-Rösle-Institut, 1962, Photo, Bild 183-A0720-0003-001, Bundesarchiv, Photo: Christa Hochneder

248 right, Zentralinstitute für Krebsforschung der Akademie der Wissenschaften der DDR und des Robert-Rössle-Instituts, 1979, Bild 183-U0228-0302 Bundesarchiv, Photo: Hubert Link

250 top © euroluftbild.de/Robert Grahn

250 below, Photo: Carla Streckwall

252, Photo: Andrew Alberts

253, Bronzeskulptur "Kore" des Bildhauers Karl Hartung, Februar 1962, Photo (Dia), 24 x 36 mm, RFDia/019-01, FU Universitätsarchiv, Photo: Reinhard Friedrich

254 left, Photo: Eva-Maria Darge

254 right, TU Berlin, Immw

258 left, Olaf Metzel, Noch Fragen?, 2011 © VG Bild-Kunst, Bonn, Photo: BBR/Jens Andreae 2013

258 right, Rolf Wicker, Esc-Enter, Detail, 2019, Photo: Eva-Maria Darge

259 left, Arun Kuplas, Bullet Holes, Installation im Foyer des Grimm-Zentrum, 2009, Photo: Arun Kuplas

259 right, Ceal Floyer, Vorsicht Stufe, 2009, PVC ready-made signs in brass optics (56 stairs in total), 230 x 60 mm, Installation view: Vorsicht Stufe, Humboldt Universität, Berlin, 2009, Courtesy the artist and Esther Schipper, Berlin © VG Bild-Kunst, Bonn, 2019, Photo © Roman März

260 top, Innenhof des Musikwissenschaftlichen Seminars der HU mit der Arbeit "in excerpere für Erich M. von Hornbostel" von Ruth Tesmer, 2019, Photo: Eva-Maria Darge

260 below, Elsbeth Arlt, Realität in den Regalen: Fußnote, Vermerk, Widmung, 2005, Photo: Matthias Heyde

260, "Flügeltor", Reinhard Haverkamp, 2019, Photo: Eva-Maria Darge

261, "Flügeltor", Reinhard Haverkamp, Detail, 2019, Photo: Eva-Maria Darge

262 top, Robert Patz, Tricksters Plan, Kojote, 2018, Photo: Robert Patz

262 center, Robert Patz, Tricksters Plan, Treppenhaus, 2018, Photo: Robert Patz

262 below, Robert Patz, Tricksters Plan, Bibliotheksansicht, 2018, Photo: Robert Patz

273, Grundsteinlegung zum Neubau der Fakultät für Bergbau und Hüttenwesen, 1955, Foto, 9 x 12 cm, F Rep. 290 (05) Nr. 0041446, Landesarchiv Berlin, Photo: Gert Schütz

275, Montagehalle für Großmaschinenbau von Peter Behrens, 1912, Photo, 40007031, bpk

276, Institut für Nichtmetallische Werkstoffe, Englische Straße 20, Abriss vor 2014, 1983, Photo 4,5 x 6 cm, F Rep. 290 (05) Nr. 0011754_C, Landesarchiv Berlin, Photo: Harald Rechenberger

277 right, Estate: Manfred Schiedhelm

278 © Deubzer König Architekten

280, Hansaviertel, Internationale Bauausstellung Berlin (IBA), Berlin-Pavillon, 1957, Photo, 9 x 12 cm, F Rep. 290 (01) Nr. 0054790, Landesarchiv Berlin, Photo: Gert Schütz

282, Photo: Bernd Wannenmacher

283, Arbeitsgemeinschaft Foerster, Mattern, Hammerbacher, Serie ArbeitsPhotos, Elsbeth Heddenhausen und Herta Hammerbacher mit Plan, Garten Elsbeth Heddenhausen (?), Photo, 23,6 x 17,9 cm, F 12536, Architekturmuseum, TU Berlin

286, Ehemaliges Scherk-Haus (Kosmetikfabrik) von Fritz Höger, 1972, Photo, 6 x 6 cm, F Rep. 290 (01) Nr. 0007044_C, Landesarchiv Berlin, Photo: Karl-Heinz Schubert

288, Photo: PR-Bild/C.Petras

289, Carl Wilhelm Gropius, Die Mohrenbrücke, Berlin, 1833, Colored steel engraving, 12,5 cm x 20,5 cm, GDR 65/152 © Stiftung Stadtmuseum Berlin

290, Ludwig-Leo-Archiv, Nr. 222 F.1, Akademie der Künste, Berlin, Photo: unknown

292 © Nöfer Architekten

293, S. Gollin, CC BY-SA 4.0, Wikimedia Commons

296 left, Karl Friedrich Schinkel, Entwurf für das Alte Palais in Berlin, approx. 1834 © Landesdenkmalamt Berlin

296 right, Karl Friedrich Schinkel, Zweiter Entwurf Karl Friedrich Schinkels für den Bau eines neuen Bibliotheksgebäudes Unter den Linden, 1835, Yd 5/105, Kartenabteilung, Staatsbibliothek zu Berlin–Preußischer Kulturbesitz © bpk/Staatsbibliothek zu Berlin

295, Hans-Scharoun-Archiv, Nr. 3897 F.17, Akademie der Künste, Berlin, Photo: unknown

297 © IHK Berlin

301, Rostlaube, Foto, 9 x 12 cm, RF/0175-02, FU Universitätsarchiv, Photo: Reinhard Friedrich

311, Otto-von-Simson-Straße 13, 17,7, x 23,8 cm, Foto/20076, FU Universitätsarchiv, Photo: Enrico Straub

317, Paul Lehmgrübner, Physikalisches Institut der Universität Berlin, Grundriss des Pfahlrostes ca 1: 85, 1874, Ink colored on transparent, 60,9 x 94,7 cm, 5574, Architekturmuseum, TU Berlin

inside cover, Berlin und Charlottenburg, 1857, SBB_IIIC_Kart_X 17806, Staatsbibliothek zu Berlin, Preußischer Kulturbesitz

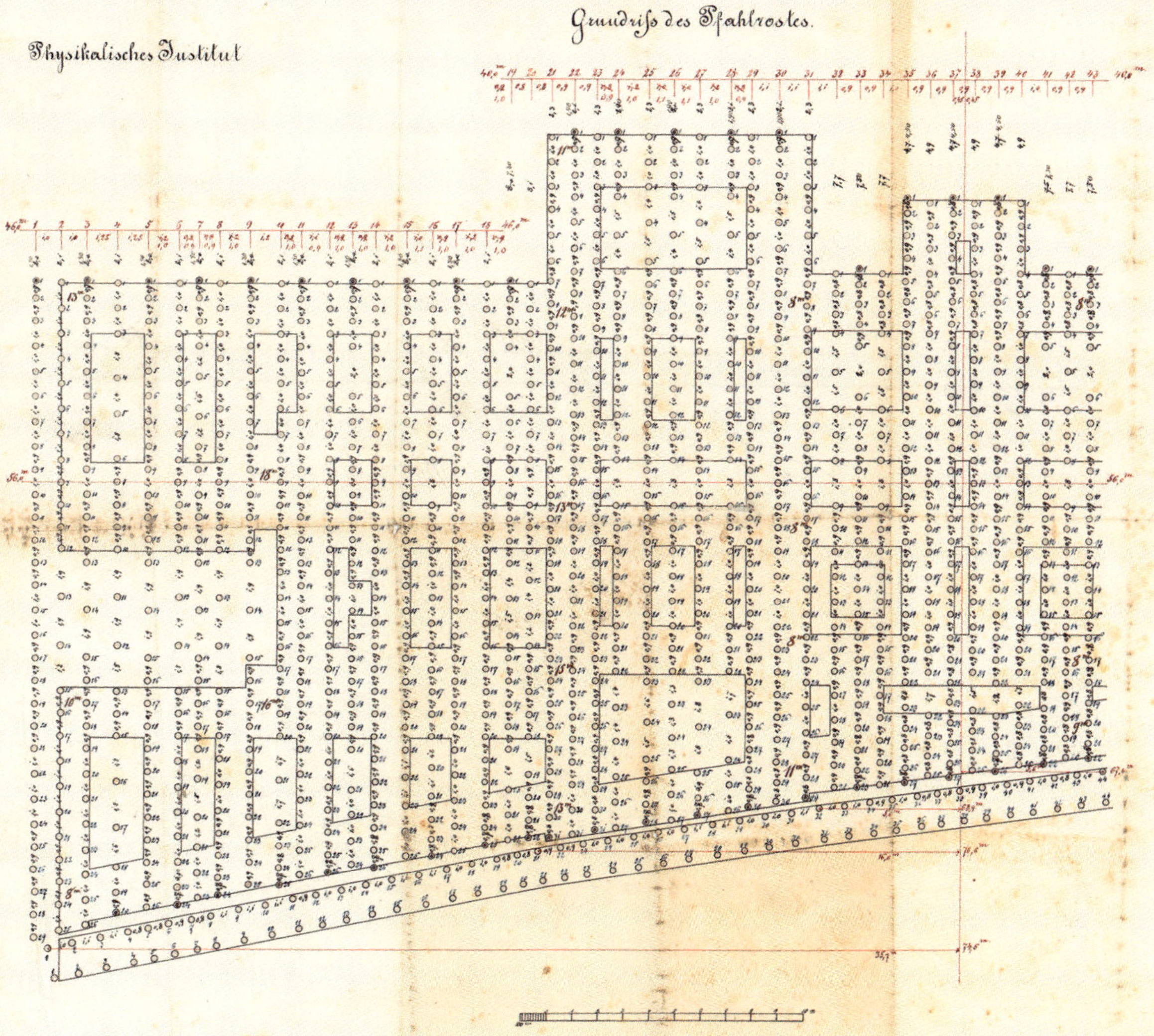

Grundriss des Pfahlrostes.
Physikalisches Institut

Imprint
© by jovis Verlag GmbH 2019

Front cover
Henry-Ford-Bau, FU, 2009, Photo: Mila Hacke, Berlin
Unknown photographer, Leopold Ahrendts, Unter den Linden. View from Opernplatz to the university, on the left the Königliche Bibliothek, n. d. (1857), Photo, IV 69/266 V, © Stiftung Stadtmuseum Berlin
Strasse des 17. Juni, taken from the Telefunkenhochhaus, 1960, Photo: unknown, presumably Willy Pragher or Friedrich Seidenstücker

Inside cover
Scan of the map "Berlin um 1910" from the publication: "Städtebauliche Entwicklung Berlins seit 1650 in Karten", Geoportal Berlin/ Berlin um 1910, EPSG: 25833 - TIFF, dl-de/ by-2-0
Map, Berlin und Charlottenburg, 1857, SBB_ IIIC_Kart_X 17806, Staatsbibliothek zu Berlin, Preußischer Kulturbesitz

Editors
Arne Schirrmacher
Maren Wienigk

Scientific Editing
Gabriele Metzler, Arne Schirrmacher, Maren Wienigk

Authors
Nils Exner (NE)
Gabriele Metzler (GM)
Sascha Morawe (SM)
Arne Schirrmacher (AS)
Maren Wienigk (MW)

Coordination
Maren Wienigk

Research
Nils Exner, Sascha Morawe, Paul Morawski, Leon Blohm, Maren Wienigk

Image Editing
Konrad Angermüller, Paul Morawski, Maren Wienigk

Copy Editing
Paul Morawski, Gabriele Metzler

Design and Typesetting
Konrad Angermüller

Translation from the German
James Campbell, Alexander Zuckrow

Project Management (jovis)
Nina Kathalin Bergeest

Proofreading
Mariangela Palazzi-Williams

Maps
Arne Schirrmacher

Lithography
Konrad Angermüller

Paper
Content: Munken Polar, 120g/m²
Cover: Invercote G, 260 g/m²

A publication by the project
Wissenschaft in der Stadt
www.wissenschaft-in-der-stadt.hu-berlin.de

In cooperation with the Humboldt-Universität zu Berlin

Funding
Die Beauftragte der Bundesregierung für Kultur und Medien
Deutsche Stiftung Denkmalschutz
Humboldt-Universität zu Berlin
Senatsverwaltung für Kultur und Europa, Berlin
Lotto Stiftung Berlin

Bibliographic information published by the Deutsche Nationalbibliothek.
The Deutsche Nationalbibliothek lists this publication in the Deutsche Nationalbibliografie. Detailed bibliographic data are available on the Internet at http://dnb.d-nb.de.

jovis Verlag GmbH
Kurfürstenstrasse 15/16
10785 Berlin

jovis books are available worldwide in select bookstores. Please contact your nearest bookseller or visit www.jovis.de for information concerning your local distribution.

ISBN 978-3-86859-605-2